The City in American Political Development

There are nearly 20,000 general-purpose municipal governments—cities—in the United States, employing more people than the federal government. About twenty of those cities received charters of incorporation well before ratification of the US Constitution, and several others were established urban centers more than a century before the American Revolution. Yet despite their estimable size and prevalence in the United States, city government and politics has been a woefully neglected topic within the recent study of American political development.

The volume brings together some of the best of both the most established and the newest urban scholars in political science, sociology, and history, each of whom makes a new argument for rethinking the relationship between cities and the larger project of state-building. Each chapter shows explicitly how the American city demonstrates durable shifts in governing authority throughout the nation's history. By filling an important gap in scholarship the book will thus become an indispensable part of the American political development canon, a crucial component of graduate and undergraduate courses in APD, urban politics, urban sociology, and urban history, and a key guide for future scholarship.

Richardson Dilworth is Associate Professor of Political Science at Drexel University, author of *The Urban Origins of Suburban Autonomy* (2005), and editor of *Social Capital in the City: Community and Civic Life in Philadelphia* (2006).

The City in American Political Development

Edited by Richardson Dilworth

Routledge
Taylor & Francis Group

NEW YORK AND LONDON

First published 2009
by Routledge
270 Madison Ave, New York, NY 10016

Simultaneously published in the UK
by Routledge
2 Park Square, Milton Park, Abingdon, Oxon OX14 4RN

Routledge is an imprint of the Taylor & Francis Group, an informa business

© 2009 Taylor & Francis

Typeset in Sabon by
Swales & Willis Ltd, Exeter, Devon
Printed and bound in the United States of America on acid-free paper by
Edwards Brothers, Inc.

Library of Congress Cataloging in Publication Data
The city in American political development / edited by Richardson Dilworth.
     p. cm.
     Includes bibliographical references and index.
     1. Municipal government – United States – History.   2. Urban policy –
United States – History.   3. Cities and towns – United States –
History.   I. Dilworth, Richardson.
JS309.C57 2009
320.8'50973–dc22   2008041121

ISBN10: 0–415–99099–8 (hbk)
ISBN10: 0–415–99100–5 (pbk)
ISBN10: 0–203–88110–9 (ebk)

ISBN13: 978–0–415–99099–8 (hbk)
ISBN13: 978–0–415–99100–1 (pbk)
ISBN13: 978–0–203–88110–1 (ebk)

To the memory of William Tweed, 1823–1878, without whom the study of urban politics would have been much less fun.

Contents

Preface

This book owes much of its existence to the Social Science History Association (SSHA) and I am grateful to the association's officers and attendees who made the annual meetings such lively and hospitable venues for discussing the role of cities in American political development (APD). During a reception at the 2004 SSHA meeting in Chicago I cornered Robert Lieberman, who, after some prodding and some wine, admitted to having a research interest in cities. I suggested that we organize a roundtable on the role of urbanization in American political development, and over the next several months I enlisted, besides myself and Lieberman, Amy Bridges, Margaret Weir, and Philip Ethington. We gathered at the 2005 SSHA meeting in Portland, Oregon, for what turned out to be a well-attended and lively panel—it seemed to resonate that urbanization and cities were interesting though under-explored elements in recent scholarship on the institutional development of the United States.

In putting together the roundtable for the 2005 meeting I began to think that an edited book would be a useful way to bring together several strains of social science and historical research under the common theme of the city's status and role in American political development. From the initial roundtable, Lieberman and Ethington had material that they thought would work as chapters, and as I began the hunt for additional authors, several subsidiary themes began to emerge. Lieberman's work suggested the need for an initial set of chapters that put cities in the United States in comparative perspective. I owe thanks to Jason Kaufman, who agreed to take up the challenge of thinking about the role of cities in both US and Canadian political development as an extension of his research that compares those two countries, and to Jerome Hodos, who adapted his comparative research on Philadelphia and Manchester so that it addressed the APD subdiscipline.

Ethington's work on the footprints of regional regimes that became his chapter with David Levitus formed the initial nucleus for an entire section on the spatial and scalar analyses of urbanization—one of the liveliest and most invigorating areas of urban research, though one still largely unused by urbanists in political science. What in my opinion has made spatial and scalar analyses so important is that they provide a new way to join political theory to the empirical study of cities. I was thus very gratified that two immensely talented theorists, Clarissa Rile Hayward and Neil Brenner, agreed to write chapters for this section.

While it was important to highlight the relatively new focus on space and scale in urban research, it was equally important to address the estimable tradition of urban research in political science. Thus preceding the section on "City, Space, and Nation" is a section on urban politics research within political science, with chapters by one relatively new political scientist, Jessica Trounstine, whose work on political monopolies offers one of the most exciting research agendas in urban politics, and two longstanding scholars, Clarence Stone and Robert Whelan, whose work has shaped what we understand today as the study of cities in political science.

The two middle sections of the book can be read as a methodological and historiographical continuum, starting with Trounstine's vigorous and rigorous reinterpretation of the machine-reform dichotomy, to Stone and Whelan's review of the urban politics literature after World War II, and then into Brenner's analysis of the regime and growth machine models, which opens up the discussion to the spatial analyses proffered by Hayward, and Ethington and Levitus. All of these chapters challenge urbanist scholars to rethink the role of institutions and institutional change in the distribution of power among city actors, the role of civic participation, the impact of historical legacies and metropolitan fragmentation on city politics, and the ways in which larger political and economic forces shape and construct politics at the city or urban level.

Last but most certainly not least, it was obvious from the beginning that there should be chapters on the role of race, ethnicity, and immigration in urban politics. I was very lucky to find three authors—Michael Jones-Correa, Alethia Jones, and Matthew Crenson—who were both willing and able to take up the challenge, crucial to understanding the role of the city in APD, of thinking about how racial, ethnic, and immigrant identities constructed in the American urban milieu translate themselves into institutional patterns at broader levels. This is an issue that can be found scattered throughout many of the other chapters, but it was important to highlight their significance in a separate section. The role of race, ethnicity, and immigration in the structuring of "deep pluralisms" is also highlighted in the conclusion by Ira Katznelson, who very instructively asks us to push even further in integrating urban politics with political theory.

In bringing together the chapters for this book I was very lucky to find a set of authors who made this a thoroughly enjoyable and intellectually exciting project. I have learned a lot from all of them and I am very grateful for their participation. Bucking the sometimes understandable assumptions about highly talented academics, there is not a single diva or miscreant in the whole bunch. They are all, in fact, beautiful people.

This book was also made possible by the conference organizers who generously provided us with panel time. I have already mentioned the SSHA, but we also held panels at the *Journal of Policy History* conference in 2005 in Charlottesville, Virginia, where Lieberman, Jones, and Stone presented drafts of their chapters. We followed that up with a panel at the 2006 meeting of the American Political Science Association where Kaufman, Crenson, Jones, and Stone presented papers, and where Steven Erie graciously and very effectively served as chair. Then in 2007 at the SSHA meeting in Chicago we were able to arrange a sort of mini-conference within a conference: two back-to-back panels with paper presentations by Lieberman, Hodos, Kaufman, Jones, Ethington and Levitus, Stone, and Trounstine. I am especially grateful to Trounstine and Lieberman, who stepped in as discussants due to my absence from the conference on account of a family emergency, and I am grateful to everyone who hauled themselves around the country to serve on panels. The tour concluded in Philadelphia in May 2007 with a day-long mini-conference at Drexel University, where Stone, Crenson, Jones-Correa, Lieberman, Trounstine, Whelan, Hodos, and Hayward all showed up to spend the entire day talking about American cities (and Manchester). Ethington and Levitus woke up at an ungodly hour so that they could join us from California via videoconference. I am grateful to Donna Murasko, Dean of the College of Arts and Sciences at Drexel, who provided the money for the conference, and for us to all go out and have a nice dinner afterward.

Thanks very much to Routledge and our editor there, Michael Kerns, who has provided unflagging support (he spent all day with us at Drexel as well), not only for our book, but more generally for APD studies within political science. By steering this project toward publication with a steady and firm hand he made my job much easier. And finally, thanks to the Drexel students who took my urban politics course in the summer of 2008 and read a draft of this book. They provided excellent feedback on what they did and did not like, and by incorporating some of their suggestions I have hopefully made this book a bit more palatable for future students.

Contributors

Neil Brenner is Professor of Sociology and Metropolitan Studies at New York University, author of *New State Spaces: Urban Governance and the Rescaling of Statehood* (Oxford University Press, 2004) and of numerous articles, and co-editor of *The Global Cities Reader* (Routledge, 2006), *State/Space: A Reader* (Blackwell, 2003), and *Spaces of Neoliberalism: Urban Restructuring in Western Europe and North America* (Blackwell, 2002).

Matthew A. Crenson is Professor Emeritus of Political Science at Johns Hopkins University. His books include *The Un-politics of Air Pollution: A Study of Non-decisionmaking in the Cities* (Johns Hopkins University Press, 1971); *The Federal Machine: Beginnings of Bureaucracy in Jacksonian America* (Johns Hopkins University Press, 1975); *Neighborhood Politics* (Harvard University Press, 1983); *Building the Invisible Orphanage: A Prehistory of the American Welfare State* (Harvard University Press, 1998); and, with Benjamin Ginsberg, *Downsizing Democracy: How America Sidelined its Citizens and Privatized its Public* (Johns Hopkins University Press, 2002) and *Presidential Power: Unchecked and Unbalanced* (Norton, 2007).

Richardson Dilworth is Associate Professor of Political Science at Drexel University, author of *The Urban Origins of Suburban Autonomy* (Harvard University Press, 2005; winner of the Best Book Award from the Urban Politics Section of the American Political Science Association), and editor of *Social Capital in the City: Community and Civic Life in Philadelphia* (Temple University Press, 2006).

Philip J. Ethington is Professor of History and Political Science at the University of Southern California, and North American Editor of the journal *Urban History* (Cambridge University Press). He is the author of *The Public City: The Political Construction of Urban Life in San Francisco, 1850–1900* (Cambridge University Press, 1994). His digital publications include "Los Angeles and the Problem of Urban Historical Knowledge," *American Historical Review* 105, no. 5 (2000), and

Urban Icons (co-edited with Vanessa Schwartz), *Cambridge Journals Online* 33, no. 1 (2006). An interdisciplinary historian, his empirical and theoretical studies have appeared in journals of geography, sociology, and political science as well as history. His photography has been published and shown internationally, including at the Los Angeles County Museum of Art and the Art Institute of Chicago. He is currently completing a dual print and online "mBook": *Ghost Metropolis, Los Angeles, 1542–2001*.

Clarissa Rile Hayward is Associate Professor of Political Science at Washington University in St Louis. She was previously Associate Professor of Political Science at Ohio State University. Her publications include *De-facing Power* (Cambridge University Press, 2000) and articles in volumes and in journals, such as the *American Political Science Review*, *Constellations*, *Critical Review of International Social and Political Philosophy*, and *Polity*. Hayward is currently completing a second book, focused on the ways democratic state actors shape political identities through institutions that racialize and privatize urban space. This research has been supported by the National Academy of Education/Spencer Foundation, the National Endowment for the Humanities, and the Institute for Advanced Study in Princeton.

Jerome Hodos is Assistant Professor of Sociology at Franklin and Marshall College. He writes about urban sociology, urban politics, globalization, and city planning, and his work has appeared in *Urban Affairs Review*, *City & Community*, and elsewhere. He is currently completing a book manuscript entitled *Second Cities: Globalization and Local Politics in Philadelphia and Manchester*.

Alethia Jones is Assistant Professor at the University at Albany, State University of New York. She holds a joint appointment in the Department of Public Administration and Policy and the Department of Political Science. She has received research fellowships from the Ford Foundation, the Massachusetts Institute of Technology, and the University of Virginia. She earned her PhD at Yale University (2005) and was affiliated with the Center for the Study of Race, Inequality and Politics. She is working on a book manuscript entitled *Bringing Immigrants In: Inclusive Policy Designs and the Politics of Community Banking*.

Michael Jones-Correa is Professor of Government and Director of the American Studies Program at Cornell University. He is the author of *Between Two Nations: The Political Predicament of Latinos in New York City* (Cornell, 1998), the editor of *Governing American Cities: Inter-ethnic Coalitions, Competition and Conflict* (Russell Sage Foundation, 2001), and the author of more than two dozen articles and chapters on immigration, race, ethnicity, and citizenship in the United

States. Professor Jones-Correa is currently working on several major projects, among them one looking at the increasing ethnic diversity of suburbs and its implication for local and national politics; another a multi-authored analyses of the 2006 Latino National Survey, a national state-stratified survey of Latinos in the United States for which he was a principal investigator; and collaborative research on new fast-growing immigrant-receiving areas. Jones-Correa has been a visiting fellow at the Woodrow Wilson Center for International Scholars (2003–2004) and at the Russell Sage Foundation (1998–1999). In 2004–2005 he served on the Committee on the Redesign of US Naturalization Test for the National Academy of Sciences.

Ira Katznelson is Ruggles Professor of Political Science and History at Columbia University. His most recent books are *Liberal Beginnings: Making a Republic for the Moderns* (with Andreas Kalyvas, Cambridge University Press, 2008), *When Affirmative Action Was White: An Untold History of Racial Inequality in Twentieth-Century America* (W.W. Norton, 2005), and *Desolation and Enlightenment: Political Knowledge after Total War, Totalitarianism, and the Holocaust* (Columbia University Press, 2003). He was President of the American Political Science Association for 2005–2006.

Jason Kaufman is a research fellow at the Berkman Center for Internet and Society at Harvard University. He is the author of *For the Common Good? American Civic Life and the Golden Age of Fraternity* (Oxford University Press, 2002) and of numerous articles covering such topics as civic associationalism in nineteenth-century United States; AIDS preventive policy and anti-discrimination law; and the cultural worlds of American high school students. His next book, *The Origins of Canadian and American Political Differences*, will be published by Harvard University Press.

David P. Levitus is a doctoral candidate in History at the University of Southern California. His dissertation focuses on the contradictions of New Deal liberalism and explores the interactions between grassroots activism and state policymaking in New York and Los Angeles.

Robert C. Lieberman is Professor of Political Science and Public Affairs at Columbia University. His most recent book, *Shaping Race Policy: The United States in Comparative Perspective* (Princeton University Press, 2005) has been awarded the Best Book on Public Policy Prize by the Race, Ethnicity, and Politics Section of the American Political Science Association. He is also the author of *Shifting the Color Line: Race and the American Welfare State* (Harvard University Press, 1998), which was awarded several prizes including the 1999 Lionel Trilling Award for the best book by a Columbia faculty member.

Clarence N. Stone is Research Professor of Public Policy and Political Science at George Washington University. He is the author or co-author of numerous books, including *Regime Politics: Governing Atlanta, 1946–1988* (University Press of Kansas, 1989; winner of the Ralph J. Bunche Award from the American Political Science Association) and *Building Civic Capacity: The Politics of Reforming Urban Schools* (with Jeffrey Henig, Bryan Jones, and Carol Pierannunzi, University Press of Kansas, 2001). From 1993 to 1998 he was Principal Investigator for Civic Capacity and Urban Education, an eleven-city study funded by the National Science Foundation. He was a Visiting Fulbright Professor at the University of Southern Denmark in 2001–2002. Stone is currently coordinating a multi-city, cross-national study of the politics of revitalizing urban neighborhoods and examining Baltimore's experience as part of the overall project.

Jessica Trounstine is Assistant Professor of Politics and Public Affairs at Princeton University. She is the author of several articles on urban politics and elections that have appeared in both the *Journal of Politics* and the *American Journal of Political Science*. Her book, *Political Monopolies in American Cities: The Rise and Fall of Bosses and Reformers* (University of Chicago Press, 2008), analyzes more than 240 cities to show that some political coalitions bias the system in their favor resulting in a loss of democratic responsiveness.

Robert K. Whelan is Visiting Professor of Urban and Public Affairs at the University of Texas-Arlington. He is co-author, with Clarence Stone and William Murin, of *Urban Policy and Politics in a Bureaucratic Age* (Prentice Hall, 1979; second edition, 1986). His current research interests include policy responses to Hurricane Katrina, and metropolitan governance in Canada.

Introduction
Bringing the City Back In

Richardson Dilworth

As of 2007 there were 19,492 general-purpose municipal governments—cities—in the United States, and they employed more people than the federal government. About twenty of those cities received charters of incorporation well before ratification of the US Constitution, and several others were established urban centers more than a century before the American Revolution.[1] Yet despite their estimable size and prevalence in the United States, the city has been a woefully neglected topic within the recent study of American politics.

The City in American Political Development seeks to redress the neglect of the city in American politics, focusing in particular on that historical institutionalist strain of scholarship that has come to be known as American political development, or simply "APD." Part I looks at the American city in comparison to cities in other countries, most notably England and Canada, as a way of exploring the relationship between cities and the nation in the definition of American exceptionalism. Part II then places in the larger context of American political development the classic debates in the study of urban politics, namely the traditional machine-reform dichotomy, the community power structure debate, and the urban political economy literature. The chapters in Part III then examine how cities and urbanization construct power that is more durable because of its arrangement in space. Finally, Part IV takes a closer look at how race and ethnicity have been defined and constructed through urban development, and how those definitions have then informed national policy.

The City in American Political Development

Each of the authors in this book demonstrate in different ways the theoretical significance of the city to the study of American political development, and indeed to the larger subject of state-building that became a revived topic of interest among social scientists in the 1980s, starting with such trailblazing books as Theda Skocpol's *States and Social Revolutions* (1979), Stephen Skowronek's *Building a New American State* (1985), and the edited volume *Bringing the State Back In* (1985), in which Skocpol declared the presence of an "intellectual sea change" that was reinvigorating state-centered scholarship in which government was perceived as an important actor in shaping social and political outcomes, rather than being simply an arena in which interest groups and social movements battled for resources, as it had been depicted in the pluralist, structural-functionalist, and neo-Marxist literature.[2] Within the study of American politics, the new focus on the state was given a platform through the journal established by Skowronek and Karen Orren in 1986, *Studies in American Political Development*.

Orren and Skowronek have more recently provided a textbook-style assessment of APD scholarship in their book *The Search for American Political Development* (2004), in which they have suggested "intercurrence" as the conceptual vehicle to push forward the research agenda of the subdiscipline they helped create. From the assertion that the state was an important and independent actor in the 1980s, state-centered scholarship burgeoned into a far-flung "new institutionalism," of which historical institutionalism, including APD, was but one component.[3] Historical institutionalism has come to focus increasingly on explaining institutional stability (often described as "path dependence") and the moments of change ("critical junctures" or "realignments") that demarcate eras of stability.[4] Orren and Skowronek capture this concern with stability and change in their definition of APD as "durable shifts in governing authority," yet they also attempt to push the agenda toward more fine-grained analyses that appreciate the contradictory forces and multiple strains of authority that churn beneath veneers of durability. Institutions should be understood as "historical composites" that embody intercurrent and often contradictory goals and values—or, in other words, "multiple orders arranged uncertainly in relationship to one another . . . a polity permeated by authority relations that have been constructed historically, a polity caught up in their contradictions and animated to seek their resolutions."[5]

With such a definition of political development, it is all the more surprising that Orren and Skowronek make no reference whatsoever to cities or city government (save for passing reference to downtown Tokyo).[6] For cities are exemplary institutions in their embodiment of multiple and contradictory authority relations: The machine versus reform, native versus immigrant, older immigrants versus newer immigrants, downtown versus the neighborhoods, pluralism versus elitism as they came to be defined in the community power structure debate, and the more general claim from the 1970s that American cities were so fragmented and composed of so many disparate and powerful interests that they were simply ungovernable.[7] And as Jane Jacobs famously pointed out, cities are important engines of economic development precisely because they embody multiple and contradictory functions, thus making them "great, confused economic laborator[ies]."[8]

Cities and American Exceptionalism

Cities also stand as one of the best examples of contradictory impulses and directions within American political development more generally. The history of the United States is characterized paradoxically by both rapid urbanization and, as Robert Lieberman illustrates in Chapter 1 of this volume, a political culture ambivalent if not hostile to large cities—an apparently odd attitude given the seeming propinquity between a national government clearly created to foster commercial development and early cities that functioned as commercial associations. As Jerome Hodos suggests in Chapter 2, this antipathy is possibly a product of the contradiction between cities that were medieval holdovers, and the more modern devices of liberal theory—most notably the social contract—that served to legitimate the new nation. The social contract implied in the US Constitution is one between citizens and the state. As James Madison made clear in his famous *Federalist*, no. 10, intermediary organizations such as cities or political parties that possessed more power than mere individuals but had no formal authority were conceived as grave threats to individual freedom and the common good. And as Madison's ally Thomas Jefferson famously wrote in a letter to Benjamin Rush: "I view great cities as pestilential to the morals, the health and the liberties of man."[9]

The uniquely foundational role of liberal theory in the founding of the United States has served as one the chief explanations of American "exceptionalism," which itself has been a durable though contentious theme in both the academic study of American political development, and in American political culture more generally.[10] As Lieberman discusses in his chapter, the United States is at least unique in purposefully placing its capital outside of a major city, thus separating political power from commerce and culture. Indeed, Constitutional Convention delegate Elbridge Gerry commented (according to the shorthand notes kept by James Madison) that he "conceived it to be the genl. sense of America, that neither the Seat of a State Govt. nor any large commercial City should be the seat of the Genl. Govt."[11]

Yet Lieberman also contends that this antipathy toward cities has been a variable theme in American political culture. At times cities have played key roles in national political coalitions, most notably during the period from the 1920s to the 1960s when big city populations looked the most like the US population overall. Lieberman thus contends that cities are problematic in American political development as long as they are racially and ethnically distinct from the rest of the country. During that relatively unique period in the twentieth century when national restrictions on immigration reduced cities' roles as ethnic entrepôts, and when it happened that more Americans lived in large cities than at any other point in history—in short, when cities looked demographically the most like the country overall—there was little conflict between urbanization and American political development.

Lieberman's understanding of the relationship between cities and American political development thus follows in the tradition of urban-centered historical studies by political scientists such as Ira Katznelson and Amy Bridges, who have seen cities not as unique in themselves, but as providing venues that magnify larger issues of racial and class conflict—as Katznelson puts it in the conclusion to this volume: "Cities present a privileged viewpoint from which to ask fundamental questions, and deploy systematic historical and social science research and evidence to answer them."[12] Thus Katznelson and Bridges both examined New York City in explaining the absence of a working-class party in the United States. In contrast, there has been as yet limited study of how American cities, as enduring institutions, may or may not fit within the exceptionalist framework. As a medieval institution that was carried over from the Old World, the city conceivably complicates the exceptionalist notion that the United States is unique for having no feudal past. The traditional story has been that cities, ill-fitted as they were in the American system of government, were rather quickly established in law as administrative adjuncts of state governments—or, as Judge John Dillon famously described them in 1868, "mere tenants at will of the legislature."[13]

The weakness of American cities has been cast in the literature as a practically inevitable outcome of cities' awkward placement as quasi-governmental, corporate entities in the American political system.[14] The solution, starting at least with John Marshall's famous decision in the 1819 *Dartmouth* case, was to separate out the private corporation, ultimately synonymous with the rights-bearing individual, and to establish the city as a public, municipal corporation, which later court cases confirmed was merely an administrative adjunct of state government with no discretionary powers—a position that came to be defined as "Dillon's Rule."

Practically every textbook on American state and local government discusses Dillon's Rule and the inherent weakness of local government. In contrast to this standard story of municipal weakness, both Hodos and Kaufman demonstrate that, when compared to cities in both Europe and Canada, American cities appear as notably autonomous local actors—it is, after all, significant that American courts had to clarify that cities were subsidiary to state legislatures. As Kaufman explains, cities in Canada had no corporate status until the mid-nineteenth century, while cities in the United States had been organized as corporations since the eighteenth century, and in many cases even earlier. Corporate status gave cities in the United States relatively more autonomy than their Canadian counterparts, and thus the successive court cases that identified them as adjuncts of state government can be interpreted as defensive measures, based on American cities' relatively prominent stature.

While Kaufman compares American and Canadian cities in order to illuminate their differences, Hodos argues that the differences between

British and American cities (in terms of their relationships to the larger systems of government in which they respectively find themselves) are best understood against the larger backdrop of their greater similarities, especially when compared to cities in Continental Europe. The "genetic similarities" between American and British cities that differentiate them from other European cities also created similar historical trajectories, as political development in both countries has been characterized by the challenges of negotiating shifting authority relations within institutional webs, features of which—most notably cities—predate the nation states. And in both countries, while the cities have been redeployed in similar ways as institutional tools of political modernization and of government reinvention, cities in both countries have also resisted the intrusion of government at higher levels, seeking to reinvent themselves as modern versions of the commercial associations they once were. Cities in Britain and the United States thus serve as examples of concurrent intercurrence, the result of a common premodern institutional legacy.

American Political Development and the Study of Urban Politics

It is notable that the period during which cities were most demo-graphically similar to the country as a whole was also the period within the American social sciences that the city became a common case study from which it was assumed larger implications could be drawn. From the inception of the discipline in the United States in the late nineteenth century up until World War II—during which time the majority of the American population came to live in urban areas, as first recorded by the Census in 1920—the city had been a central concern within political science. The *American Political Science Review* had a section on "municipal affairs" that appeared in most issues,[15] and the first president of the American Political Science Association, Frank Goodnow, devoted much of his scholarly attention to cities.[16] Later presidents, such as Charles Merriam (a reform-oriented Chicago alderman) and William Bennett Munro, were also centrally concerned with city government. As Merriam noted in his 1926 presidential address: "One of the most striking advances in research during the last twenty-one years has been that centering around the problem of the modern city . . . In no field has there been more scientific and practical political research than here."[17]

As Merriam's comments suggest, the city had been a subject of interest precisely because it represented a unique institutional form in the American political system. Similarly, James Bryce's famous comment in *American Commonwealth* (1888) that "the government of cities is the one conspicuous failure of the United States" speaks to a concern for the institutional particularities of municipalities—or, as Bryce called them, "mechanical defects in the structure of municipal governments."[18] The antidote was institutional reform specific to the problems of cities. Early issues of the *American Political Science Review* thus practically brim over with institutionalist studies of commission government, city manager systems, home rule systems, and municipal ownership of utilities.

The interest in cities was eclipsed by the concern with the rise of fascism in Europe and US involvement in World War II. After the war the interest in cities returned, precisely at the moment that such traditional industrial centers as Philadelphia, Detroit, and Baltimore reached their peak populations. Indeed, Clarence Stone and Robert Whelan in their chapter claim that the 1950s and 1960s are (incorrectly, they argue) perceived as the "golden age" in the study of urban politics. Yet for the most part cities were no longer viewed as unique institutional forms as much as microcosms of the larger society that could serve as convenient case studies. The pre-eminent political scientist after World War II, Robert Dahl, for instance, used for a major study of American pluralism a single city, New Haven, justified by the simple explanation that it "lay conveniently at hand."[19] The debate over the distribution of power in American society that flourished during the postwar decades was one that rested mostly on competing depictions of power and political participation in individual cities and towns. As Paul Peterson summarized this approach:

> Every political scientist lives in a city, in a town, or at least in a village; by studying the politics around him, he can—with only modest research resources—gather the rich contextual information necessary for high-quality interpretive analysis, which he then generalizes to the nation as a whole.[20]

As Stone and Whelan describe in their chapter, the pluralist strain of this "community power structure" debate, championed by Dahl, Edward Banfield, and others, imagined city politics as a process of progressive modernization and assimilation where immigrants and other newcomers to the city arrived with a "private-regarding ethos" but gradually assumed a more "public-regarding ethos" as they worked their way up the socioeconomic ladder. Yet as Stone and Whelan point out, even as this theory of modernization was being formulated it was being challenged by alternate depictions of the city as embodying continuous and durable inequalities, especially with regard to race.

The beginnings of the "urban crisis"—middle-class "white flight" and corporate disinvestment from American cities, the resultant financial crises of city governments such as New York City's near-bankruptcy in 1975, and the riots of the late 1960s and early 1970s—moved the scholarly discussion away from processes of assimilation to what Stone and Whelan describe as a "political economy" perspective. This new perspective on urban politics was also more state-centered than the pluralist literature, which reflected the postwar behaviorist rejection of institutional explanations, and it once again asserted the relative uniqueness of cities.[21] For instance, in his influential book *City Limits* (1981) in which he sought to hammer the final nail in the coffin of the community power structure debate, Paul Peterson argued that city politics was largely determined by structural forces over which cities had little control. Cities, Peterson noted, were institutionally distinct from nations in that they had no control over their borders and little leverage over economic forces, and they were thus constrained to pursuing "developmental policies" designed to attract labor and capital, while they were also compelled to deflect residents' demands for "redistributional policies." A later formulation of the political economy perspective that sought to move away from the economic determinism of Peterson was the "regime" model pioneered by Stone, which envisioned city politics as largely a process of coordinating different interests to forge an informal group of leaders who had the resources and power to govern. Stone argued that informal arrangements were necessary to urban governance because he argued, like Peterson, that city governments themselves were not provided the institutional capacity to govern without the help of nongovernmental groups, being in most cases the business community.[22]

In contrast to the arguments of Peterson and Stone that cast city government as institutionally weak, Jessica Trounstine brings the local state back in more forcefully by arguing in her chapter that control over city government was a valued asset among competing groups, who, once they had control, sought to make institutional changes to maintain their power. Trounstine uses this claim to challenge the classic dichotomy between "machine" and "reform" regimes, and in doing so provides not only a new revisionist account of this classic divide but also, and possibly most importantly, provides a new institutionalist take on a subject that was central to early political science. For much of the institutionalist thrust of early political science was motivated by the hope that constitutional provisions—commission and city manager government, home rule, civil service, non-partisan and at-large elections, voter registration—could thwart the "corruption" of the classic political machines. Trounstine agrees with the classic accounts in finding that these institutional reforms were significant, but differs in arguing that they served the same purposes as the classic tools of political machines, such as patronage and gerrymandering. Once elected, reform and machine politicians alike sought to alter electoral institutions so as to increase the likelihood of their reelection; both regime types sought to prevent shifts in governing authority by bolstering their institutional durability. The result in both cases was monopolistic municipal government dominated by one party or faction and thus increasingly less responsive to the needs of the populations they governed. Trounstine's chapter thus provides a new account of how shifts in governing authority within cities are made durable through institutional change.

Cities and the Spaces of American Political Development

Notable in Trounstine's account as well is the fact that the cities with machine regimes (Chicago, New York, New Haven, Kansas City, and Philadelphia) differ in their spatial distribution from the cities she covers that had reform regimes (San Jose, Austin, San Antonio, and Dallas). Thus while the specific institutional mechanisms deployed by either machine or reform regimes may have both been used to maintain power within cities, the two types of regimes each collectively formed broader regional cultures. Philip Ethington and David Levitus build on this point in their chapter by arguing that cities and their metropolitan regions have served, at least since the New Deal, as the nodal points of culturally specific regional regimes upon which politicians have achieved national power, thus achieving their "metonymic moment" when a regional political culture becomes nationally dominant. American political development should thus be seen as a complex territorial story, not simply one of "levels" (local, state, federal) or "scales," but of nodes and paths that organize the linkages between resources, representation, leadership, and the exercise of power. The Republican realignment of the 1960s was built on such a metonymic shift where the regional regime of the New Deal, anchored in part by large Eastern and Midwestern cities, ceded control to the regional regime that was anchored in the metropolitan regions of the Sunbelt, which eventually became the national regime of the "New Right." And as Ethington and Levitus note, building on Trounstine, politicians of the Sunbelt campaigned as reformers against "big government" centered in Washington, D.C. and its apparent failings as the "urban crisis" spread.

By introducing space as an orchestrating mechanism within shifts in governing authority, Ethington and Levitus thus expand on Orren and Skowronek's observation that political development is best explored through descriptions "of authority relations as they are arranged on a site."[23] Their chapter is preceded by the more theoretical treatments of the relation between space and political development in the chapters by Neil Brenner and Clarissa Rile Hayward. Brenner builds on Stone and Whelan's chapter by interrogating the scalar and spatial assumptions of the urban political economy literature. Understood as the lived experience of capitalism, urbanism brings what David Harvey has called a "structured coherence" to a mode of production that otherwise negates by constantly reinventing the distinctions between local, national, and global scales. Whereas most political scientists who focus on national-level institutions rely on a "methodological nationalism," that in its aspatiality and inattention to scale reifies an outdated Westphalian vision of the world, urbanist scholars rely similarly on a "methodological localism" that focuses on the role of economic development because it imagines cities as fixed, aspatial containers, bereft of much more than tangential relations to other levels of power. The local focus in the urban political economy literature can thus be faulted at times for taking local scale as an analytical category rather than a product of political development itself that needs to be interrogated and unpacked in order to understand urbanism as the spatial production of capitalism.

Hayward builds on Brenner's critique by examining the spatial construction of power in the case of racial identity. While "scientific" theories of racial hierarchy that became popular in the nineteenth century didn't stand the test of time, they were inscribed in the spatial pattern of urbanization through racially segregated housing, especially by the restrictive covenants—deeds that specified owners could only sell their homes to specific racial groups, usually restricted to Caucasians—that became popular in American cities in the first decades of the twentieth century.[24] Discredited theories of racial hierarchy have thus survived in the spatial expression of urbanization, and they survived in particular through the commodification of urban land. By maintaining the racial homogeneity of neighborhoods, restrictive covenants maintained property values. The values of the discredited theories of racial hierarchies were thus transmuted into monetary values for homes, and no longer had to be justified (as they could not be) through narratives. Narrative identities of racial superiority and inferiority were thus deeply embedded into the American urban landscape.

As is well known, the value of race as expressed in housing was just as much a product of government policy as it was of free markets. In 1933 the federal government created the Home Owners Loan Corporation (HOLC) to refinance more than 1 million mortgages at risk of default. Building on the popular restrictive covenants, the HOLC established as part of its lending criteria appraisal standards that consistently downgraded notably non-Caucasian central city neighborhoods while favorably evaluating the newer outlying, and more uniformly white, suburbs. The HOLC was disbanded in 1936, and in its place the Federal Housing Administration (FHA) established a massive mortgage guarantee program with similarly racialized appraisal standards in a rating system that made mortgages relatively cheaper for newly constructed homes, most notably in the newer suburbs. Thus the division between city and suburb that became more pronounced after World War II also became a spatially defined racial division—so much so that one big-city mayor famously referred to suburbs in the 1950s as a "white noose" strangling the country's cities.[25] Yet as Hayward points out, for suburbanites, the legal separation of suburbs as municipalities independent of the cities they surround is yet another layer of the racial construction of urban space that allows for the denial that race is a collective problem, but rather one particular to racialized cities.

Race, Ethnicity, and American Political Development

Hayward thus brings the discussion back to Chapter 1 by expanding on Lieberman's observation that cities are accepted within American political culture only at moments when there is a close demographic similitude between cities and the nation as a whole. Yet as Hayward suggests, the more common demographic dissimilitude of cities can be seen not only as a product of who happened to live in cities at certain times, but also an attempt to structure urban space so as to compartmentalize racial and ethnic conflict so that they can be defined as aberrations within the narrative of progressive assimilation that has been a longstanding ideal within American political development. As Stone and Whelan point out, the story of orderly and progressive assimilation—"modernization"—in urban politics was most salient in the 1950s, precisely the moment when cities most resembled the country as a whole.

Each of the three chapters in the final section of the book demonstrates different ways in which race and ethnicity were constructed in specific cities, and how those constructions then informed national policy. Michael Jones-Correa compares the impact of the racially and ethnically charged riots at both the beginning and end of the twentieth century, from 1917 to 1921 and from 1980 to 1993 respectively, which he argues followed similar trajectories in terms of how they helped to shape national policies affecting cities. While the earlier race riots accelerated the adoption of racial restrictive covenants that later informed and guided HOLC and FHA underwriting policies, the riots from the 1980s and 1990s spurred federal initiatives in private urban investment, namely Enterprise and Empowerment zones, that were adapted from local strategies. In both periods, then, Jones-Correa uncovers a common pattern of local responses to ethnic and race riots that shaped and informed national policy.

Matthew Crenson argues that the unique race relations that define the history of Baltimore helped to shape the national government's response to civil rights. As a border city that attracted both Southern plantation owners and Quaker merchants, Baltimore's elite could not discuss race beyond a basic agreement on recolonization and, later, on nativism—so as to talk about immigration rather than race. At the same time, Baltimore had the largest free black population of any American city prior to the Civil War. The combination of a large free black population and a white city leadership that declined to discuss or deal with race meant that black Baltimoreans were far more preoccupied fighting with one another than uniting around their common racial identity. Thus black civil rights leaders from Baltimore, most notably Thurgood Marshall and Clarence Mitchell, had skills in compromise and negotiation rather than in mass mobilization, reflected in Marshall's efforts in litigation and Mitchell's efforts in lobbying, neither of which required mass appeals. At a more general institutional level, the unique form of racial politics developed in

Baltimore informed the larger strategy of the National Association for the Advancement of Colored People (NAACP).

In the final chapter, Alethia Jones traces the urban origins of United States Postal Savings Banks (PSBs) at the turn of the twentieth century. Challenging the traditional story of policy formulation within political science that focuses on policy actors and how they structure programs to meet specific clienteles, Jones argues that the origins of PSBs can only be adequately understood by also examining the policy targets, namely politically weak immigrants who did not have the power to lobby Congress. The immigrant origins of PSBs are uniquely urban not only because most immigrants lived in cities, but also because immigrants, possessing composite identities as both local and international actors, represented the very complexities of space that define urbanization. PSBs were international in the sense that they mimicked the government banking functions that were familiar to European immigrants, and they were local in the sense that they were intended to provide greater stability than the largely unregulated or loosely regulated neighborhood banks that had sprung up in city neighborhoods across the country. In responding to a uniquely urban need, PSBs also created a new standard for state banking regulations and thus nationalized the banking system, paving the way for later New Deal reforms. The purpose of the PSBs (which were eliminated in 1966) of creating greater stability from fear of bank runs was generalized in 1933 by the creation of the Federal Deposit Insurance Corporation, which thus carries within its legacy the urban origins of PSBs.

Notes

1. The contemporary count of municipal government is from the United States Census's 2007 Census of Governments, located at http://www.census.gov/govs/www/cog2007.html (accessed June 30, 2008). The figure of "about twenty" cities having corporate charters prior to ratification of the Constitution comes from Gerald Frug, *City Making: Building Communities without Building Walls* (Princeton, NJ: Princeton University Press, 1999), p. 36.
2. Theda Skocpol, "Bringing the City Back In: Strategies of Analysis in Current Research," in Peter B. Evans, Dietrich Rueschemeyer, and Theda Skocpol, eds., *Bringing the City Back In* (New York: Cambridge University Press, 1985), pp. 4–5. See also Kathleen Thelen and Sven Steinmo, "Historical Institutionalism in Comparative Politics," in Sven Steinmo, Kathleen Thelen, and Frank Longstreth, eds., *Structuring Politics: Historical Institutionalism in Comparative Analysis* (New York: Cambridge University Press, 1992). For an important critique of Skocpol and others, see Gabriel A. Almond, "The Return to the State," *American Political Science Review* 82 (September 1988): 853–874.
3. Peter A. Hall and Rosemary C.R. Taylor, "Political Science and the Three New Institutionalisms," in Karol Sultan, Eric M. Uslaner, and Virginia Haufler, eds., *Institutions and Social Order* (Ann Arbor: University of Michigan Press, 1998), pp. 15–44.

4. On path dependence see Paul Pierson, *Politics in Time: History, Institutions, and Social Analysis* (Princeton, NJ: Princeton University Press, 2004), ch. 1; on critical junctures see John Hogan, "Remoulding the Critical Junctures Approach," *Canadian Journal of Political Science* 39 (September 2006): 657–679; and on realignment, specifically as it relates to the study of American political development, see Karen Orren and Stephen Skowronek, *The Search for American Political Development* (New York: Cambridge University Press, 2004), pp. 59–64.

5. Orren and Skowronek, *The Search for American Political Development*, quotes on pp. 108, 114, 120.

6. Ibid., p. 22.

7. Douglas Yates, *The Ungovernable City: The Politics of Urban Problems and Policy Making* (Cambridge, MA: MIT Press, 1977).

8. Jane Jacobs, *The Economy of Cites* (New York: Vintage Books, 1969), p. 92.

9. Jefferson to Rush, September 23,1800, in Albert Ellery Bergh, ed., *The Writings of Thomas Jefferson* (Washington, DC: Thomas Jefferson Memorial Association, 1907), vol. 10, p. 173; quoted by Lieberman in Chapter 1 of this volume.

10. See Orren and Skowronek, *The Search for American Political Development*, pp. 57–59.

11. James Madison, *Notes of Debates in the Federal Convention of 1787*, July 26, 1787. Available at http://avalon.law.yale.edu/subject_menus/debcont.asp.

12. See also Ira Katznelson, *City Trenches: Urban Politics and the Patterning of Class in the United States* (New York: Pantheon, 1981); and Amy Bridges, *A City in the Republic: Antebellum New York and the Origins of Machine Politics* (New York: Cambridge University Press, 1984), pp. 5–6. As Katznelson noted of the social turbulence that defined the 1960s: "The city was portrayed as the locale of a myriad of social ills, as if these shortcomings were uniquely or inherently urban, and as if cities and their problems were not condensed versions of the relations that characterize the society as a whole" (*City Trenches*, p. 3).

13. *City of Clinton v. The Cedar Rapids and Missouri River Railroad Co.*, 24 Iowa 455 (1868), quoted in Anwar H. Syed, *The Political Theory of American Local Government* (New York: Random House, 1966), p. 68, and by Hodos in Chapter 2 of this volume.

14. See, for instance, Frug, *City Making*, pp. 39–48.

15. See, for instance, John A. Fairlie, "Municipal," *American Political Science Review* 1 (November 1906): 114–122; Fairlie, "Municipal Notes," *American Political Science Review* (August 1907): 683–693; William B. Munro, "Municipal Affairs," *American Political Science Review* 2 (February 1908): 274–283; and Munro, "Notes on Current Municipal Affairs," *American Political Science Review* 3 (May 1909): 245–252.

16. See, for instance, Goodnow's books *Municipal Problems* (New York: Macmillan, 1897), *City Government in the United States* (New York: Century Company, 1906), and *Municipal Government* (New York: Century Company, 1909).

17. Charles E. Merriam, "Progress in Political Research," *American Political Science Review* 20 (February 1926): 1–13.

18. James Bryce, *American Commonwealth* (Indianapolis: Liberty Fund, 1995; originally published in 1988 by Macmillan and Company), vol. 1, ch. 51.

19. Robert A. Dahl, *Who Governs? Democracy and Power in an American City*, second edition (New Haven: Yale University Press, 2005), p. xiii. Later authors have explicitly used Dahl's justification for their own case studies,

such as Gregory E. McAvoy, *Controlling Technocracy: Citizen Rationality and the NIMBY Syndrome* (Washington, DC: Georgetown University Press, 1999), p. 11.

20. Paul E. Peterson, *City Limits* (Chicago: University of Chicago Press, 1981), p. 3.
21. For an influential example of the rejection of institutional explanations, see Robert A. Dahl, *A Preface to Democratic Theory* (Chicago: University of Chicago Press, 1956), pp. 135–137.
22. Clarence N. Stone, *Regime Politics: Governing Atlanta, 1946–1988* (Lawrence: University Press of Kansas, 1989), pp. 3–11.
23. Orren and Skowronek, *The Search for American Political Development*, pp. 24–25.
24. For a recent and very readable review of nineteenth- and early twentieth-century theories of racial hierarchy, see Louis Menand, *The Metaphysical Club: The Story of Ideas in America* (New York: Farrar, Straus and Giroux, 2001), ch. 5, and for a discussion of racial covenants, see Michael Jones-Correa, "The Origins and Diffusion of Racial Restrictive Covenants," *Political Science Quarterly* 115 (2000–2001): 541–568.
25. As quoted, among other places, in the United States Commission on Civil Rights, *Book 4: Report on Housing* (Washington, DC: Government Printing Office, 1961), p. 1.

Part I
American Exceptionalism and the City

1 The City and Exceptionalism in American Political Development

Robert C. Lieberman

In 1813, in the middle of their extraordinary correspondence on the evolving government of the fledgling republic they both helped to found, Thomas Jefferson wrote to John Adams:

> Before the establishment of the American states, nothing was known to History but the man of the old world, crowded within limits either small or overcharged, and steeped in the vices which that situation generates. A government adapted to such men would be one thing; but a very different one, that for the man of these States. Here every one may have land to labor for himself if he chooses; or, preferring the exercise of any other industry, may exact for it such compensation as not only to afford a comfortable subsistence, but wherewith to provide for a cessation from labor in old age. Every one, by his property, or by his satisfactory situation, is interested in the support of law and order. And such men may safely and advantageously reserve to themselves a wholesome control over their public affairs, and a degree of freedom, which in the hands of the *canaille* of the cities of Europe, would be instantly perverted to the demolition and destruction of everything public and private. The history of the last twenty-five years of France, and of the last forty years in America, nay of its last two hundred years, proves the truth of both parts of this observation.[1]

This quotation reveals most fully and subtly Jefferson's deep antipathy to cities and his conviction that they were profoundly harmful to the political life of a nation with democratic aspirations. Democracy, he believed, required an independent citizenry, self-sufficient, virtuous, and fully capable of self-government. These qualities resided in the countryside of the yeoman farmer, not in cities, which he thought pestilential, crowded places that bred corruption, dependence, and tyranny. Some years earlier he wrote even more bluntly and shockingly to Benjamin Rush, a leading citizen of one of North America's largest and most cosmopolitan cities, that the yellow fever epidemic then afflicting several American cities would discourage the growth of great cities in our nation, and I view great cities as pestilential to the morals, the health and the liberties of man. True, they nourish some of the elegant arts; but the useful ones can thrive elsewhere; and less perfection in the others, with more health, virtue and freedom would be my choice.[2]

In these passages and elsewhere, Jefferson expressed the already-common theme of American exceptionalism, the conviction that American society was fundamentally different from the sclerotic feudalism of the Old World. In the great capitals of Europe such as Paris and London political, economic, cultural, and social power mingled to create singular centers of national dominance that held sway over their national peripheries, symbolizing the dominance of the absolutist courts of European monarchs, which Jefferson particularly feared. Jefferson's antipathy toward cities and the connection he made between cities and aristocratic corruption anticipated Tocqueville, the first systematic American exceptionalist. "America," Tocqueville wrote, "does not have a great capital whose direct or indirect influence makes itself felt over the whole extent of its territory," distinctly drawing a contrast between the United States and his home country of France, where Paris held sway politically, economically, socially, and culturally over the entire country. The lack of a metropolis, Tocqueville went on to say, "I consider to be one of the first causes of the maintenance of republican institutions in the United States" because cities—like Paris during the French Revolution—were especially prone to disorder and, in the extreme, the dangerous plebiscitary action of easily manipulable crowds.[3] Cities thus posed a dual danger for American democracy: aristocratic despotism on the one hand and mob rule on the other. For Jefferson, as for others of the founding generation, the future of the republic lay in the sturdy independence of the American countryside.

Jefferson's cultural and political hostility toward cities has been a constant theme in American political life ever since. Cities, moreover, have repeatedly and consistently been at the center of national political, economic, and cultural controversies. Jefferson himself, along with James Madison, clashed with Alexander Hamilton in the 1790s over the location of the national capital and the role of commerce and finance, centered in cities such as New York and Philadelphia, in the political economy. Draft riots in New York City in 1863 highlighted conflicts across lines of class and race that threatened the precarious unity of the Union's war effort, and urban violence has continued to be a national flashpoint, inflaming divisive tensions within American society.[4] In the Progressive era, cities were the focal point of fundamental conflicts over the form and content of American governance and political institutions—conflict over political parties and municipal reform, immigration and race, labor rights, poverty, and public health.[5] And in the late twentieth and early twenty-first centuries, cities have again come under assault from national political leaders and governing coalitions, a trend visible both in policies—the slow but dramatic decline in federal support for city governments, for example—and in often pungent expression: "God damn New York," Richard Nixon said in a taped conversation in 1972, complaining that the city was full of "Jews, and Catholics, and blacks and Puerto Ricans." This new round of national antipathy for cities was neatly summed up in the banner headline on the front page of the New York *Daily News* on October 30, 1975, summarizing the president's refusal to bail the city out of impending bankruptcy: "Ford to City: Drop Dead."[6]

But Americans have not always been so consistently and relentlessly anti-urban in their political sensibilities. This picture of American anti-urbanism obscures substantial and significant variation in the place that cities have occupied in American national politics over time and across lines of region, race, and ideology. Against this background of profound fear and loathing, cities have at times been essential parts of the American state—of national governing coalitions that have exercised power and shaped public policy, of associational networks that connect public authorities to civil society, and of the common cultural notion of the state.[7] During a few periods in American political history—in particular the late nineteenth century and the New Deal era—cities, and their residents and political elites, were especially powerful presences in American politics. At these moments, cities seem to have been central to the national political regime in ways that defied the general anti-urban bias that affects American politics both culturally and institutionally.[8] In these periods, urban voters and party organizations were critical to national electoral and governing coalitions; their representatives carried unusual weight in Congress (despite Congress's structural representational bias toward geography and against dense concentrations of people); and contributed substantially to the ideological and cultural valence of policy debates. In addition to providing more than their usual share of inputs in American national politics in these periods, cities also received more outputs than at other times, especially in terms of policy benefits but also of prestige and attention. In short, in these periods particularly, the American city was a key component of the American state; this was, however, a rather uncommon state of affairs. These observations, moreover, puncture the Jeffersonian mythology of American exceptionalism by suggesting that American politics is, at least under some circumstances, susceptible to the same political forces that have made European cities centers of power and prestige.

What was it about these periods—if indeed these periods were as I describe them—that made them moments of urban triumph, in which cities overcame the cultural and institutional odds that the basic structure of American politics seems to lay against them? What configurations of political conditions prevailed to make this happen, and what can we learn from these patterns both about the prospects for cities and their residents in the new suburban (or exurban or posturban) era in which American politics now finds itself and about American political development more generally? In this chapter, I do not even begin to answer these questions but rather to lay the groundwork for a possible approach to them. I will first lay out briefly some of the conceptual, analytical, and empirical issues that these questions pose, with a view toward developing an agenda for research. I will then present a broad empirical sketch of some of the key demographic and political characteristics of the major American cities from the beginning of the republic until the present. This empirical portrait will further sharpen the analytical questions with which I begin. Finally, I will suggest possible further directions for connecting the city and the state in American political development.

Cities in the Study of American Political Development

One of the principal issues in American political development that this study potentially engages is the status of ideology or political culture and institutions as potentially competing or conflicting explanatory factors and analytical modes. The basic cultural anxiety about cities that Jefferson expressed has long been a dominant theme, or at least a prominent motif, of American political culture. It coincided with the partisan struggles that Jefferson, along with his fellow Virginia squire James Madison, waged with Alexander Hamilton in the 1790s on issues including the creation of the First Bank of the United States and the construction of an interlocking system of public and private finance, Hamilton's proposals to promote commerce and manufacturing, and especially the location of the national capital. In the last of these battles, the cosmopolitan Hamilton favored New York but would have settled for Philadelphia, both centers of culture and commerce to which he thought power was naturally and necessarily connected. Jefferson and Madison preferred to separate power from commerce and culture, preventing the creation of a single urban center like Paris or London around which the provincial hinterlands would revolve. They instead sought to create a new capital on the unpromising swampy banks of the Potomac River that quite by design lacked the commercial core that typically nurtured the growth of powerful cities, even when their origins were military or ecclesiastical, or even political.[9] This anti-urban ideological bias has persisted, as Grant McConnell noted, in the mythology of the small constituency, rooted in a Jeffersonian image of small communities as "repositories of social virtue."[10] Cities, by contrast, have often been portrayed as sites of vice and corruption. At the same time, this mythology of rural virtue has parallels in the imagery of the countryside of "Merrie Olde England" and "la France profonde," suggesting that anti-urban cultural patterns, while important, may not be sufficient to explain national differences in the political power and prestige of cities in national regimes.

At the same time, the institutional structure of American politics is also biased against cities, or against any densely concentrated areas of population. The representational structures of the Senate and the Electoral College, which allocate votes to territorial units rather than people, confer extra power on sparsely populated states. Before the Supreme Court's "one person, one vote" decisions of the early 1960s, this imbalance was, in many instances, exacerbated by states that replicated this territory-based districting scheme that privileged rural counties over cities.[11] Some analysts have argued that the decentralized and fragmented institutional structure of the American state has systematically nurtured and enhanced the privileged position of rural agricultural interests (although others have challenged this interpretation).[12]

The question that emerges from these overlapping and reinforcing forces is how and why American cities have been able to overcome both the ideological and institutional barriers to their power. Both of these anti-urban currents in the American political tradition—the cultural and the institutional—are generally posited to be relatively stable, ordered patterns that organize large swaths of political life over reasonably long spans of time. But to the extent that these patterns are stable, they cannot explain the apparent ups and downs of the political fortunes of cities over time. What is it that changed at those moments when cities fared better in national politics? Were these moments when pro-urban cultural forces surged and prevailed? If so, how did they overcome pervasive institutional barriers? Or were these moments primarily the consequence of institutional changes that challenged prevailing cultural norms about cities? These questions not only frame the key causal axis of this inquiry, they also connect this project to some of the most central and urgent questions at the forefront of the subfield of American political development.[13]

These considerations suggest a range of potential explanations for over-time variation in the political fortunes of cities. First, there might be variations in cultural patterns and ideological beliefs about cities. It is a grave mistake, as Rogers Smith has shown, to consider the American political tradition as monolithic; American political culture, rather, consists of multiple strands whose contest for dominance shapes political arrangements and outcomes.[14] In order to paint a complete picture of this phenomenon and assess the role of political culture and ideas in affecting the shifting power and prestige of cities in the American state, it will be necessary to identify, unpack, and measure these competing ideological strands, one that regards cities as dangerous, dirty, and corrupt and another that celebrates cities as civilized, tolerant, and dynamic—a challenge that I acknowledge but do not begin to undertake here.[15] Second, the political and institutional circumstances of cities have clearly been deeply susceptible to change over time and these political changes, doubt-less interacting in complex ways with shifting cultural sensibilities, are also necessary for mounting a causal explanation. Although empirically these two strands may often be difficult to entangle—as in the case of Progressive reform, which involved both ideological claims about cities and institutional engineering of them—they are analytically distinct and need as far as possible to be treated separately, to better to assess their independent and interactive causal effects.

I offer here a first, and admittedly rough, approach to measuring the institutional and political contours of the city–state relationship. (I regard the assembly and description of this data as this chapter's main purpose, as a preliminary step toward future work that might make use of these data in an explanatory argument.) There are several dimensions of the political evolution of American cities that form a useful starting place for consideration of potential institutional causes. First is simply the demo-graphic transformation of American cities in relation to the rest of the country—their growth and decline and the shifting characteristics of their populations, particularly their racial and ethnic diversity. Diversity—ethnic, racial, and cultural—is one of the key politically salient features of American cities, noted by both pro- and anti-urban forces alike. Measuring the extent of that diversity, in terms both of absolute numbers and of divergence from or convergence with the rest of the country will be essential to developing and testing hypotheses about diversity as a factor in shaping the relationship between cities and the state. In a demo-cratic political system, moreover, the size of any subgroup of the popu-lation is a principal basis for that group's power and ability to protect and foster its interests. Size, however, is not everything in democratic politics; institutional arrangements are crucial in translating numbers into votes into power, and the institutional matrix in which American cities are embedded amply bears out this point. A second dimension, therefore, is the way in which cities fit into the representational structure of American politics. How are urban populations represented in American national policymaking institutions? Do those institutions dilute the strength of urban voices in American politics, or do they provide opportunities for urban interests to be influential, if not decisive, in national policy debates and power struggles? Finally, cities are not the same everywhere in the United States; the patterning of urban work, space, and politics differs from region to region and era to era, and these differences may be systematically connected to the overall weight of cities in American political life.

At least one final measurement issue looms, and that is the dependent variable, which I have variously described as the level of urban partici-pation, prestige, power, or influence in the American national state. There are a number of ways that this outcome, or cluster of outcomes, might be measured: policy enactments or other policy benefits (such as funding or other material goodies) that flow to cities; levels of participation by urban voters and representatives in national policymaking processes; and levels of urban power in the regime. Clearly these are difficult concepts to measure and will need to be refined in order to make the larger project at hand a feasible one. Moreover, the risk of endogeneity is high, as these outcomes inherently blend into many of the potential underlying explanatory factors, both ideological and political. I do not address this measurement challenge here; I merely note it as an analytical issue and a necessary next step.

An Empirical Survey of American Cities, 1790–2000

To measure the shifting political fortunes of American cities requires a consistent empirical definition of what constitutes a city. This is not as straightforward a question as it might seem. Some places clearly deserve to be called cities, densely populated human agglomerations that serve as economic and cultural focal points for a surrounding region—large metropolises such as New York City, of course, but also Little Rock, Arkansas, or Boise, Idaho. Others place of comparable size to Little Rock and Boise, however, might seem less clear candidates to be called cities because they are less central to the political economies of their surrounding regions—Huntington Beach, California, say, or Chandler, Arizona.[16]

Cross-national comparison adds further complication to the question of what constitutes a city. No matter how cities are defined—whether by sheer population size or by economic or political centrality to a surrounding region—the United States undeniably contains many of them, and for much of American history one would be hard-pressed to identify a single nationally dominant city over a long span of time. In other countries, by contrast, single cities have tended to dominate. In population terms, for example, Paris is more than 2.5 times the size of France's next-largest city (Marseille), while London is more than seven times larger than its nearest competitor in the UK (Birmingham).[17] By comparison, New York is slightly more than twice the size of Los Angeles. The drop-off in size from top city is faster outside the United States: the ratio of the largest city to the tenth-largest is 10.0 in France (Paris–Lille) and 21.7 in the UK (London–Leicester), compared with 8.4 in the United States (New York–Detroit). In some countries, population changes are further compounding this centralizing tendency, as in Japan, where the national population is shrinking but the population of Tokyo is growing. Moreover, many of the great European metropolises are national centers not only of population but also of commerce, culture, and political power, clearly standing in a hierarchical relation to other cities in the country— again, London and Paris stand as the paradigmatic examples. These comparisons further highlight the potential distinctiveness of American urbanism—in particular the relative dispersion of urbanism across the

American landscape (both geographical and political)—and the importance of considering cities collectively as a distinctive political actor in American political development.

This task, however, poses important measurement issues. The empirical challenge is to define a universe of cities systematically that describes the urban arc of American political development and approximates a reasonable boundary between urban and sub- or ex-urban, even as that boundary becomes fuzzier in the post-industrial political economy of the twenty-first century. There are two possible measurement approaches: absolute and relative, each with its own virtues and defects.

An absolute scale for measuring cities would involve setting a fixed population threshold—say, 100,000—and counting only cities that meet that threshold in any given year. This approach has the potential advantage of allowing the inclusion only of substantial urban agglomerations by setting the threshold high enough to exclude small municipalities. The risk, however, is that using a fixed numerical threshold over time might mask substantial variation in the size a place must be to be considered a major city. Consequently, an absolute approach might either unreasonably exclude cities from an earlier period (when the population was smaller and a city that today would be called small was considered big) or include cities in a later period that are too small to be reasonably considered important urban centers, or both. To illustrate this dilemma, take 100,000 as a population threshold. At first blush, this seems a reasonable, if arbitrary, line separating large cities from small cities and other sorts of places. But not until the 1820 Census, when New York clocked in at 123,706, did a single American city break the 100,000 barrier. This measure, then, would exclude not only New York before 1820 but also Philadelphia, Boston, Charleston, and Baltimore, all estimable cities in this period and important commercial, political, and cultural centers in the early republic. On the flip side, by 2000 this cutoff is clearly too low: it would include places such as Livonia, Michigan; Arvada, Colorado; West Covina, California; and McAllen, Texas, none of which would make anyone's list of important urban centers in the United States (not yet, anyway). Raising or lowering the threshold would not help; doing so would simply make it even harder for early cities to count or easier for later ones.[18]

The alternative approach, and the one I adopt here, is to define cities relative to changes in overall population by setting the threshold size for inclusion not at an absolute population level but at a fixed percentage of the total national population. This approach not only still allows for the identification of significant urban agglomerations but also now allows the definition of what counts as a city to change as the overall size of the country—and hence a reasonable measure of what counts as a "big" city—changes. The virtues and defects of this approach are the obverse of the absolute approach: a relative cutoff might include some very small places in early years and exclude significant cities in later years when the population, and hence the threshold is larger. For example, using a threshold of one-tenth of 1 percent of the total United States population includes Middleborough, Massachusetts (population 4,526), in 1790 but excludes Corpus Christi, Texas (population 277,454) in 2000. Despite these anomalies at the margins, however, this admittedly arbitrary standard, 0.1 percent of the total national population, actually produces a fairly reasonable list of American cities over time. The threshold city size for inclusion has grown from 3,929 in 1790 to 281,422 in 2000.[19] Most important, the relative standard effectively holds constant over time the minimum ratio of country to city size, which is important to avoid selection bias in explaining variation in the political importance of cities: any such variation found in these data will not be the result solely of choosing only "mega-cities" in an earlier, more sparsely populated era and many "quasi-cities" in later years.[20]

This criterion, at least 0.1 percent of the total national population in any given census year, produces a set that includes 115 different cities.[21] Four cities—Baltimore, Boston, New York, and Philadelphia—appear on the list in each of the twenty-two censuses. Only three other cities—Honolulu, New Orleans, and San Francisco—appear on the list for every year since their states joined the Union. At the other extreme, six cities cross the threshold only once: Marblehead and Middleborough, Massachusetts (both in 1790); St Joseph, Missouri (1900); Mobile, Alabama (1960); and Moyamensing, Pennsylvania, and Williamsburgh, New York (both in 1850, four years before they were consolidated into Philadelphia and Brooklyn, respectively). Six cities have, at various times, been even an order of magnitude larger, reaching a population of more than 1 percent of the national total: New York (every year since 1800), Philadelphia (1860–1960), Brooklyn (1870–1890; Brooklyn became part of New York City in 1898), Chicago (1880–2000), Detroit (1930–1950), and Los Angeles (1930–2000). And even in this group, New York is something of an outlier; the largest city in the country since independence, New York had more than 5 percent of the country's population from 1910 to 1950, more than twice its nearest rival during those years, Chicago.

These data can, first, provide a general picture of the changing prominence of cities in the United States. Figure 1.1 plots both the number of cities and their share of the total national population over time. The dominant trend is dramatic growth, from seventeen cities comprising less than 5 percent of the country's population in 1790 to approximately sixty cities containing more than one in four Americans in the middle of the twentieth century. Since 1950, the number of cities has remained constant, but the urban share of the total population has declined substantially, from 27.0 percent at its peak in 1930 to 16.9 percent in 2000. This pattern corresponds to the temporal arc of American industrialism, which fueled the growth of the great American cities in the nineteenth and early twentieth centuries and whose dissipation produced urban decline and the rise of suburbs, exurbs, and edge cities in the last half of the twentieth century.[22] This pattern also suggests at the crudest and most straightforward level that sheer numbers can help account for urban influence in American political development: the New Deal era, roughly from the 1930s to the 1960s, stands out as the peak moment for cities considered simply as a share of the American nation.

By a related measure, the United States is currently among the least urban of the world's advanced industrial nations. Figure 1.2 displays the urban percentage of the populations of thirty countries, covering most of the expanded European Union and Organization for Economic Cooperation and Development (OECD) countries. The data in Figure 1.2 are calculated the same way as the American data in Figure 1.1, counting cities with at least 0.1 percent of the total national population (although with a city population floor of 50,000).[23] Urban population in the United States is roughly comparable to that of France but considerably lower than that of the UK or of other major industrial countries such as Germany and Japan. Moreover, these aggregate urbanization figures conceal notable differences about the concentration of urban populations in a single metropolis. Again, most comparable to the United States is France, whose largest city, Paris, has less than 4 percent of the country's population (down from nearly 7 percent in the early twentieth century). Less than 3 percent of the total US population lived in New York City in 2000. By contrast, approximately one in nine people in the UK lived in

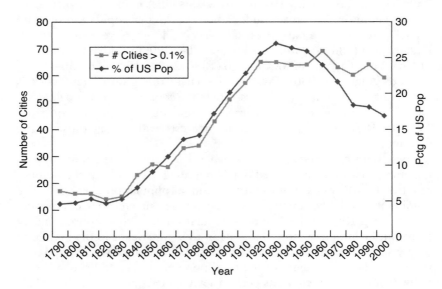

Figure 1.1 Number and population of major cities, 1790–2000

London according to the most recent national census, a pattern of concentration that has remained more or less unchanged since the mid-nineteenth century. Moreover, regardless of population density or dispersal, many countries contain single cities that combine national capital, financial and economic centers, and unrivaled cultural preeminence within countries—not only London and Paris but also cities such as Tokyo, Berlin, Seoul, and Mexico City. This pattern of singularly dominant cities was commonplace in pre-twentieth century Europe, where cities such as Paris, Vienna, and London exerted a strong centripetal attraction on European politics, economy, and society for centuries.[24] These cross-national distinctions underscore the distinctiveness of the American pattern of urbanization, in which urban prominence has been considerably more dissipated and dispersed, compounding the puzzle of the urban political surges of the late nineteenth and mid-twentieth centuries.

The aggregate picture of American urbanization, however, conceals some interesting regional variation, and Figure 1.3 plots the urban share of the population for each of the four regions defined by the Census Bureau.[25] Until the late twentieth century, the Northeast was far and away the leading urban section of the country, with more than one-third of its population living in large cities from 1890 until the 1950s. The Northeast, however, began its period of urban decline somewhat sooner than the rest of the country, falling farther and faster from its peak (42.7 percent in 1920) than other regions. The Midwest and the West followed similar patterns, growing steadily through the nineteenth and into the early twentieth centuries and peaking somewhat later and lower than the Northeast. While Midwestern cities declined as sharply as Northeastern

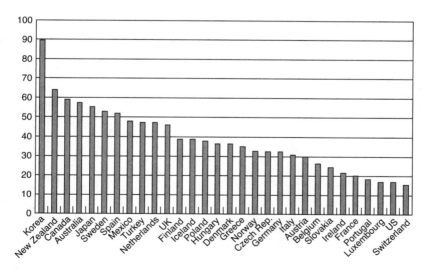

Figure 1.2 Urbanization rates

cities, urbanization in the West has not declined as sharply, and even grew between 1980 and 1990, with the result that the West is now the most urban region of the country. The South has been a consistent outlier throughout American history, with much lower levels of urbanization and much slower, although still steady, growth. Urban growth in the South lasted longer into the twentieth century than in the country's other regions, turning downward only in the last third of the century, some three or four decades after the rest of the country. These regional differences suggest that there is more to the rise and decline of cities in the national regime than simply the size of the urban population. There has been a pronounced shift, these data indicate, from Northern and Eastern cities—older, industrial, densely packed—toward the newer, more spread out cities of the South and West. Regional differences in the political economy, as Richard Bensel has shown, have long been an important driving force in American political development, and it may be that these differences will equally shape the political lives of cities and their relations with the national state.[26] City politics, moreover, differs dramatically across regions; cities of the South and West have been historically much less prone to be organized around strong traditional party organizations; the famous city machines in American political history have typically been located in the Northeast and Midwest, while city politics in the South and West has tended to be either apartisan or even reform-minded.[27] Clearly regional differences have shaped the politics of cities and we might well expect regional shifts in urban population to shape the overall place of cities in the American state.

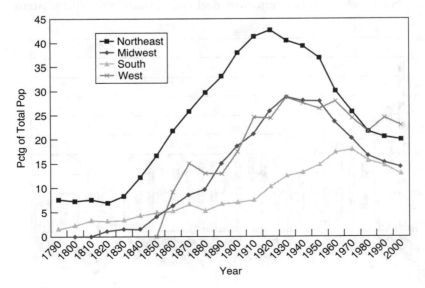

Figure 1.3 City population by region, 1790–2000

Cities loom large in American political consciousness not only because they are large but because they are gathering places of difference, across lines of class, nationality, and especially race. In late nineteenth-century racial "science," African-Americans were generally seen as a rural people, out of place in the city and especially prone, for example, to its characteristic diseases such as tuberculosis. As African-Americans increasingly moved from the countryside to the city over the course of the twentieth century, they became increasingly associated with social rather than biological pathologies—relating especially to family structure, work ethic, and aptitude—that underlay the phenomenon of the "urban underclass."[28]

Comparatively, moreover, this phenomenon—the physical, economic, and political isolation of racial, ethnic, and national-origin minorities— is not necessarily an exclusively urban one. In France, for example, North African immigrants in the post-World War II era were typically concentrated (deliberately) in the suburban outskirts of major cities, first in temporary workers' hostels and later in dense public housing developments. Thus the flashpoint of racial and religious tensions in French society have been in the suburbs, as in the 2005 civil unrest that began in Clichy-sous-Bois, a suburban commune about 16 kilometers northeast of Paris, and spread quickly through the *banlieues* surrounding Paris and other French cities. Britain, by contrast, more closely resembles the United States in the urbanization of its minority population, with ethnic and racial minorities more densely clustered in large cities, from the violence in Nottingham and the Notting Hill neighborhood of London in 1958 to Brixton in South London several times in the 1980s and 1990s and the declining industrial cities of the Midlands (Birmingham and Bradford, among others) in the early 2000s. These comparisons sharpen questions about the relationship among cities, race, and politics in American political development: How might the racial composition of cities interact with political institutions to shape the place of cities in American political life?

American cities have not always been more racially diverse than the rest of the country; in fact, for much of American history—from the early nineteenth century to the mid-twentieth—the reverse was true. Figure 1.4 compares the nonwhite population percentage of American cities with the total national nonwhite population share, and shows that only in the very early years of the republic and again since World War II have cities been less white than the nation as a whole (the figure includes 95 percent confidence intervals around the city nonwhite percentages in order to show that city–national differences are statistically significant in every census year except 1940).

Before the Civil War, however, most nonwhites in the United States were African-American slaves; during this period the percentage of the nonwhite population that were slaves never fell below 86.3 percent (in

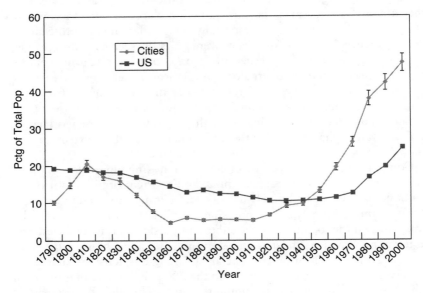

Figure 1.4 City nonwhite population, 1790–2000

1830). Slavery, moreover, was almost exclusively a rural phenomenon, associated with plantation agriculture and cultivation especially of cotton but also of rice, sugar, indigo, and other labor-intensive crops; the urban percentage of the national slave population never rose above 2.8 percent (in 1810). Free blacks, on the other hand, were disproportionately likely to live in cities (although not overwhelmingly so—between 20 and 25 percent of them usually did). This concentration of free black population was a distinctive demographic feature of cities in the antebellum period, as Figure 1.5 shows (from 1870 onward, of course, Figures 1.4 and 1.5 are identical). Figure 1.5 again reveals the period between the Civil War and the mid-twentieth century as distinctive—the era of American history when cities were whiter than the rest of the country, coinciding with their expanded political influence. (As Figures 1.6 and 1.7 show, Southern cities were considerably more nonwhite than cities in other regions until the post-World War II period; since the 1970s, there has been essentially no regional differentiation in the nonwhite percentage of urban populations.[29])

Another axis of urban difference is immigration. Cities have often been the predominant destination for immigrants to the United States, and urban population data reflect this. Figure 1.8 compares the percentage of the urban population born outside the United States with the foreign-born percentage of the total national population. In every census since 1860 (the first year in which data on nativity are available at the city level), cities were more heavily populated by immigrants than the rest of the

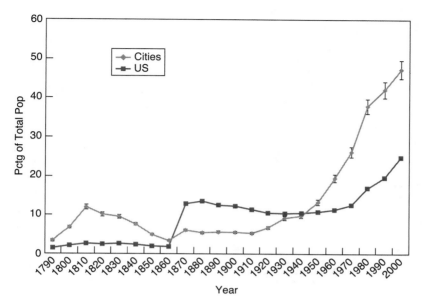

Figure 1.5 City free nonwhite population, 1790–2000

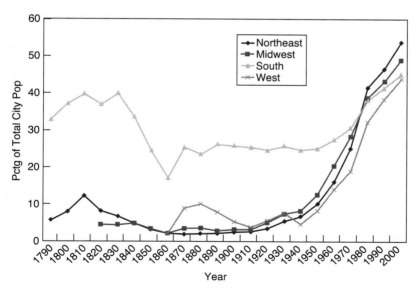

Figure 1.6 Nonwhite city population by region, 1790–2000

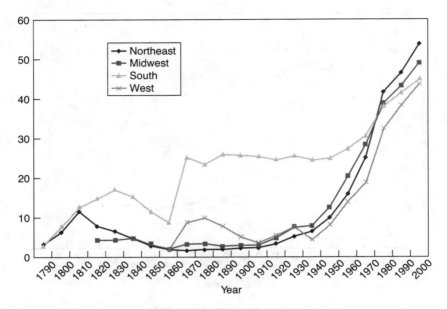

Figure 1.7 Free non white city population by region, 1790–2000

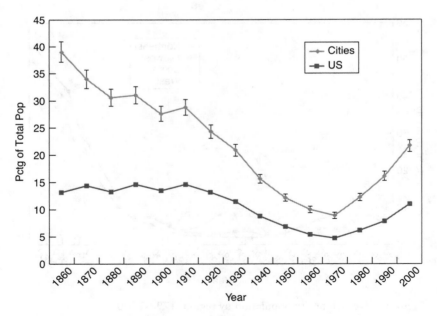

Figure 1.8 City foreign-born population, 1860–2000

country.[30] In the nineteenth century and into the early twentieth, the foreign-born percentage of cities was approximately twice that of the country as a whole. But during the great immigration trough of the middle of the twentieth century, corresponding roughly to the period of legal immigration restriction from 1924 to 1965, the gap between cities and the nation closed; cities in this period were less distinctive that at other times in American history. Figure 1.9 breaks these data down by region and shows that again Southern cities have been historically distinctive, with very low levels of foreign-born population. Northeastern cities have generally been the most heavily foreign-born (the higher line for the West in late nineteenth century reflects the distinctive character of San Francisco, which is the only Western city in the data set until 1890). Since the 1970s, however, the foreign-born populations of Western and Southern cities have grown especially quickly, reflecting the importance of immigration from Latin America and Asia in reshaping the political geography of the United States.

This picture of disproportionate diversity in American cities again resonates with Tocqueville's fears about the distinctive dangers of urban populations:

> The low people who inhabit these vast cities [Philadelphia and New York] form a populace more dangerous even than that of Europe. It is composed first of freed Negroes, whom law and opinion condemn

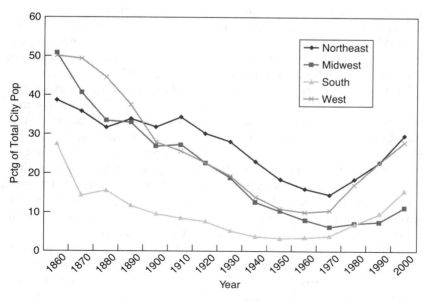

Figure 1.9 Foreign-born city population by region, 1860–2000

to a state of hereditary degradation and misery. One also encounters within it a multitude of Europeans whom misfortune and misconduct drive toward the shores of the New World each day; these men bring our greatest vices to the United States, and they have none of the interests that could combat their influence. Inhabiting the country without being citizens of it, they are ready to take part in all passions that agitate it; so for some time we have seen serious riots break out in Philadelphia and New York. Such disorders are unknown in the rest of the country, which is not anxious about them, because up to the present, the population of the towns has not exercised any power or influence on the countryside.

I nevertheless regard the greatness of certain American cities and, above all, the nature of their inhabitants, as a genuine danger that threatens the future of the democratic republics of the New World, and I do not fear to predict that it is through this that they will perish, unless their government comes to create an armed force that, while remaining submissive to the wills of the national majority, is still independent of the people of the towns and can reduce their excesses.[31]

Tocqueville here connects the characteristic outsider status of urban populations—domestic minorities and immigrants—with the distinctive political structure and development of the American democratic institutions. The salvation of American democracy from the danger of cities, he suggests, will come from the operation of representative institutions in which even the largest cities are not, politically speaking, emanations of national power but are, rather, independent political units subject to the same Madisonian political forces as any other group. It is this political structure that has, for American cities, provided both constraint (as Tocqueville hoped) and opportunity (as subsequent history shows).

These demographic data suggest a number of hypotheses about the connections between cities and the American state. But the city–state relationship is not merely demographic but predominantly political, and population figures, while highly suggestive about the historical arc of the urban moment in American political development, beg a question of fundamental importance about the causal political mechanisms that might connect cities to the national regime. Population size and weight might in themselves be an indicator of voting strength, but because of the ways the American state aggregates votes and converts them into political power at the national level, sheer numbers are not sufficient as a measure even of potential political influence.[32] What matters, consequently, is not only the number of city dwellers in the United States but the ways in which electoral institutions translate those numbers into representation, which consequently affects the potential for cities to participate in governing and policymaking coalitions.

Again, comparison can be illuminating. The United States is not the only country in which representative institutions are biased in favor of land over people. In fact, in the modern era the United States is extraordinarily scrupulous in demanding that the size of House of Representative districts within each state be equal "as nearly as is practicable," as the Supreme Court instructed in 1964.[33] Pro-rural bias in legislative representation has, of course, been a theme of British politics for centuries, dating back to the era of nineteenth-century parliamentary reform that moved substantially toward balanced representation first of the urban bourgeoisie and then of the working class—as any reader of Anthony Trollope well knows. The underrepresentation of cities and their commercial interests was central to representation controversies, as Edmund Burke's 1774 speech to the electors of Bristol attests. This shared history suggests the importance of examining the interaction of electoral systems (and political institutions more generally) with urbanization and the political status of cities as a critical factor in political development.

For this purpose, the relevant political unit is not cities per se but states, which are the fundamental political unit of the American state and the basis for political representation. But how do we measure the extent to which state-based representation reflects urban populations? As a first cut, Figure 1.10 displays the share of House and Senate seats and electoral votes that come from states that contain at least one of the cities in the data set.[34] For most of American history, it seems, a majority of national representation has at least been associated with states containing a major

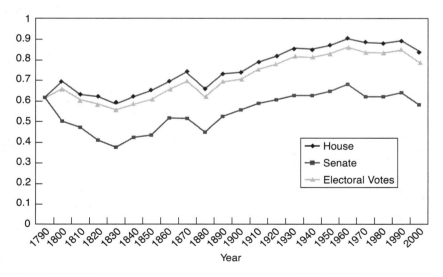

Figure 1.10 Urban states and national representation, 1790–2000

city, not a terribly helpful or revealing result in assessing the capacity of cities to shape national politics and policy or in explaining variation in this capacity. (The figure does, however, display graphically the rural bias inherent in the Senate and, to a lesser extent, the Electoral College).

But simply counting whether or not a state contains a large city is not a sufficient test of whether it should count as an indicator of urban representation or political strength. Even states with large cities, after all, are not equivalent in their urban-ness. Consider Virginia, for example, which has contained at least one major city in every census since 1800 (Richmond, Norfolk, and more recently Virginia Beach); these cities have never accounted for more than about 13 percent of the state's population. Illinois, by contrast, has had only one major city, but since 1890 Chicago has accounted for at least 23 percent of the state's population (and more than 40 percent from the 1910s to the 1950s). Figure 1.11 shows the variation in the urban percentage of state populations for states containing at least one major city. The center line of the plot for each year shows the median urban state population percentage, which peaks at over 27 percent in 1920; the plot also shows the maximum and minimum for each year (the top and bottom points of each line) and the first and third quartiles (the top and bottom of the box). These data confirm that there has been substantial variation in the urban density of states, which ought to affect the weight of urban representation in the national state. We ought not, then, to equate all states containing cities in measuring urban political influence in national politics.

Figure 1.12 recalculates urban representational strength for states with urban populations of at least 20 percent (another arbitrary cutoff but one that, based on the data shown in Figure 1.10 makes a reasonable

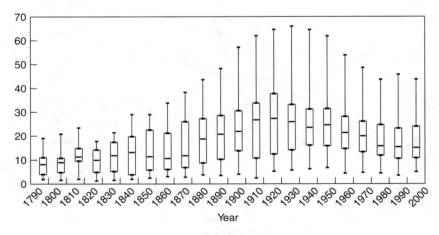

Figure 1.11 State urban percentages, 1790–2000

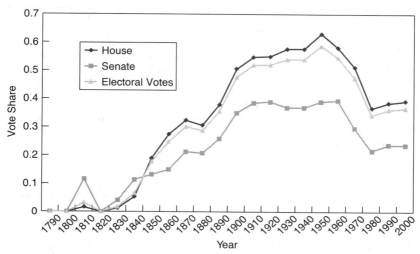

Figure 1.12 Urban states and national representation (20 percent threshold), 1790–2000

historical distinction between historically more and less urban states and suggests a threshold above which state elected officials might reasonably have to accommodate urban interests). This figure reveals much more limitation and variation in the representational strength of cities in the American regime. Here the first half of the twentieth century stands out as the peak of urban voting strength in American national political institutions; during this period urban states constituted 40 percent of the Senate and a bare majority of the House and the Electoral College. (It is important not to put too much weight, if any, on the absolute numbers here; a majority of seats does not imply any reason to expect urban representatives to vote as a bloc with any consistency. But over-time variation is an indication of greater or lesser *potential* for urban interests to form an essential or even pivotal part of a governing or policymaking coalition.[35])

Another indicator of urban penetration of the national state is the extent to which cities are breeding grounds for national political leadership. If cities are well integrated into the national regime, we should observe politicians whose careers are based in cities to rise to positions of prominence and power in national politics. As a first and relatively informal measure of this phenomenon, Table 1.1 lists the urban-based politicians who became president of the United States. "Urban-based" here is defined as either living or working or in one of the cities in the data set or holding public office, whether elected or appointed, in a jurisdiction that includes all or part of a city (at least partly the period when the city was at or over the 0.1 percent threshold).[36] Urban politicians have, in fact, been reasonably successful in rising to the nation's highest office; one in

Table 1.1 Presidents of the United States with urban political backgrounds

President	City and affiliation(s)
2. John Adams (1797–1801)	Boston. Practiced law; represented in Massachusetts state legislature
6. John Quincy Adams (1825–1829)	Boston. Practiced law
10. John Tyler (1841–1845)	Richmond. Represented in House, 1817–1821
13. Millard Fillmore (1850–1853)	Buffalo. Lived; practiced law; represented in House, 1833–1835, 1837–1843
19. Rutherford B. Hayes (1877–1881)	Cincinnati. City solicitor, 1857–1859; represented in House, 1865–1867
21. Chester Alan Arthur (1881–1885)	New York. Lived; practiced law; Collector of the Port of New York, 1871–1878
22/24. Grover Cleveland (1885–1889)	Buffalo. Lived; practiced law; Mayor, 1882
23. Benjamin Harrison (1889–1893)	Indianapolis. Lived; practiced law.
26. Theodore Roosevelt (1901–1909)	New York. Born; lived; President, Board of Police Commissioners, 1895–1897
27. William Howard Taft (1909–1913)	Cincinnati. Practiced law
32. Franklin D. Roosevelt (1933–1945)	New York. Lived (secondary); practiced law
33. Harry S Truman (1945–1953)	Kansas City. Judge, Jackson County Court, 1922–1924; Presiding Judge, 1926–1934
35. John F. Kennedy (1961–1963)	Boston. Represented in House, 1947–1953
38. Gerald R. Ford (1974–1977)	Grand Rapids. Represented in House, 1949–1973
41. George H.W. Bush (1989–1993)	Houston. Represented in House, 1967–1971
44. Barack Obama (2009–)	Chicago. Lived; represented in state legislature, 1997–2004; represented Illinois in Senate, 2004–2008

Sources: Biographical Directory of the United States Congress (http://bioguide.congress.gov); Kenneth C. Martis, *The Historical Atlas of United States Congressional Districts, 1789–1983* (New York: Free Press, 1982).

three presidents (sixteen of forty-three, or seventeen of forty-four, depending on how many times you count Grover Cleveland) have had urban political backgrounds. Whether this represents good news or bad news for cities depends on the benchmark for measuring proportional success; over time cities have represented well under one-third of the national population (Figure 1.1), although urban states have accounted for more than one-third of the electoral votes since the late nineteenth century (Figure 1.12). What is particularly striking and suggestive about this list, however, is the temporal clustering. From 1877, when Cincinnati's Rutherford Hayes entered the White House, to 1913, when Cincinnati's William Howard Taft left, the urban occupancy of the presidency was interrupted only by James Garfield's six months in office in 1881 and William McKinley's term from 1897 to 1901. Before and after this period, urban representation in the presidency is intermittent. A secondary temporal cluster is the New Deal period, spanning the Franklin Roosevelt, Truman, and Kennedy administrations (interrupted by Eisenhower).[37] Again, these patterns suggest periods of greater urban participation in the national regime, moments in American political history when cities and their residents potentially wielded power and influence in national politics and policymaking.

Conclusion

These data begin to outline the arc of cities and their connection to the state in American political development and the possibilities and limits of exceptionalism in thinking about the relationship between American cities and the American state. Between roughly the Gilded Age and the New Deal era, cities earned a central, if not always honored, place in the American regime. During this period, not uniformly or consistently but to a greater extent than before or since, they both provided key inputs to the national state—votes, organization, leaders, policy ideas—and benefited from its key outputs—policies, spoils, and power.[38] But these data also point in broad terms toward a set of theoretical conjectures and hypotheses about the forces in American politics that account for this historical arc, forces that have to do with the demographic, institutional, and ideological patterns that both emanate from cities and their residents and react to them. Disentangling these issues and finding causal relationships between these forces and the political fortunes of cities and their residents will also help to address the conundrums of exceptionalism—Do the unique features of American urban politics derive, as Jefferson might have supposed, from the distinctive tensions in American political culture between agrarian ideals and urban realities? Or do they emerge from more concrete—and comparable—patterns of politics that we can uncover historically? The view of political development that this theoretical and empirical outline suggests is one that avoids the extreme opposites of whiggish liberal progressivism on the one hand and the jeremiad on the other. Rather, it seeks to uncover what Karen Orren and Stephen Skowronek call "durable shifts in governing authority," changes whose direction and pace are not fixed by some overarching logic.[39] At the same time, however, it potentially breaches and bridges Orren and Skowronek's seemingly impenetrable divide between institutional and cultural explanations for such change. Finally, the enterprise set forth here is an urgent one not only for expanding the horizons of American political development but also for addressing, and ultimately reversing, the political misfortunes of American cities in the twenty-first century.

Notes

1. Jefferson to Adams, October 28, 1813, in Albert Ellery Bergh, ed., *The Writings of Thomas Jefferson* (Washington, DC: Thomas Jefferson Memorial Association, 1907), 13: 401–402. This connection between cities and corruption was a constant theme in Jefferson's thought. In 1787, he wrote to James Madison: "I think our governments will remain virtuous for many centuries as long as they are chiefly agricultural; and this will be as long as there shall be vacant lands in any part of America. When they get piled upon one another in large cities, as in Europe, they will become corrupt as in Europe." Jefferson to Madison, December 20, 1787, in Julian P. Boyd, ed., *Papers of Thomas Jefferson* (Princeton, NJ: Princeton University Press, 1955), 12: 442.
2. Jefferson to Rush, September 23, 1800, *Writings*, 10: 173.
3. Alexis de Tocqueville, *Democracy in America*, trans. Harvey C. Mansfield and Delba Winthrop (Chicago: University of Chicago Press, 2000), p. 266.
4. Iver Bernstein, *The New York City Draft Riots: Their Significance for American Society and Politics in the Age of the Civil War* (New York: Oxford University Press, 1990); Roger Lane, *The Roots of Violence in Black Philadelphia, 1860–1900* (Cambridge, MA: Harvard University Press, 1986); National Advisory Commission on Civil Disorders, *Report of the National Advisory Commission on Civil Disorders* (Washington, DC: Government Printing Office, 1968); Thomas J. Sugrue, *The Origins of the Urban Crisis: Race and Inequality in Postwar Detroit* (Princeton, NJ: Princeton University Press, 1996).
5. Jacob Riis, *How the Other Half Lives: Studies Among the Tenements of New York* (New York: Charles Scribner's Sons, 1890); Lincoln Steffens, *The Shame of the Cities* (New York: McClure, Philips, 1904); Upton Sinclair, *The Jungle* (New York: Doubleday, 1906); Ira Katznelson, *City Trenches: Urban Politics and the Patterning of Class in the United States* (New York: Pantheon, 1981).
6. Demetrios Caraley, "Washington Abandons the Cities," *Political Science Quarterly* 107 (1992): 1–30; Nixon quoted in Jack Newfield, "Bush to City: Drop Dead," *Nation* April 19, 2004. See also Margaret Weir, "The Politics of Racial Isolation in Europe and America," in Paul E. Peterson, ed., *Classifying by Race* (Princeton, NJ: Princeton University Press, 1995), pp. 217–244; Peter Dreier, John Mollenkopf, and Todd Swanstrom, eds., *Place Matters: Metropolitics for the Twenty-first Century* (Lawrence: University Press of Kansas, 2001).
7. J.P. Nettl, "The State as a Conceptual Variable," *World Politics* 20 (1968): 559–592.
8. This claim is, for now, based on a largely impressionistic reading of the historiography of American national politics. As will become clear, it is one of my purposes in this project to develop systematic and valid measures of the city's contribution to the state, and vice versa.
9. Stanley Elkins and Erik McKitrick, *The Age of Federalism: The Early American Republic, 1788–1800* (New York: Oxford University Press, 1993), esp. ch. 4; Ron Chernow, *Alexander Hamilton* (New York: Penguin Press, 2004).
10. Grant McConnell, *Private Power and American Democracy* (New York: Alfred A. Knopf, 1966), p. 93.
11. *Baker v. Carr*, 369 US 186 (1962); *Reynolds v. Sims*, 377 US 533 (1964).

12. McConnell, *Private Power and American Democracy*; Theodore J. Lowi, *The End of Liberalism: The Second Republic of the United States*, second edition (New York: W.W. Norton, 1979); John Mark Hansen, *Gaining Access: Congress and the Farm Lobby, 1919–1981* (Chicago: University of Chicago Press, 1991); Kenneth Finegold and Theda Skocpol, *State and Party in America's New Deal* (Madison: University of Wisconsin Press, 1995); Adam D. Sheingate, *The Rise of the Agricultural Welfare State: Institutions and Interest Group Power in the United States, France, and Japan* (Princeton, NJ: Princeton University Press, 2001).

13. See Robert C. Lieberman, "Ideas, Institutions, and Political Order," *American Political Science Review* 96 (2002): 697–712; Karen Orren and Stephen Skowronek, *The Search for American Political Development* (Cambridge: Cambridge University Press, 2004); Rogers M. Smith, "Which Comes First, the Ideas or the Institutions?," in Ian Shapiro, Stephen Skowronek, and Daniel Galvin, eds., *Rethinking Political Institutions: The Art of the State* (New York: New York University Press, 2006); Desmond S. King and Rogers M. Smith, "Racial Orders in American Political Development," *American Political Science Review* 99 (2005): 75–92; Robert C. Lieberman, *Shaping Race Policy: The United States in Comparative Perspective* (Princeton, NJ: Princeton University Press, 2005).

14. Rogers M. Smith, *Civic Ideals: Conflicting Visions of Citizenship in U.S. History* (New Haven: Yale University Press, 1997).

15. See Lewis Mumford, *The City in History: Its Origins, its Transformations, and its Prospects* (New York: Harcourt, Brace and World, 1961); Jane Jacobs, *The Death and Life of Great American Cities* (New York: Random House, 1961).

16. In 2000, Boise, Little Rock, Huntington Beach, and Chandler each had a population in the neighborhood of 180,000.

17. According to the most recent national censuses.

18. An extreme example is the Census's old "urban" classification, which it defined before 1950 as any incorporated place of 2,500 or more persons. In the first census, in 1790, there were only twenty-four such places in the country; by the time this standard was abandoned in 1950, there were more than 4,000.

19. The total US population in the 1790 Census was 3,929,214; in 2000 it was 281,421,906.

20. An alternative standard for choosing cities that considers not simply size but also regional centrality is certainly plausible, and possibly even preferable. Such an approach might approximate the Census's definition of metropolitan areas: "a large population nucleus, together with adjacent communities that have a high degree of economic and social integration with that nucleus" (metropolitan areas are officially designated by the Office of Management and Budget [OMB]). Cities, then, could be defined as the nuclei around which metropolitan areas form, regardless of (or in conjunction with) population size. These official Census–OMB/Bureau of the Budget metropolitan definitions go back as far as 1950. Replicating this definition for the census years before 1950 would require extensive historical reconstruction involving data on growth, employment, and commuting patterns between outlying and central places, among other things. The 0.1 percent threshold reasonably approximates this standard using population data that are much more straightforward and readily available from the Census.

21. The complete list of cities that appear in the data set for each decennial census year from 1790 to 2000 is available from the author.

42 *Robert C. Lieberman*

22. William Julius Wilson, *The Truly Disadvantaged: The Inner City, the Underclass, and Public Policy* (Chicago: University of Chicago Press, 1987); Kenneth T. Jackson, *Crabgrass Frontier: The Suburbanization of the United States* (New York: Oxford University Press, 1985).
23. The data displayed in Figure 1.2 are calculated from the remarkable compilation of urban population data collected by computer scientist Thomas Brinkhoff and reported at http://citypopulation.de. Using an absolute population threshold for defining changes the results slightly, though not substantially. No matter how you measure it, cities loom larger in most other industrial countries.
24. Paul M. Hohenberg and Lynn Hollen Lees, *The Making of Urban Europe, 1000–1950* (Cambridge, MA: Harvard University Press, 1985).
25. The regions are the Northeast (the six New England states plus New Jersey, New York, and Pennsylvania); the Midwest (Indiana, Illinois, Iowa, Kansas, Michigan, Minnesota, Missouri, Nebraska, North Dakota, Ohio, South Dakota, and Wisconsin); the South (the eleven Confederate states plus Delaware, the District of Columbia, Kentucky, Maryland, Oklahoma, and West Virginia); and the West (Alaska, Arizona, California, Colorado, Hawaii, Idaho, New Mexico, Montana, Nevada, Oregon, Utah, Washington, and Wyoming).
26. Richard Franklin Bensel, *Sectionalism and American Political Development: 1880–1980* (Madison: University of Wisconsin Press, 1984).
27. David R. Mayhew, *Placing Parties in American Politics: Organization, Electoral Settings, and Government Activity in the Twentieth Century* (Princeton, NJ: Princeton University Press, 1986); Amy Bridges, *Morning Glories: Municipal Reform in the Southwest* (Princeton, NJ: Princeton University Press, 1997).
28. US Department of Labor, Office of Policy Planning and Research, *The Negro Family: The Case for National Action* (the "Moynihan Report") (Washington: Government Printing Office, 1965); Wilson, *The Truly Disadvantaged*; Daryl Michael Scott, *Contempt and Pity: Social Policy and the Image of the Damaged Black Psyche* (Chapel Hill: University of North Carolina Press, 1997); Martin Gilens, *Why Americans Hate Welfare: Race, Media, and the Politics of Antipoverty Policy* (Chicago: University of Chicago Press, 1999).
29. These data measure "race" only in its crudest form, considering only the distinction between whites and all others as reported by the Census. Particularly in the last third of the twentieth century, these data almost certainly conceal significant and important variation in the racial and ethnic makeup of cities as the nonwhite population of the United States has diversified significantly to include larger numbers of Asians and Asian-Americans as well as Latinos (who, according to Census categories, are also assigned a racial classification, typically either white or black).
30. The year 1850 was the first for which the Census reported nativity (place of birth) data, but only for states and not for smaller political subdivisions.
31. Tocqueville, *Democracy in America*, p. 266.
32. William H. Riker, *Liberalism Against Populism: A Confrontation Between the Theory of Democracy and the Theory of Social Choice* (San Francisco: W.H. Freeman, 1982).
33. *Wesberry v. Sanders*, 376 US 1 (1964), 6–8. This ruling was later refined and held to require extreme mathematical precision in *Kirkpatrick v. Preisler*, 394 US 526 (1969); and *Karcher v. Daggett*, 376 US 725 (1983).
34. A number of simplifying assumptions were necessary to calculate these proportions. The number of states was assumed to be the number of states at

the time the Census was conducted (and this number was doubled to give the number of Senate seats). The number of House seats was set at the number of seats generated by the apportionment conducted immediately *after* the Census in question (except for 1920, when there was no reapportionment after the Census and congressional apportionment remained the same as that following the 1910 Census). The number of electoral votes is simply the sum of the House and Senate seats (plus an additional three for the District of Columbia for 1970 and after; the District was given three electoral votes by the Twenty-Third Amendment to the Constitution, ratified in 1961, but still has no voting representation in either chamber of Congress). Thus these data represent only decennial snapshots of representational strength and do not reflect adjustments due to the addition of new states between censuses.

35. By analogy, Cameron, Epstein, and O'Halloran have shown that African-American majorities in legislative districts are not necessary for legislative influence. Charles Cameron, David Epstein, and Sharyn O'Halloran, "Do Majority-Minority Districts Maximize Substantive Black Representation in Congress?," *American Political Science Review* 90 (1996): 794–812. A more refined and precise measure of urban political influence might be the actual vote shares for presidential or other candidates that came from cities, which is a possible direction for future research.

36. William Henry Harrison does not appear in the table but comes very close to fitting the criteria for inclusion. He represented Cincinnati in the House of Representatives from 1816 to 1819; Cincinnati first reached the 0.1 percent threshold for inclusion in the data set in 1820. Gerald Ford, by contrast, just barely makes it in. He was first elected to the House from Grand Rapids, Michigan, in 1948 and served until becoming vice president in 1973; the last year Grand Rapids appears in the data set is 1950.

37. Franklin Roosevelt's political identification with New York City is somewhat tenuous. He mainly lived on his family's estate in Hyde Park, New York, some 75 miles north of New York City, and his first elective office was as a state senator from rural Dutchess County. But he also maintained a townhouse in New York City for most of his adult life and practiced law there after studying at Columbia Law School and before beginning his political career.

38. On American cities as important sites in the national and international nexus of Progressive policy ideas, see Daniel T. Rodgers, *Atlantic Crossings: Social Politics in a Progressive Age* (Cambridge, MA: Harvard University Press, 1998).

39. Orren and Skowronek, *The Search for American Political Development*, p. 123.

2   Against Exceptionalism

Intercurrence and Intergovernmental Relations in Britain and the United States

Jerome Hodos

The field of American political development (APD) started as an attempt to explain "American exceptionalism"—the idea that American political culture and institutions were somehow unique when compared with Western European societies. While the field has moved on to define itself in a more sophisticated way as the study of "historical institutionalism"— the development of political institutions over time—the explicitly comparative claims at its base are in need of further examination.[1] In this chapter I compare how the United States and the United Kingdom have historically attempted to integrate cities into their political structures, and I argue that we would do better to interpret the American polity as part of an Anglo-American cultural-political family than as a unique entity.

From an urban point of view the American polity is largely descended from British precedents. There are marked similarities across the two countries in the varieties of self-government town residents adopted, the philosophical rationales for integrating pre-capitalist institutions into the bourgeois state, and the amount and kind of formal autonomy that cities in both countries possess. This is true despite the difference between American federalism and the unitary structure of British government. Differences in institutional structure are less important than one might think, and American exceptionalism amounts to less than meets the eye.

Moreover, the trajectories of change in central–local relations over time have also been remarkably coincident. The puzzle for both countries has been how to incorporate pre-existing cities into a modern political order; the answer was to treat them as feudal relics and try to subordinate them. Both states "swallowed" those pre-existing cities only with great difficulty, and have to this day never fully digested them. State attempts at subordination took place over centuries and were never entirely successful, as cities have repeatedly tried to challenge or renegotiate their subjugation to the state.[2] In what follows I explore these issues both at the national scale and with reference to specific cities, primarily Philadelphia and Manchester.

What Is APD?

Karen Orren and Stephen Skowronek define political development as "a durable shift in governing authority."[3] Certainly changes in the division of authority between central, state and local governments ought to count in this definition, yet the terms *city*, *urban*, *federalism*, and *intergovernmental relations* do not even appear in the index to Orren and Skowronek's book. The authors argue, furthermore, that from its original concern with American exceptionalism the subfield of APD has become less triumphalist, more critical, and more diffuse. There is no longer any necessary reason for political development to be *American* political development—its insights could conceivably be applied to the political history of any country. Thus the field is ripe for a return to comparative analyses, particularly with regard to cities.

Several scholars, among them Paul Kantor and Paul Peterson, have analyzed intergovernmental relations in the US in terms of the constraints placed upon cities by structural features of the American polity. At the most general level, the problem is that cities are not nations: they have open borders, and cannot control flows of capital, jobs, or people. Therefore, they must compete with each other to offer environments that are attractive to employers and residents. Competition places limits on cities because exit is an available option for anyone dissatisfied with urban policies.[4] Despite claims of dependency, however, comparative analysts have generally viewed American cities as uniquely powerful by virtue of their strong, directly elected mayors, extensive taxing authority, and independence from the central state. Thus the domestic and the comparative literature on urban autonomy seem to be at odds with each other.

The most common resolution of this argument relies on the nature of federalism: cities' political strength in the United States is counterbalanced by their relative weakness vis-à-vis capital, because the American federal system allows cities (and state governments) to compete against each other. Cities in the US, for example, have greater reliance on local tax revenues, but therefore must rely more on strategies to maximize their fiscal bases (i.e. luring investment). In the UK, by contrast, cities have traditionally been viewed as strong with respect to capital, but fiscally and politically weak vis-à-vis the central government.[5]

A more historical analysis, however, illuminates some genetic similarities that may carry greater weight. Cities as an institutional form certainly predate the nation-state. They were incorporated into the state *post hoc*, in a difficult and often conflictual process that persisted for centuries.[6] Accommodations between states and cities were often occasional or contingent, worked out via protracted back-and-forth jockeying for power. State–city relations, then, are a prime example of Orren and Skowronek's concept of *intercurrence*, according to which different parts of the American state developed to serve distinct purposes, and thus may not fit together very well. This is true not just for the United States, but also for Britain. The division of responsibility between different sub-parts of the polity is not always clearly demarcated, and thus the "multiple orders" of the American and British states conflict and "impinge" upon each other.

Despite the federal/unitary distinction, therefore, American urban patterns have significant commonalities with those of other English-speaking countries. These deeper patterns extend back centuries and include not just similar institutions but also similar trajectories of change over the entire modern history of these nations. (Interestingly, all of the largest British settler states—Canada, Australia, and the United States—adopted federalist structures.) In general, local governments are most restricted and least powerful in the Anglophone countries; in all cases they are subject to some version of the *ultra vires* doctrine (explained on p. 52).[7] The Anglo-American pattern represents a particular solution to the "problem" of urban autonomy.

The Medieval British Legacy

There are three main sources for British urban patterns. First, the town or village, and the more basic form of the parish, were small, local assemblies of villagers who combined to take care of essential local services, such as provision for the poor or road maintenance. Second, the borough began as an administrative and military center organized by the king or lords, and evolved into a grouping of traders and producers.[8] Some boroughs, such as London, over time won privileges of self-government and exemptions from various taxes. Most, however, were governed for the administrative convenience of the nobility or clergy who held sway over them.

The third source of British intergovernmental patterns was the transmission of Continental urban developments to England via the Norman Conquest, which began the transformation of the most established boroughs, such as Cardiff and Bristol, into chartered corporations. The City of London, for example, won self-government in 1190, and its charter gave it substantial additional powers, including ownership of Southwark and Middlesex, control over the whole of the Thames, and a monopoly over markets for 7 miles.[9] By virtue of the granting of charters, boroughs as a class became more differentiated from towns, villages, and parishes; the pre-existing bifurcation of local governance in England was reinforced, and would be reinscribed over the succeeding centuries.

The urban polity was everywhere designed as a vehicle for enhancing the autonomy of the bourgeoisie and protecting it from lordly interference. But the urban corporation's top-down character in England meant that cities were significantly less autonomous there than elsewhere—they never, for example, formed independent city-states, as on the Italian peninsula. The state in England and in Anglo settler colonies would retain a stronger hand, and urban autonomy was thus weaker.

There were multiple, gradually increasing attempts by higher-level governments to exert authority over cities. In 1682, for example, Charles II challenged the legitimacy of the corporate charters of London and other cities, and subordinated all cities to his control. In 1688, when the Stuarts were overthrown, Parliament replaced the king as the supreme state authority, and the inviolability of charters from royal abrogation was reinstituted.[10] However, the issue of Parliamentary power over corporations was left unresolved. As a result, "for the whole of the eighteenth century, hardly any Municipal Corporation could feel assured that any particular element in its constitution . . . would be upheld by the Courts at Westminster."[11]

The lack of clarity over the status of corporate charters was even more pronounced in the American colonies. English settlers brought with them the dual system of local governance. Some founded unincorporated local governments, with rights to participation originally based on membership in a local congregation but gradually altered to a basis in property ownership; this is the origin of the New England township. But over time the number of urban corporations grew, through two mechanisms. First, a small number of patrician, mercantile cities developed closed corporations; there were, by the time of the Revolution, about two dozen of these cities, with Philadelphia, founded in 1682, being the most prominent. These municipal corporations were independent of central administrative control and nearly always run by small groups of merchants in their own interest.[12]

Second, the New England colonies illegitimately issued their own charters for townships. The legal cloud under which these New England corporate charters existed was further complicated by the uncertain status of corporations in Britain. Though the King's power over corporations was significantly reduced and partially passed to Parliament, he tried to maintain a greater level of authority over the colonies. The royal administration demanded the right to oversee and veto any charter, and in fact vetoed several. Many of these vetoes were ignored. New Englanders, in issuing charters through their legislatures, were participating in the great historical shift of authority away from kings and toward elected legislative bodies.[13] In addition, the colonists' desire for autonomy expressed itself as a usurpation of royal authority that recalled the uprisings in medieval cities, centuries before. The powers of the central state to regulate and subjugate cities were sharply contested.

The lack of clarity over urban autonomy was shaped by three additional factors, all of which tended to weaken the cities vis-à-vis higher governments. First, many urban corporations closed their franchises, and became self-perpetuating, oligarchic bodies. Nearly three-fourths of England's municipal corporations became closed corporations by the end of the eighteenth century, as did Philadelphia. The elected common councils declined throughout the eighteenth century, as did the number of freemen or burgesses. One of the driving forces for this change was the rise of the country gentry, who often served as the Crown's representatives, and who diminished the towns' independence by including themselves in town governance.[14]

Second, chartered cities lost functions such as road maintenance and poor relief:

> Parliament preferred to entrust the new functions of regulation and taxation, not to the Municipal Corporations, but to entirely new bodies, established for the special purposes desired, on which the Mayor and some other representatives of the Corporation were merely *ex officio* members in a permanent minority.[15]

This process occurred not just in England, but also in the American colonies: as early as 1712, the Pennsylvania legislature vested independent commissions with special power for carrying out specific duties.

Third, liberal political philosophers grew increasingly hostile toward the corporate towns, seeing them as unresolved holdovers of the feudal era. While corporations were useful for pursuing specific goals, they were also suspect, because they invested groups with special privileges and because they created status groups that ill fit with the growing interest in individual liberty and formal equality. Thomas Hobbes wrote in *Leviathan* (1651) of "the great number of Corporations; which are as it were many lesser Common-wealths in the bowels of a greater, like wormes in the entrayles of a naturall man."[16] The movement to subjugate the corporations to popularly accountable bodies targeted precisely the privileged statuses that were the heart of the corporate form. The ambiguous status of corporations would be resolved in the US by splitting the corporation in two—the "private" corporations we now recognize, and a "public" corporate form for municipal governments. The public form was subjected to heavy state oversight, and both forms became widely available to the population via general incorporation laws, so that their privileged status characteristics decayed.[17]

The Nineteenth Century's Tug of War

In the nineteenth century the similarities in how Britain and the US treated their cities became more obvious. Much of the century consisted of a tug of war between cities and higher governments for authority, with cities gradually losing ground. Both countries faced the dilemma of how to regularize the unsystematic pattern of charters so as to rationalize and modernize intergovernmental relations. The first instances of political modernization were explicit attempts to overcome feudal legacies, particularly legacies of exclusion and disfranchisement. One change was the full enshrinement of legislative (rather than executive) control over cities. In England, Parliament consolidated its control over incorporation and annexation law, and grew less wary of using it. In the US, this was a city–state government relationship, as the federal government entirely abandoned any direct relationship to cities. After independence, state legislatures moved quickly to consolidate their power by reissuing city charters.[18] The legislatures, as the people's bodies, grabbed power at a time when governors and executives were in disrepute because of their history as agents of the King. Pennsylvania was particularly active in this regard; the state forced a new charter on Philadelphia in 1789.

Another trend was the growth of democratic forms of city government. After 1775 no new cities had closed corporations; their charters called for popularly elected officials, and most had property rather than occupational franchise requirements. Philadelphia's new charter, for example, ended its closed corporation form. Throughout the early 1800s property requirements for the franchise declined, until all white males were eligible. A similar trend toward more democratic cities appeared in England. Rapidly increasing discontent with the political and administrative failures of what one commentator called "a shabby, mongrel aristocracy" forced a wave of reforms in the 1830s, instantiated particularly in the 1832 parliamentary reforms and in the 1835 Municipal Corporations Act. As a result of the 1832 reforms, for example, Manchester got two seats in the Commons, and the franchise qualification was reduced to £10.[19]

Both countries also established more uniform procedures for chartering cities in the first place. In the US a "general law" for the incorporation of cities, which made most charters standard or uniform, was instituted in state after state. Louisiana was first, in 1808, and then Indiana and Ohio in 1817; thirteen states had such laws before the Civil War. In England, the Municipal Corporations Act of 1835 expanded the size of the municipal franchise (to prevent closed corporations), enumerated city government functions (police, streets, markets, and the like), and specified elections and terms of office for certain positions. It also made provisions for charters for new cities; the procedure became an application to the Privy Council, which would review it and decide whether or not to grant it.[20] But neither country abolished the old special-act charters; the question of how to alter those city governments to fit modern needs for a rationalized state would be an ongoing problem.

In reality, however, the Act enabled full, charter-style autonomy only for ten cities—Liverpool, Birmingham, Manchester, Leeds, Sheffield, Bristol, Bradford, Nottingham, Kingston-upon-Hull, and Newcastle. Thus it set a precedent for treating some large cities as more deserving of self-government than others; this bifurcation of cities would be true across the Atlantic as well. It also gave to the town councils responsibility for most local functions, cutting down on the multiplication of independent commissions.[21] Manchester, for example, won its charter of incorporation in October 1838, despite a fierce political struggle, with opposing petitions in favor of and against incorporation presented to Parliament. In 1839 the police commissioners denied the newly elected city council entrance to the town hall, and the churchwardens refused to turn over the rate books. This forced Parliament to pass a special bill in 1839 giving the central government control over all policing for two years; then, in 1841, the new municipal government was recognized as the sole holder of police power.[22] In both Manchester and Philadelphia, then, the political struggle to overturn feudal arrangements was carried out and eventually decided by a higher level of government, resulting in new charters, more democratic city government, and broad bourgeois control of the city.

As cities grew, controversies arose over which level of government would provide new services, and over increasing urban political power, both de facto and in terms of legislative representation. The larger city governments, newly empowered by more democratic charters, swiftly moved to increase their authority, especially in terms of service provision and territorial expansion. In fact, for much of the antebellum or early Victorian era Parliament and the American states were generally receptive to requests by cities for additional powers. State governments passed hundreds or even thousands of private bills relating to single cities, primarily at local request.[23] Higher governments gave permission for cities to expand services, to start municipal enterprises, and to conduct annexations. Perhaps the first example of such an increase in city government provision of municipal services was Philadelphia's construction of the Schuylkill Water Works in 1799–1801, but similar enterprises expanded rapidly in the ensuing decades. Cities took control of police and fire services, of water and gas provision, and often of local transportation as well. In 1846, Manchester bought the rights to governance from the Lord of the Manor for £200,000, so that the city could control the markets. The city owned gas and water works, and won Parliamentary approval to borrow against the gas works revenue to undertake street improvements. In the 1870s and 1880s, the city pursued a scheme to build a giant aqueduct to draw drinking water from Thirlmere, over 100 miles away.[24]

In the most grandiose schemes, cities incurred large debts for mercantile development strategies.[25] Both Philadelphia and Manchester became part-owners of massive infrastructure projects—the Manchester Ship Canal and the Pennsylvania Railroad—that extended their influence for hundreds or even thousands of miles beyond their borders. In addition, many cities conducted territorial expansions by annexation. The city of Philadelphia pushed for the consolidation of all of Philadelphia County's jurisdictions into one metropolis, to facilitate policing and tax collection. This plan passed in 1854, and the scope of Philadelphia government multiplied immensely. Manchester, too, pursued annexations in the late nineteenth century.

Clearly, massive urbanization from the 1830s forward changed the balance of power and the scale of urban problems. But the growth of urban power caused increasing consternation at higher levels of government. Both state governments and the British Parliament became unsure of the democratic capacities of immigrants and the poor in cities, and the administrative capacities of city governments to cope with new problems such as public health. They began to interfere with cities in multiple ways: changing the incorporation rules, taking away responsibilities, interfering in the selection of municipal officers, and codifying new legal doctrines to guarantee urban subordination.

Such interference, especially in the United States, was often less about good government than about corruption or partisan advantage. Most city charters could be altered or even abolished by simple act of the legislature, and state governments often passed laws that affected localities without giving localities much input. In Philadelphia, for example, state government chartered street railway companies, but did not allow the city to veto the charters or regulate company operations, including fares. State government politicians also often passed laws to help their own political party at the local level, via such measures as state takeovers of local police departments (this even happened to New York City in the 1850s). At the worst extreme, so-called "ripper legislation" abolished locally elected officials and gave the state the right to appoint them. The Pennsylvania legislature, in 1901, abolished the mayoralty in Pittsburgh, Scranton, and Allegheny, and replaced it with a state-appointed "recorder."[26]

Over time, there was so much complaint about how American state legislatures misused special acts affecting cities that they were outlawed in state constitutions. But higher-level governments continued to intrude on local affairs by establishing a wide range of independent, special-purpose boards and authorities to carry out expanded municipal functions. In England, the early Victorian decades saw both the Poor Law reform of 1834, which established larger-area Poor Law Unions, and the rise of sanitary principles, which led to the establishment of health districts and the entire public health apparatus. One should add to this, in both countries, the establishment of permanent local police and fire services, mandatory public schooling, and the like. Higher governments often considered local authorities incompetent to assume these new, enlarged functions, and removed them from local control. As a result, some functions, such as schooling in both countries, were given autonomous status; school boards were directly elected but not under the control of the mayor or city council. Other functions were removed from local control entirely, and centralized; in England in the 1870s, this included local prisons.[27] There has thus been recurring disagreement and conflict over whether cities should be in control of their own services or not.

Parliament and state governments were able to pursue this fragmentation and subjugation of local governance because, by fundamental doctrine, they determined what cities could and could not do. The climax of state government interference was reached with the declaration of "Dillon's Rule" in 1868. Iowa Supreme Court Justice John Dillon wrote:

> Municipal corporations owe their origin to, and derive their powers and rights wholly from, the legislature. It breathes into them the breath of life, without which they cannot exist. As it creates, so it may destroy. If it may destroy, it may abridge and control . . .. We know of no limitation of this right so far as corporations themselves are concerned. They are, so to phrase it, the mere tenants at will of the legislature.

American cities are therefore creatures of the states, with no legal powers except those assigned by the states.[28]

Dillon's Rule is similar to the *ultra vires* doctrine that governs state–city relations in the UK. In Britain, "local councils have only been able to do what statute permits—a doctrine known as *ultra vires*, a Latin term which translates 'beyond the powers.'" English cities get whatever powers they possess from Parliament—if Parliament doesn't grant them authority, they can't exercise it.[29] Thus, in both England and in the US, the single most important principle governing relations between cities and higher levels of government firmly establishes the subordination of local government. Cities may do only what the legislature gives them power to do—they have no general power to pursue their citizens' welfare. Such doctrines definitively mark the surpassing of old, feudal conceptions of urban autonomy.

Thus, while *ultra vires* hamstrung the British city from above, American cities were hamstrung from above and below (or alongside). American state governments not only limited city powers directly via applications of Dillon's Rule, but also offered smaller communities legal tools to protect themselves from annexation and encroachment. Municipal general incorporation laws, which allowed any locality to incorporate itself if it so desired, were the spur to American political fragmentation; by 1900 over 70 percent of incorporated places had populations of less than 3,000. Furthermore, in the late nineteenth and early twentieth centuries, many states adopted redistricting rules that permanently diluted urban population strength, and gave rural areas disproportionate representation in state legislatures.[30] This dilution was equivalent to the long-standing underrepresentation of British cities in Parliament. The big cities' attempted solution to this problem was to try to free themselves from higher-level oversight, through a range of policies that can be collected under the principle of "home rule."

Home Rule and 1888

The largest cities in particular have long both claimed to be and been treated as separate entities, and they tried to re-establish a firmer legal footing for their own authority. This effort took several forms—the establishment of *city classes* in the US, which singled out the largest cities for special treatment and powers; *home rule* provisions, which gave large cities greater control over their charters and freedom from the worst forms of state government interference; and the 1888 Local Government Act in England, which effectively mixed various of these provisions for British cities. All of these measures had one overriding feature in common: they classified cities in order to separate out the biggest ones.

State after state reacted to the laws and constitutional provisions prohibiting special or private acts for individual cities by classifying them. These classifications, typically based on population, placed the largest city in the state into its own category, so that legislation for that class affected only that city. Pennsylvania, for example, adopted city classifications in 1895. Under the state's rules, Philadelphia was the only first-class city, and Pittsburgh was the only second-class city. Scranton was given a special designation as "Second Class A," and all other cities were third class.[31]

Classification provisions were sometimes combined with "home rule" measures. Home rule is a state government constitutional provision that gives cities the right to write and to change their own charters. In such cases, the state legislature cannot take the cities' powers away—and they become, in some sense, truly autonomous and self-governing. Indeed, the *Pennsylvania Legislator's Municipal Deskbook* even calls home rule "an incursion on state supremacy." Missouri was the first state to adopt a home rule provision in its constitution, designed specifically for St Louis. Though home rule spread across the United States, Pennsylvania was typically slow to adopt governmental reforms. Philadelphia, for example, did not achieve a home rule charter until 1951, and Pennsylvania's other local governments were not allowed to adopt home rule until 1957.[32]

In England, the Local Government Act of 1888 also bifurcated the British urban system; this bifurcation was a simplification of the pre-existing patchwork of local authorities. It created "county boroughs"— cities with populations of at least 50,000—that effectively served as their own counties, not under the thumb of the counties they were located in. The number of such county boroughs grew from sixty-one in 1888 to eighty-three in 1934. Simultaneously, it subordinated the smaller, weaker "municipal boroughs," originally established in 1835. These municipal boroughs are overseen by counties, but have several autonomous functional responsibilities, such as roads, health, and early education. The 1888 Act, interestingly, also made English counties more like American states, giving them more power over the districts within their boundaries.

As part of the law, many central funds were passed through the counties, rather than going directly to the local authorities—including those for some formerly local responsibilities such as road maintenance, poor relief, and sanitation.[33] Municipal corporations thus come in two varieties after 1888: county boroughs (fully independent, equal to counties), and municipal boroughs (independent, but under supervision of a county). This duality is similar to the US distinction between home rule cities and the townships or boroughs formed according to general incorporation laws.

The long struggle between cities and higher levels of government, therefore, ended in a lopsided draw. Higher governments mostly won the war, but the national urban systems in both countries were split into two categories of cities. This split pattern rationalized the colonial and early modern systems in similar ways, and achieved greater authority for higher-level governments, but only at the price of ceding to the largest cities their right to be treated differently. These cities over time acquired greater administrative capacity, and governmental fragmentation began to decrease as functions were consolidated into city governments proper.[34] This system would undergo significant modification in the twentieth century as the scope of government expanded overall.

The Keynesian and Post-Keynesian Eras

The Depression of the 1930s forced a further realignment of state–city relations. In both countries (for the first time in the US) this realignment took the form of increasing central state assistance to and monitoring of local affairs. Local governments swelled as they took national money to provide ever-increasing services. Unemployment and rising poverty in American cities fueled urban demands for federal aid; the US Conference of Mayors, for example, was founded in 1933, largely in order to lobby for increased federal assistance.[35] The Keynesian era, however, offered cities a tradeoff: increased administrative powers and resources in exchange for less autonomy, since policy priorities would be determined at the national rather than the local level. The full Keynesian program eventually meant four things: increased administrative power and service delivery by city governments; the rise of urban governance at a regional spatial scale, including transport infrastructure, broader planning powers, and urban renewal; stronger direct links between central government and city government, in the US often bypassing the state governments; and a challenge to urban autonomy as urban priorities were increasingly determined at the national level.

First, both countries increased the scale and scope of urban government, and massively expanded relief and social assistance programs, giving local government hefty responsibility for delivering those programs. And even before World War II, they began using central government money to rebuild cities through infrastructure and slum clearance programs. The National Industrial Recovery Act of 1933 was the first national law to really allow federal spending for infrastructure and reconstruction in American cities; it required 25 percent of each state's funding to go toward city-based projects.

Second, the expanded range of local government activities was often accompanied by increased planning capacity and the rise of regional governance. In the UK, Keynesianism meant full employment, plus infrastructure and services spending, tending toward a regional spatial scale. In the US, it involved transportation funding first (including for airports), then urban renewal, with increased resources for urban planning and redevelopment.[36] Herman Finer in England, and Lewis Mumford and Clarence Stein's Regional Plan Association in the US, among others, argued that supra-county, regional governance was a good idea, and that the functional desirability of economic coordination would lead to larger spatial units for infrastructural services such as transportation and utilities. In Philadelphia, starting in the late 1930s, the city planner Edmund Bacon and other "Young Turks" argued for political reforms that would give the city new economic and spatial planning capabilities.[37] Philadelphia's transition to Keynesian principles combined a late adoption of home rule in 1951 with political reform, a change in governing party (from Republican to Democrat), and a new, powerful planning commission. Bacon became director of city planning in the new regime and he shepherded most of the city's postwar renewal activity, including mass transit, housing construction and renovation, and the development of downtown commercial and retail projects.

Third, Keynesianism also boosted direct central–local linkages. The UK had already, in 1929, substantially increased its revenue sharing with local governments. The US federal government began direct cash grants to cities in 1932; these payments ballooned from $10 million to $941 million in 1963, and expanded further after that. The massive rise in central aid comes with an important catch, of course: increased funding means that city governments are not self-sustaining financially. In many cases city governments came to prefer dealing with the federal government to dealing with their own state governments, and the city–federal relationship increasingly aimed to bypass the state governments altogether.[38] De facto if not de jure, cities became third partners in American federalism, and they did so in a set of direct relations with the federal government on a series of issues—such as housing and urban renewal—in which state governments have historically had very little interest or competence.

Finally, this central–local partnership entailed a new conceptualization of intergovernmental relations in both countries. In the United States the new doctrine came to be called "cooperative federalism," in which different levels of government might jointly act on certain issues, making each partner more effective, so that sharing power was not a zero-sum game. This vision is, in effect, a functionalist view: Cities are "integrated parts in a governmental structure and a corpus of functions larger and more important than themselves. They have practically no functions or purpose outside this context."[39] Thus Keynesianism simultaneously promised to deliver more administrative power, but less local autonomy. Urban self-government would decline in favor of national planning and determination of the functional needs of regions, and city bureaucracies would become much more encompassing as primary agencies of service delivery. This bargain was perhaps clearer in England than in the United States. The national welfare state was constructed by removing particularistic powers from local governments and replacing them with national, universal benefits. Local governments were not supposed to be independent power centers, but were primarily supposed to carry out centrally made planning decisions and deliver benefits. Neil Brenner has called this pattern of intergovernmental relations "spatial Keynesianism."[40]

Keynesian approaches reached their height in the 1970s. In the US, government aid ballooned when President Nixon adopted general revenue sharing in 1972, which gave money to cities directly without any demands on how it should be spent. In Britain, high Keynesianism arrived with the creation of Greater London in 1965, and with the Local Government Act of 1972, which created full regional governments with real powers, called "metropolitan county councils," in six of the country's largest cities: Liverpool (Merseyside), Birmingham, Sheffield (South Yorkshire), Manchester, Newcastle (Tyne and Wear), and Leeds (West Yorkshire). The Greater Manchester Council, for example, was formed out of Manchester and nine surrounding local authorities, which were carved from the counties of Cheshire and Lancashire. This planning apparatus came into being, however, just as Keynesianism was on its last legs; in that sense, it was destroyed at its peak rather than suffering a gradual decay.[41]

The Death of Keynesianism and the Rise of Neoliberalism

Economic and social changes in the 1970s weakened the political underpinnings of Keynesian approaches, eventually leading to conservative governments that dismantled the intergovernmental arrangements of the preceding decades. Deindustrialization accelerated, labor unions declined, and local governments faced rapidly rising expenditures and shrinking tax bases. As the middle class grew and suburbanized in both countries, it tipped the political balance against the cities and sundered the Keynesian political coalition. Suburbanization was combined in the US with political fragmentation, since general incorporation laws allowed smaller and smaller units to become self-governing and avoid annexation.[42] This changing geographic and class pattern helped destroy Keynesianism, ushered in the era of Thatcher and Reagan, and institutionalized yet another shared shift in intergovernmental relations.

The years between 1977 and 1986 constituted the crucial period in abandoning the Keynesian intergovernmental pattern. In a striking departure, center-left governments in both the US and the UK issued urban policy white papers that sought to move away from Keynesian principles. Jimmy Carter's Commission on a National Agenda for the Eighties, for example, declared in 1980: "[There] are no 'national urban problems,' only an endless variety of local ones." The Commission actively endorsed the shift toward the Sunbelt, and argued that policy shouldn't try to combat the decline of the Rustbelt. In Britain, the 1977 white paper *Policy for the Inner Cities* similarly analyzed the structural causes of urban decline, and recommended pro-market approaches to urban policy. The Keynesian, national spatial policy of equalizing differences across regions was repudiated in favor of a focus on particular, high-growth urban regions that accepted or even accentuated cross-regional unevenness.[43]

In the 1980s, Ronald Reagan and Margaret Thatcher both forced cities to concentrate on economic development and the enhancement of the private sector, rather than engage in redistributive social spending. They borrowed urban policies from one another—Enterprise Zones, urban development corporations, public–private partnerships, and competitive central government grants for redevelopment (President Clinton's Empowerment Zones, Britain's City Pride program)—and used fiscal policy to discipline and subjugate cities. The first Reagan budget cut aid to cities by 23 percent, and the US simply dismantled much of its urban policy, adopting "a strategy of urban disinvestment." Thatcher tried to cap the rates that local authorities could charge, and also reduced their grant aid if their budgets went over her spending targets. Her policies made local authorities more dependent on centrally given grants, which means that central government in the UK has held increasingly powerful purse strings over time. While in 1990 rates provided over 50 percent of local authority income, the proportion declined by 2002 to under 20 percent. In effect, while Reagan defunded urban programs as much as possible, Thatcher centralized urban policymaking in the national state so as to break the backs of left and Labour city governments.[44]

Ultimately, in addition to increasing reliance on market forces, the institutional and intergovernmental changes of the 1980s were also directed at hobbling urban administrative power and subjecting cities even more to higher authority, in part because the cities were generally run by the opposing political party. In some ways the new higher-government intrusions into urban affairs are reminiscent of the nineteenth century. Under Thatcher, reforms gutted local authorities and disabled regional policy, and government in the UK has become "one of the most centralized systems in the world."[45] Reagan sought to give the states more control over spending, which tended to leave cities out in the cold. And state governments have not been shy about interfering increasingly with local government; Philadelphia in particular has been subject to intrusions by the Pennsylvania legislature. In 1991, Pennsylvania founded PICA, the Pennsylvania Intergovernmental Cooperation Authority, which oversees Philadelphia's budget and borrowing. In recent years, the state has taken over the Philadelphia Parking Authority by changing who nominates its board—largely to seize control of the authority's patronage appointments—and has also forcibly taken control of the city's public school system.[46]

As in earlier decades of reasserted higher-level power, the fragmentation of urban governance by means of special-purpose authorities has also been on the rise. Thatcher used political fragmentation as a conscious strategy to weaken city governments; she founded the centrally funded urban development corporations (UDCs) precisely to pursue urban redevelopment in preference to social spending, and to avoid popular and Labour Party demands. Manchester received not one but two of these UDCs, the Central Manchester and the Trafford Park Development Corporations.[47] And in 1986, Thatcher administered the *coup de grâce* to Keynesian strategies—she dismantled the conurbations, dismembering regional government.

Thatcher and Reagan's hostility to urban power was, of course, well understood by cities, and some of them, especially the largest ones, began campaigns of resistance. Some cities even tried to reclaim centuries-dormant foreign policy powers for themselves by becoming nuclear free zones or sanctuary cities.[48] Others took neoliberal arguments about globalization at their word, and tried to recover older international economic roles independent of the nation-state that had decayed during the Keynesian era. Of all British cities, Manchester was most successful at embracing the neoliberal turn, and in addition has gone a long way toward reinvigorating its old role as a regional hegemon. It has used economic development planning to reassert its dominance over other local authorities, particularly Salford and Trafford, and for much of the 1990s city council leader Graham Stringer even bent Thatcher's development corporations to his will.[49] In pushing cities to be more self-reliant, however, states are opening a can of worms: What happens when (not if) those cities decide that subordination to national interests is a constraint rather than a benefit? Will cities be able to force the pendulum of intergovernmental relations to swing back in their favor?

The Future of Urban Autonomy

The persistent tendency across the last five centuries has been to try to subordinate city power to central state power—but this tendency has always been resisted. Intergovernmental relations have been a tug of war between states seeking to incorporate and rationalize their territory, and cities jealous of their fragile liberties. Institutionally, the means states used to impose control over cities were often haphazard or expedient rather than systematic, and therefore residues of the old urban autonomy persisted well into the modern era. Thus, I have argued here that state–city relations in the US and the UK are *both* examples of APD's concept of intercurrence, in which the different parts of the state exist in tension and conflict with one another. The institutional "fit" between cities and states, especially for the largest and most powerful cities, has always been fraught and imperfect, never smooth.

I have also argued that intergovernmental relations in the US and UK, as well as the patterns of change in these relations over time, are more similar than different—despite the difference in state structure between the two countries. Rather than "American exceptionalism," I suggest that there is an Anglo-American cultural family of states with heavily subordinated cities. In a further departure from conventional thinking, I want to suggest the possibility that this family resemblance may be growing, due to the impact of neoliberalism and devolution.

The last two decades have seen a devolutionary trend in which subnational governments are being given increased responsibility for various state functions. Devolution is, in fact, already a core principle in the US—that is the whole meaning of state government. And strategies of devolution are currently advancing in the United Kingdom through measures such as empowered regional parliaments in Scotland and Wales. The political progress of the European Union (EU) is only likely to further devolution in Britain, given the EU's adoption of the subsidiarity principle and its willingness to fund redevelopment aid for regional governments. These trends suggest that the importance of the states in the US system may be less "exceptional" in coming decades.[50]

Since the early 1990s, the pendulum has been swinging uncertainly toward greater city autonomy. But it is not clear that devolution and regionalism will lead specifically to *urban* autonomy. Regionalism's meaning for cities depends on whether regions are drawn in such a way as to put major cities at their centers. The institutional shape of devolved intergovernmental relations, however, is likely to be based on regions in the UK and on state governments in the US, rather than on a form approaching the older, chartered medieval city-states.[51] Both state governments in the US and regional governments in the UK may increase the "political space" they occupy, and stifle moves toward urban autonomy. A door has opened, but it is not clear whether cities will be able to step through it.

Notes

1. Karen Orren and Stephen Skowronek, *The Search for American Political Development* (New York: Cambridge University Press, 2004).

2. By "state" I mean national government, like the United States or France; "state governments" mean American states such as Pennsylvania.
3. Orren and Skowronek, *The Search for American Political Development*, p. 123.
4. Paul E. Peterson, *City Limits* (Chicago: University of Chicago Press, 1981); Paul Kantor, *The Dependent City Revisited* (Boulder, CO: Westview Press, 1995); Martin Shefter, *Political Crisis/Fiscal Crisis: The Collapse and Revival of New York City* (New York: Basic Books, 1985), pp. 232–235.
5. Relevant sources include: Frank Gaffikin and Barney Warf, "Urban Policy and the Post-Keynesian State in the United Kingdom and the United States," *International Journal of Urban and Regional Research* 17, no. 1 (1993); Jacques Lagroye and Vincent Wright, "Introduction: Local Government in Britain and in France—the Problems of Comparisons and Contrasts," in Jacques Lagroye and Vincent Wright, eds., *Local Government in Britain and France* (London: George Allen & Unwin, 1979); Bas Denters and Lawrence E. Rose, eds., *Comparing Local Governance* (Basingstoke: Palgrave Macmillan, 2005); Patrick Le Gales, *European Cities* (Oxford: Oxford University Press, 2002); Christopher Leo, "City Politics in an Era of Globalization," in Mickey Lauria, ed., *Reconstructing Urban Regime Theory* (Thousand Oaks, CA: Sage, 1996); Warren Magnusson, *The Search for Political Space* (Toronto: University of Toronto Press, 1996); Herman Finer, *English Local Government* (New York: Columbia University Press, 1934), pp. 189–192.
6. Orren and Skowronek, *The Search for American Political Development*, pp. 112–116. On state formation, see Charles Tilly, *Coercion, Capital and European States* (Cambridge, MA: Basil Blackwell, 1990).
7. For a comparative analysis focused on Canada, see Magnusson, *The Search for Political Space*.
8. Max Weber, *The City* (New York: Free Press, 1958), p. 94; Henri Pirenne, *Medieval Cities* (Princeton, NJ and Garden City, NY: Princeton University Press and Doubleday, 1956 [1925]); Carl Stephenson, *Borough and Town* (Cambridge, MA: Medieval Academy of America, 1933); Finer, *English Local Government*.
9. Sidney Webb and Beatrice Webb, *The Manor and the Borough*, 2 vols. (Hamden, CT: Archon Books, 1963 [1908]), p. 288; Stephenson, *Borough and Town*; Frederic W. Maitland, *Township and Borough* (Cambridge: Cambridge University Press, 1898); Finer, *English Local Government*.
10. Weber, *The City*; Ted R. Gurr and Desmond S. King, *The State and the City* (Chicago: University of Chicago Press, 1987); Le Gales, *European Cities*; Pirenne, *Medieval Cities*; Peter Clark and Paul Slack, *English Towns in Transition, 1500–1700* (London: Oxford University Press, 1976); Charles Tilly and Wim P. Blockmans, eds., *Cities and the Rise of States in Europe, A.D. 1000 to 1800* (Boulder, CO: Westview Press, 1994); Gerald E. Frug, *City Making* (Princeton, NJ: Princeton University Press, 1999), pp. 34–36; Jon C. Teaford, *The Municipal Revolution in America* (Chicago: University of Chicago Press, 1975).
11. Webb and Webb, *The Manor and the Borough*, p. 270.
12. On the New England township, see Charles M. Kneier, *City Government in the United States* (New York: Harper & Brothers, 1947); Teaford, *The Municipal Revolution in America*.
13. Jason Kaufman, "Corporate Law and the Sovereignty of States," *American Sociological Review* 73 (June 2008): 402–425.
14. This was one of the origins of the "rotten boroughs" that were reformed in 1832. See Webb and Webb, *The Manor and the Borough*; Clark and Slack,

English Towns in Transition, 1500–1700, pp. 134–140; Finer, *English Local Government.*

15. Webb and Webb, *The Manor and the Borough*, p. 395. On the American trend, see Edward P. Allinson and Boies Penrose, *The City Government of Philadelphia* (Baltimore: Johns Hopkins University, 1887); Eric H. Monkkonen, *America Becomes Urban* (Berkeley: University of California Press, 1988).
16. Hobbes quoted in Frug, *City Making*, p. 34.
17. Gerald E. Frug, "The City as a Legal Concept," in Lloyd Rodwin and Robert M. Hollister, eds., *Cities of the Mind* (New York: Plenum, 1984); Frug, *City Making*; Kaufman, "Corporate Law and the Sovereignty of States."
18. See Frug, *City Making*; Teaford, *The Municipal Revolution in America.*
19. Quoted in Webb and Webb, *The Manor and the Borough*, p. 700; V.A.C. Gatrell, "Incorporation and the Pursuit of Liberal Hegemony in Manchester 1790–1839," in Derek Fraser, ed., *Municipal Reform and the Industrial City* (New York: St Martin's, 1982); Arthur Redford, *The History of Local Government in Manchester*, 3 vols. (London: Longmans, Green & Co., 1940); Teaford, *The Municipal Revolution in America*; Charles R. Adrian and Ernest S. Griffith, *A History of American City Government: The Formation of Traditions, 1775–1870* (New York: Praeger, 1976); Allinson and Penrose, *The City Government of Philadelphia.*
20. Webb and Webb, *The Manor and the Borough*; Adrian and Griffith, *A History of American City Government*; Kneier, *City Government in the United States*; Jon C. Teaford, *City and Suburb* (Baltimore: Johns Hopkins University Press, 1979).
21. Webb and Webb, *The Manor and the Borough*, pp. 749–753; Finer, *English Local Government*, pp. 63–66. London's metropolitan government system— the County Council, the City, and the twenty-eight metropolitan boroughs— was created by act of Parliament in 1899.
22. On the political dispute, see Redford, *The History of Local Government in Manchester*; Gatrell, "Incorporation and the Pursuit of Liberal Hegemony in Manchester 1790–1839"; W. Medcalf, "On the Municipal Institutions of the City of Manchester," *Transactions of the Manchester Statistical Society 1853–54* (1854) 17–32; available from http://www.archives.org/details/transactionsofma1875mancuoft. Incorporation was explicitly pursued by local Liberal elites as a way to break the Tory stranglehold over the municipality, and therefore to lay the ground for their assault on Parliament as a whole. Thus autonomous cities were critical for the bourgeois power base—power would flow from cities upward to the central state. Richard Cobden, the movement's chief militant, even wrote a pamphlet entitled *Incorporate Your Borough*; see Gatrell, "Incorporation and the Pursuit of Liberal Hegemony in Manchester 1790–1839," p. 38; Redford, *The History of Local Government in Manchester.*
23. Adrian and Griffith, *A History of American City Government*; David R. Berman, *Local Government and the States* (Armonk, NY: M.E. Sharpe, 2003), p. 54; Kneier, *City Government in the United States*; Nancy Burns and Gerald Gamm, "Creatures of the State: State Politics and Local Government, 1871–1921," *Urban Affairs Review* 33, no. 1 (1997).
24. Gurr and King, *The State and the City*; Teaford, *The Municipal Revolution in America*; Webb and Webb, *The Manor and the Borough*; Medcalf, "On the Municipal Institutions of the City of Manchester"; Redford, *The History of Local Government in Manchester.*
25. Kantor, *The Dependent City Revisited*; Monkkonen, *America Becomes Urban*, p. 4. On Philadelphia's expansion, see Allinson and Penrose, *The City Government of Philadelphia.*

26. Frug, "The City as a Legal Concept"; Berman, *Local Government and the States*; Kneier, *City Government in the United States*.
27. Monkkonen, *America Becomes Urban*; Redford, *The History of Local Government in Manchester*, vol. II, pp. 300–301; Adrian and Griffith, *A History of American City Government*.
28. Quoted in Berman, *Local Government and the States*, p. 2. See also Frug, "The City as a Legal Concept"; Kneier, *City Government in the United States*.
29. David Wilson, "The United Kingdom: An Increasingly Differentiated Polity?," in Denters and Rose, eds., *Comparing Local Governance*, p. 157; Finer, *English Local Government*.
30. Teaford, *City and Suburb*, Table 2, p. 66; Roscoe C. Martin, *The Cities and the Federal System* (New York: Atherton Press, 1965); Kneier, *City Government in the United States*.
31. On special-act charters, see Berman, *Local Government and the States*; Adrian and Griffith, *A History of American City Government*, p. 41. On Pennsylvania city classes, see Pennsylvania Department of General Services, "The Pennsylvania Manual" (2002); Pennsylvania Local Government Commission, *Pennsylvania Legislator's Municipal Deskbook* (third) (2006); available from http://www.lgc.state.pa.us/deskbook.html (accessed April 1, 2008); Pennsylvania State Association of Township Supervisors, *Pennsylvania Municipalities: In a Class by Themselves* (n.d.); available from http://www.psats.org/today_About_PA_Municipalities.pdf (accessed April 1, 2008).
32. In some states, however, home rule can be taken away by simple act of the legislature; see Kneier, *City Government in the United States*; Berman, *Local Government and the States*; Pennsylvania Local Government Commission, *Pennsylvania Legislator's Municipal Deskbook*; Pennsylvania Department of General Services, "The Pennsylvania Manual."
33. Sidney Webb and Beatrice Webb, *English Local Government: The Story of the King's Highway* (London: Longmans, Green & Co., 1920); Finer, *English Local Government*.
34. Finer, *English Local Government*.
35. Mark Gelfand, *A Nation of Cities* (New York: Oxford University Press, 1975).
36. Rob Atkinson and Graham Moon, *Urban Policy in Britain* (New York: St Martin's, 1994); John J. Gunther, *Federal–City Relations in the United States* (Newark: University of Delaware Press, 1990); Martin, *The Cities and the Federal System*.
37. Carolyn Adams et al., *Philadelphia: Neighborhoods, Division and Conflict in a Postindustrial City* (Philadelphia: Temple University Press, 1991); Robert A. Beauregard, "City Planning and the Postwar Regime in Philadelphia," in Mickey Lauria, ed., *Reconstructing Urban Regime Theory*.
38. Martin, *The Cities and the Federal System*; Gurr and King, *The State and the City*; Kantor, *The Dependent City Revisited*; Berman, *Local Government and the States*. The largest cities, such as New York and Chicago, also won the postwar argument over whether cities or states should win federal airport funds; see Martin, *The Cities and the Federal System*.
39. Finer, *English Local Government*, p. 9; Martin, *The Cities and the Federal System*.
40. Neil Brenner, *New State Spaces* (New York: Oxford University Press, 2004), p. 115; Mike Goldsmith, "The Changing System of English Local Government," in Lagroye and Wright, eds., *Local Government in Britain and France*. For an argument that a similar regionalist approach was adopted in Canada—though, like in the US, the urban–regional policy focus was eventually discarded in favor of a state–provincial one—see Magnusson, *The Search for Political Space*.

41. Berman, *Local Government and the States*; Goldsmith, "The Changing System of English Local Government"; Allan Cochrane, *Whatever Happened to Local Government?* (Buckingham: Open University Press, 1993); Sue Goss, *Local Labour and Local Government* (Edinburgh: Edinburgh University Press, 1988).

42. Berman, *Local Government and the States*.

43. The Commission quoted in Gunther, *Federal–City Relations in the United States*. On British policy see Timothy Barnekov, Robin Boyle, and Daniel Rich, *Privatism and Urban Policy in Britain and the United States* (New York: Oxford University Press, 1989); Atkinson and Moon, *Urban Policy in Britain*; Brenner, *New State Spaces*.

44. Barnekov, Boyle, and Rich, *Privatism and Urban Policy in Britain and the United States*, p. 139; Gunther, *Federal–City Relations in the United States*; Berman, *Local Government and the States*; Gurr and King, *The State and the City*; Cochrane, *Whatever Happened to Local Government?*; Wilson, "The United Kingdom: An Increasingly Differentiated Polity?"; Gaffikin and Warf, "Urban Policy and the Post-Keynesian State in the United Kingdom and the United States"; Alan DiGaetano and Paul Lawless, "Urban Governance and Industrial Decline: Governing Structures and Policy Agendas in Birmingham and Sheffield, England, and Detroit, Michigan, 1980–1997," *Urban Affairs Review* 34, no. 4 (1999); Stephen Quilley, "Manchester First: From Municipal Socialism to the Entrepreneurial City," *International Journal of Urban and Regional Research* 24, no. 3 (2000).

45. Mike Goldsmith, "A New Intergovernmentalism?," in Denters and Rose, eds., *Comparing Local Governance*, p. 238; Adam Tickell, Jamie Peck, and Peter Dicken, "The Fragmented Region: Business, the State and Economic Development in North West England," in Martin Rhodes, ed., *The Regions and the New Europe* (Manchester: Manchester University Press, 1995).

46. On Pennsylvania's various seizures of power, see Berman, *Local Government and the States*, pp. 33, 68.

47. Wilson, "The United Kingdom: An Increasingly Differentiated Polity?" Manchester was distinctive also in the way that the city's Labour government took control of the development corporations' plans; see Quilley, "Manchester First: From Municipal Socialism to the Entrepreneurial City."

48. Magnusson, *The Search for Political Space*; Heidi Hobbs, *City Hall Goes Abroad* (Newbury Park, CA: Sage, 1994).

49. Michael Katz, *The Price of Citizenship* (New York: Metropolitan/Henry Holt, 2001); Quilley, "Manchester First: From Municipal Socialism to the Entrepreneurial City"; Steve Quilley, "Entrepreneurial Turns: Municipal Socialism and After," in Jamie Peck and Kevin Ward, eds., *City of Revolution* (Manchester: Manchester University Press, 2002); Graham Haughton and Aidan While, "From Corporate City to Citizens City? Urban Leadership After Local Entrepreneurialism in the United Kingdom," *Urban Affairs Review* 35, no. 1 (1999); Iain Deas and Kevin Ward, "Metropolitan Manoeuvres: Making Greater Manchester," in Peck and Ward, eds., *City of Revolution*.

50. DiGaetano and Lawless, "Urban Governance and Industrial Decline"; Le Gales, *European Cities*.

51. Paul Kantor, "Can Regionalism Save Poor Cities? Politics, Institutions, and Interests in Glasgow," *Urban Affairs Review* 35, no. 6 (2000).

3 Town and Country in the Redefinition of State–Federal Power

Canada and the United States, 1630–2005

Jason Kaufman

One thing many studies of American political development lack is a comparative dimension. This is all the more so in the case of urban affairs. Numerous multi-city studies exist, but they rarely, if ever, transcend America's national border.[1] America's closest neighbor, politically and culturally speaking, is Canada, and it is to Canada that I turn here in seeking to contextualize the particularities of the American experience.

As with many things, this "most similar case" comparison overturns several commonly held beliefs about American politics. Given the liminal status municipal governments occupy with respect to state and national government, a focus on cities is indeed quite revealing about durable shifts in governing authority. The municipal domain provides an especially tractable place to study what Orren and Skowronek call "the elaboration of concepts that join institutions, history, and politics."[2]

The turn-of-the-last-century political scientist, William B. Munro, noted that the United States was "the world's chief laboratory for experimentation in municipal government," and the foregoing analysis attempts to explain why. This gets to the very heart of Orren and Skowronek's professed desire to emphasize the study of stasis and change in American political development. The convergence of jurisdictional ambiguity concerning the role and nature of American city government, American municipalities' equally uncertain relationship to their respective state governments, and the rural slant of American federal politics, will all be highlighted as contributing factors, particularly in contrast with the Canadian case.[3]

Most prominent studies of comparative US–Canadian politics—those by Seymour Martin Lipset, Louis Hartz, and Werner Sombart, for example—barely touch on the urban dimension. The aforementioned William Munro is an exception to this rule. His 1929 Marfleet Lectures at the University of Toronto looked explicitly at comparative US–Canadian politics, and one of these lectures, "City Government in Canada," is admirable in its detailed comparison of municipal political structures in

Canada, Britain, and the United States. Whereas Munro primarily stresses structural differences in municipal government, however, I look more broadly at the marriage of "institutions, history, and politics" here. Munro's analysis comes up a bit short in attributing nearly all of the structure of Canadian municipal politics to "American influence." The strength of his analysis is description as opposed to explanation.[4]

By comparing the role of urbanization in Canadian political development with that of the United States, we gain valuable new insight into the different roles cities can and do play in the erection and transformation of political power in and between national and sub-national political domains. As centers of economic and political activity, cities play a crucial—but variable—role in national networks of prominence and power. Historically, this has resulted in different roles for urban elites in Canadian and American national development.

An important caveat here, of course, is that the field of municipal governance was itself changing throughout the period in question— roughly four centuries of European rule in northern North America—*as well as* the fact that there was and is a great deal of variance within countries as well as within states and provinces. My goal here is not to enumerate every nook and cranny of urban politics in these two countries but to briefly point out some salient trends while posing equally important topics for further research. Case-specific comparisons are sorely needed to explore these ideas in full.

Such a comparison must confront a number of obstacles at the outset, from triangulating between differences related to place—which should probably include considerations such as climate, topology, and demography—to those related to economics, domestic politics, international politics, race, class, status, ethnicity, and national identity. There are many things that separate the United States and Canada. Isolating the independent effects of urbanization and "place" is no mean feat.

One might first consider some of the things that Canada and America have in common vis-à-vis municipal government. In both cases, national government has relatively little jurisdiction over city government. This lack of urban-centralization is readily apparent in both countries' constitutions, neither of which says overly much about local politics. This difference is especially salient in light of the experience of countries such as France and England, where centralized, national authority over local government is generally the rule. Weak national jurisdiction over municipalities has led both the US and Canada to not only a great deal of experimentation and diversity but also a surprising degree of uniformity, presumably the combined effect of cross-national immigration and imitation.

Another commonality of the northern North American experience is the enormous territorial expansion both countries experienced over the course of the nineteenth century, thus presenting novel problems of accession and administration not generally experienced in modern Europe. Since territorial jurisdictions were generally established before municipal ones, western cities remained subordinate from the start, though, as I will discuss shortly, there are important differences here as well.

Finally, both countries became predominantly "urban," demographically speaking, at about the same time—the 1920s—thus generating new problems and precepts in municipal governance. From public health to public transit, city managers now found themselves faced with a bevy of responsibilities never imagined by their forebears. In both cases, however, the effects of urbanization and industrialization actually made cities *more*, rather than less, dependent on higher units of government. The rise of the automobile and the suburb have only exacerbated this process by raising questions about the proper size and reach of city government in greater metropolitan affairs.

In the face of these common challenges and constraints, Canadian and American cities have nonetheless evolved in vastly different institutional contexts, thus shaping the particular way city governments have grown and changed to meet them.

Important differences in the organization of local government actually predate the creation of national states in both Canada and the United States, and in ways that are telling for their long-term trajectories. For starters, revisionist historians now tell us that the various townships of early colonial New England were organized not as agrarian proto-democracies but as private, for-profit business corporations in which only shareholders—often absentee landowners—were permitted to vote. Thus, Tocqueville's so-called "New England town meetings" were actually more like shareholders meetings than "schools for democracy." Because the New England Puritans believed strongly in the corporate-organizational form as a model for political organization, they liberally used it to generate and legislate the many townships and colonies of the seventeenth and eighteenth centuries. Not surprisingly, this model later evolved into one prominent in not only American municipal organization but also business, religious, and civic association as well.[5]

This is one of the most interesting, and poorly understood, aspects of the early American experience, one that deserves more attention. Scholars such as Hendrik Hartog, John Frederick Martin, and Leonard P. Curry have launched valuable forays into the study of early American municipal corporations and city charters, but there is much yet to be learned. How exactly the corporate-township model affected the finances, legal status, and administrative capacity of early American cities is little known. So too is the impact this legal form had on the Founders' thinking about the role of local government in the new nation.[6]

One thing we *do* know about the Founders' thoughts on the municipal issue is that they appear to have thought relatively little about it: the

Constitution says virtually nothing at all about the administration of towns and cities, leaving supervision thereof to the respective states. Whether this was because the Founders' trusted the states to manage internal affairs or simply because they did not foresee the rising role of urban centers is not clear. The Founders were, for the most part, anti-urban in outlook, particularly those allied with Jefferson's vision of a rural, agrarian republic. Their failure to grapple sufficiently with the issue of municipal government may reflect a wish that it would go away or fade in importance as the nation grew, a wish wholly betrayed by reality. Ironically, this lacuna is most evident in the plans for the nation's capital, Washington DC, a city bestowed with no state oversight, limited budgetary power, and ambiguous jurisdiction—features that continue to plague it to this day.[7]

In contrast, proto-Canadian cities, such as Quebec, Montreal, Halifax, Kingston, St John, and York (the latter-day Toronto), were founded on more conventional (i.e. centralized, royalist) terms. Incorporation did not become a feature of Canadian municipal government until the mid-nineteenth century. Prior to that, cities were considered subordinate conglomerations subject to provincial authority and control. Cities in New France had no jurisdictional autonomy whatsoever and were governed, following the French model, by a policy of "almost unlimited central control." From the English accession of 1760 to the 1840s, Canadian cities were generally governed by royally appointed Courts of Quarter Sessions, mostly staffed by retired army officers appointed magistrates for life.[8]

American cities' jurisdictional autonomy relative to that of Canadian cities flies in the face of widely accepted legal doctrine concerning American municipalities. "Dillon's Rule," the eponymous creation of a native Iowan, Justice John Forrest Dillon, represents American municipalities as the dependent creations of the American states. Technically, this is true; all municipal corporations exist at the behest of their respective state governments. Once created, however, corporate entities gain relative autonomy from the bodies that create them. Though landmark court decisions such the *Dartmouth College* case served to create a distinction between public and private corporations, thus portraying municipal corporations as creatures of the state, the corporate shell nonetheless protected American municipal corporations from some unwanted interference. The American "home rule" movement was, in effect, a real-world corrective to Dillon's misperception; because cities had independent status as "legal fictions" qua corporations, they could challenge state oversight, just as could any other corporation. Seen in comparative perspective, American municipal governments are not nearly as weak as Dillon's Rule would have us believe.[9]

An alternative interpretation of Dillon's Rule would say that this doctrine surfaced in the United States exactly because of the ambiguity underlying American municipalities' legal status. In other nation states, such as Canada and Britain, the subordinate role of cities was clear enough to make such analyses unnecessary. Dillon aimed to stress municipalities' weakness vis-à-vis state government because that status was rather ambiguous and quite easily challenged, as seen in the subsequent home rule movement. Canada and England have no comparable doctrine, it would seem, because there was no comparable need to clarify the jurisdictional status of city governments. Comparative analysis with other common law countries thus provides an important corrective to the popular perception that American city governments are unusually weak. By comparative standards, they are actually relatively strong.

Nevertheless, while it might thus appear that cities were less influential in the political development of Canada than the United States, there are mitigating factors that deserve consideration as well. Canadian cities had relatively little political autonomy under the French and British colonial systems, but provincial elites tended to spend most of their time there, thus keeping urban affairs in the limelight of Canadian political debate. Since provincial business and government were so often contiguous with major Canadian cities, Canadian politics evolved with the concerns of city-dwellers firmly in mind, in contrast to the American case, where a continually expanding frontier and a decidedly rural political elite tended to keep urban affairs on the proverbial back burner. Canada's western frontier was not open to settlement until 1870, when the Hudson's Bay Company relinquished its monopoly charter thereto, so Canadian politics further lacked the rural, western character of American politics, with its frontiersmen and territorial politicians.

In the United States, Southern plantation owners and westward pioneers had a say in national affairs equal to their (largely northeastern) urban counterparts. This was partly a result of the fact that the American trans-Appalachian frontier was opened to settlement long before the Canadian west. In the United States, many state constitutions guaranteed rural voters disproportionate sway over urbanites. The location of state capitals outside some states' primary population centers—Albany in New York, for example, and Harrisburg in Pennsylvania—further limited American urbanites' influence on state politics.

One result of America's relatively haphazard settlement process, both before and after the Revolution, was that rural areas played a major role in the politics of the new nation. Geography, rather than population, often prevailed in the determination of American political representation, thus providing rural settlers a disproportionate influence in the national Senate, as well as many state legislatures. In Canada, by contrast, elite compacts allowed urbanites to dominate provincial politics, and its English-style parliament allowed city-dwellers to run for provincial and national office in rural ridings. Presumably, provincial governments applied themselves to municipal affairs more consistently and earnestly than their American counterparts. This may help explain Canada's continuing advantage in city-specific policy areas such as commuter infrastructure, anti-sprawl legislation, and education and health care for the poor and needy. American state legislatures do not have the same explicit obligation to tackle urban affairs, so issues such as commuter rail, poverty relief, and metropolitan planning all too often suffer.

A second relevant factor that requires consideration is the structure of Canadian provincial–local jurisdiction itself: while the United States Constitution says virtually nothing about local government, the British North America Act of 1867 (Canada's de facto, though as yet unratified, Constitution) explicitly places municipal institutions and local government under the authority of their respective provincial governments. The Canadian Constitution also enumerates the powers of the provinces in ways not foreseen by the American Constitution. Direct taxation, public health, "municipal institutions" (i.e. city government and its incumbent responsibilities), liquor licensing, and education are all expressly designated provincial responsibilities in Canada. In America, the states are merely granted all powers not explicitly allocated to the national government in the Constitution.[10]

One consequence of the Canadian system of explicitly delegating powers to the provinces is that the provinces have generally been more predisposed than the American states to assure that public resources are evenly distributed. Whereas education spending in the United States varies greatly by school district, for example, Canadian provincial governments provide "equalization payments" to "poor" school districts within their purview, as they tend to do with health and infrastructure spending as well. The United States Supreme Court confirmed the legality of locally variable school financing in the landmark case of *San Antonio Independent School District v. Rodriguez*. Americans living in resource-poor school districts suffer from the lack of legally mandated fiscal cooperation between adjacent jurisdictions. Revenue-sharing between districts is standard practice in Canada.[11]

In contrast to the foregoing areas of public administration that the Canadian provinces govern, criminal law is, by contrast, designated a national function in Canada, though enforcement of the law remains a provincial responsibility. It is worth noting (and studying in much more detail) the fact that the Royal Canadian Mounted Police (RCMP) not only have no centralized federal counterpart in the United States (save, perhaps, the Federal Bureau of Investigation, plus smaller agencies such as the Bureau of Alcohol, Tobacco, and Firearms) but also "contract out" their services to most of the provinces—only Ontario and Quebec, as well as parts of Labrador and Newfoundland, maintain their own provincial police forces at present. Notably, numerous city governments in Canada also pay the Mounties to serve as their local police force. Policing is thus far more centralized in Canada than in the United States. To my knowledge, the consequences of this distinction have yet to be assessed. One might hypothesize that Canadian police forces are more efficient as a result of the top-down mandate of the RCMP.

Since prison-building, too, is a federal rather than a provincial responsibility—with the exception of facilities for prisoners sentenced for less than 2 years—there is less tendency for Canadian provincial and local politicians to look to prisons as a key source of economic renewal. Though there are many contributing causes to this difference, the unique role of the American states in building and staffing prisons, as well as manning and operating local police forces, presumably contributes to America's tendency to look to incarceration, as opposed to more rehabilitative responses to anti-social behavior. Treatment services for drug users and tolerance for minor drug-related activity are characteristic of most Canadian jurisdictions today, though drug trafficking is still prosecuted heavily. American cities that have contemplated similar policies have been repeatedly opposed by the Justice Department. Needle exchanges for intravenous drug users, for example, are extremely uncommon in US cities; they are, however, quite common in Canadian cities. These are topics that deserve much further analysis, particularly in a comparative light.

A third ramification of differences in the formal allocation of sub-national political power is more qualitative, and thus harder to see, but important nonetheless. Because the powers of Canadian municipal councils are formally proscribed by provincial government, Canadian city government tends to run in a less partisan manner than American city governments. "Although council members may be elected with political party support they seldom run as party candidates in most Canadian municipalities nor do they openly or officially work together as party groups in council," writes Crawford.[12] Though single parties often dominate American city politics, there is no comparable sense of being above, or beyond, the reach of party politics—American machine politics should not be mistaken for non-partisanship.

Presumably, Canadian municipal non-partisanship is a result of the fact that the Canadian Constitution portrays municipal councils as functionary appendages of provincial government, rather than distinct governments in their own right—i.e. leadership roles in municipal government are regarded more as bureaucratic postings than partisan winnings:

> Because there is no party alignment, councils do not divide consistently on the various issues but usually each member votes on the issues before council as he [or she] feels inclined, or as he feels his personal political interests require. There are no government issues which take precedence because there is no "Government."[13]

Though partisanship has crept into Canadian municipal affairs of late, the general proclivity of these non-partisan municipal councils is to avoid initiating new programs without provincial impetus. Party politics drive many policy initiatives in American cities, by contrast, even in those cities with de facto single-party rule. Urban boosterism is an established way of life in American municipal politics; it is far less relevant in the Canadian context, particularly because provincial governments, coupled with non-partisan municipal councils, hold the reins to so many crucial areas of urban affairs.

Furthermore, notes Crawford:

> The lack of an opposition [in Canadian municipal government] means that there is no one person or group whose duty it is to look for the flaws in the proposals made to council and thereby to protect the citizens against ill-advised action. ... Frequently proposals of dubious value are adopted by councils, not because the members approve of them, but for want of any one who will assume the thankless task of criticizing and opposing them. At the same time, the absence of party in municipal government may be a factor contributing to its sensitivity to public opinion. Councils are notorious for their ability to change their minds and to reverse their decisions.[14]

Partisanship, log-rolling, and *ad hominem* attacks are strikingly prevalent in American city politics. City boosterism, or the promotion of urban business by political entrepreneurs, business elites, manufacturing and trade associations, is another unusual feature of American municipal politics related to cities' jurisdictional autonomy and partisan politics.

At one more level of remove, an important ramification of these differences is that American cities have been greater incubators for policy innovation and political entrepreneurship than their Canadian counterparts. Canadian cities have formal obligations to their citizens defined by provincial government; further action, though possible, must be executed without formal legal sanction. Since American states do not hold similar power over municipal government—particularly following the home rule movement of the late nineteenth century—city politicians have a freer hand to experiment and innovate. At the same time, however, the absence of state sanction sometimes hampers policies intended to promote the social welfare of citizens: American cities must often initiate such policies without guarantee of state funding or support. This observation is another corrective to received wisdom about American political development: while the American states are often perceived as "policy laboratories," American cities are where a good deal of American public policy is actually crafted and implemented. This is another subject deserving of further attention.[15]

An interesting example of US–Canadian differences in political "style" can be found in the response of both countries to the exigencies of the Great Depression. In the United States, poor relief was quickly and easily framed as a national responsibility, thus enabling Franklin D. Roosevelt's federal "New Deal" programs. The paucity of Constitutional language about state powers facilitated the expansion of federal oversight in this domain. In Canada, by contrast, poor relief was constitutionally relegated to the provinces, which in turn framed public relief as the responsibility of local government. (The English Poor Law model of punitive, local aid remained in place in Canada until the mid-twentieth century despite being abandoned in England in the 1830s.) When unemployed, hungry men and women flocked to Canadian cities with active social welfare programs, such as Vancouver and Edmonton, the city councils (legally) responded by arguing that migrant supplicants were only eligible for relief in their primary place of residence. Thousands were turned away or carted off to crude provincial work camps.

Ultimately, however, Canadian provincial governments mended their ways in the 1940s and 1950s by initiating large-scale social welfare programs such as universal health and unemployment insurance. These were policy areas in which the Canadian system granted the provinces explicit jurisdiction, thus making it easier to initiate and justify policy innovations therein. Social programs of this size or scope are relatively rarely implemented in the American states, presumably (in part) because their constitutional power to do so is not fully enumerated. There are obvious exceptions, though: in comparison with Canada, American state involvement in social welfare policy pales in comparison with the role of Washington. The federal government is responsible for innovation and implementation of many key social welfare programs in the United States. Given the degree of poverty, inequality, and crime in most American cities, municipal governments are often left filling major gaps in the social safety net.

Admittedly, and in conclusion, these brief comments on the role of municipal government in Canadian and American political development raise as many questions as answers. Of further interest are issues such as differential responses to, and incentives for, suburbanization. How, for example, have provincial limits on city power influenced the rise of greater metropolitan zones in Canada, as opposed to the United States? Highway and road-building, parking, zoning, and power-sharing are all key elements of the peripheralization of North American cities. Though I am in no position to answer, or even assess, these differences, I desperately hope others will.

Also of interest are matters such as inter-jurisdictional responses to natural disasters, national defense crises, and public health emergencies. In the United States, for example, individual city governments had to create their own institutional responses to HIV/AIDS, thus heightening their learning curve and duplicating (and sometimes countermanding) efforts at the state and federal levels. In Canada, one would presume, provincial governments were better able to coordinate and control prevention and treatment regimes at the regional and local levels. Comparative studies of governmental response to natural disasters and public health crises like these would be most profitable.

Finally of interest will be the ways in which Canadian and American municipal organizations have transformed themselves of late in response to the heightened demands put upon them by taxpayers, politicians, and national and sub-national legislatures. Under Mayor Mike Harris, for example, Toronto underwent an effort to make its city government look more like that of multi-jurisdictional American metropolises such as New York City. Harris' efforts were unpopular and have been largely undone, but the temptation may remain for Canadian politicians to emulate their American counterparts. Unfortunately, and for reasons that deserve better understanding in their own right, American mayors and city councils do not seem nearly as likely to copy their northern neighbors vice versa, though they could surely benefit by doing so. Lack of support from state government coupled with the grueling demands of American city politics make such efforts exceedingly unlikely.

Comparative study will undoubtedly reward those willing to juggle the extra material, particularly in areas where *both* American and Canadian cities appear to have evolved in molds quite different from their Western European counterparts. I very much hope others will be compelled to follow these leads and pursue these topics in depth.

Acknowledgments

I wish to thank Richard Dilworth for his incisive comments on earlier drafts of this chapter and Hendrik Hartog for originally introducing me to the fascinating subject of public law. All errors, factual and otherwise, are purely my responsibility.

Notes

1. Recent noteworthy exceptions include: Alan DiGaetano and Elizabeth Strom, "Comparative Urban Governance: An Integrated Approach," *Urban Affairs Review* 38 (2003): 356–395; Jon Pierre, "Comparative Urban Governance: Uncovering Complex Causalities," *Urban Affairs Review* 40 (2005): 446–462; Jeffrey M. Sellers, "Re-Placing the Nation: An Agenda for Comparative Urban Politics," *Urban Affairs Review* 40 (2005): 419–445; Katherine M. Johnson, "'The Glorified Municipality': State Formation and the Urban Process in North America," *Political Geography* 27 (2008): 400–417; Bishwapriya Sanyal, ed., *Comparative Planning Cultures* (New York: Routledge, 2005); Leo Van Den Berg, Erik Braun, and Alexander H. J. Otgaar, eds., *City and Enterprise: Corporate Community Involvement in European and US Cities* (Burlington: Ashgate, 2003); Anita A. Summers, Paul C. Cheshire, and Lanfranco Senn, eds., *Urban Change in the United States and Western Europe: Comparative Analysis and Policy* (Washington, DC: Urban Institute Press, 1999); Michael Keating, *Comparative Urban Politics:*

Power and the City in the United States, Canada, Britain, and France (Brookfield: Elgar, 1991).

2. Karen Orren and Stephen Skowronek, *The Search for American Political Development* (New York: Cambridge University Press, 2004), p. 107.

3. William B. Munro, *American Influences on Canadian Government* (Toronto: Macmillan, 1929), p. 100.

4. Munro, "City Government in Canada," in *American Influences on Canadian Government*.

5. John Frederick Martin, *Profits in the Wilderness: Entrepreneurship and the Founding of New England Towns in the Seventeenth Century* (Chapel Hill: University of North Carolina Press, 1991); Jason Kaufman, "Corporate Law and the Sovereignty of States," *American Sociological Review* 73 (June 2008): 402–425; Jason Kaufman, *The Origins of Canadian and American Political Differences* (Cambridge, MA: Harvard University Press, 2009).

6. Leonard P. Curry, *The Corporate City: The American City as a Political Entity, 1800–1850* (Westport, CT: Greenword Press, 1997); Hendrik Hartog, *Public Property and Private Power: The Corporation in the City of New York in American Law, 1730–1870* (Chapel Hill: University of North Carolina Press, 1983); Martin, *Profits in the Wilderness*.

7. Stanley Elkins and Eric McKitrick, *The Age of Federalism* (New York: Oxford University Press, 1993); Kenneth R. Bowling, *The Creation of Washington, D.C.: The Idea and Location of the American Capital* (Fairfax, VA: George Mason University Press, 1991).

8. Kenneth Grant Crawford, *Canadian Municipal Government* (Toronto: University of Toronto Press, 1954), pp. 20, 23, 33, 38–39.

9. John Forrest Dillon, *Treatise on the Law of Municipal Corporations* (Chicago: J. Cockcroft, 1872); Gerald Frug, "The City as a Legal Concept," *Harvard Law Review* 93, no. 6: 1057–1154; Hartog, *Public Property and Private Power*.

10. Jason Kaufman, *Origins of Canadian and American Political Differences*; Robert C. Vipond, *Liberty and Community: Canadian Federalism and the Failure of the Constitution* (Albany, NY: SUNY Press, 1991); Ronald L. Watts, "The American Constitution in Comparative Perspective: A Comparison of Federalism in the United States and Canada," *Journal of American History* 74, no. 3 (1987): 769–792.

11. 411 US 1 (1973).

12. Crawford, *Canadian Municipal Government*, p. 55.

13. Ibid., p. 55.

14. Ibid., p. 56.

15. Cf. Jacob Hacker, *The Divided Welfare State: The Battle Over Public and Private Social Benefits in the United States* (New York: Cambridge University Press, 2002); Theda Skocpol, *Protecting Soldiers and Mothers: The Political Origins of Social Policy in the United States* (Cambridge, MA: Belknap Press, 1992).

Part II
Rethinking Urban Politics

4 Challenging the Machine–Reform Dichotomy
Two Threats to Urban Democracy

Jessica Trounstine

One of the classic themes in the study of urban political history is the clash between the Boss and the Reformer. According to traditional accounts machines dominated local politics through party organizations, created corrupt and inefficient government, and were supported by immigrant masses who had been bribed into loyalty.[1] Municipal reformers on the other hand sought clean government run by experts and supported by a knowledgeable, decisive electorate, which would allow elected officials freedom to pursue growth and development.[2] Yet, despite these important differences, machine and reform coalitions shared many more characteristics than the conventional wisdom would suggest.

The machine–reform dichotomy has been a subject of debate since reformers first began penning critiques of machines at the turn of the nineteenth century.[3] In these accounts machines epitomized corrupted democracy and reformers the cities' white knights. A second generation of scholarship challenged these early normative claims. Theorists such as Robert Merton argued that machines dominated for extended periods of time because they provided integral social functions such as the provision of welfare, the creation of informal networks between business and government, and the centralization of power.[4] Simultaneously, a new generation of scholarship on municipal reform reanalyzed the movement as an effort by businessmen and the middle class to regain governing authority. To achieve this goal reformers sought to disenfranchise poor, working class, and immigrant voters.[5] Then scholarship deriding machines reemerged while reform was reinterpreted as a complex, multifaceted movement.[6] More recently urban historians have suggested that machines dominated the minds of reformers more frequently than they dominated cities. However, even in revisionist accounts machine and reform politicians tend to be analyzed in opposition to one another and frequently at one historical moment.

Studying political machines and municipal reform side by side and over time allows us to see how alike they were. After coming to power, both types of coalitions sought to prevent durable shifts in governing authority by biasing political institutions in their favor.[7] In approximately 30 percent of America's largest cities the result was the elimination of effective competition and the domination of governance by a single coalition for multiple terms.[8] During periods of dominance, with reelection virtually guaranteed, machine and reform coalitions became less responsive to the populations they governed.

The development of dominance in machine and reform cities exemplifies the importance of timing and the processes of path dependence and positive feedback emphasized by scholars of American political development. The period during which a coalition established governing authority significantly affected (or attenuated) its options for biasing the system. The demographic and economic makeup of a city, the prevailing distribution of authority, and institutional setting made some strategies more attractive and successful than others.[9] Over time, dominance became self-reinforcing. The presence of biased institutions coupled with smashing electoral victories and low turnout discouraged challengers from attempting to enter the political fray at all. Ultimately though, the inflexibility in the structures and strategies of dominance undermined the ability of incumbents to maintain power as dissatisfaction became widespread among city residents and elites. Once a coalition became reliant on specific mechanisms to prevent shifts in governing authority, it became increasingly difficult for the coalition to choose any other path. In many cases a regime's inability to change its tactics ultimately led to its defeat.

In this chapter I show that both machine and reform politicians sought to increase the certainty of reelection by advantaging incumbents at all stages of the voting process. The strategies that these coalitions used allowed them to maintain dominance for long periods of time while excluding large segments of the population from the benefits of municipal governance. I begin by laying out a theoretical framework for understanding the similarities between machine and reform politics. Then I provide historical evidence of the various mechanisms each type of coalition relied upon to preserve power. Finally, I explain the effects of dominance: incumbents were reelected with near certainty and large segments of the population were denied access to municipal services and benefits. The divergent characterizations scholars have offered of machine and reform politicians can be reinterpreted as alternative means to achieve the same goal—a durable shift in governing authority.

A Theory of Dominance

As is the case in the sporting world, the institutions that govern political contests have the potential to determine which contestants are most likely to win elections, what skills and strategies will be most valuable, and who gets to participate. Thus, political institutions vary in the degree to which they ensure competitive elections and responsiveness to voters. Some institutions, biased institutions, simultaneously decrease competition (increasing the probability that incumbents will retain power) and decrease the need for incumbents to be responsive to voters. We should expect politicians to favor institutions that advantage them and to select strategies that enhance their chances of victory given the context in which they run. These strategies might consist of being responsive to voters or they might be the implementation of biased institutions.

If a coalition chooses to enact or rely on bias to insulate its governing authority it selects from among a number of options that can be categorized by the decision points in a democratic electoral system—generating preferences regarding government performance (information bias), translating preferences into votes (vote bias), and converting votes into seats (seat bias).[10]

Information bias refers to a system in which the government has a systematic advantage in controlling information about its record of performance and thus, citizen's preferences. State-controlled media and low information elections (e.g. nonpartisan elections) are examples of such mechanisms. In essence, information bias suggests an advantage for incumbents in the dissemination of information about government activity and available alternatives.

Vote bias describes a systematic advantage for incumbents in the way votes are cast. When a coalition uses government resources (for example, patronage employees) to promote the organization of its supporters or inhibit the organization of its opposition, it is engaging vote bias. Mechanisms such as poll taxes, registration laws, and vote fraud are other examples of this type of bias. Additionally, this category includes barriers to competition for challengers, such as lowering officials' pay or physically intimidating candidates. Barriers to competition bias outcomes toward the governing regime because voters have no other options.

The final step in the electoral process is the translation of votes into seats. This type of bias has been extensively studied in the literature on apportionment and representation particularly with regard to the US Congress.[11] The system's seat bias is determined by the degree to which the share of seats won exaggerates the share of votes won in favor of the incumbent coalition. Measures that create or increase malapportionment, gerrymandering, or reserved seats in the government's favor increase the incumbent coalition's probability of retaining governing authority. Additionally, the elimination of districts in legislative elections can increase incumbents' advantage when used in combination with voting restrictions. In this case at-large elections offer a substantial advantage to the incumbent coalition because all seats represent the same limited electorate. Table 4.1 displays strategies that have been used to increase the probability of incumbents maintaining governing authority in American cities.

Two bundles of strategies have been common in American history. Machine coalitions achieved control primarily through the use of government resources for political ends while reform coalitions dominated

Table 4.1 Biasing strategies

Information bias	Vote bias	Seat bias
Media control (ownership, regulation)	Vote bribery	Annexing in government's favor
Suppression of voluntary associations	Obscure polling place sites	Gerrymandering
Control over judicial system/prosecutors	Use of government resources to prevent opponent organization or enhance incumbent organization	Malapportionment
Low information elections (e.g. nonpartisan)	Impairment of election monitoring	Decreasing size of legislature
	Disqualification of candidates	At-large elections
	Candidate requirements (signatures, thresholds)	Increasing appointed offices
	Low pay for office holders	
	Violence keeping voters from polls or forcing vote choice	
	Electoral falsification (ghost/repeat voting, inflating totals, discarding ballots)	
	Registration requirements	
	Suffrage restrictions (literacy tests, poll taxes, language or race requirements, citizens only)	
	Assassinating/threatening/imprisoning opponents	

government by relying on rules that limited the opportunity for dissenters and minority populations to participate in elections.

The strategies selected and relied upon by machine and reform organizations differed because they faced different institutional constraints and political contexts. In short, the timing and location of dominance mattered a great deal. Machines lacked home rule, were frequently thwarted by state officials of opposing parties, and sought power in cities with large, diverse populations of working-class and poor voters, many of whom were first and second generation immigrants. A reliance on patronage for winning reelection made sense in this environment. Reformers benefited from flexible city charters, supportive state governments, and more homogeneous communities in which opponents to reform platforms could be excluded from the electorate through suffrage restrictions and vote dilution.

The following sections provide a more in-depth analysis of each type of bias used by governing coalitions in Chicago, New York, New Haven, Kansas City, Philadelphia, San Jose, Austin, San Antonio, and Dallas. The first five cities were dominated by machines and the latter four cities by reform regimes. The following discussion is organized by biasing category (information bias, vote bias, and seat bias) and by coalition type (machine or reform).

Controlling Information

Machines sought to control information to shape voters' preferences using a number of different mechanisms. For example they placed organization loyalists in official positions that held investigative authority such as local-level prosecutors, grand juries, or state attorneys general. When investigations did occur, machines used control over city agencies to destroy evidence, provide extended leaves to potential witnesses, and otherwise prevent prosecutorial cooperation. The machine's relationship to the criminal underworld was sometimes utilized to kill informants.[12] Another mechanism of information control was influence over the news media. Machines attempted to achieve favorable news coverage by bribing editors or reporters, contributing heavily in advertising funds, or by offering publishers or editors public jobs. Libel suits against papers were also used to control the presentation of harmful information. In a few cases machines resorted to murdering investigative reporters.[13]

Reformers used less obviously corrupt methods for controlling information and shaping the preferences of voters in favor of their incumbent organizations. At the turn of the century, many reform organizations secured the enactment of nonpartisan local elections, arguing that parties should be irrelevant to urban administration. Because reformers argued that they had identified the most appropriate approach to good government, political institutions that made governance conflictual, such as parties, served to stymie progress. One reform leader argued the purpose of the nonpartisan movement was "to unite decent voters in an effort to take the city government out of politics."[14] By "politics" reformers meant "patronage and selfish intrigue of those who lived on the public payroll and were therefore considered hindrances to community development."[15]

In converting elections to nonpartisan contests, reformers sought to minimize divisions in the electorate and among elites. The lack of party cues to assist voters in the formation of preferences resulted in systems biased in favor of candidates with independent wealth or fame and incumbents, advantaging reform coalition members.[16] Additionally, the less structured environment for competition in a nonpartisan system served to decrease interest and knowledge among constituents, making it difficult for challengers to activate opposition to the incumbent regime.[17] Without parties to train new leaders and teach voters political skills, nonpartisan elections increased the probability that membership in the incumbent organization was the only path to access the system.

The most powerful reform weapon in shaping the preference of voters was control over the local media. Newspaper editors and owners were the leaders of the reform movement in many cities. In San Jose, San Antonio, Dallas, and Austin, reform-owned newspapers refused to report stories that challenged the dominance of the local elites.[18] The local papers in all four reform cities endorsed reform charters, and news stories about city hall tended toward unabashed editorializing. According to a review of city manager government in Dallas, the publisher of the *Dallas News* "threw the full weight of his paper behind" the movement.[19] Every day leading up to the charter election the *News* published a front-page article explaining some aspect of the proposed change and urged its adoption. On the eve of charter reform in San Jose, the *Mercury Herald* printed a front-page article that argued the election would reveal

> whether the people of San Jose want boss rule or popular rule; whether the jobs of city hall shall go to henchmen who do nothing for their pay but politics for their master, or to be clean capable men who are good citizens and are accustomed only to a fair wage for fair service.[20]

Everywhere, local news organizations shared the vision of the common good that reformers proposed to enact; but frequently only after reformers strategically purchased opposition news outlets. In Austin the leaders of the opposition owned the evening paper and reported anti-reform speeches in great detail.[21] This changed after reform leaders purchased the paper in 1924. In 1896, the San Jose Good Government League was organized to win control of the city for the forces of reform but failed in part because the city's newspapers published articles critically analyzing the reform plan. Such problems ended after reform leaders J.O. and E.A. Hayes purchased two of the city's three newspapers and ended printed opposition to the reform charter and candidates in the newly consolidated *San Jose Mercury Herald*. The editor of the *Herald* resigned after discovering that the new owners intended to impose an editorial policy with "political implications."[22] The Hayes family completed their news monopoly in 1942 when they purchased the town's third and last independent newspaper, *The News*. Two years later the reform coalition finally achieved dominance. By coordinating the support of papers, reformers were "shielded from criticism by enthusiastic and boosterish local mass media" and successfully biased the system in their favor.[23]

Biasing Votes Using Government Resources

The second stage of the voting process requires voters to translate their preferences into votes on election day. Coalitions can take steps to ensure that incumbent office holders are advantaged when ballots are cast by limiting the ability for residents or challengers to participate in electoral contests.

In order to bias outcomes toward their organizations, governing coalitions in many political systems focus on trading divisible benefits (such as public jobs) for support, thereby using government resources to engender loyalty to the incumbent regime and pay political workers. Patronage becomes an even stronger strategy for bias when the coalition uses the benefit coercively, threatening recipients with losing their jobs if they do not perform political functions, requiring that job holders pay a portion of their salary into party coffers, and/or using political appointees to further bias the political system through practices such as vote fraud and intimidation. When workers are assured of economic security if and only if they support the incumbent coalition they are extremely unlikely to engage in political opposition.[24] The loyalty generated by such uncertainty over maintaining one's job is likely to be even more dramatic when the employee has few options for work in the private sector. In this way, coercive patronage serves to bias the system in favor of incumbents.

Party-based coalitions in Chicago, Kansas City, New York, New Haven, and Philadelphia employed patronage coercively. In Kansas City nearly all machine leaders and workers held public jobs, some contributing up to 50 percent of their salaries to the party's campaign funds.[25] In Chicago Mayor Cermak pressured employees to contribute 1 to 2 percent of their salaries.[26] Later in the city's history, Mayor and Boss Richard J. Daley made certain that his patronage appointees would remain loyal to him by threatening their jobs and controlling which government decisions they made.[27] By using government resources to organize and maintain the coalition, machine organizations successfully biased electoral outcomes in favor of incumbent coalitions.

However, patronage was not sufficient to guarantee long-term dominance for urban coalitions because various factions and opposition parties used the same strategies. Shifting governing authority using patronage required that a coalition control *access* to patronage, often through relationships with higher levels of government. Where organizations had difficulty securing and/or controlling patronage, they did not survive without alternative electoral strategies. For instance in New York, anti-Tammany governors doled out patronage to various wings of the Democratic Party until the late 1890s. Tammany finally consolidated governing authority only after a new governor supportive of the organization channeled patronage to Tammany leaders at the turn of the century.[28]

Control over the bureaucracy through patronage workers also allowed coalitions in Chicago, Kansas City, New York, New Haven, and Philadelphia to control delivery of municipal benefits and application of city laws. New York's machine made sure that the city's attorney used the power of the office to go after political challengers or their supporters for violations of mundane city ordinances. Near election time "a general raid ... [was] made on the whole body of store keepers and others in the district, care, of course, being taken not to trouble any who are known to be of the right stripe." Storekeepers were then offered the option of settling their violations in exchange for their vote at the next election. Any fines paid by violators were funneled into the machine's reelection fund.[29]

Legal and illegal businesses knew that they needed the machine on their side to pass inspections, secure utility extensions, ignore closing laws, sell liquor during Prohibition, run lotteries, and so on.[30] A 1917 editorial in the *New York Times* explained Tammany's system:

> Bootblacks, pushcart men, fruit vendors, soda water stand and corner grocery keepers, sailmakers, dry goods merchants, and so forth, "all had to contribute to the vast amounts that flowed into station houses, and which, after leaving something in the nature of a deposit there, flowed on higher." ... The police was a collecting agency for Tammany Hall every day of the year.[31]

Such a system ensured that businesses would organize electoral support for the machine. Incumbent politicians, reliant on their patronage work-force, could use selective application of the law to enhance their pro-bability of reelection.

However, excessive corruption served to undermine a machine's author-ity if it became too offensive to voters or attracted the attention of higher levels of government. Successful machines were careful to use corruption to ensure loyalty, not to aggregate enormous wealth.[32] Properly controlled, patronage workforces could act as a strong deterrent to opposition, biasing outcomes in favor of incumbents using public funds.

Machines also profited from their skill in employing electoral fraud and repression. Stories abound of politicians at the turn of the century throw-ing uncounted ballots into the river, registering and voting on behalf of the dead or departed, and paying for individual votes.[33] Kansas City's Boss Tom Pendergast garnered 50,000 phantom voters in the late 1940s.[34] Between 1930 and 1934 the number of voters in the second ward went from 8,128 to 15,940 without a significant population increase.[35] In Richard J. Daley's first election for mayor, the *Chicago Tribune* published photographs of Democratic ward boss, Sidney "Short Pencil" Lewis, erasing votes cast for Daley's Democratic opponent in the primary. Daley's Republican opponent Robert Merriam sought to have Daley disqualified because of the fraud. But, the Democratic machine controlled the Board of Elections, and the commissioner chastised Merriam rather than Lewis or Daley. The chief election commissioner charged: "Merriam is following Hitler's tactics which consisted of this—it you tell a lie often enough, people will begin to believe you."[36]

In addition to fixing the votes of people who arrived at the polls, machines preferred for their opponents to stay at home on election day, also enhancing the vote bias of the system. Gary Cox and Morgan Kousser argue that party workers turned from mobilizing supporters with illegal tactics to discouraging opponents with threats when the enactment of the Australian ballot made verifying votes too difficult.[37] Some machines avoided the problem by refusing to oil the voting machine lever for the opposition candidate. The squeak of an un-oiled lever immediately identified opposition supporters to the polling officials.[38] In other cases machines supported the passage of laws that legally limited the size of the electorate when it served their needs.[39] By constructing their ideal electorate through fraud and intimidation, machines biased the system in favor of their incumbent organizations.

Bosses also frequently frustrated their competitors' attempts to organize. Machines used threats and arrests, denial of meeting or parade permits, and selective enforcement of laws to limit insurgencies against their organizations. They relied on state laws that protected existing parties at the expense of new coalitions. For example, in Chicago, an independent needed 60,000 to 70,000 signatures to get his name on the ballot, compared with the regular party requirements of only 2,000 to 4,000. Next, the independent needed the machine-controlled Chicago Elections Board to approve the entire list of signatures.[40] In 1931 five minor candidates filed to run for mayor against the machine's founder Anton Cermak. As President of the County Board, Cermak controlled the Board of Election Commissioners, which declared the petitions of all five candidates illegal.[41] These rules worked as barriers to entry for challengers, thus favoring the machine's incumbent candidates.

Reformers Shape the Electorate with Institutions

Where machines used informal and extralegal tactics such as patronage ties, bribery, and threats to shape election outcomes in their favor, politicians in San Jose, Austin, Dallas, and San Antonio relied on legal mechanisms of bias that determined who had the right to cast ballots. Reformers proposed, lobbied for, and supported passage of suffrage restrictions at the state and local level including literacy tests, abolition of alien suffrage, registration requirements, poll taxes, obscure polling places, and measures that decreased the visibility or comprehensibility of politics such as non-concurrent, off-year elections.[42] Reform changes to city electoral and governing institutions had the effect of limiting opportunities for opponents to voice dissent and ensured that those who cast ballots shared reformers' demographics and policy goals.

In Austin only 37 percent of adults over the age of 21 had the right to vote in 1933 because of suffrage restrictions including the poll tax and literacy test.[43] San Antonio required property ownership for bond elections until 1969 and in tax elections until 1975.[44] In California mobile and migrant workers were the focus of increased residency requirements for voters in the 1870s.[45] In 1911 the Progressive legislature established biannual registration.[46] In 1894 California's Republican-controlled state house enacted a literacy requirement that barred from voting anyone who could not write his name and read the Constitution in English.[47] The *Los Angeles Times* applauded the amendment saying "here is one of the greatest reforms of our age . . . for the illiterate herd of voters will no longer haunt the polls on election day . . . and therefore the honest voter will have a chance to carry the election."[48]

Santa Clara County, where San Jose is located, implemented an additional four dollar poll tax in the late 1890s.[49] A local populist newsletter criticized the tax for its disfranchising effects on "free white men eligible for naturalization" meaning European immigrants and low-income whites. The article made clear it was *not* concerned about "Chinamen or negroes."[50] Such barriers to registration and voting significantly decreased the size of the electorate and especially impacted participation among poor and working-class residents and people of color.

By 1900 San Jose and the Santa Clara Valley had already established their position as the agricultural heartland of California. Canneries and orchards employed large numbers of Chinese, then Japanese, and finally Mexican immigrants throughout the twentieth century. Chinese workers in particular were targeted for restriction from social and political life. Led by laborers and grangers from San Francisco, California's constitution was amended in 1879 to include a series of anti-Chinese provisions. Chinese were prohibited from voting, owning land, working in certain occupations, and municipalities were authorized to exclude Chinese from city bounds or to designate specific areas of the city where Chinese residents could live.[51]

The anti-Chinese movement found support in San Jose. The city's Chinatown was burned to the ground in 1887 and forced to relocate outside of the city. Community members largely believed the fire was a result of arson tacitly approved by the city council and mayor because the ethnic enclave stood in the way of downtown development. The fire department successfully saved every non-Chinese-owned business in the path of the fire but not a single Chinese-occupied structure. In a 1902 pamphlet entitled "Sodom of the Coast," leaders of the reform movement targeted gambling operations and graft centered in the Chinese community in an effort to overhaul the city government.[52] Throughout the first half of the twentieth century the reform-owned *San Jose Mercury Herald* printed articles in support of excluding Asian immigrants, preventing aliens from owning land, and warning of the "yellow peril."[53] Such anti-Chinese and

Japanese sentiment suggests that San Jose's leaders would have supported the state-level changes that narrowed the electorate.

In addition to state suffrage restrictions, San Jose reformers were likely aided by the fact that the laboring class worked seasonally and tended to leave the city after harvest. Elections were held when agricultural workers were not living in the city—late winter and early spring.[54] According to one source in 1939 the permanent agricultural workforce in San Jose was 3,000 people. During harvest season this ballooned to 40,000 workers.[55] Holding elections when the migrant workforce was not in residence excluded this segment of the community from direct political participation. Pickers and canners earned wages at the bottom of the city's pay scale, and given that the working class constituted the most vocal opposition to reform charters, it seems likely that reformers would have been aided by limiting their participation.[56]

Reform incumbents also benefited from institutionalized mechanisms that increased barriers to competition through charter revision and city ordinances. This legally biased the system in favor of certain types of people who were the most likely supporters of the reform agenda. Reformers decreased the pay for elected and appointed city offices and increased candidate qualifications through charter revisions. For example, in Austin council members were required to post $10,000 bonds before taking office in the early 1900s.[57]

These changes meant that office holders all worked other jobs that had flexible hours and/or had some independent source of wealth. The result was that city councils tended to be populated by upper-class professionals and small business owners, the same groups leading the reform movement. Between 1944 and 1980, a large proportion of San Jose's leadership community attended the local Jesuit high school, graduated from the local Jesuit college, and lived in one of two wealthy, white neighborhoods. They were part of a "good old boys network" of civic-minded men who "really cared about the city," but who were not representative of the entire community.[58] The changes reformers made to government erected barriers to enter the political fray, encouraged certain types of people to become active participants in governance and actively discouraged others, biasing outcomes in favor of reform candidates.

Machines and Reformers Insulate Their Seat Shares

In the final stage of the voting process, the translation of votes to seats, incumbent political coalitions often have immense power in biasing the system because they can insulate coalition members from challenges. In machine cities gerrymandering was used to bolster the chances of incumbent coalitions. For instance, during the 1920s New York's Boss Charles Francis Murphy drew district lines to dilute the votes of Italian neighborhoods. In the 1960s and 1970s, Daley's machine relied on creative district line drawing to ensure that neighborhoods with black and Latino majorities were dominated by white, machine loyal representatives.[59]

Reformers in San Jose, Austin, Dallas, and San Antonio increased incumbents' probability of retaining control using different mechanisms. They implemented at-large elections, transformed elected seats to appointed ones, and used strategic annexations. By abolishing districts and choosing citywide elections, reform charters ensured that minority preferences, even those of substantial size, remained unrepresented in the city legislature. At-large elections also had the effect of shifting representation toward voters rather than residents. In a district system, regardless of the number of voters in a given area of the city, the area is assured of representation on the council. In an at-large election this is no longer the case. Thus, in reform cities where turnout had already been decreased through suffrage restrictions and registration requirements, it became even less likely that certain areas would be represented. Given the nature of the suffrage restrictions, these areas of the city tended to be low income, working class, and communities of color.

In many reform cities, the abolition of districts or wards generated some of the most vocal opposition and contentious argument against the reform charters. Opponents of Austin's 1908 reform charter argued that "under the aldermanic system the citizens are assured direct representation in the affairs of the municipality, and direct control over ward improvements. Ward representation is in line with the democratic doctrine of local self-government."[60] In 1924 Austin's reform charter passed by a tiny margin of twenty votes out of 4,906 ballots cast. Five of the city's seven wards defeated the charter, but the two wealthy areas of town passed it by a three to one margin. Because the election was citywide the supporters won.

San Jose reformers abolished the ward system in 1915 to reduce the influence of certain districts.[61] The coalition displaced by San Jose's reformers had been able to control city government because it maintained strong support in the city's older, central wards. Reformers came to dominate the second and third wards. According to one observer, the latter was a "traditional stronghold of the better elements, with strict moral views and continued efforts to secure a government which they believe honest and impartial."[62]

In revising the charter, San Jose reformers lost in the central wards but won large numbers of votes in the second and third wards, as well as in newly annexed territory, thereby cinching the citywide victory. According to the political editor of the *San Jose Mercury News* the at-large system "served the interests of the folks who had established it, not the average person in town . . . [reformers] didn't want the small, parochial interests of more narrowly based groups to have any influence in politics."[63] At-large elections required more campaign funds, more extensive organization, and bigger mobilization operations in order to win and so tended to bias outcomes in favor of reform incumbents.

Reformers also benefited from the use of strategic annexation that maintained an electorate supportive of their administrations. As they grew, cities such as San Jose, San Antonio, Dallas, and Austin selectively expanded their city boundaries and chose not to annex particular outlying communities. San Jose's first planned annexation was a one hundred foot wide strip of land leading to the city of Alviso where San Jose hoped to build a port in 1912. Though the port was never built, San Jose did construct a technologically advanced sewage treatment plant on the site, which then became the tool by which other communities could be convinced to be annexed to the city. Given that annexation decisions were made in order to "grow and be able to pay the bill,"[64] poorer communities and undevelopable land were not priorities. San Jose reform leaders sought to "capture the cross roads which the administration told us were going to be the shopping centers of the future—where the sales tax would be."[65] Not surprisingly while San Jose had access to its treatment plant in Alviso, it did not annex the actual city, a poor agricultural community, until the late 1960s. When the annexation did occur it was in response to Alviso's attempt to annex the sewage treatment plant to its own borders.

San Jose annexed vast tracts of suburban land; incorporating 1,419 outlying areas by 1969. Yet, as of 2005 there were pockets of county land surrounded on all sides by the city of San Jose. Outside of the official city bounds, these areas have been excluded from participating in local governance. In other cities annexation decisions had a more direct and obvious political effect. San Antonio's annexation practices were challenged by the Justice Department under the Voting Rights Act in 1976 because they diluted a growing Mexican American population in the city.[66] Annexations created and maintained a community and electorate that tended to support reform goals. Had these excluded communities become part of the city, reformers might have lost elections. Thus, annexations biased the system in favor of incumbent reformers by determining whose votes translated into seats and whose views would not be counted.

Finally, reformers biased government toward the incumbent regime by transforming many elected positions into appointed offices. Reform charters eliminated popularly elected mayors or turned them into ceremonial heads and invested all executive power in city managers appointed by the council. The purpose of this change was to create a more efficient government. An editorial in the *Dallas News* urged voters to support the new charter by asking: "Why not run Dallas itself on business schedule by business methods under business men? The city manager plan is after all only a business management plan." The article goes on to explain: "[T]he city manager is the executive of a corporation under a board of directors. Dallas is the corporation. It is as simple as that. Vote for it."[67]

The elimination of elected leaders generated extensive controversy. In many cities municipal employees and labor organizations opposed reform charters and the strength of the city manager position because they did not feel that their interests would be protected. In San Jose the reform charter granted the city manager the authority to appoint all of the city's officials without approval from the council and the power to prepare the annual budget. At the same time the council served on a part-time basis, for very low pay, and was elected at-large in nonpartisan elections. The charter instructed councilors to interact with municipal employees "solely through the city manager." For further clarity, the charter explains: "[N]either the Council nor its members . . . shall give orders to any subordinate officer or employee, either publicly or privately."[68] As a result the manager had an enormous information and resource advantage over the elected legislators. Even if dissenting voices were elected in small numbers to the city council, the control of the city remained tightly bound to the reformist city manager and his administration. In Austin the first council elected following the city manager charter revision was unpopular with the voters because it was not responsive to their needs. One observer noted:

> The council that worked with Manager Johnson was not a repre-
> sentative body at all . . .. It was a super-managerial board. It refused
> to provide the type of political leadership necessary to keep the
> administration responsive to public opinion, and to maintain satis-
> factory public relations . . .. The council did eliminate "politics" in
> the sordid sense of the word by ending patronage . . . it also
> eliminated politics in the democratic sense of the word.[69]

David Eakins explains the consequences of this drive to increase the competence of the political system: efficiency "both in theory and in practice meant heeding some citizens and not others . . . [and] the cost of greater efficiency was less democracy."[70] Eliminating politics resulted in an elimination of the pressure and ability to incorporate disaffected and disgruntled constituents. Such strategies of bias effectively insulated incumbent coalitions from shifts in public sentiment and protected their governing authority.

Bias Had Electoral and Distributional Consequences

When coalitions biased the system in their favor, they won. In every year between 1931 and 1979 the same faction of the Democratic Party controlled the mayoralty and the city council in Chicago. In Philadelphia the Republican organization dominated between 1860 and 1950, at times winning more than 80 percent of the vote. Tammany Hall governed New York from 1918 through 1932; the machine's margin of victory climbing at virtually every election.

The effects of reform consolidation are similar. Like their machine counterparts, reform candidates won repeatedly, with landslide victories. In Dallas 86 percent of 182 city council members elected between 1931 and 1969 pledged allegiance to the Citizens' Charter Association. This nonpartisan slating group held a majority on the council every year except a brief period between 1935 and 1938. San Antonio's Good Government League won 95 percent of the eighty-eight council races between 1955 and 1971. Between 1944 and 1967 in San Jose seventy-five councilors were elected to office; seventy-two were members of the dominant coalition.

Additionally, turnout declined in both machine and reform cities as peripheral groups were demobilized by those in power and discouraged from participating by the lack of choices.[71] Given the long time periods governed by bias, these results suggest that outcomes were clear well in advance of election day, reinforcing the authority of the regimes. After insulating their coalitions from shifts in power, machine and reform organizations turned their attention away from a large, diverse electoral coalition.

Under machine dominance core coalitions were targeted for a disproportionate share of municipal benefits and others suffered. In Chicago African Americans were denied services, government jobs, and elected offices. Blacks made up 40 percent of the city population in 1970, but only 20 percent of the municipal workforce. In 1972 African Americans brought suit against Daley for discriminatory hiring practices and won.[72] As of 1974 Latinos made up only 1.7 percent of the full-time city payroll but composed about 10 percent of the population.[73] After 1976, when the machine was in its final stages of life, minorities' share of patronage positions grew; more than one-third of new hires were people of color.[74]

In addition to patronage, machines supported policies that benefited some groups of residents to the detriment of others. In many cities urban renewal represented the provision of benefits to core coalition members and city elites at the expense of peripheral groups. For every new building that was erected, a slum was cleared, displacing more than a million residents over the course of the federal program. These decisions were not made independent of the racial and ethnic makeup of neighborhoods. In New Haven alone Wolfinger estimates 7,000 households and 25,000 residents were moved to make way for urban renewal. As first Mayor Lee and then DiLieto pursued redevelopment, spending over $200 million of public funds, New Haven became the fourth poorest city in the country. By 1989 its infant mortality rate rivaled third world countries in some neighborhoods, and the citywide average was the second highest in the nation.[75]

While New York Italians heavily supported the Tammany machine in the 1920s they received the most menial of patronage positions—garbage men, street cleaners, and dock workers. Similarly, Chicago's African American community won few concessions from the consolidated Daley machine even after providing a large portion of the Democratic vote and the margin of victory in 1955 and 1963. Blacks demanded, but were refused, a halt to police brutality and discrimination, appointment to high-level political positions, and living wage jobs. "Mr. Mayor we would like to point out," the *Daily Defender* said, "that in comparison with other cities . . . Chicago is sadly lacking in the utilization of its finest and most well-qualifies [sic] Negro citizens in responsible positions in your administration."[76]

Similarly, under reform dominance those excluded from the governing coalition won little from municipal leaders. Because reformers had spent much energy and many resources separating politics from government, dissent was eliminated in the very structure of the city's institutions. By unifying the executive and legislative branches of government and making council seats at-large, all of those in power were beholden to the same constituency. Such a structure made it appear as though the cities were homogeneous and unified, but many cities with reform governments had large populations of poor and minority residents who did not always share reform views. Intense debates erupted over the placement of public works, the location of new roads and freeways, the provision of parks, libraries, and schools, and the role of labor unions in municipal government.

While reform coalitions maintained agendas that promoted growth and development, benefiting business and middle-class whites, they ignored the social needs of many residents and neglected the city's burgeoning physical problems.[77] One of the clearest examples of this pattern is seen in Southwestern annexation policies. As cities such as San Jose annexed new communities at the behest of developers, poorer communities closer to the center were not provided with basic municipal services. The Latino neighborhood known as the Mayfair district in San Jose flooded in 1952 creating a significant public health threat.[78] The same creek overflowed its banks again in 1955, 1958, and 1962. The year that the dominant coalition collapsed, 1979, the water district finally filed an application to protect the nearly 4,000 homes and businesses in the area from further damage.[79] In the early 1970s, residents of Alviso, a heavily Latino area, blocked a bridge demanding that crossers pay a toll to pay for needed repairs that the city of San Jose had refused to provide.[80]

Austin's 1969 Model Cities program first focused on paving and drainage in center city neighborhoods. Yet the predominately African American west side of Austin did not have paved streets in some areas until 1979.[81] Meanwhile, city government provided sewerage, streets, and utilities for all of the new developments. The busy annexation mill in San Antonio doubled the city's size between 1940 and 1950 but leapfrogged over older, poorer, and more heavily Latino neighborhoods. During these years reformers promised Latino leaders that they would build drainage projects in return for support in bond elections. The bonds passed and the money was allocated, but the projects were never built.[82] As late as the 1980s, Mexican American communities in San Antonio were beset by flooding due to inadequate drainage systems.

Conclusions

In both machine and reform cities coalitions selected strategies to ensure reelection that had long-term effects on the political arena. Securing dominance made governing coalitions less attentive to the broader public. When the electoral system became uncompetitive, groups outside of the dominant coalition could not easily contest the hand that they were dealt. Biased systems allowed dominant organizations to reduce the size of their electoral coalitions, conserve resources, and reward key players. Secure from threats to their governing authority, coalitions directed benefits of municipal government toward core members and coalition elites at the expense of peripheral groups. First Jews and Italians, and then blacks, Latinos, and Asian Americans were limited from participating in the political process and from receiving equal shares of government benefits. The lesson for American political development is clear—those in power can be expected to build defenses against durable shifts in governing authority, and when they succeed, as both machine and reform coalitions did, portions of the population are likely to suffer.

Notes

1. James Bryce, "Rings and Bosses," *The American Commonwealth* (Indianapolis: Liberty Fund, 1995; originally published in 1988 by Macmillan and Company), vol. 2, chapter 63.
2. Amy Bridges, *Morning Glories: Municipal Reform in the Southwest* (Princeton, NJ: Princeton University Press, 1997).
3. Lincoln Steffens, *The Shame of the Cities* (New York: Hill and Wang Publishing, 1957; originally published in 1904).
4. Robert K. Merton, *Social Theory and Social Structure* (New York: The Free Press, 1957).
5. Samuel P. Hays, "The Politics of Reform in Municipal Government in the Progressive Era," *Pacific Northwest Quarterly* 55, no. 4 (1964).
6. On machines see Steven Erie, *Rainbow's End: Irish Americans and the Dilemmas of Urban Machine Politics, 1840–1985* (Berkeley: University of California Press, 1988). On reform see John D. Buenker, *Urban Liberalism and Progressive Reform* (New York: Charles Scribner's Sons, 1973); Kenneth Finegold, *Experts and Politicians: Reform Challenges to Machine Politics in New York, Cleveland, and Chicago* (Princeton, NJ: Princeton University Press, 1995); James Connolly, *The Triumph of Ethnic Progressivism: Urban Political Culture in Boston, 1900–1925* (Cambridge, MA: Harvard University Press, 1998).

7. By institutions I mean rules, structures, and procedures for creating, implementing, and enforcing collective action.
8. Jessica Trounstine, *Political Monopolies in American Cities: The Rise and Fall of Bosses and Reformers* (Chicago: University of Chicago Press, 2008).
9. For further explanation see ibid.
10. For a similar argument see Gary W. Cox, "Public Goods, Targetable Goods and Electoral Competition," unpublished typescript, 2001.
11. See for example Gary W. Cox and Jonathan N. Katz, *Elbridge Gerry's Salamander: The Electoral Consequences of the Reapportionment Revolution* (Cambridge: Cambridge University Press, 2002); Bernard Grofman, W. Koetzle, and T. Brunell, "An Integrated Perspective on the Three Potential Sources of Partisan Bias: Malapportionment, Turnout Differences, and the Geographic Distribution of Party Vote Shares," *Electoral Studies* 16, no. 4 (1997): 457–470; Gary King and Robert Browning, "Democratic Representation and Partisan Bias in Congressional Elections," *American Political Science Review* 81, no. 4 (1987): 1251–1273.
12. V.O. Key, "Political Machine Strategy Against Investigations," *Social Forces* 14, no. 1 (1935): 120–128.
13. Ibid.
14. "Tired of Bossism," *Los Angeles Times* June 30, 1888, p. 1.
15. Harold Stone, Don Price, and Kathryn Stone, *City Manager Government in Nine Cities* (Chicago: Public Administration Service, 1940), p. 268.
16. Charles R. Adrian, "A Typology for Nonpartisan Elections," *Western Political Quarterly* 12, no. 2 (1959): 449–458; Brian Schaffner, Matthew Streb, and Gerald Wright, "Teams without Uniforms: The Nonpartisan Ballot in State and Local Elections," *Political Research Quarterly* 54, no. 1 (March 2001): 7–30.
17. Brian Schaffner and Matthew Streb, "The Partisan Heuristic in Low-Information Elections," *Public Opinion Quarterly* 66, no. 4 (2002): 559–581; Seymour Martin Lipset, Martin Trow, and James Coleman, *Union Democracy: The Inside Politics of the International Typographical Union* (New York: The Free Press, 1956).
18. Bridges, *Morning Glories*; Philip J. Trounstine, personal interview by author, 2003.
19. Stone, Price, and Stone, *City Manager Government in Nine Cities*, p. 267.
20. Quoted in Valerie Ellsworth and Andrew Garbely, "Centralization and Efficiency: The Reformers Shape Modern San Jose Government," in David Eakins, ed., *Businessmen and Municipal Reform: A Study of Ideals and Practice in San Jose and Santa Cruz* (San Jose: Sourisseau Academy for California State and Local History, San Jose State University Original Research in Santa Clara County History, 1976), p. 14.
21. Harold Stone, Don Price, and Kathryn Stone, "City Manager Government in Austin, Texas," a Report Submitted to the Committee on Public Administration of the Social Science Research Council, Washington, DC, 1937.
22. Clyde Arbuckle, *Clyde Arbuckle's History of San Jose: Chronicling San Jose's Founding as California's Earliest Pueblo in 1777, through Exciting and Tumultuous History which Paved the Way for Today's Metropolitan San Jose; the Culmination of a Lifetime of Research* (San Jose: Memorabilia of San Jose, 1985), p. 42.
23. Bridges, *Morning Glories*, p. 140.
24. Lipset, Trow, and Coleman, *Union Democracy*.
25. Lawrence H. Larsen and Nancy Hulston, *Pendergast!* (Columbia: University of Missouri Press, 1997).

26. Alex Gottfried, *Boss Cermak of Chicago: A Study of Political Leadership* (Seattle: University of Washington Press, 1962).
27. Mike Royko, *Boss: Richard J. Daley of Chicago* (New York: Signet Press, 1971).
28. Peter McCaffery, "Style, Structure, and Institutionalization of Machine Politics: Philadelphia, 1867–1933," *Journal of Interdisciplinary History* 22, no. 3 (1992): 435–452; Erie, *Rainbow's End.*
29. "Tammany Election Funds; Where Some of them Come From. How the Corporation Attorney's Office is Worked for Electioneering Purposes," *New York Times* August 27, 1877, p. 8.
30. Erie, *Rainbow's End;* Harold F. Gosnell, "The Political Party versus the Political Machine," *Annals of the American Academy of Political and Social Science* 169 (1933): 21–28; Roger Biles, "Edward J. Kelly: New Deal Machine Builder," in Paul M. Green and Melvin G. Holli, eds., *The Mayors: The Chicago Political Tradition* (Carbondale: Southern Illinois University Press, 1995).
31. "The Golden Prime of Tammany," *New York Times* October 28, 1917, p. E2.
32. Dick Simpson, *Rogues, Rebels and Rubber Stamps: The Politics of the Chicago City Council from 1863 to the Present* (Boulder, CO: Westview Press, 2001); Martin Shefter, "The Emergence of the Political Machine: An Alternative View," in Willis D. Hawley et al., eds., *Theoretical Perspectives on Urban Politics* (Englewood Cliffs, NJ: Prentice Hall, 1976).
33. A search of the *Chicago Tribune* for articles containing the words fraud, election, and mayor turned up 334 articles between 1849 and 1950.
34. Alan Reitman and Robert B. Davidson, *The Election Process: Voting Laws and Procedures* (Dobbs Ferry, NY: Oceana Publications, 1972).
35. It is likely that the surge of Democratic popularity brought many new voters into the electorate; however, this ward was predominately African American, and blacks did not abandon the Republican ticket in large numbers elsewhere until 1936. (See Larsen and Hulston, *Pendergast!*)
36. Clay Gowran, "Merriam Charges Election Board Bias: Rips Holzman as Spokesman for Opponent," *Chicago Tribune* February 27, 1955, p. 1.
37. Gary Cox and Morgan Kousser, "Turnout and Rural Corruption: New York as a Test Case," *American Journal of Political Science* 25, no. 4 (1981): 646–663.
38. Erie, *Rainbow's End.*
39. Erie argues (ibid.) that because city governments had limited resources an expanding electorate made retaining office tenuous. He provides examples in places such as New York and Pennsylvania where machine leaders supported suffrage restriction in order to limit demands on their organizations.
40. Royko, *Boss: Richard J. Daley of Chicago.*
41. Gottfried, *Boss Cermak of Chicago: A Study of Political Leadership.*
42. It is important to note that suffrage restrictions were not confined to states and cities where reformers came to monopolize cities. All of the states that housed political machines had at one time or another limited the right to vote to certain groups (whites, property holders, men, etc.). The point here is that reformers benefited from these restrictions because their political opponents were denied the opportunity to participate in elections.
43. Bridges, *Morning Glories.*
44. Roberts Brischetto, Charles L. Cotrell, and R. Michael Stevens, "Conflict and Change in the Political Culture of San Antonio in the 1970s," in David R. Johnson, John A. Booth, and Richard J. Harris, eds., *The Politics of San Antonio: Community, Progress, and Power* (Lincoln: University of Nebraska Press, 1983).

45. Alex Keyssar, *The Right to Vote: The Contested History of Democracy in the United States* (New York: Basic Books, 2000).
46. Progressives made registration somewhat easier in other respects. They decreased the amount of time one needed to register before the election from 3 months to 40 days, increased registration locations, and standardized the process.
47. The act included a grandfather clause that allowed anyone currently enfranchised to vote. It is likely that the generational turnover following the passage of this act aided the San Jose reformers immeasurably in the passage of the reform charter in 1915.
48. R. Garner Curran, "The Amendments. Several Very Important Questions to Be Voted on at the Next Election," *Los Angeles Times* September 29, 1892, p. 9.
49. Stephen J. Pitti, *The Devil in Silicon Valley: Northern California, Race, and Mexican Americans* (Princeton, NJ: Princeton University Press, 2003).
50. Quoted in ibid., p. 84.
51. Keyssar, *The Right to Vote*; Connie Young Yu, *Chinatown, San Jose, USA* (San Jose: San Jose Historical Museum Association, 1991).
52. Yu, *Chinatown, San Jose, USA.*
53. Tom McEnery, personal interview by author, 2003.
54. San Jose City Clerk Record of Elections and the City of San Jose Commission on the Internment of Local Japanese Americans, *With Liberty and Justice for All: The Story of San Jose's Japanese Community* (San Jose: Commission on the Internment of Japanese Americans, 1985).
55. City of San Jose, *With Liberty and Justice for All.*
56. Pitti, *The Devil in Silicon Valley*, pp. 82, 222.
57. Bridges, *Morning Glories*, p. 65.
58. Susan Hammer, personal interview by author, 2003.
59. Erie, *Rainbow's End.*
60. Austin Dailey Statemen, December 27, 1908 quoted by Bridges, *Morning Glories.*
61. Philip J. Trounstine and Terry Christensen, *Movers and Shakers: The Study of Community Power* (New York: St Martin's Press, 1982), p. 83.
62. Robert Thorpe, "Council-Manager Government in San Jose California," MA thesis, Stanford University, 1938, p. 6.
63. Trounstine personal interview.
64. Mayor George Starbird paraphrasing manager Hamann in a 1972 speech given at the San Jose Rotary Club; transcript entitled "The New Metropolis," available at the San Jose Public Library.
65. Starbird, "The New Metropolis," p. 4.
66. US Attorney General, Objection Letter to City of San Antonio. April 2, 1976.
67. Stone, Price, and Stone, *City Manager Government in Nine Cities*, p. 286.
68. San Jose City Charter, Section 411.
69. Stone, Price, and Stone, "City Manager Government in Austin, Texas," p. 24.
70. Eakins, *Businessmen and Municipal Reform*, p. 3.
71. Trounstine, *Political Monopolies in American Cities.*
72. Erie, *Rainbow's End.*
73. Joanne Belenchia, "Latinos and Chicago Politics," in Samuel Gove and Louis Masotti, eds., *After Daley: Chicago Politics in Transition* (Chicago: University of Illinois Press, 1982), pp. 118–145.
74. I.M. Pace, "Employees in Top Salary Range Jump 500 Percent in Two Years, over One Third of City Hall's New Hires are Minority in 1976," *Chicago Reporter* 6 (June/July 1977).

75. Mary Summers and Philip Klinkner, "The Election of John Daniels as Mayor of New Haven," *PS: Political Science and Politics* 23, no. 2 (1990): 142–145.
76. "Memo to Mayor Daley," *Daily Defender* June 23, 1956, p. 9.
77. Carl Abbott, *The New Urban America: Growth and Politics in Sunbelt Cities* (Chapel Hill: University of North Carolina Press, 1987).
78. Glenna Matthews, *Silicon Valley, Women, and the California Dream: Gender, Class, and Opportunity in the 20th Century* (Stanford, CA: Stanford University Press, 2003).
79. The project was completed in 2006. Santa Clara Valley Water District, Lower Silver Creek Flood Protection Project, handout. Available at www.valley water.org/media/pdf/watershed_monthly_progress_report_pdf/11–03%20-%20LSilver3.271Handout.pdf (accessed September 12, 2006).
80. J. Douglas Allen-Taylor, "Watchin' the Tidelands Roll Away," *Metro* August 20–26, 1998. Available at http://www.metroactive.com/papers/metro/08.20.98/cover/alviso-9833.html (accessed September 12, 2006).
81. Anthony Orum, *Power, Money, and the People: The Making of Modern Austin* (Austin: Texas Monthly Press, 1987).
82. Johnson, Booth, and Harris, eds., *The Politics of San Antonio*.

5   Through a Glass Darkly
The Once and Future Study of Urban Politics

Clarence N. Stone and Robert K. Whelan

In a shift from "the lost world of municipal government" to the field now known as urban politics, several major figures in political science played large roles.[1] Among them were such prominent scholars as Robert A. Dahl, Wallace S. Sayre, Herbert Kaufman, Edward C. Banfield, and James Q. Wilson.[2] In the eyes of some observers, their work of the early 1960s was the golden age of urban political study. Yet the school of thought to which these works contributed so heavily, classic pluralism, was not the main foundation on which subsequent urban scholarship built. Hindsight tells us that the "golden age" bore little long-lasting fruit.

Whereas pluralism failed to provide an instructive theoretical lens to guide research in the years that followed, a conceptual shift to urban political economy proved to be far more fertile. Still, with ongoing evolution in the urban condition, it may now be time for a theoretical refocusing. Hence in this chapter we look back critically at the ways in which city politics has been studied. In particular we see a need to discard some past assumptions, rethink the nature of political change, and give more attention to politically marginal segments of the urban population, and consider what their position can tell us about the nature of the urban political order.

While important insights have been gained over the years, the quest for an adequate theoretical lens continues. Our aim here is to identify some promising elements for a research framework for the future. We do this in three steps. One is to examine shortcomings in classic works. The second is to revisit briefly urban political economy studies from the 1970s and to take stock of some of their strengths and weaknesses. In this vein we recast the position of the urban regime concept to place it in a more explicit historical context. The third is to look widely at the urban political order with attention to *interpenetrations* of government, civil society, and the economy. We then ask why marginality persists in a formally democratic system and consider prospects for change.

As a promising alternative to past frameworks, we suggest American political development (APD), chiefly as set forth by Orren and Skowronek.[3] Whereas pluralism assumes a highly autonomous process of politics[4] and urban political economy privileges the causal force of the economic system, APD offers a polity-centered approach in which politics is thoroughly interwoven with the economic *and social* features of a complex body of arrangements for governing. In putting political change at center stage, APD suggests caution about pursuing parsimony at the cost of adequacy of explanation.[5] It brings history to bear as a counterbalance to any tendency toward narrow grounds of explanation.

Orren and Skowronek warn against any notion of a monocausal process of development. As they put it, "master ideas or processes alleged to arrange political affairs for extended periods of time" should be viewed with skepticism.[6] Orren and Skowronek offer the alternative of "inter-currence"—the coexistence of multiple orders, typically originating at different times and in tension with one another—as a focal concern. As a way out of endless complexity, Orren and Skowronek suggest that analytical efforts center on "durable shifts in governing authority."[7]

By bringing these various strands of analysis together and tracking major shifts in governance, we get a fresh look at the political development of cities. What Robert Salisbury once called "the new convergence of power"—a main street/city hall coalition around the reshaping of the central city—was at the heart of a post-World War II shift in how US cities are governed.[8] It was also a shift that accentuated the political marginality of substantial segments of the population. Now, more than a half century later, it seems appropriate to consider whether urban politics is entering a new phase that could culminate in yet another shift. If so, what are its markers? We believe that APD offers an instructive perspective in responding to that question.

Classic Pluralism

When classic pluralism emerged as the discipline's dominant paradigm,[9] it bore the strong markings of a passive 1950s and provided little insight into the oncoming period of social turmoil and urban disorder. Although talk of an urban crisis had surfaced by the 1950s, the main thrust of pluralism was to celebrate American politics as widely representative and American political practice as highly resilient. Nothing seemed amiss in the capacity of cities to meet the kinds of change becoming evident. As the 1960s further unfolded, for the champions of pluralism underlying assumptions continued to trump observable reality.[10] Thomas Kuhn tells us that an established paradigm does not readily yield to emergent anomalies. So it was with pluralism. It is instructive, then, to see what pluralism encompassed and examine the assumptions it rested on.[11]

Who Governs? was the most elaborately theoretical of the city studies.[12] For Dahl the finding that cities such as New Haven are not governed by a covert ruling elite is only the surface of a complex body of political explanation. As viewed by Dahl, a change process gave birth to pluralism; it emerged from a transformation in society, often given the shorthand of modernization. Over time politics ceased to be an arena of deference to society's patrician class and instead became an autonomous process centered on popular elections. In Dahl's treatment, modernization meant increased democratization of elections combined with role differentiation to replace rule by notables.[13] With political activity severed from both social notability and business leadership, this separation of society's major functional roles dispersed power in such a way that no one group could exercise control, but many groups could defend their immediate interests. Overarching control was made difficult by the fact that different groups had varying power resources. Wealth, technical expertise, and popularity each advantaged a different sector of society. In the pluralist narrative the political danger was not domination, but immobility from the fragmentation of a highly differentiated society.

Dahl's pluralism has a further layer. Embedded in *Who Governs?* is a Parsonian form of structural functionalism.[14] Consider how consensus on fundamentals fits into Dahl's overall scheme of things. According to Dahl, New Haven had a "prevailing system of beliefs to which all the major groups in the community subscribe."[15] With consensus at work, conflict was confined to narrow gauge and shifting issues. As Dahl read the situation, a skillful leader like Mayor Richard Lee could pursue a large-scale, public-minded agenda. According to Dahl, Mayor Lee benefited from a trend in which there was a shift in political orientation from highly particular to collective benefits. This trend enabled the spread of policies that "emphasized shared benefits to citizens in general rather than to specific categories."[16] Banfield and Wilson talked of a parallel move from a private-regarding to a public-regarding ethos. In both instances a broad consensus and collective benefits rested on a process of growing assimilation into the middle class and its values.

Role differentiation and value consensus were thus essential counterweights to one another, and both were vital elements in modernization. Standing alone, role differentiation could lead to an inability to govern. Thus, in the pluralist model of politics, the two elements combined with elections to assure that power would be dispersed, but without undoing the capacity of the community to govern itself. Elections, role differentiation, and consensus combined provide a form of governing both widely representative and effective in problem-solving.

In Dahl's New Haven study, the testing of the pluralist model was selective, and several of its assumptions went largely unexamined. Key findings included: (1) efforts to exert influence largely followed lines of policy specialization; (2) public officials, not economic elites, made the major explicit decisions; and (3) mayoral officeholders evolved over time from notables to those who possessed common-touch popularity (often with an immigrant-stock/ethnic dimension). For a complicated theoretical argument, this constitutes quite limited empirical support.

Assumptions were more wide-ranging: (1) politics is an autonomous process largely independent of interpenetrations by economic and social factors;[17] (2) however, political development is driven by a master process of modernization; (3) since elections are the central political process and determine who holds the key positions of authority, the outcome of mayoral contests track the flow of power over time; (4) decision outcomes indicate power; (5) legal authority is especially important and through the actions of elected officeholders is widely responsive to citizen concerns;[18] (6) rising levels of education and income bring about assimilation into a middle-class system of values, and, through accompanying forms of socialization, individuals become value carriers. All in all, despite a degree of complexity, this model rests on a narrow conception of what is politically relevant and how.

Urban Political Economy

As the 1960s unfolded and then gave way to the 1970s, the tenets of pluralism proved to be sharply at odds with the flow of events. Conflict was patently not confined to low-key, narrow-gauge issues; a deep racial divide became evident, belying the notion of a shared world view,[19] and a post-reform politics of fractured interests and identities thoroughly eclipsed the notion that consensus-based public mindedness was on the rise.[20] New York City's fiscal crisis of 1975 provided a focusing event, not just putting economic issues at the forefront, but also dispelling the notion of an autonomous politics. With a Financial Control Board in charge of ameliorating the city's debt crisis, the role of economic elites no longer appeared remote and minor.

Political economy nudged pluralism off center stage, and attention gravitated toward James O'Connor's depiction of modern democratic politics as caught in an irresolvable tension between the accumulation needs of capital and the state's need for popular legitimacy. Instead of consensus, O'Connor posited endemic conflict.[21] And Ira Katznelson put forward the critical view that ruling forces employed social-control mechanisms that are neither spontaneous nor benign.[22]

Whereas pluralists Sayre and Kaufman had depicted a New York City in which service-demanders held the upper hand over revenue-providers, urban scholars became increasingly concerned with the economic foundation for revenue production. Recovering pluralist Charles Lindblom put forward the idea that an unrelenting need for investment in economic growth gives business a "privileged position" in public affairs.[23] Debate began to center on the question of how much slack there might be in what Jones and Bachelor termed "the social cables that bind the local polity and the local economy."[24] Martin Shefter published a seminal article in which the need to win elections had to contend with multiple and not easily reconciled imperatives. In addition to winning elections, urban politicians encounter needs to promote the city's economic health and preserve the city's credit, contain group conflicts, and maintain social peace generally.[25]

Although the notion of an autonomous political process lingered with Rufus Browning, Dale Rogers Marshall, and David Tabb's *Protest Is Not Enough*,[26] Paul Peterson's *City Limits* provided an influential counterpoint.[27] Peterson argued that city politics was largely determined by the economically competitive position of localities within a federal system, a system that did little to provide financial equalization. For Peterson, the overriding interest of the city in responding to this competition trumped other policy considerations. As a form of economic determinism, Peterson's book launched a still unresolved debate about the interplay between structure and agency.[28] And with cities undergoing a transition from an industrial era to a post-industrial period, the economic imperative to pursue growth claimed a place (although disputed in its particulars) at the center of the urban political stage that it still holds. Counter to Peterson's view that policy choices are driven by a shared economic need among city inhabitants, sociologist Harvey Molotch argued that city policy often emanates from action by "the growth machine," a self-serving coterie of business interests organized to pursue private profit-making by a narrowly conceived form of development.[29] And, as argued below, the concept of an urban regime added another twist. Further, the arrival of a political-economy perspective put the city in a wider context of national policy and a global economy.[30]

Urban political economy thus departed sharply from pluralism as an approach to the study of city politics. In a post-pluralist framework: (1) the context of a capitalist economy is fundamentally important; (2) far from being autonomous, politics is powerfully linked to the economy; (3) a major concern is how the economic imperative to pursue growth is interpreted, applied, and balanced against other considerations; (4) a pluralist understanding of modernization gives way to a developmental perspective centered on political-economic relations; (5) benign consensus and encompassing assimilation are put aside in favor of an open-ended potential for conflict and for biased and contested social control; and (6) replacement conceptually of actors as carriers of values acquired through socialization by actors as agents embedded in structures while also engaged in situationally specific struggles.

While differing from pluralism in several aspects, an urban political-economy approach constitutes no tightly conceived paradigm. Instead it harbors competing schools of thought. One version puts features of the capitalist economy as the encompassing explanatory core. This version of urban political economy is thus fiercely at odds with a polity-centered approach found in APD. Note also that it differs from Peterson's market-driven determinism. Whereas Peterson sees the market in play as an autonomous (non-political) set of forces operating strictly on principles of supply and demand, an alternative school of thought treats the market as a framework within which a political struggle occurs among an unevenly matched set of contenders.[31]

Strengths and Limitations in Urban Regime Analysis

In its various forms, urban regime analysis grew out of an urban political-economy approach, but can gain from a widened scope of analysis. Its point of departure is the need to bridge the divide between private control of investment and popular control of public office. Starting with Martin Shefter's antecedent work on Tammany Hall,[32] scholars have shown further that bridging that state–market divide brings civil society into play as well. Political activity is not narrowly state-centered.

An interpenetration of civil society and political activity is also displayed plainly in sociologist Robert Crain's analysis of the politics of school desegregation.[33] Crain found that a city's experience with desegregation depended on how a community's civic elites align with school politics. If they were engaged, the process went peacefully. If they were disengaged, the process deteriorated readily into violence. Unrestrained political activists exploited racial hostility to garner support with little concern for wider or long-term consequences.[34]

It is no surprise, then, that Stone's regime analysis of Atlanta's biracial coalition was drawn toward a consideration of the interpenetration of that city's civic structure and political activity.[35] Biracial cooperation was mediated through extensive civic networks, and the prominent role of business in agenda-setting rested heavily on a thorough-going connection between civil society and political activity.[36] Atlanta's governing coalition was thus much more than a simple accommodation between elected officeholders and the controllers of investment capital, and "the city too busy to hate" had an agenda far more expansive than simply economic growth.

Stone defines an urban regime as an informal arrangement for governing. As such, a strong regime has a capacity to pursue a priority agenda by relying on a cross-sector coalition of the kind that first can provide the multiple resources needed for addressing a top policy priority and second that can devise a mode of cooperation and coordination to keep a governing coalition active and aligned behind its agenda. Put into historical context, this conception of governing turns out to be particularly useful for examining US cities as they embarked on a widespread effort to redevelop and accommodate themselves to deep-running changes in the urban economy.

Let's turn, then, to the theme of "the new convergence of power," and how and why it came about in the post-World War II period. This is the period when the automobile became *overwhelmingly* dominant and suburbs grew very rapidly. It thus became a time that brought business leaders concerned over the fate of the central business district together with politicians anxious about the city's economic future. It is also a period in Chicago, New Haven, Boston, Pittsburgh, St Louis, and many other places in which patronage-oriented politicians and reform-minded business executives put away their past antagonisms and formed a strategic alignment. The structure of governance shifted, and in various configurations, "the new convergence" came together to alter land use, embrace the expressway, and promote a different kind of central business district.

Originating more than a half century ago, "the new convergence" is no longer new and shows signs of fading. But, if we turn the clock back a few decades, we can see that the post-World War II struggle to reshape the city brought to a close a political era centered on machine versus reform politics. A radically reconfigured alliance took its place. In his famous study of New Haven, Robert Dahl called that city's version of an emergent arrangement "the executive-centered coalition." Richard Lee, the mayor of New Haven in that period, described his city's governing alliance this way:

> We've got the biggest muscles, the biggest set of muscles in New Haven . . .. They're muscular because they control wealth; they're muscular because they control industries, represent banks. They're muscular because they head up labor. They're muscular because they represent the intellectual portions of the community. They're muscular because they're articulate, because they're respectable, because of their financial power, and because of the accumulation of prestige which they have built up over the years as individuals in all kinds of causes whether United Fund, Red Cross or whatever.[37]

Consider this period through APD eyes. The "new convergence" constituted a durable shift in governing arrangements. Politics realigned. Yet, as suggested by Orren and Skowronek, multiple orders coexisted. New Haven illustrates the pattern. In order to pursue a far-reaching redevelopment agenda, Mayor Lee not only needed a muscular coalition of cross-sector membership, but he also had to devise a mode of co-existence between the old and the new. He did this by constituting the redevelopment agency as an independent body answerable to the mayor but not the board of aldermen, an arrangement that was feasible because the agency's work was funded mainly by federal and foundation grants. Thus the board of aldermen was largely frozen out of the redevelopment arena, but, as Dahl reports, Mayor Lee could not extend his policy reach by gaining approval for a new city charter. Old and new forms operated side by side, with the mayor's executive authority greatly constrained over wide areas of governance.[38]

The "new convergence" remade cities physically but left social reconstruction largely unaddressed. Moreover, across many cities it left a legacy of racial divide and grassroots distrust for authority. Years later, as one observer put it, "the ghost of urban renewal is always present."[39]

The regime concept captures well the construction of muscular coalitions for redevelopment. However, with its focus on convergence at the top, it largely left out of the picture the grassroots and how they coped with a remade, post-industrial city. Ward-based organizations and neighborhood political clubs eventually gave way to new forms of association and interaction among those on the lower rungs of the ladder of social stratification. Thus much has been left unexamined,[40] and the initial move of urban regime analysis toward exploring the interpenetrations of government, market, and civil society needs to be extended.

What about interpenetrations when interactions fall well below the level of pursuing a priority agenda, that is, when people are coping with limited resources, marginal standing, and a lack of sustained attention from top leaders? Here is where we need insights gained from ethnographic studies and observations of and by grassroots groups and those working at the street level. The interpenetrations of state, market, and society that come into play in setting a priority agenda such as redevelopment do not form an order at one with the interpenetrations found in the day-to-day actions of those at the political margins. What lines of connection extend across the boundaries of race and class? What does the political order look like from the bottom up? Orren and Skowronek offer the sound guidance that we should pay attention to multiple orders. We need to remember, however, that not only do orders vary by the time in which they take shape, but they also vary across the reach of the policy process.

Thinking about Civil Society from the Bottom Up

With an assumption that government and politics constitute an autonomous activity, classic pluralism never found a bridge to two landmark studies of civil society, also of an early 1960s vintage. *The Death and Life of Great American Cities*, a critique of planning professionals, by author and activist Jane Jacobs came out the same year as *Who Governs?*[41] The following year sociologist Herbert Gans published *The Urban Villagers*, a look at life in a working-class neighborhood and at why urban renewal was socially injurious.[42] With their highly critical stances, both books offered compelling reasons to question that a pluralist consensus was on the rise. Far from celebrating urban redevelopment as a broadly shared vision of city revitalization, both books highlighted its destructive side. Both showed planners and policy professionals as out of touch with residents. In his work Gans demonstrated that professional planners and members of the working class in Boston's West End saw the world in radically different ways. Jacobs, for her part, showed how little the professionals understood the way a tenuous pattern of social relationships could serve such aims as public safety. Though neither book focused on African American populations, both showed how government action could become a source of deepened disaffection and discontent. Within a few years, the Kerner Commission Report painted in the racial particulars, thereby countering the notion that assimilation was bringing about a society of dispersed inequalities, divided only by a succession of narrowly defined and ever-shifting issues.[43]

Urban political economy provided a framework through which scholars could question classic pluralism, but it was not well positioned to highlight civil society, particularly the manifold ways in which it is layered. While Robert Putnam—initially by way of a study of Italian regional governments—put a spotlight on social capital,[44] it fell to later writers to bring a bottom-up view of civil society into focus and direct attention to the dynamics surrounding stratified relations. Consider two trenchant analyses of race and stratification and where they take us that urban political economy hasn't. Both Cathy Cohen's study of AIDS as a case of the politics of marginality and Mary Pattillo's treatment of race and class in the gentrification of a Chicago neighborhood provide us a bottom-up view of civil society and its complex part in the politics of inequality.[45]

Both scholars call for moving beyond a simple dichotomy between the dominant and the dominated. Cohen gives attention to the varied ways in which marginality can be politically structured, and Pattillo centers her work on the role of actors in the middle—on brokers who mediate relations between elites at the top and those in society's lower ranks. She tells us that "the middle is the place where the actual face-to-face work of inequality transpires."[46]

Cohen and Pattillo alike make use of frameworks in which inequality is fundamental, but works in complicated ways. Consider marginality and its relation to a polity-centered approach. Cohen talks about historical experiences of exclusion and subordination out of which marginality is forged. She then defines marginality as a condition of "deficiency in the economic, political, and social resources used to guarantee access to the rights and privileges assumed by dominant groups."[47] In a view from the top, economic, political, and social resources and their various consequences may appear to be neatly differentiated. Not so from the bottom—they are experienced as highly intertwined.

Cohen sets forth three analytical pillars to consider in the politics of marginality: (1) a history of unequal power relations; (2) the development and importance of indigenous structures within the marginalized group; and (3) the absence of a unidirectional, top-down form of control and the presence instead of a dynamic and evolving body of relationships constituted from struggles between forces of domination and those of resistance.

Stratification occurs not just in differentiating dominant players from those in lesser positions, but also in relations within the marginal group.[48]

The latter accounts for varied forms of marginality; stratification within the marginal group provides actors who can play the broker role. Pattillo argues that internal stratification means a black political identity rests on shared struggle that consists of more than a sense of linked fate; it also involves discussion, debate, and sundry forms of engagement around what blackness means. As she puts it, there is "no 'black' way of doing things."[49] Given the framework offered by Cohen and Pattillo, scholars need to be attentive to the resources, abilities, and inclinations of those in the bottom ranks of the system of social stratification.

Consider how concrete policy experiences can undermine trust. In tracing Chicago's redevelopment experience, Pattillo points out that "promises are political acts." As such, over time "they are pronounced, manipulated, retracted, and denied within a context of unequal abilities to define the situation."[50] Even at the early stage of redevelopment (the 1950s), distrust of officialdom was high. To those on the lower rungs of society, unfulfilled promises have a very long history—their accumulated experience means that a rhetoric of good intentions readily evokes suspicion rather than confidence, cynicism rather than an inclination to cooperate. In short, people in the lower strata fit no mold of trusting citizens, eager to receive benefits from a benign government (or for that matter a benign society). Their reaction to policy initiatives is colored by a history of neglect, unmet promises, and more than occasional instances of blatant disregard.[51]

By no means should it be assumed that the designs of policy makers proceed to application without being affected by the accumulated and differentiated experiences of various segments of the populace, in addition to the varied concerns of those all along the chain of official implementation.[52] Thus, what to the official makers of policy may seem like a shared policy occurrence may in fact differ greatly by social circumstance. For example, Cathy Cohen points out that "AIDS is a very different disease in poor black communities than in white gay male communities."[53] A failure to grasp that fact is reflected in the varying ways and differing speeds with which aspects of the AIDS issue were understood and addressed.

Policy is not made and carried out on a blank slate. Socio-economic inequalities enter the picture in multiple ways. Bear in mind that at the local level especially, policies are often de facto co-produced.[54] Official agents of the government, whether directly or indirectly, depend heavily on the populace. Level of trust and patterns of interaction are fundamental.[55] Also, as Jane Jacobs argues, police and other agents of the government find that the demands of their tasks depend heavily on what citizens provide. Take Jacobs a step further and consider the tensions between law-enforcement agents and lower-income communities, especially those of color. On the community side, "don't snitch" tee shirts and a persisting reluctance to testify about unlawful behavior expose one source of tension. On the law-enforcement side, an individualist under-standing of crime and of the police role constitutes another source.[56] Thus the disjuncture between the order headed by civic and political elites and the order prevalent among the lower strata can be severe.

Still at points of contact, neither state nor lower-strata communities are monolithic. Nor is their relationship frozen. As Boston's youth anti-violence campaign shows, mutual distrust can give way to active co-operation.[57] Multiple strands of relationship run within the wider social order, and no one is all-determining.

One strand concerns how blame is understood. For an illustration let us return to ethos theory, especially Banfield's elaborated version. This takes us back to an earlier assumption that people are carriers of values derived from their position in society and the socialization they have experienced. Banfield talked about a present-time orientation (essentially an inability to defer gratification) in a way that connected it closely to the idea of a culture of poverty.[58] In Banfield's assessment any public effort to address poverty was doomed to failure because those who are per-sistently poor have a non-productive mindset and thus are unable to pursue a middle-class path of upward mobility. In this view, because a mindset is transmitted to the younger generation at a very early age, there is little that government programs can do without radical intervention in the parent–child relationship.

Contrast Banfield's view with the "conditional approach" offered by sociologist Mario Luis Small.[59] In his study of a Boston public housing project, Small found that much theorizing about poverty is simplistic. Instead of a single prevalent mindset, he found heterogeneous views of the world and how it operates. Behaviors varied within a given time, and over time as well.[60] Instead of uniform social isolation and apathy among the poor, Small found many residents to have ties beyond the neighborhood, and most tellingly he discovered a subgroup actively involved in efforts to expand programs, improve the neighborhood, and enlarge opportunities for residents. Many of this group had been part of an earlier reform mobilization or were part of a household involved in that mobilization. Thus a subgroup had a positive vision of what the community could be— in short, a future-time orientation.

The idea of a prevalent culture of poverty is further contradicted by a recent study of the underground economy in a Chicago neighborhood, by sociologist Sudhir Venkatesh.[61] In contrast to the view that urban residents can usefully be viewed as value-carriers (bearers of a culturally transmitted ethos), he found that behavior, including time horizons, was largely guided by a scarcity of material resources. Moreover, this scarcity gave rise to no amoral pattern of conduct. Quite the contrary, there was a wide net of mutual assistance and a shared body of norms about obligations to others.

In short, close-up studies of poverty neighborhoods indicate that these communities are not incapable of a constructive relationship with government, though mending that relationship is not apt to be quick, easy, or cheap. Old assumptions and their implications stand in need of re-examination. As historian Alice O'Connor puts it, we need to reorient "research away from the problems and pathologies that plague low-income communities and toward a better understanding of how these conditions are maintained or made worse."[62] Strands of connection can be built around lower-strata assets,[63] though sometimes arrangements bear a strong resemblance to ward and patronage connections of the past.[64]

Consider what we have known for many decades, dating back to the urban disorder of the 1960s and earlier.[65] The range of alienating policies and program treatments experienced by the lower ranks of the social order is wide and deep. This experience has aggravated if not created a troubled government–society relationship. This relationship has become a profound part of the current ordering of politics. Its causes are complex and go back further than recent forces of globalization, though it is certainly the case that deindustrialization, for instance, has contributed greatly to the difficulties faced by those who dwell in the central city. However, the evolution of a capitalist economy does not stand alone as a causal factor; at the very least we have to add race and government-service professionalism to the equation to account for the current state of government–civil society relations.[66]

At the same time we should remember that there are instructive instances in which this ruptured government–civil society relationship has been repaired, though often only over a limited policy span. At the current stage of research, these instances stand as limited-scale case studies about a potential, not pieces in a systematic *model* for assessing how the urban political order might be in a process of re-forming.

Still we should not overlook the point that today's policy landscape is populated with multiple forms of connection between different layers of the larger political order, and some are efforts to mend government–civil society relations. Community policing, school reform, affordable housing, and neighborhood conservation are highly visible fronts in this struggle. Community development corporations (CDCs), advocacy groups, charter schools, community-based organizing, contracting out to nonprofits, black churches as mobilizing and mediating forces, and various forms of citizen engagement are part of the picture.[67]

Lacking, however, is an encompassing framework that brings these disparate elements into a coherent picture. A move toward such a picture calls for traveling along a different path from both classic pluralism and urban political economy, hence Cohen and Pattillo are useful starting guides. Still they leave much uncharted. The following are some significant course markers:

1. At the heart of the policy challenge left by the shift to a post-industrial city is a damaged set of government–society relations.

2. Not only damaged, these relations are hard to alter because they are heavily infused by society's system of stratification.
3. The operation of the stratification system rests on multiple foundations, only some of which trace directly to the workings of a capitalist economy. Race and professionalism are separate and conceptually distinct strands, though practice weaves the various strands together.
4. One source of reinforcement for the current pattern of govern-ment–society relations is the tendency for upper-strata groups to "blame the victim," that is, to see members of the lower strata as responsible for their own problems and as a source of risk to others.[68]
5. Another source of reinforcement is that the present pattern rests in part on a legacy of defective reform efforts and a history of deficient connections between the lower strata and the mainstream.
6. Causal conditions are structured but not intractable, and behaviors spring not from a single source (such as a given culture) but a con-junction of factors.
7. The importance of structural forces notwithstanding, we are following no inevitable trajectory. Instead, as contemporary scholarship increas-ingly suggests, outcomes are socially constructed and historically constituted. That there are multiple urban orders and connections means that change is always in process, and strategic interventions have a potential to alter seemingly entrenched tendencies.

The thrust of the discussion to this point has been toward a need for a broad conception of the urban political order. The polity approach of Orren and Skowronek carries us in that direction. The interpenetration of state, market, and society provides an alternative to economic or social determinism, and steers clear of an assumption that government and politics form an autonomous sphere.[69] Moreover, Orren and Skowronek warn against any effort to treat jumbled forms of interpenetration as a highly integrated arrangement. They offer an intercurrence of multiple orders as an alternative macro-view. And they join historian Alice O'Connor and others in calling for close attention to the role of "human and political agency."[70]

Conclusion

The urban classics of the 1960s made flawed assumptions about the nature of the local political arena. Urban political economy made some useful correctives but did not go far enough. Although some of its schools of thought are less narrowly constituted than others, none delves into civil society in the depth that some key sociological studies have. Hence there is much that urban political science can learn, particularly from a bottom-up view of civil society and how the lower strata fit into the political order. For its part, urban history contributes to an enlarged view of that order by painting on a wide canvas, with due attention to federal policy, the city's regional setting, and the multi-sector foundations of local politics. In place of the single dominant path of development found in classical pluralism, analysis today can take a cue from historians and explore the manner in which varied factors come together. The inter-currence concept of Orren and Skowronek provides a needed framework for considering the ways in which outcomes depend on how multiple factors mesh, clash, and coexist.

Still, the "mother lode" of grand theory remains as a strong temptation. That the market is such a powerful force reinforces the temptation, and the positing of an overriding neoliberal project constitutes one version of an overly economy-centered explanation. Although we by no means dismiss the influence of the market, we regard this version of political economy as illustrative of a flawed approach, unduly narrowing the base of explanation.

Consider an application of Jason Hackworth's argument about the global economy. In his view, following the public debt crisis of the 1970s, a once-dominant Keynesian liberalism was done in by the ascendance of neoliberalism. In Hackworth's assessment of political change in New York City: "The austerity program instituted after the city's debt crisis shook apart the once solid New Deal coalition in the city."[71] Important as the financial crunch was, privileging the explanatory power of economic factors in this way reduces a complex restructuring of politics to a single factor when much more was at work. In this specific instance of the splintering of the New Deal coalition, other authors show how race played a major role.[72]

Turning points and periodization are part of what urban political development should consider, but not in the form of oversimplifying the restructuring of city politics. As Orren and Skowronek caution, any present time rests on layers of past events—therefore "any realistic depiction of politics in time will include multiple orders."[73] In the restructuring of city politics, we contend that the ways in which race, class, and professionalization mix and sort out politically are what need to be studied. For instance, coming out of the 1960s, struggles over the reshaping of urban-service agencies along with racial divides and demographic change all played a part in realigning political loyalties in New York and other cities. During what Hackworth calls the neo-Keynesian period, technocratic professionalization was identified as a major source of division.[74] Economic change aside, the interplay between race/ethnicity and the operating rules of public agencies put enormous pressure on the New Deal coalition.

Periodization raises other issues; the temptation may be strong to focus on current change and pay little heed to what seems unchanging. However, past layers of politics are a significant force. Although there is good reason to ask if the 1970s were years of major clashes that in combination set the stage for the city politics that followed, we believe it is useful to consider continuities as well. In particular we think there is evidence of a persisting ecology of disadvantage that took a distinctive form as World War II came to a close. Convergent power at the top helped bring about increased powerlessness at the bottom, as old lines of connection weakened.

Though some of the particulars vary by place, the presence of a marginalized urban population of substantial size is an ongoing phenomenon. Its foundations are clearly racial as well as economic. The separation of the politics of home from workplace, what Ira Katznelson calls "city trenches," is another contributing factor,[75] as is a seemingly unwavering but racially tinged attachment to a belief in individual responsibility as the key to poverty and distress. Scholars may have abandoned explanations in the form of individuals as value-carriers, but the nation's policy discourse has not. All of these are matters worthy of further exploration, with special attention to how various policies and institutional arrangements intertwine and reinforce an ecology of disadvantage.

Yet, in spite of a formidable array of forces, as a final (and less pessimistic) note, we put forward for consideration the possibility that, the neo-liberal project notwithstanding, the position of society's lower strata may be in an early stage of change. Whether this change is for the better remains to be seen. In any case, we see much wisdom in Paul Pierson's reminder that sometimes it has been "gradual interconnected social processes that created conditions for a set of triggering events."[76] Change by accretion is not to be ignored, but neither, of course, is the possibility of unyielding continuity.

Still the question remains as to whether the long period of urban transformation following World War II, that is, the remaking of the industrial city into a post-industrial place, has sufficiently wound down to invite a fresh periodization and characterization, and, if so, what that might possibly be. With the insight that comes from looking back, urban historians have given us a new look at this period of urban makeover. Among other things, in contrast with the more elite-centered research of regime analysis, historians have given major attention to the city–suburb relation and thereby put the spotlight on what we might call residential politics, particularly the rise of home-owners as a powerful political identity. Race and immigration, national policy, state practices of allowing and encouraging local-government fragmentation, and market choices have combined to give us metropolitan areas containing sharply clashing interests, weak means to respond to inter-local conflicts, and inhospitable ground for wide-ranging public mindedness to take hold. Growing complexity and social differentiation have made it increasingly urgent to think of the central city and its suburbs as integral parts of a single political universe. Metropolitan politics is not simply an ancillary feature of city politics but increasingly a main arena.

In that context particularly, looking back over the time since World War II, we can see that, contrary to classical pluralism, inequalities have been anything but dispersed. Instead, clustered inequalities have become a threat to social cohesion, hampered the performance of urban schools, and posed enduring problems for law enforcement. In the period of postwar transformation, many city agendas were dominated by a "convergence of power" between city hall and major business interests with the result that urban neighborhoods were neglected, less affluent city populations bore social disruption and economic dislocation, and intergroup tensions flourished. Lower socio-economic status populations remain to a degree disconnected from mainstream opportunities and often are alienated from the service agencies of city government, especially the police. Instead of the kind of politically mediated mutual adjustment between groups predicted by pluralism, we have instead had an ongoing version of "winner takes all."

Yet the contemporary urban scene in America is not totally bleak. There are signs of an emerging era of urban reconstruction. Neighborhood and community organizing has proved to be a durable force.[77] Working through such entities as CDCs, the nonprofit sector is a significant contributor to affordable housing and neighborhood conservation. Despite decreased federal funding, community policing continues as a presence in local law enforcement. The improvement of urban education remains the mechanical rabbit that the hounds of reform are unable to catch, but there are a few promising developments—not the least of which is that school performance is now a matter of national concern. Advocacy for children and youth, early childhood education, and youth-development programs seem to be on the upswing. Though federal grants remain a force in decline, federal tax law and the Community Reinvestment Act occupy a significant place. And one of the distinctive features of the urban scene in America is the part played by philanthropy. Though this is hardly a matter for unbounded optimism, it is a subject much in need of research. And it could be that foundations, particularly community foundations, are a growing force. In some instances, they are the initiating means by which problems of inequality are addressed.

With the refashioning of the central business district no longer the policy magnet it once was, there is opportunity now to consider the urban condition more broadly than in the past, bearing in mind the argument of Orren and Skowronek that any given time is home to multiple and not necessarily congruent orders. As part of this process, we have suggested that urban scholars alter or expand the political-economy framework to give more attention to civil society. And we should remember as well that civic life itself is almost certain to be composed of multiple orders.

Notes

1. The transition has important roots in Lawrence Herson's "The Lost World of Municipal Government," *American Political Science Review* 51 (June 1957): 330–345.
2. Key works were Robert A. Dahl, *Who Governs?* (New Haven: Yale University Press, 1961); Wallace Sayre and Herbert Kaufman, *Governing New York City* (New York: Russell Sage, 1960); Edward C. Banfield, *Political Influence* (Glencoe, IL: Free Press, 1961); and Edward C. Banfield and James Q. Wilson, *City Politics* (New York: Vintage Books, 1963).
3. Karen Orren and Stephen Skowronek, *The Search for American Political Development* (New York: Cambridge University Press, 2004).
4. For a recent succinct statement of pluralism on this point, see Rufus P. Browning, Dale R. Marshall, and David H. Tabb, *Racial Politics in American Cities* (New York: Longman, 2003), p. 13.
5. On this count, it is useful to pay heed to the tradeoffs in Thorngate's postulate; see Karl Weyck, *The Social Psychology of Organizing* (Reading, MA: Addison Wesley, 1979), pp. 35–37.
6. Orren and Skowronek, *The Search for American Political Development*, p. 16.
7. Ibid., pp. 1–32
8. Robert H. Salisbury, "Urban Politics: The New Convergence of Power," *Journal of Politics* 26 (November 1964): 775–797.
9. Richard M. Merelman, *Pluralism at Yale* (Madison: University of Wisconsin, 2003).
10. A peculiar pattern took shape. For a time the community power debate continued, but the intense conceptual controversy at its center had little apparent role in guiding future research.
11. Thomas Kuhn, *The Structure of Scientific Revolutions* (Chicago: University of Chicago Press, 1970).
12. It was preceded by Robert Dahl's *A Preface to Democratic Theory* (Chicago: University of Chicago Press, 1956), and was in some ways an application of that book's theoretical argument.
13. Role differentiation, in Dahl's words, "ended a period when social status, education, wealth, and political influence were united in the same hands. There was never again anything quite like it" (*Who Governs?*, p. 24).
14. Talcott Parsons, *The Social System* (Glencoe, IL: Free Press, 1951).
15. Dahl, *Who Governs?*, p. 84. Dahl also talks about the extent to which democratic systems, with elections as the regulator, provide belief systems within which *leaders* are confined. See also the discussion of New Haven political leader John Golden on p. 75, and the emphasis on "common values and goals" on p. 92.
16. Dahl, *Who Governs?*, p. 61. More widely Dahl observes: "In pluralistic, democratic political systems with wide political consensus the range of acceptable strategies is narrowed by beliefs and habits . . ." (*Who Governs?*, p. 225). Even for the earlier period of New Haven in which ethnic conflict was at a peak, Dahl talks about "the yearning for assimilation and acceptance" (*Who Governs?*, p. 33). Thus, in *Who Governs?*, consensus is a pervasive theme, along with dispersed inequalities.
17. To be noted, however, is that, in an interview years after the publication of *Who Governs?*, Dahl acknowledged that he should have paid greater attention to "limiting factors," that is, how public decision-makers "need to take into account the decisions and influences of the market system" (interview in Robert J. Waste, *Community Power* [Beverly Hills, CA: Sage, 1986], p. 192).

18. Interestingly, Dahl notes that patterns of political participation correspond with socio-economic characteristics, but makes little of this point (*Who Governs?*, pp. 282–293).
19. J. Phillip Thompson, III, *Double Trouble* (New York: Oxford University Press, 2006).
20. Clarence N. Stone, Robert K. Whelan, and William J. Murin, *Urban Policy and Politics in a Bureaucratic Age* (Englewood Cliffs, NJ: Prentice-Hall, 1979, 1986).
21. James O'Connor, *The Fiscal Crisis of the State* (New York: St Martin's Press, 1973).
22. Ira Katznelson, "The Crisis of the Capitalist City: Urban Politics and Social Control," in Willis D. Hawley et al., *Theoretical Perspectives on Urban Politics* (Englewood Cliffs, NJ: Prentice-Hall, 1976), pp. 214–229.
23. Charles Lindblom, *Politics and Markets* (New York: Basic Books, 1977).
24. Bryan D. Jones and Lynn W. Bachelor, *The Sustaining Hand* (Lawrence: University Press of Kansas, 1993), p. 253.
25. Martin Shefter, "New York City's Fiscal Crisis," *The Public Interest* 48 (Summer 1977): 98–127. See also his book, *Political Crisis/Fiscal Crisis: The Collapse and Revival of New York City* (New York: Columbia University Press, 1992).
26. Rufus Browning, Dale Rogers Marshall, and David Tabb, *Protest Is Not Enough* (Berkeley: University of California Press, 1984).
27. Paul Peterson, *City Limits* (Chicago: University of Chicago Press, 1981). A kindred analysis extended to the suburbs is Mark Schneider's *The Competitive City: The Political Economy of Suburbia* (Pittsburgh: University of Pittsburgh Press, 1989).
28. Particularly useful sources on the general debate are Philip Abrams, *Historical Sociology* (Ithaca, NY: Cornell University Press, 1982); William H. Sewell, Jr, "A Theory of Structure," *American Journal of Sociology* 98 (July 1992): 1–29; and Colin Hay, "Structure and Agency," in David Marsh and Gerry Stoker, *Theory and Methods in Political Science* (New York: Palgrave, 1995), pp. 189–206.
29. Harvey Molotch, "The City as a Growth Machine," *American Journal of Sociology* 82 (September 1976): 309–331.
30. John H. Mollenkopf, *The Contested City* (Princeton, NJ: Princeton University Press, 1983); Saskia Sassen, *The Global City* (Princeton, NJ: Princeton University Press, 1991); Susan E. Clarke and Gary L. Gaile, *The Work of Cities* (Minneapolis: University of Minnesota Press, 1998); H.V. Savitch and Paul Kantor, *Cities in the International Marketplace* (Princeton, NJ: Princeton University Press, 2002); Jeffrey M. Sellers, *Governing from Below* (New York: Cambridge University Press, 2002); and Neil Brenner, *New State Spaces* (New York: Oxford University Press, 2004).
31. Jason Hackworth, *The Neoliberal City* (Ithaca, NY: Cornell University Press, 2007).
32. Martin Shefter, "The Emergence of the Political Machine: An Alternative View," in Willis D. Hawley et al., *Theoretical Perspectives on Urban Politics* (Englewood Cliffs, NJ: Prentice-Hall, 1976), pp. 14–44.
33. Robert Crain, *The Politics of School Desegregation* (Chicago: Aldine, 1968).
34. Note, however, that suburban experiences fit a different pattern. See, for example, Becky M. Nicolaides, *My Blue Heaven* (Chicago: University of Chicago Press, 2002).
35. Clarence N. Stone, *Regime Politics* (Lawrence: University Press of Kansas, 1989).

36. The interconnection is also at the heart of Floyd Hunter's early study of Atlanta, *Community Power Structure* (Chapel Hill: University of North Carolina Press, 1953).
37. Quoted in Dahl, *Who Governs?*, p. 130.
38. On the consequences of this limited authority for John Daniels, New Haven's first and so far only, African American mayor, see Douglas W. Rae, "Making Life Work in Crowded Places," *Urban Affairs Review* 41 (January 2006): 271–291; Cathy J. Cohen, "Social Capital, Intervening Institutions, and Political Power," in Susan Saegert, J. Philip Thompson, and Mark Warren, *Social Capital and Poor Communities* (New York: Russell Sage, 2001), pp. 267–289; and Mary Summers and Philip Klinkner, "The Election and Governance of John Daniels as Mayor of New Haven," in Huey L. Perry, *Race, Politics, and Governance in the United States* (Gainesville: University of Florida Press, 1996), pp. 127–150.
39. Mary Pattillo, *Black on the Block* (Chicago: University of Chicago Press, 2007), p. 8.
40. Significant exceptions include: Cathy J. Cohen and Michael C. Dawson, "Neighborhood Poverty and African American Politics," *American Political Science Review* 87 (June 1993): 286–302; Michael Jones-Correa, *Between Two Nations* (Ithaca, NY: Cornell University Press, 1998); Cathy J. Cohen, *The Boundaries of Blackness* (Chicago: University of Chicago Press, 1999); Archon Fung, *Empowered Participation* (Princeton, NJ: Princeton University Press, 2004); and Peter F. Burns, *Electoral Politics Is Not Enough* (Albany: State University of New York Press, 2006).
41. Jane Jacobs, *The Death and Life of Great American Cities* (New York: Random House, 1961).
42. Herbert Gans, *The Urban Villagers* (New York: Free Press, 1962).
43. Kerner Commission Report, *The Report of the National Advisory Commission on Civil Disorders* (Washington, DC: GPO, 1968).
44. Robert Putnam, *Making Democracy Work* (Princeton, NJ: Princeton University Press, 1993).
45. Cohen, *Boundaries of Blackness*; Pattillo, *Black on the Block*.
46. Pattillo, *Black on the Block*, p. 307.
47. Cohen, *Boundaries of Blackness*, pp. 37–38.
48. One might add that there may be more than one marginal group, further complicating intra-marginality relations. See, for example, Susan Clarke et al., *Multiethnic Moments* (Philadelphia: Temple University Press, 2006).
49. Pattillo, *Black on the Block*, p. 303.
50. Ibid., p. 256.
51. See the related argument about cumulative discontent by African Americans with liberal reform in Matthew Countryman, *Up South: Civil Rights and Black Power in Philadelphia* (Philadelphia: University of Pennsylvania Press, 2006).
52. For a telling instance of how implementation is variously constructed, see the treatment of AIDS prevention by Cohen, *Boundaries of Blackness*, and Michael Brown, "Reconceptualizing Public and Private in Urban Regime Theory," *International Journal of Urban and Regional Research* 23 (March 1999): 70–87.
53. Cohen, *Boundaries of Blackness*, p. 345.
54. Stephen Macedo et al., *Democracy at Risk* (Washington, DC: Brookings Institution Press, 2005), pp. 95–96.
55. Anthony S. Bryk and Barbara Schneider, *Trust in Schools* (New York: Russell Sage Foundation, 2002).

56. Steve Herbert, *Citizens, Cops, and Power* (Chicago: University of Chicago Press, 2006).

57. Jenny Berrien and Christopher Winship, "An Umbrella of Legitimacy," in Gary S. Katzmann, *Securing Our Children's Future* (Washington, DC: Brookings, 2002), pp. 200–228.

58. Edward C. Banfield, *The Unheavenly City* (Boston: Little, Brown, 1970).

59. Mario Luis Small, *Villa Victoria* (Chicago: University of Chicago Press, 2004).

60. On many counts his findings concur with those on Chicago's Robert Taylor Homes by Sudhir A. Venkatesh, *American Project* (Cambridge, MA: Harvard University Press, 2000).

61. Sudhir A. Venkatesh, *Off the Books* (Cambridge, MA: Harvard University Press, 2006).

62. Alice O'Connor, "Swimming against the Tide," in Ronald F. Ferguson and William T. Dickens, *Urban Problems and Community Development* (Washington, DC: Brookings Institution Press, 1999), p. 119.

63. John P. Kretzmann and John L. McKnight, *Building Communities from the Inside Out* (Evanston, IL: Institute for Policy Research, Northwestern University, 1993).

64. Nicole P. Marwell, *Bargaining for Brooklyn* (Chicago: University of Chicago Press, 2007).

65. On this matter there is a clear paper trail, consisting of commission reports (e.g. the National Advisory Commission on Civil Disorders 1968), social science accounts (e.g. Kenneth B. Clark, *Dark Ghetto* [New York: Harper & Row, 1965]), and in-depth journalism (e.g. Paul Jacobs, *Prelude to Riot* [New York: Vintage Books, 1966]; Joseph P. Lyford, *The Airtight Cage* [New York: Harper & Row, 1966]; and Robert Conot, *Rivers of Blood, Years of Darkness* [New York: Bantam Books, 1967]).

66. For instance, see how a code of professional police conduct can stand as a barrier to community policing—Herbert, *Citizens, Cops, and Power*. On professionalism more generally as a barrier to government–citizen relations, see David Marquand, *Decline of the Public* (Cambridge: Polity Press, 2004).

67. On black churches, see Omar M. McRoberts, *Streets of Glory* (Chicago: University of Chicago Press, 2003); R. Drew Smith and Frederick C. Harris, *Black Churches and Local Politics* (Lanham, MD: Rowman & Littlefield, 2005); and Michael L. Owens, *God and Government in the Ghetto* (Chicago: University of Chicago Press, 2007).

68. Pattillo notes that marginalized groups "are blamed for the decadence and decline of the American city, resulting in a stream of regressive, if not punitive, policies" (*Black on the Block*, p. 19; see also p. 264).

69. Of course, there are separately configured entities and significant autonomy in day-to-day operations. The lack of autonomy comes from the way in which decision-makers incorporate context into their actions as well as from overt interactions between and among the three spheres.

70. O'Connor, "Swimming against the Tide," p. 119. See the parallel arguments by Ira Katznelson, "Structure and Configuration in Comparative Politics," in Mark Lichbach and Alan Zuckerman, *Comparative Politics* (New York: Cambridge University Press, 1997); Robert H. Bates et al., *Analytic Narratives* (Princeton, NJ: Princeton University Press, 1998).

71. Hackworth, *Neoliberal City*, p. 34.

72. In addition to numerous historical studies covering various cities, see especially on New York City, Jonathan Rieder, *Canarsie* (Cambridge, MA: Harvard University Press, 1985).

73. Orren and Skowronek, *The Search for American Political Development*, p. 17.

74. Kerner Commission Report, *The Report of the National Advisory Commission on Civil Disorders*, pp. 284–288.
75. Ira Katznelson, *City Trenches* (Chicago: University of Chicago Press, 1981). For a west coast version of the separation, see Nicolaides, *My Blue Heaven*.
76. Paul Pierson, *Politics in Time* (Princeton, NJ: Princeton University Press, 2004), p. 85.
77. Marion Orr, ed., *Transforming the City* (Lawrence: University Press of Kansas, 2007).

Part III
City, Space, and Nation

6 Is There a Politics of "Urban" Development?

Reflections on the US Case

Neil Brenner

Like all commodities under capitalism, cities are often naturalized, both in scholarly analysis and in everyday life: The social processes required to produce them are forgotten or hidden. The built environment thus acquires the "aura" of a pregiven materiality, mysteriously devoid of the concrete social relations that engendered it.[1]

In the field of North American urban political science, this urban fetishism has frequently assumed the form of methodological localism—the tendency of scholars to focus on local governmental institutions without investigating the supralocal institutional-regulatory frameworks and spatial divisions of labor within which such institutions are embedded. To some extent, these localist methodological tendencies flow from the understandable concern of urban political scientists to legitimate their subfield within a disciplinary environment that has long been dominated by methodological nationalism—an equally problematic tendency to naturalize the national scale of political life.[2] Yet, even when this localist turn stems from a well-justified concern to circumvent the blind-spots of methodological nationalism, it contains serious methodological limitations of its own. Insofar as the subfield of urban politics focuses predominantly or exclusively on local political institutions or processes, it is in danger of being ensnared within the formally analogous methodological trap of localism. Within such an epistemological framework, the local or urban scale is taken for granted as a pregiven, relatively discrete container of political-economic processes; its supralocal conditions of possibility, contexts of development, and consequences are bracketed.[3] However, to the degree that urban political dynamics are actually conditioned by, and in turn condition, supralocal institutions and processes, the notion of a discrete "urban" politics is a mystification: It represents processes, dynamics, and struggles that originate outside of cities, and that effectively ricochet through them, as being internally generated and/or enclosed within their jurisdictional boundaries.

One of the major epistemological agendas of critical urban theory is to deconstruct this fetish of the city by revealing the sociospatial processes that underpin the creation and continual transformation of urban landscapes, including those through which processes of urban governance unfold.[4] This project of defetishization requires the adoption of a multi-scalar methodological framework to investigate, and thus to denaturalize, those regulatory problems, strategies, and struggles that are commonly characterized as "urban" or "local." Within such a framework, cities may well remain a central object and terrain of investigation, but they are grasped by being positioned analytically within broader, supra-urban political-economic fields—for instance, of worldwide capital accumulation and national state power. On the one hand, putatively urban processes are often themselves multiscalar, stretching beyond any single municipality into a tangled jigsaw of metropolises, regions, national urban networks, and worldwide spatial divisions of labor. At the same time, urban formations are in turn shaped by diverse supralocal processes, institutions, and arrangements, from worldwide flows of investment, trade, and migration, to state jurisdictional boundaries, intergovernmental divisions, and various kinds of spatial policies. This multiscalar methodological orientation acknowledges the strategically essential role of the urban scale within modern capitalism, but emphasizes its embeddedness within broader landscapes of political-economic activity. From this point of view, rather than being seen as a pregiven social fact, the very intelligibility of the urban as a discrete arena of political-economic life represents an historically contingent *product* of strategies to establish such a formation. In David Harvey's terms, such strategies entail efforts to construct an urbanized "structured coherence"—that is, a relatively durable, locally concentrated framework of institutional and spatial organization—within otherwise relatively inchoate, multiscalar configurations of capital, infrastructure, population, and governance.[5]

For present purposes, I consider the implications of this methodological orientation for deciphering the politics of urban development in the US context. In a first step, I consider the problem of localism, and I specify several ways in which this tendency is manifested within certain strands of the two major approaches to the study of US urban politics, urban regime theory, and urban growth machine theory.[6] Against methodologically localist interpretations, I argue that the growth-oriented character of US urban politics is the product of *national* state institutions and political geographies, the character of which is then specified. On this basis, through a state-theoretical reading of Logan and Molotch's classic 1987 work *Urban Fortunes*, I suggest that growth machines must be understood as national politico-institutional constructs rather than as internally generated products of purely "urban" or "local" mobilizations.[7] More generally, this analysis suggests that the apparently "urban" character of growth machines, both in the US and elsewhere, must be investigated and explained, rather than being presupposed. A concluding section summarizes some of the epistemological, methodological, and comparative implications of the foregoing discussion.

Localism in Question

Urban regime theory and growth machine theory represent the two most important analytical frameworks through which urban development has been analyzed within US political science.[8] Developed in the US during the 1980s as critiques of traditional ecological and structuralist Marxist approaches to urban studies, both theories isolate certain sets of actors and organizations at the urban scale, and examine their diverse boosterist activities in promoting economic growth: Their goal is to "uncover rather than merely assert the role of politics in urban theory."[9] In this sense, both theories represent critical reformulations of traditional elite theory in the context of urban politics.[10]

Urban regime theory, as developed influentially by political scientists such as Stephen Elkin, Clarence Stone, and Heywood Sanders, emphasizes (1) the privileged position of business interests in the formation of municipal socioeconomic policies and (2) the changing division of labor between markets and state institutions in processes of urban development.[11] Empirical research within the urban regime framework has examined the ways in which public and private interests mesh together through a range of formal and informal civic arrangements, cooperative alliances, and partnerships that are in turn embodied in, and reproduced through, specific types of urban growth coalitions or regimess (e.g. pluralist, federalist, or entrepreneurial in Elkin's typology; or caretaker, progressive, or corporate in Stone's framework).[12]

Urban growth machine theory, developed in the paradigmatic work of sociologists John Logan and Harvey Molotch, is focused less on policy outcomes than on the process of urban development itself.[13] For Logan and Molotch, the city operates as a growth machine insofar as localized coalitions—generally composed of property owners ("rentiers") and other auxiliary, place-bound supporters (developers, universities, local media and newspapers, utility companies, labor unions, small retailers, and the like)—form and attempt to promote land uses that enhance the exchange-value of local real estate tracts. Although challenges to the growth agenda and the ideology of "value-free" development may be articulated in the name of use-values by neighborhood organizations, slow-growth, and other NIMBYist (not-in-my-backyard) local movements, Logan and Molotch emphasize the overarching power of "place-entrepreneurs" and, in most instances, the local government, in circumventing such oppositional forces. On this basis, Logan and Molotch contend that urban growth machines have played a key role in shaping the landscape of urban development throughout US history, despite their deeply polarizing and often socially and environmentally destructive effects.

Since the mid-1980s, urban regime theory and growth machine theory have generated an impressive body of research on the politics of local economic development, particularly in the US, but also, increasingly, in comparative international perspective.[14] Consistent with their goal of circumventing the limitations of traditional structuralist approaches, both theories focus on the activities, alliances, and agendas of local political-economic elites *within* cities. This has led several commentators to underscore the problem of "localism" with each of these research traditions. For instance, Alan Harding suggests that both regime theory and growth machine studies are "essentially localist" due to their overwhelming emphasis on intralocal political dynamics:

> [T]hey often underplay the importance of externally imposed structures that predispose local actors to particular forms of behavior and the role played by more variable non-local sources of influence on urban development, for example the changing demands of higher levels of government or external investors.[15]

Concomitantly, Bob Jessop, Jamie Peck, and Adam Tickell argue that studies of urban growth machines tend to attribute "causal power to local political networks and thereby suggest . . . that spatial variations in urban fortunes are merely a byproduct of the geographies of charismatic city leadership or effective urban networking."[16]

And finally, Andrew Wood presents a closely analogous line of critique through his suggestion that

> regime and coalition approaches . . . assert the autonomy of urban or local politics as a legitimate focus for study without properly theorising the basis for that politics. Urban politics is simply politics that takes place in cities rather than being a politics of the city.[17]

I am sympathetic to these authors' concern to decipher the supralocal institutional parameters for urban development. However, I believe that their critique of "localism" in studies of US urban development requires more precise specification.

From my point of view, there are at least three analytically distinct ways in which an "urban" analysis can be described as localist:

- First, *ontological* localism entails the claim that local entities, institutions, or processes are in some sense autonomous from, and/or more causally significant than, entities, institutions, or processes organized at supralocal scales.
- Second, *methodological* localism is premised on the assumption that, even though the local may be intertwined with and conditioned by supralocal entities, institutions, or processes, it can and must be isolated from the latter for analytical purposes, as a means to decipher its "internal" structures and determinants. As indicated at the outset of this chapter, to the degree that this analytical maneuver

is accomplished without explicit justification or explanation, methodological localism may also entail a *naturalization* of the local scale, that is, its presentation as a pregiven or self-evident site for social-scientific inquiry.

- Third, *empirical* localism entails the choice of locally scaled entities, institutions, or processes, such as cities, as a focal point for research. It *may* (but does not necessarily) entail underlying ontological claims regarding the nature of the local, a naturalization of the local scale, and/or specific methodological claims about how the local should most appropriately be studied.

In these terms, it is evident that most proponents of urban regime theory and urban growth machine theory avoid ontological forms of localism. Neither theory is tied intrinsically to the claim that urban processes are ontologically autonomous from, or causally primary over, any other scale of political-economic life. Concomitantly, it seems equally clear that both theories do exemplify empirical forms of localism, for the simple reason that they focus on cities and/or local governance processes, which are justifiably viewed as a key site of politics. This empirical localism appears quite defensible because, as all of the contributors to this volume demonstrate, cities have long been important sites of political-economic activity and institutional experimentation in US history; it therefore makes sense to devote intellectual resources to their investigation.

This leaves open the considerably thornier question of methodological localism, which lies at the heart of the critiques raised by the authors quoted above. To what extent do urban regime theorists and/or urban growth machine theorists neglect to illuminate the supralocal contexts and determinants of urban development processes? To what extent do authors working in these traditions treat the local in isolation from broader political-economic institutions and forces? To what degree do they take the local for granted, as a pregiven or self-evident site? In short, to what extent does the (defensible) empirical localism of urban regime theory and urban growth machine theory slide into a (problematic) methodological localism?

Despite the lines of interpretation suggested in the passages quoted above, I believe that a close reading of the relevant literatures reveals a more complicated state of affairs, in which different authors working within each of the research traditions under discussion confront these issues in rather divergent ways. For instance, much of the case study-based literature applying regime theory and growth machine theory arguably does veer towards methodological localism. Extralocal institutional parameters are generally presupposed as the analysis focuses primarily or exclusively upon intralocal coalitions and conditions within a particular city. By contrast, macrohistorical or comparative deployments of these approaches are more likely to avoid methodological localism, or to embrace it only in a relatively circumscribed manner. A concern with multiple cities, longer term temporal frames, and/or divergent national contexts seems to attune scholars more explicitly to the broader spatial and institutional fields within which urban politics are constituted.

Yet, whatever their research agenda or methodological orientation, nearly all theorists of urban regimes and growth machines generally *do* appear to recognize—in more or less detail, and with greater or lesser degrees of reflexivity—the nationally specific "institutional envelope" within which local coalition formation has been configured in the US.[18] The key issue, then, is the extent to which such analysts address the *theoretical* significance of this empirical observation, in the context of their specific arguments about urban political-economic dynamics. The charge of methodological localism is only justified in cases in which the local is unreflexively presupposed and/or in which national institutional arrangements are relegated to an external "background" structure.

The National Institutional Parameters for Urban Development

The concern to avoid methodological localism stems from a relatively straightforward proposition: The "localness" of coalition formation and growth politics in US cities, as elsewhere, is not a pregiven empirical attribute of the coalitions in question, but a mediated *result* of national institutional structures and political geographies that, quite literally, create a space in which local growth coalitions may be established. Indeed, it can be argued that urban growth machines are "creatures" of the (national) state insofar as national political-institutional structures (1) play a major role in delineating the spatial units within which growth coalitions are formed and (2) establish a system of land-use regulations and restrictions that decisively condition local actors' degree of commitment to, and dependence upon, a growth agenda. It is essential, therefore, to situate the formation of urban growth coalitions not only within the changing worldwide spatial divisions of labor associated with capitalist production systems, but also within the evolving spatial divisions of regulation associated with national state structures.[19]

These claims can be illustrated with reference to the long-term role of the US national state in mediating the politics of urban development in US cities. For present purposes, I bracket the consequences of US cities' evolving positions in geoeconomic divisions of labor for local growth machine dynamics, a crucial issue that is now being actively and productively investigated by urban scholars.[20] Instead, my concern is to outline some of the nationally specific institutional arrangements—many of which were consolidated through intense intergovernmental and legal struggles during the course of the nineteenth century[21]—that have most directly facilitated the proliferation of urban growth machines within the US state apparatus:

- *The institutionalized power of private capital.* Private developers and real estate speculators in the US are given an inordinate authority to make decisions involving land uses, capital investment, and job locations. This tradition of urban privatism reflects an institutionally entrenched belief within the US state that the private sector is best equipped to assess investment opportunities and locations, to organize the technical expertise and management skills required for economic development, and to maximize the efficiency of economic operations. This situation is embodied in, and further exacerbated by, the lack of a major non-business political party in the US that resembles the social democratic, trade union-based parties that have played an important role in European local politics.[22] For these reasons, state policies in the US have long been mobilized quite extensively in order to create new avenues for privately organized capital investment within cities, whether through urban renewal programs, housing policies, urban development action grants, or a range of other federal, state, and local incentives policies. Such policies subsidize capital investment by minimizing private risk and covering key overhead costs, but generally without subjecting firms to extensive regulatory constraints or public controls. Additionally, urban regeneration programs in the US have prioritized capital-led initiatives to promote (re)investment over labor-oriented policies, often through the establishment of "partnerships" and other co-operative arrangements between public agencies and major business organizations.[23] This prioritization of market-led forms of economic governance on each level of the US state has been an essential institutional precondition for the proliferation of urban growth machines throughout the US urban system. Urban growth machines are less likely to form in national states that impose tighter regulatory constraints upon local land markets and local investment decisions.
- *The institutional structure of US federalism.* The federal structure of the US state dictates that political power and responsibilities are shared among national and subnational administrative levels. Whereas capital and labor are highly mobile between jurisdictions within the national economy, subnational political units such as states and the municipalities are allotted important regulatory powers, in policy areas such as public health, welfare, education, and economic development, which enable them directly to influence the locational patterns of industries and population. Although federal urban policies have existed since the New Deal, their implementation has been left largely to the states and the municipalities.[24] Moreover, in stark contrast to most other advanced industrial countries, there is no nation-wide spatial planning system in the US and there are few federal equalization or redistributive programs that promote the relocation of capital and population into declining, disadvantaged

areas.[25] Within this decentralized political system, then, the public agencies that can most immediately influence intra-national locational patterns (both of capital and of population) are the states and the municipalities.[26] Economic development initiatives by states and municipalities intensified considerably after World War II in conjunction with a wave of industrial relocations from the unionized, high-cost regions of New England to the non-unionized rural South. The world economic recession and the onset of deindustrialization during the late 1960s and early 1970s created a new urgency for external investment, particularly within crisis-stricken regions and cities. Accordingly, state-level and local economic development initiatives were massively intensified during this era and have subsequently become standard policy tools for subnational governments throughout the country.[27] The federalized territorial structure of the US state must therefore be viewed as a key institutional parameter within which local (and state-level) growth machines have been encouraged to form in US cities. Urban growth machines are less likely to form in national states in which municipalities lack such extensive powers autonomously to influence capital investment and to promote economic development.

- *Decentralized municipal finance.* Municipalities in the US are heavily dependent upon locally collected taxes—property taxes, in particular—in order to finance local public goods.[28] Although the structural dependence of the state upon capital for tax revenues is a universal feature of capitalist social formations, this dependency is articulated in a profoundly localized spatial form within the US intergovernmental system due to the highly decentralized character of local government finance.[29] It is this circumstance, above all, that underpins the propensity of local governments in the US to support property-developing growth machine strategies, for real estate provides a crucial source of local property tax revenues. The strategic importance of the property tax to local government revenue in the US has long underpinned a pattern of "municipal mercantilism" in which localities compete aggressively to encourage land uses within their jurisdictions that yield higher tax inputs.[30] Due to the impact of postwar intergovernmental transfer programs and post-1970s tax revolts, among other factors, the percentage of total municipal revenues that are derived from property taxes has declined steadily during the course of the twentieth century.[31] Nonetheless, this percentage still remains relatively high by international standards. Urban growth machines are much less likely to form in national states in which municipal revenues are not directly contingent upon local property values and local economic growth.

- *Bond markets and municipal credit ratings.* Since the mid-nineteenth century, US municipalities have relied extensively upon the private

bond market in order to raise credit for major capital improvements
in public infrastructure (schools, highways, bridges, hospitals, sports
stadiums, and the like). As of the late twentieth century, roughly one-
fourth of local spending in US cities was derived from the municipal
bond market, and was thus directly contingent upon the willingness
of individuals and corporations to invest in local public goods.[32]
This arrangement grants important powers and responsibilities to
private bond-rating agencies, such as Moody's Investor's Service and
Standard & Poor's Corporation, which determine the interest rates
for municipal bonds within different localities. As Alberta Sbragia
explains:

> The logic used by [municipal bond] lenders in assessing risk—and
> the criteria they deem important—is often expressed by groups
> (business and taxpayer groups especially) that see a city more as
> a financial enterprise than as a dispenser of services.[33]

Insofar as bond-rating agencies' assessments of the local business
climate directly impact the cost of municipal bonds, local politicians
have an important incentive to promote local economic development
and thus to support and participate within local growth machines.[34]
Urban growth machines are less likely to emerge in national states in
which private bond markets do not serve as an important source of
municipal credit and thus as a constraint upon local state activities
and budgetary priorities.

• *Suburbanization, metropolitan jurisdictional fragmentation, and
home rule.* Urban development in the US has long proceeded in
tandem with large-scale processes of suburbanization that have
continually thrust huge clusters of population and industry beyond
extant municipal boundaries.[35] Until the late nineteenth century,
suburban development was managed through municipal annexation
strategies, in which suburbs were incorporated into city cores through
the extension of municipal boundaries. During the first quarter of the
twentieth century, the principle of suburban autonomy—or "home
rule"—became increasingly predominant.[36] This permitted affluent
property-owners—as well as industrialists in search of non-unionized
labor—to create new municipal units within suburbanizing zones, to
introduce various local regulations (zoning laws, for instance) to
influence land uses within these jurisdictions, and thus to protect the
value of their real estate investments. During the postwar period, in
close conjunction with massive federal subsidies to suburbanites in
the form of highway policies and home mortgage tax breaks, jurisdictional fragmentation intensified dramatically within US metropolitan areas, leading in turn to a deepening polarization of urban
regions among countless governmental units competing for fiscal

resources and capital investment. Whatever the disagreements between public choice theorists and consolidationists regarding the relative efficiency of these arrangements, both schools concur in their observation that metropolitan jurisdictional fragmentation extends competition between governmental units onto a highly localized geographical scale. Whereas the institutional features of the US state mentioned previously serve primarily to generate a competition between cities located in different regions of the national economy, metropolitan jurisdictional fragmentation creates the geographical conditions for growth machines to compete for jobs and investments within city-regions as well. The result is an exceptional level of sociospatial and racial polarization within US metropolitan areas, as political boundaries become veritable walls segregating classes and racial/ethnic groups.[37] Yet, in a national political system in which regulatory capacities are decentralized, in which municipalities rely extensively upon locally collected taxes, and in which metropolitan areas are also fragmented among multiple administrative units, local governments would appear to have little choice but to continue to compete aggressively for the tax base both at inter-regional and intra-regional scales. In national states that do not permit such an extreme fragmentation of metropolitan areas under conditions of high fiscal decentralization, it is unlikely that growth machines oriented towards this type of zero-sum interlocality competition could form.

From this perspective, then, the politics of local growth machines are derived as much from nationally entrenched institutional structures and practices within the US state apparatus as from the "human activism" of place-entrepreneurs.[38] No matter how shrewd the rentiers within US urban growth machines might be in finding new ways to enhance the exchange-value of their real estate, a nationally specific configuration of state spatial organization has been an essential condition of possibility and active impetus for most of their activities. Interlocality competition among US cities must therefore be viewed as a key expression and embodiment of the peculiar formation of national state power that has underpinned each historical wave of capitalist industrialization and urbanization within the US space-economy. This framework of national state power may even entail an "iron cage" of sorts for local political actors insofar as only a fundamental reform of national political institutions could realistically interrupt the logic of aggressive growth machine competition upon which US urban development has long been grounded.[39]

Urban Fortunes and the Political Geographies of Urban Development

Against this background, the seminal contribution to the study of urban growth machines, Logan and Molotch's *Urban Fortunes*, can be critically reinterpreted as an historically nuanced account of how the politics of urban development have been intertwined with an entrenched but evolving matrix of national state spatial and institutional organization. Logan and Molotch are most centrally concerned with the political economy of *place*, understood as a localized land-use nexus that is dominated by rentiers and their political allies.[40] However, their analysis is filled with astute references to the variegated national contexts and consequences of urban growth machine activities. For this reason, a focused examination of the supralocal dimensions of Logan and Molotch's account can open up some useful insights into the political and institutional geographies of urban development in US history.

As noted, Logan and Molotch devote extensive analytical and empirical attention to the vicious battle among diverse local agents—rentiers, politicians, corporate executives, residents, and so forth—for control over urban land uses. They introduce national institutional structures into their analysis mainly in order to illuminate the external political and organizational environment in which such local power struggles unfold. Yet references to the national institutional envelope of land-use regulation and, by implication, growth machine formation, recur throughout Logan and Molotch's analysis, and the issue is examined in considerable detail in their chapter on "How Government Matters."[41] Indeed, even though *Urban Fortunes* is intended more as a work of urban political economy than as a contribution to state theory or political geography, it contains an incisive analysis of how urban growth machines have been conditioned by, and have in turn shaped, the changing spatialities of the US state.[42] On my reading, Logan and Molotch explore this issue on at least three distinct levels—*deep structures* of state space and land-use regulation; *historically specific regimes* of state space and land-use policy; and *conjunctural struggles* over state spatial organization and land-use policy.

1. *Deep structural features of US state space.* On various occasions, Logan and Molotch allude to many of the features of the US state structure that were summarized in the previous section. These entrenched features of state spatial and institutional organization— in particular, local fiscal and administrative autonomy, metropolitan jurisdictional fragmentation, and the principle of home rule—are said to have played a key role in engendering the formation of urban growth machines and the resultant logic of interlocality competition among cities throughout US history.[43]

2. *Historically specific regimes of land-use policy.* Logan and Molotch likewise discuss the ways in which, since the maturation of the industrial city, a range of federal and local state policies has been introduced in order to influence urban land uses.[44] The resultant regimes of state regulation have decisively molded the political geographies within which urban growth machine activities have been

organized by channeling certain types of development into particular locations, both within and among metropolitan areas. Although Logan and Molotch do not deploy the conceptual vocabulary of regimes, their account implicitly traces three broad and partially overlapping historical formations of federal and local land-use policy:

- *Nineteenth-century industrial urbanization.* During the early industrial era, local growth machines jockeyed to attract key federal infrastructural investments (railroads, canals, ports, and the like) and thus to enhance their strategic economic importance within the national economy.[45]

- *Twentieth-century suburbanization and metropolitan fragmentation.* A new formation of land-use policies emerged during the period of organized capitalism in the twentieth century in conjunction with planning reform movements, the expansion of suburbanization, and the increasing jurisdictional fragmentation of metropolitan areas. Here Logan and Molotch trace the role of restrictive local policies (zoning, growth control, environmental policies, and so forth) and federal incentives policies (housing and urban renewal, urban development action grants, block grants, tax increment redevelopment, and so forth) in influencing the geographies of land use and thus in creating a stratified urban and suburban hierarchy.[46] This policy regime, which was fully consolidated during the postwar period, provided national and local politicians with a wide array of techniques through which to influence the distribution of local land uses within their jurisdictions and thus "to serve the exchange interests of local elites."[47]

- *The 1980s and beyond.* More briefly, Logan and Molotch allude to the new historical formation of land-use policy that was being established during the 1980s, under Reagan's New Federalism, as they were writing their book. Under the Reagan administration, the federal government introduced various strategies that were intended to force localities to promote local economic development projects—for instance, by diminishing federal urban subsidies and thus tightening local budgetary constraints; by lowering federal standards in welfare, occupational safety, and environmental protection; and through the establishment of enterprise zones within distressed inner cities. These new arrangements are interpreted as federal attempts to circumvent the forms of local anti-growth resistance that had emerged during the preceding two decades.[48]

Whereas each of the aforementioned federal and local regimes of land-use policy facilitated and intensified the activities of local growth machines, Logan and Molotch suggest that the second and third regimes also met with stiff resistance from anti-development forces. Hence, their account implies that national state institutions have long constituted a central arena of political contestation in which the geographies of urban development are fought out. For, in the US context, national state institutions are responsible for establishing, enforcing, and modifying the system of land-use regulations within which growth machine activities are circumscribed.

3. *Conjunctural struggles over the spatial (re)configuration of political institutions.* Finally, Logan and Molotch emphasize the role of localized struggles over jurisdictional boundaries, land-use regulations, and intergovernmental relations in the context of the more entrenched structures of national state spatiality summarized above.[49] Growth machine interests may attempt to rework the organization of political space at national, metropolitan, and local scales in order to enhance the exchange-values of urban land. Meanwhile, anti-growth alliances may attempt to introduce federal and local state resources, regulations, and restrictions to counter such initiatives and thus to preserve place-based use-values. These struggles are always fought out in locally specific ways, which are shaped decisively by the strategies pursued and the alliances sought by the major actors involved. Issues such as the drawing of suburban jurisdictional boundaries, the configuration of zoning and growth-control regulations, and the form and distribution of federal urban subsidies thus become central stakes in political struggles over the geographies of urban and metropolitan development. In this sense, the spatial structures of the US state do not merely animate the activities of urban growth machines, but may themselves be reshaped through the struggles provoked by those activities.

In sum, the spatial and institutional configuration of the US state has long figured centrally in producing the urban scale as a strategic site for growth machine activities within the US political-economic landscape. Whereas Logan and Molotch's book is focused most directly on explaining how and why the city serves as a *growth machine*, the preceding discussion reveals that, in so doing, they also begin to provide an account of why it is that the *city* serves as a growth machine. The salient point here is thus not only that "the State actively sustains the commodity status of land" but that its political-geographical structures and institutional organization also serve (1) to distribute land uses across national, regional, and local scales and (2) to impel the formation of profoundly localized, growth-oriented territorial alliances.[50] Molotch's subsequent comparative work powerfully reinforces these points by showing how nationally specific intergovernmental structures, fiscal arrangements, and land-use regulations in the US, the UK, France, Italy, and Japan entail significantly divergent rules for rentier participation in local development, leading in turn to major cross-national differences in the character of urban politics.[51] Such comparative investigations make even more explicit an analytical proposition that is subtly interwoven throughout the text of *Urban Fortunes*: the very existence of urban growth machines, and their specific politico-institutional form, hinge upon national rule-regimes that regulate land uses at all spatial scales within the national territory.[52] This interpretation is not intended to diminish the importance of locally rooted political strategies and struggles, rather, it is presented as a basis for situating the latter within the (national) institutional envelope that defines their most basic political parameters. This reading of Logan and Molotch's work is summarized schematically in Figure 6.1.

Coda: "Urban" Development as a Multiscalar Political Strategy

Insofar as urban regime theory and urban growth machine theory have helped illuminate some of the key political dynamics associated with the production of urban space, they have contributed forcefully to the project of demystifying urban life under modern capitalism. However, due to the methodologically localist tendencies of at least some contributions to these research traditions, such approaches have only partially succeeded in defetishizing the putatively urban dimensions of what is generically labeled "urban politics." In this chapter, I have argued that the pro-duction of the urban cannot be adequately understood as a locally generated or self-contained outcome; it also represents a key moment within broader, multiscalar processes of capitalist development and state regulation. Therefore, the fetish character of the city can be fully demystified only through modes of analysis that reflexively illuminate the conditions of its production at *all* spatial scales—from worldwide spatial divisions of labor to national and subnational institutional geographies and regulatory strategies, and locally rooted political struggles.

The task of superseding the fetish character of the urban is hugely complex: It involves simultaneous, reflexive consideration of the diverse political-economic, institutional, and socio-technological processes, at various spatial scales, that have created a chronically yet unevenly urbaniz-ing world. In this chapter, we have touched upon only one dimension of this wide-ranging research agenda—the need to investigate the role of national political institutions and geographies in engendering a specifically urbanized (or localized) form of growth politics. I have suggested that, even though this issue is not of central theoretical concern to most students of urban growth machines, the paradigmatic work of Logan and Molotch contains neglected but extremely valuable methodological foundations for confronting it—including (1) a three-tiered conceptualization of how state structures impact urban land-use patterns and (2) the rudimentary

Structural factors Deeply entrenched features of state spatial organization in the USA that animate, channel and mediate growth machine activities and, more generally, interlocality competition	• The institutionally entrenched tradition of urban privatism provides business interests with major decision-making powers over urban land uses. • The institutional structure of US federalism provides relatively autonomous capacities to the states and the municipalities to engage in economic development initiatives and other strategies to influence the location of capital and population. • The decentralized system of local government finance underpins an extensive reliance of municipalities upon locally collected property taxes and private bond markets. • The jurisdictional fragmentation of metropolitan space and the principle of home rule further intensify interlocality competition between city cores and suburban peripheries.
Historically specific regimes of land-use policy Distinct but partially overlapping formations of federal and local policies to influence the geography of urban land uses and thus to enhance the exchange-values of places	19th century industrial urbanization • Growth machines compete for federal subsidies in order to construct large-scale transportation and communications infrastructures. 20th century suburbanization and metropolitan fragmentation • Growth machines mobilize a range of restrictive policies (such as zoning, growth control and environmental regulations) in order to influence local land uses within their jurisdictions. • The federal government mobilizes various incentives policies (such as urban renewal, public housing, urban development action grants, revenue sharing) in order to impel growth machines to pursue particular approaches to urban development. The 1980s and beyond • The federal government attempts to circumvent anti-growth opposition by imposing new fiscal pressures upon localities and by lowering federal standards in policy spheres such as welfare, occupational safety and environmental protection.
Conjunctural, localized forms of political contestation Strategies and struggles to enhance the use-values or exchange-values of specific places by modifying existent forms of state spatial and institutional organization	• Pro- and anti-growth forces contest urban/suburban jurisdictional boundaries at various spatial scales. • Pro- and anti-growth forces contest the form and geographical distribution of zoning and growth-control regulations at various spatial scales. • Pro- and anti-growth forces contest the form and geographical distribution of federal urban policies at various spatial scales.

Figure 6.1 State structures and the political geographies of urban growth machines in the US

elements of a periodization of the relationship between state structures and growth machine dynamics during the history of US urbanization since the late nineteenth century (see Figure 6.1).

This discussion of the national structuration of US urban development builds upon an emergent, highly informative literature on this issue that includes both historical investigations and contemporary analyses.[53] In drawing upon this work here, my central concern has been less to offer a comprehensive overview of the evolving national/urban interface in the US (on which see Chapter 8 by Ethington and Levitus, this volume), than to underscore its essential *epistemological* relevance to the very constitution of "urban politics" as a discrete research field. Indeed, the preceding discussion suggests that the subdisciplinary label "urban politics" is fundamentally misleading insofar as it implies that the urban represents a distinct or relatively autonomous institutional terrain. Against such constructions, the urban has been conceptualized here as a medium and expression of diverse, supralocal political-economic processes—including strategies of capital accumulation and state spatial regulation—which in turn shapes and reshapes such processes. This is one sense, I believe, in which Henri Lefebvre's suggestive conception of the urban as a site of "mediation" can be understood.[54] From this perspective, the urban maintains its "structured coherence"—and, thus, its epistemological intelligibility both in social science and in everyday life—only due to political strategies that attempt to establish it as such.[55] As we have seen, urban growth machines represent a paradigmatic example of such political strategies.

These epistemological and methodological considerations have particular salience in the current moment of worldwide capitalist development, in which the national structuration of urbanization processes is being profoundly recalibrated in conjunction with accelerated geoeconomic integration, an increasing neoliberalization of regulatory arrangements, processes of national state retrenchment, and the proliferation of regionally and locally specific forms of industrial crisis.[56] In the US context, "entrepreneurial" forms of urban policy have been superimposed upon the distributive land-use struggles and governance arrangements that prevailed during the industrial and Fordist–Keynesian accumulation regimes.[57] This intensified activation of local economic development strategies among US cities has been impelled in no small measure through the restructuring of national state spaces—from Reagan's New Federalism in the 1980s to various post-federal programs of welfare devolution and fiscal retrenchment in the 1990s.[58] A closely analogous proliferation of local economic initiatives, likewise animated through national politico-spatial transformations, has been occurring since the early 1980s in many Western European states.[59] Given the long commitment of European welfare states to redistributive regional policies that attempted to integrate local economies within national systems of governance, to equalize the national tax base, and thus to alleviate intra-national territorial inequalities, this "new urban politics" represents a rather striking developmental break.[60] In the face of these transformations, urban or local growth machines appear to have become an important politico-institutional feature on the otherwise still quite variegated landscapes of territorial regulation across much of post-Fordist Western Europe.[61] The analysis in this chapter suggests, however, that the consolidation of a new urban politics, both in the US and beyond, must be understood above all in relation to the (evolving) national institutional envelopes within which they are embedded. The political arenas of "urban" development are constituted through the making and remaking of national state spaces. There is indeed a politics of urban development, and this politics generally does involve local institutions, strategies, and struggles—but their conditions of possibility lie elsewhere.

Notes

1. See Maria Kaika and Erik Swyngedouw, "Fetishizing the Modern City: The Phantasmagoria of Urban Technological Networks," *International Journal of Urban and Regional Research* 24, no. 1 (2000): 120–138.
2. For a more detailed overview of the evolution of approaches to urban politics in postwar US political science, see Stone and Whelan's Chapter 5 in this volume. On methodological nationalism, see Andreas Wimmer and Nina Glick-Schiller, "Methodological Nationalism and Beyond: Nation-state Building, Migration and the Social Sciences," *Global Networks* 2, no. 4 (2002): 301–334; and John Agnew, "The Territorial Trap: The Geographical Assumptions of International Relations Theory," *Review of International Political Economy* 1, no. 1 (1994): 53–80.
3. Throughout this chapter, I use the terms "local" and "urban" interchangeably.
4. Foundational contributions to this research tradition include Henri Lefebvre, *The Urban Revolution*, trans. Robert Bononno (Minneapolis: University of Minnesota Press, 2003 [1970]); and David Harvey, *The Urban Experience* (Baltimore: Johns Hopkins University Press, 1989).
5. See Harvey, *The Urban Experience.*
6. For excellent overviews of these research traditions, see Mickey Lauria, ed., *Reconstructing Urban Regime Theory: Regulating Urban Politics in a Global Economy* (New York: Sage, 1997); and Andy Jonas and David Wilson, eds., *The Urban Growth Machine, Critical Perspectives, Two Decades Later* (Albany: State University of New York Press, 1999).
7. See John Logan and Harvey Molotch, *Urban Fortunes. The Political Economy of Place* (Berkeley and Los Angeles: University of California Press, 1987). For an analogous argument on the case of the Netherlands, see Pieter Terhorst and Jacques van de Ven, "The National Urban Growth Coalition in the Netherlands," *Political Geography* 14, no. 4 (1995): 343–361.
8. See Lauria, *Reconstructing Urban Regime Theory*; and Jonas and Wilson, *The Urban Growth Machine.*
9. See Andrew Jonas, "A Place for Politics in Urban Theory: The Organization and Strategies of Urban Coalitions," *Urban Geography* 13, no. 3 (1993): 282.
10. See Alan Harding, "Elite Theory and Growth Machines," in David Judge, Gerry Stoker and Hal Wolman, eds., *Theories of Urban Politics* (London: Sage, 1995), pp. 35–53.

11. See Stephen Elkin, *City and Regime in the American Republic* (Chicago: University of Chicago Press, 1987); Clarence Stone, *Regime Politics: The Governing of Atlanta, 1946–1988* (Lawrence: University Press of Kansas, 1989); and Clarence Stone and Heywood Sanders, eds., *The Politics of Urban Development* (Lawrence: University Press of Kansas, 1987).
12. See Elkin, *City and Regime;* and Stone, *Regime Politics.*
13. See Logan and Molotch, *Urban Fortunes.*
14. See Lauria, *Reconstructing Urban Regime Theory;* Jonas and Wilson, *The Urban Growth Machine;* and Stone and Sanders, *The Politics of Urban Development.*
15. Alan Harding, "Urban Regimes in a Europe of the Cities?," *European Urban and Regional Studies* 4, no. 4 (1997): 294.
16. Bob Jessop, Jamie Peck, and Adam Tickell, "Retooling the Machine: Economic Crisis, State Restructuring and Urban Politics," in Jonas and Wilson, eds., *The Urban Growth Machine,* p. 144.
17. Andrew Wood, "Questions of Scale in the Entrepreneurial City," in Tim Hall and Phil Hubbard, eds., *The Entrepreneurial City* (New York: John Wiley & Sons, 1998), p. 277.
18. See Murray Low, "Growth Machines and Regulation Theory: The Institutional Dimension of the Regulation of Space in Australia," *International Journal of Urban and Regional Research* 18 (1999): 451–469.
19. See Kevin Cox and Andrew Mair, "Locality and Community in the Politics of Local Economic Development," *Annals of the Association of American Geographers* 78, no. 2 (1988): 307–325.
20. For an overview, see Neil Brenner and Roger Keil, eds., *The Global Cities Reader* (New York: Routledge, 2006).
21. Alberta Sbragia, *Debt Wish: Entrepreneurial Cities, U.S. Federalism and Economic Development* (Pittsburgh: University of Pittsburgh Press, 1996).
22. Alan Harding, "Review Article: North American Urban Political Economy, Urban Theory and British Research," *British Journal of Political Science* 29 (1999): 673–698.
23. Peter Eisinger, "City Politics in an Era of Devolution," *Urban Affairs Review* 33, no. 3 (1988): 308–325.
24. John Mollenkopf, *The Contested City* (Princeton, NJ: Princeton University Press, 1983).
25. John Friedmann and Robin Bloch, "American Exceptionalism in Regional Planning, 1933–2000," *International Journal of Urban and Regional Research* 14, no. 4 (1990): 576–601.
26. See Peter Eisinger, *The Rise of the Entrepreneurial State* (Madison: University of Wisconsin Press, 1988); Sbragia, *Debt Wish.*
27. See Robert Goodman, *The Last Entrepreneurs. America's Regional Wars for Jobs and Dollars* (New York: Simon and Schuster, 1979); Eisinger, *The Rise of the Entrepreneurial State;* and Susan Clarke and Gary Gaile, *The Work of Cities* (Minneapolis: University of Minnesota Press, 1998).
28. See Dennis Judd and Todd Swanstrom, *City Politics: Private Power and Public Policy* (New York: Longman, 1998).
29. See Claus Offe, *Contradictions of the Welfare State* (Cambridge, MA: MIT Press, 1980).
30. See Sbragia, *Debt Wish.*
31. See Judd and Swanstrom, *City Politics.*
32. Ibid., p. 338.
33. Alberta Sbragia, "Politics, Local Government and the Municipal Bond Market," in Alberta Sbragia, ed., *The Municipal Money Chase: The Politics of Local Government Finance* (Boulder, CO: Westview Press, 1983), p. 102.

34. See ibid.
35. See Kenneth Jackson, *Crabgrass Frontier* (New York: Oxford University Press, 1985); and Robert Fishman, *Bourgeois Utopias* (New York: Basic Books, 1987).
36. See Anne Markusen, "Class and Urban Social Expenditure: A Marxist Theory," in William Tabb and Larry Sawers, eds., *Marxism and the Metropolis* (New York: Oxford University Press, 1979), pp. 90–112.
37. See Jackson, *Crabgrass Frontier*; and Markusen, "Class and Urban Social Expenditure."
38. See Logan and Molotch, *Urban Fortunes*, p. 11.
39. Recent advocates of such a reform include David Rusk, *Inside Game/Outside Game. Winning Strategies for Saving Urban America* (Washington, DC: Brookings Institution Press, 1998); Bruce Katz, "Enough of the Small Stuff: Toward a New Urban Agenda," *Brookings Review* 18, no. 3 (2000): 6–11; and Peter Dreier, John Mollenkopf, and Todd Swanstrom, *Place Matters: Metropolitics for the 21st Century*, second edition (Lawrence: University Press of Kansas, 2004).
40. See Logan and Molotch, *Urban Fortunes*, p. 12.
41. Ibid., pp. 147–199.
42. The concept of state space is elaborated at greater length in Neil Brenner, *New State Spaces: Urban Governance and the Rescaling of Statehood* (New York: Oxford University Press, 2004); and Neil Brenner, Bob Jessop, Martin Jones, and Gordon MacLeod, eds., *State/Space: A Reader* (Boston: Blackwell, 2002).
43. See Logan and Molotch, *Urban Fortunes*, pp. 2, 27, 147–151, 178–180.
44. Ibid., pp. 147–199.
45. Ibid., pp. 52–57.
46. Ibid., pp. 153–199.
47. Ibid., p. 178.
48. Ibid., pp. 244–247.
49. Ibid., p. 37.
50. Ibid., p. 27.
51. See Harvey Molotch, "Urban Deals in Comparative Perspective," in John Logan and Todd Swanstrom, eds., *Beyond the City Limits: Urban Policy and Economic Restructuring in Comparative Perspective* (Philadelphia: Temple University Press, 1990), pp. 175–198; Harvey Molotch and Serena Vicari, "Three Ways to Build: The Development Process in the United States, Japan and Italy," *Urban Affairs Quarterly* 24, no. 2 (1988): 188–214.
52. The concept of a rule-regime is proposed by Jamie Peck, "Political Economies of Scale: Fast Policy, Interscalar Relations and Neoliberal Workfare," *Economic Geography* 78, no. 3 (July 2002): 332–360. Further elaborations can be found in Neil Brenner, Jamie Peck, and Nik Theodore, "Variegated Neoliberalization: Geographies, Modalities, Pathways," unpublished manuscript.
53. See Gerald Frug, *City Making: Building Cities without Building Walls* (Princeton, NJ: Princeton University Press, 2002); Dreier, Mollenkopf, and Swanstrom, *Place Matters*; Clarke and Gaile, *Work of Cities*; Eisinger, *The Entrepreneurial State*; as well as Mollenkopf's classic text, *The Contested City*.
54. See Lefebvre, *The Urban Revolution*. See also, more recently, Ash Amin and Nigel Thrift, *Cities: Reimagining the Urban* (London: Polity, 2002); and John Allen, Allan Cochrane, and Doreen Massey, *Rethinking the Region* (London: Routledge, 1998).
55. See Harvey, *The Urban Experience*.

56. See Brenner, *New State Spaces*.
57. See Harvey, *The Urban Experience*.
58. See Clarke and Gaile, *Work of Cities*; and Eisinger, *The Entrepreneurial State*.
59. See, for example, Margit Mayer, "Post-Fordist city politics," in Ash Amin, ed., *Post-Fordism: A Reader* (Cambridge, MA: Blackwell, 1994), pp. 316–337; Aram Eisenschitz and Jamie Gough, *The Politics of Local Economic Development* (New York: Macmillan, 1993); and Paul Cheshire and Ian Gordon, "Territorial Competition and the Predictability of Collective (In)action," *International Journal of Urban and Regional Research* 20, no. 3 (1996): 383–399.
60. See Brenner, *New State Spaces*.
61. See Alan Harding, "Urban Regimes and Growth Machines: Towards a Cross-national Research Agenda," *Urban Affairs Quarterly* 29, no. 3 (1994): 356–382. It should be noted, however, that the agenda of many urban growth machines in the post-Fordist period appears to have expanded significantly, both in the US and elsewhere. While property values still matter immensely to key players in local territorial alliances, the project of increasing ground rents is now being intertwined more tightly with initiatives to construct highly specialized, innovative local and regional milieux in which specific types of globally competitive firms may prosper. Such strategies to promote the conditions for local territorial competitiveness, which I have elsewhere termed "urban locational policies," may be pursued in a variety of ways, depending upon their target variables—such as allocative efficiency, growth efficiency, or innovative efficiency—as well as upon their social base within local class relations (see Brenner, *New State Spaces*; Eisenschitz and Gough, *The Politics of Local Economic Development*; and Bob Jessop, Kurt Nielson, and Ove Pedersen, "Structural Competitiveness and Strategic Capacities: Rethinking State and International Capital," in Jerzy Hausner, Bob Jessop, and Kurt Nielsen, eds., *Institutional Frameworks of Market Economies* (Brookfield, VT: Avebury, 1993), pp. 23–44. In this sense, the place-based exchange-values emphasized by Logan and Molotch can no longer be understood purely in terms of property values; today they encompass a broader spectrum of factors and conditions that impact what might be termed "place-competitiveness" (see Jessop, Peck, and Tickell, "Retooling the Machine").

7 Urban Space and American Political Development

Identity, Interest, Action

Clarissa Rile Hayward

This chapter asks: "What is special about urban space as a site of American political development?" As Karen Orren and Stephen Skowronek note, "sites" of development need not be physical places. Defining a site as "a prior political ground of practices, rules, leaders, and ideas, all of which are up and running," Orren and Skowronek suggest that a policy network can be a site, for instance, as can a political institution.[1] But when the relevant site of development *is* a physical place, this chapter's principal claim is, that makes a difference. Taking seriously the view—adopted by a wide range of social and political theorists—that space is not just "where politics happens," a "container" within which social and political relations are situated, it makes the case that spaces and places are "prior grounds" of a distinctive type, which significantly shape social and political relations of power.[2]

The chapter focuses, in particular, on the spatialization of racial hierarchy in the contemporary metropolis, and on its relation to three concerns that have been central to the study of American political development: the construction and the maintenance of identities (in the first section), the definition of interests (second section), and the enabling and the constraining of political action (third section). At the same time, it focuses on three properties of space/place that make it distinctive as a site of development. The first is the materiality of physical spaces and places: the fact that people experience them corporeally. This property lends space a distinctive capacity as a mechanism for maintaining and for reproducing *identity*. The second trait is the legal status places enjoy as property: the fact that, in capitalist regimes, they typically are owned and bought and sold in the form of commodities. This property lends place a distinctive capacity as a mechanism for shaping *interests*. The third and final trait is space's relation to practices of governance, and in particular to practices of democratic governance. That governance is spatially grounded, even as relations of power transcend the boundaries defining particular spaces and particular places, lends space a distinctive capacity as a mechanism for shaping political *action*. Together, this chapter argues, these traits enable spaces and places to function as sites of development that produce and maintain relatively durable hierarchies, including, but not limited to, relatively durable racial hierarchies.

Space/Place and Identity

The first of the three properties on which the chapter focuses, then, is the *materiality* of space and place: the fact that people experience physical spaces and places with their bodies. This materiality lends place and space distinctive capacities as mechanisms for the maintenance and for the reproduction of identity.

Why? Let us begin with the claim, advanced by theorists such as Alasdair MacIntyre, Paul Riceour, and Charles Taylor, that identities are narrative in their structure.[3] For an action to have meaning, these theorists underscore, it must be interpreted. For interpretations of multiple actions by a given actor to be rendered intelligible—to be related in some comprehensible way, both to one another and to the agent who is defined as their author—they must be placed in a narrative context: a story about "who I am" as a unique individual. The same holds for collective identities. People experience what it is that is distinctive about the social collectivities with which they identify as narratives about "who we are" in a social sense: about "our" defining characteristics (as Americans, for example, or as African-Americans) about our origins, our history, our values, and our ends.[4]

When a constructed identity not only is circulated as a story, however—when it also is *institutionalized* in a spatial form—then it acquires a resilience it would not otherwise enjoy. Consider one example of a spatial form that institutionalizes a constructed identity: the so-called "black" American ghetto. Ghettos were forged in the US over the course of the last century by private actors (such as land speculators, developers, and realtors) and also by agents of the American state, who engaged in practices such as racial zoning and enforcing racially restrictive covenants.[5]

The former practice is perhaps the more notorious of the two. In 1910, Baltimore was the first American city to pass a law aimed specifically at segregating and isolating by race. Over the next 7 years, other cities followed suit.[6] But the latter practice—the use of racially restrictive covenants—was the longer-lasting, and the more significant. Beginning near the turn of the century, and through its middle decades, developers wrote racial restrictions into the deeds of countless properties in targeted subdivisions, and in particular urban and suburban neighborhoods. They did so specifically with a view to creating—and to marketing—racial exclusivity.[7] In 1928, when the Institute for Research in Land Economics and Public Utilities conducted the first large-scale study of deed restrictions, it found that about half of the deeds analyzed included some form of racial restriction.[8] By mid-century, some 80 percent of vacant land in Chicago, Los Angeles, and suburban New York was governed by racial covenants. In St Louis alone, 559 city blocks were so governed, with covenants particularly common in areas near the boundaries of majority-black neighborhoods.[9]

These actions—actions that, together, helped construct the "black" ghetto—were informed by a racial identitarian story, which circulated widely in the early decades of the twentieth century. That story was constructed in response to major demographic shifts of the time, especially the Great Migration of Southern blacks to Northern cities starting around the time of World War I, and the dramatic reduction in the number of Southern and Eastern European immigrants to those same cities following the Immigration Act of 1924.[10] Now it was not Italians or other so-called "new immigrants," but African-Americans who took the lowest paying and the least desirable jobs. Now it was not "foreigners," but black Americans, who moved into the oldest and the most dilapidated housing. Now it was not principally Southern and Eastern Europeans, but black migrants from the Southern states whom business owners exploited as "scabs" when their workers went on strike.

In response, established residents of Northern cities began to revise the racial stories that they told, and to do so in at least three significant ways. First, they began to de-emphasize putatively racial divisions among those whom eventually they would come to regard as "*white* ethnics," and to focus their attention on what they increasingly understood to be a black/white racial divide.[11] Second, they revised, in light of the conditions of industrial urbanism, the list of traits and behaviors that they claimed biological race caused. These now included, not just scabbing (which was racialized as "turning nigger"), but also failure to maintain the physical condition of one's residence, and more generally an incapacity for home ownership and an unfitness for admission to high status (white) neighborhoods.[12] Third and finally, they now suggested—and this even in cities where, for decades, blacks and whites had lived side by side—that the proper relation between "the races" was one of strict separation. Humans, the claim was, naturally congregate with those of their own race. Deviations from this pattern threaten both neighborhood stability and property values. Therefore, positive steps should be taken to correct them.[13]

This racial story was told, and it was re-told on multiple levels, through the early decades of the twentieth century. It was circulated among business elites—among real estate agents, for instance, and real estate lenders and appraisers, and also among elected officials and members of the nascent profession of city planners. It was circulated in popular discourse, as well, for example in local newspapers and in magazines such as *Good Housekeeping*, which wholeheartedly celebrated homes in racially exclusive residential communities.[14]

A story such as this one can racialize people's understandings of their social identities. But it can do so effectively only if and to the extent that people find it compelling. Every time an identity-story is told, every time an identity-story is re-told, it is opened up to (potential) challenge from its audience. With every telling, that is to say, a narrative of collective identity invites questions. "What is a 'black' person," for example, and "how do you know that blacks and whites should not live side by side?" An identity that circulates in narrative form is inherently vulnerable to contestation and to change.

This particular narrative—this racial identitarian narrative—which was so widely circulated in the early decades of twentieth century, *was* contested, and it *was* challenged, so much so that, by mid-century, it had been almost entirely discredited. By the 1940s, narratives of race as biological difference—which had been rationalized by providing an allegedly scientific basis for the differential treatment of persons based on membership in racial categories—had been decisively undermined at the level of scientific discourse. Over the next two decades, what is more, the normative stories that had served to justify and to legitimize racial hierarchies, also came under siege. If race is a collective identity-story, then by century's end, it was widely acknowledged that it was not a very good story.

But race lived on. One important reason race lived on, is that prior to its being discredited, this early twentieth century narrative of racial identity and difference was, quite literally, built into the urban and suburban fabric. It was institutionalized in rules and in laws (such as racial zoning laws). It was built into material forms, such as racialized urban and suburban spaces. It was (to borrow a term from Pierre Bourdieu's lexicon) "objectified," made into object form. Or in other words, made into material form.[15]

Bourdieu illustrates his notion of the objectification of identitarian assumptions in material form with the examples of, on the one hand, the division between the Kabyle house and the public world (the assembly, the field, the market), and on the other, the division of spaces interior to the house itself.[16] In constructing such divisions, his claim is, (in building walls, in relegating particular persons and particular activities to one side or the other), people create in material form expressions of both identity-categories and also the social meanings they attach to those categories. They designate specifically "male" spaces, for example, and they make these the spaces of politics, and of production and exchange. They designate "female" spaces, and they make these the spaces of domestic work, and of sex and reproduction. As social actors engage in practical activities in spaces such as these (as they cook and care for the sick and the dying in the Kabyle household, or, to return to the present example, as they work and drive and shop in the white suburban enclave), they learn and they re-learn *extra-discursively* the meanings—the beliefs, the values, the perceptual and classificatory claims—that have been built into those spaces.

If people continue to act as if they believe in race, if people continue to experience the social world through a racial lens, this is not the case not simply because *they are told racial identity-stories*. It is also because they learn racial identities *practically*, through everyday contact with the material forms in which these stories have been objectified. When people learn to function as competent social actors in urban and suburban spaces that have been racialized—in "black" ghettos, in racially exclusive "white" enclaves, or for that matter in those urban neighborhoods designated "Chinatowns"—part of what they learn is not the *story* of race so much as racial "common sense."[17]

Space/Place and Interest

The materiality of space, then, lends it a capacity to help maintain constructed identities. This is the first of the three traits that work together to make space distinctive as a site of development. The second is its status as property: the fact that, in capitalist regimes, places—both land and also the structures people build on land—typically are owned, and typically are bought and sold as commodities.[18] That place takes the form of property lends it a distinctive capacity as a mechanism for shaping interests. Even more specifically (and to continue with the American urban example), this quality of space interacts with its materiality to make it an important mechanism for racializing interests.

Recall the racial identitarian story cited above. This story, during the years when it was circulated, had an important economic dimension. Some racial groups, it asserted, pose a grave threat to property values. Because their racially rooted attributes cause the deterioration of the places in which they live, it is risky to invest in those areas of a city to which they have access, or to which they likely will in the foreseeable future. This economic corollary of the racial identity-story was told countless times in the early decades of the century, at the conferences, in the journal articles, in the text books of the increasingly professionalized real estate industry. According to one influential text, for instance:

> Among the traits and characteristics of people which influence land values, racial heritage and tendencies seem to be of paramount importance. The aspirations, energies, and abilities of various groups in the composition of the population will largely determine the extent to which they develop the potential value of the land.[19]

To cite just one more example, another mid-century text book, in a question for students of real estate that was appended at the end of a chapter, asked: "In which of the following neighborhoods would you prefer to invest?" Neighborhood A the text characterized as "zoned for single-family residences. No deed restrictions are in force," while in Neighborhood B, it posited, "Deed restrictions have been established controlling the type of houses which may be built and restricting occupancy to members of the Caucasian race." Neighborhood B was the "correct" answer.[20]

The narrative that linked investment risk to race was not only taught to real estate professionals in their classrooms. It was also written into the Code of Ethics of the National Association of Real Estate Boards (NAREB), according to which: "A Realtor should never be instrumental in introducing into a neighborhood a character of property or occupancy, members of any race or nationality, or any individuals whose presence will clearly be detrimental to property values in the neighborhood."[21]

In the wake of the Great Depression, this narrative was institutionalized by New Deal Agencies, such as the Home Owners Loan Corporation (HOLC) and the Federal Housing Administration (FHA), which have been widely credited with nationalizing the practice known as "redlining."[22] The latter agency, for instance, clearly advised in its *Underwriting Manual* that racial segregation in the surrounding neighborhood was a necessary condition for a favorable rating for a property that was to receive a federal loan guarantee. In its 1938 *Underwriting Manual*, the FHA specified that neighborhood ratings should reflect the presence of "Adverse Influences," which it defined to include "incompatible racial and social groups." It specifically recommended the use of racially restrictive covenants to promote segregation.[23] In the postwar years, the FHA, together with the Veteran's Administration (VA) channeled the vast majority of state-backed mortgages to the racially exclusive white suburbs that were built around American cities at that time. From the start of the program through to the early 1960s—a period during which the FHA insured mortgages on close to one-third of new housing in the United States—African-Americans received less than 2 percent of state-insured mortgages. Even these, it is worth noting, went disproportionately to segregated areas in the American South.[24]

Programs such as these affected people's interests profoundly. The FHA and VA mortgage programs, for instance, because they lowered down payments and interest rates, and because they significantly extended amortization periods, made it possible for many middle- and working-class white Americans to purchase private homes for the very first time. It is hardly an exaggeration, however, to say they did so *on the condition that those homes be sited in racially exclusive white neighborhoods.* They thus not only *affected* people's interests, but further helped to *create* a new constellation of racialized interests, which centered principally on home ownership and on property values.

One might think of interests such as these as interests in what the legal theorist Cheryl Harris has called "whiteness as property."[25] Whiteness in this country, Harris's claim is, accords people legally protected privileges they would not enjoy if not for their racial status. She offers the examples of access to the very best schools and the very best jobs. Whiteness as property, through much of the last century, the present example suggests, enabled the racially privileged to reap the material benefits of state-subsidized home ownership in a dual housing market.

It is worth underscoring, however, that prior to their construction, the making of "white places" was *not* necessarily in the interests of all to whom white racial status eventually would be ascribed. Racial segregation and urban disinvestment in the early and the middle decades of the last century constrained, not only the housing choices of African-Americans, but also those of so-called "ethnic whites." In many instances, the fear of racialized others that racist narratives incited prompted Italian-Americans, Irish-Americans, Polish-Americans, and others to abandon neighborhoods in which they had invested substantial resources and had established important social networks.

Indeed, through the early decades of the century, new immigrants had good reason to forge alliances, *not* with the unambiguously white, but with African-American migrants from the Southern states. They had good reason, that is, to ally themselves against the privileged, and with those who, like them, had everything to gain from challenging race- and class-based social hierarchies. David Roediger, cited in previous notes, highlighting multiple instances of cross-racial labor organization in the early decades of the century, conceives of coalition-building around white supremacy in that era as a kind of collective action problem.[26] It was a nontrivial challenge, he emphasizes, for those who would promote racial exclusivity as a marker of value, to induce home owners to agree to sign away their rights to sell to a large class of potential buyers. In urban neighborhoods that bordered nascent ghettos—neighborhoods where covenants typically were very heavily employed—many property owners were recent Southern and Eastern European immigrants. Winning their cooperation was not, in Roediger's words, compatible with "[f]ine distinctions as to which European groups were most desirable."[27]

Hence, although some covenants excluded long lists of groups, many followed what, from the point of view of those aiming to market racial exclusivity relatively widely, would have been the dominant strategy: they excluded only those on the bottom of the American racial hierarchy. From the point of view of new immigrants, one can think about the strategic context they faced at that point in time as exhibiting the logic of a collective action dilemma. They may have stood to gain the *most* from a radical challenge to the racial hierarchy. But a leveling of—even any substantial change to—that hierarchy, which would have required relatively enduring inter-group coordination and cooperation, would have been difficult to effect. Hence when these bearers of "in-between" racial status received overtures to join whites—overtures accompanied by the promise of the benefits of whiteness as property—they defected.

It is by now commonplace to note that the phenomenon known as "white flight" was not simply the product of the irrational prejudices of individual home buyers. Nor, I want to underscore, was it an outcome that followed inexorably from the fixed interests of property owners. Instead, "white flight" was an instrumentally rational response to a contingent set of interests: interests that themselves were constructed by politically influential private actors (such as NAREB) and by democratic state actors (such as the HOLC and the FHA).

Space/Place and Action

The third trait that makes space distinctive as a site of political development is its relation to practices of governance, and in particular to practices of democratic governance. Power relations transcend the boundaries people construct when they demarcate places: nation-state boundaries, for instance, or boundaries defining urban and suburban municipalities. Yet at the level of the nation-state, as well as at the sub- and the trans-national levels, political jurisdictions typically are defined territorially. That territory grounds most practices of democratic governance, even as power relations transcend territorial boundaries, lends space a distinctive capacity for shaping political action.[28] In the context of American cities and their suburbs, this quality of space enables those who are privileged to act in ways that concentrate collective problems in places that form the bottom of spatial hierarchies. It enables them to do so, what is more, while denying some people whom those problems profoundly affect the political capacity to address them.

By "collective problems," I mean problems that are collective in a causal sense, such as the very high rates of joblessness and the concentrated poverty that characterize many older central cities in the US. When black Southern migrants moved to Northern and Midwestern cities, their ghettoization strained an already-strained urban infrastructural and social service delivery system. The direction of private and public investment away from older cities, to their suburbs, and also to the newer cities of the American South and Southwest, led the former to bleed, not just their wealthy and their middle-class residents, but also the manufacturing firms that had been so crucial to their economic well-being.[29] Joblessness rose in central cities. With joblessness came poverty, and with concentrated poverty, a host of problems that taxed city schools, police, health systems, and other public services.

Of course, this centrifugal movement of people and of capital would not have affected cities so dramatically had they been able to expand their boundaries to keep pace with decentralization. But municipal incorporation laws had been liberalized by that time, and an arsenal of new legal weapons helped to protect incorporated municipalities against annexation.[30] Hence the decentralization of residents and businesses decimated urban tax bases. Faced simultaneously with shrinking revenues and with heightened service demands, cities confronted what, increasingly, was identified as an "urban crisis."[31] In the postwar decades, they found themselves inadequate to the task of addressing the pressing problems they confronted: problems the roots of which lay well beyond their borders.

The dramatic decline in manufacturing jobs in the postwar American city thus was not caused by the decisions and the actions of city residents and city officials alone. Rather, it was caused by decisions made and actions taken well beyond city boundaries. Similarly, the decline of urban tax bases that accompanied the postwar decentralization of businesses and residences was not caused only or principally by those who lived in and/or those who governed American cities. Nor was the stress that was put on urban school systems and other public services by the influx of rural migrants to urban centers. Nor was the shortage of affordable, open housing in many of the country's major metropolitan regions. These and related problems were caused by a range of actions that were taken beyond city boundaries, including the actions of the private agencies (such as NAREB) and the federal agencies (such as the FHA and the HOLC) cited above.

People who are privileged by extant power relations, however (the wealthy and the middle class, those who are constructed as "white"), can—and they often do—act in ways that localize these problems on the "other" side of the territorial boundaries that define political jurisdictions. The privileged can—and they often do—retreat to relatively homogeneous incorporated suburban municipalities. There they can engage in exclusionary zoning practices, for example by requiring large lot sizes and set-backs or by disallowing multifamily housing. They can opt out of supporting public housing, as well, and they can even opt out of supporting public transportation within the boundaries of their municipalities. They can pool their tax monies, and they can use these to provide schooling and other public services, which they can make available to residents only.

The privileged thus can transform what are, in a causal sense, collective problems, into the problems of people who live and work in older cities, and especially in the ghettoized sections of those cities. They can make decisions that profoundly affect people who do not reside in their municipalities, while effectively excluding them from participating in the processes through which those decisions are made.

In the American urban context, this third quality of space (its imbrication with practices of democratic governance) interacts with the first two (with its materiality and with its status as property), not merely to localize, but also to *racialize* collective problems.[32] Analysis of discourse on the so-called "urban crisis," for example, shows that by the time of the riots of the mid-1960s that crisis was interpreted and debated, across the ideological spectrum, in largely racial terms.[33] By 1967, Nathan Glazer could confidently assert that "the Negro Problem" was the "most decisive of the social problems that we think of when we consider the urban crisis."[34] That same year, Irving Kristol declared that "what we call the 'urban crisis' is mostly just a euphemism for problems *created by* the steady influx of Southern Negroes into Northern and Western cities."[35]

Note Kristol's (implausible) causal claim: the migration of African-Americans caused the urban crisis. This and similar comments, which are prevalent in both elite and popular discourse about "urban decline," illustrate how siting in the "black" ghetto what were, in a causal sense, collective problems had the effect of transforming them, in an experiential sense, into "black" problems.

Conclusion

This chapter has highlighted (to return to Orren and Skowroneck's terminology) the *durability* of the racialization of space. Despite non-trivial challenges to racial identity-stories—both scientific and also normative challenges to the racist narratives that were in circulation at the turn of the twentieth century—racial hierarchy continues to shape political conflict, and political possibility, in the twenty-first century American metropolis.

It is worth underscoring, however, that space/place as a site of development not only can indurate, but also can *legitimize* racial hierarchy. Place's status as property can make racial inequalities appear to be no more than the product of the exercise of market freedoms. At the same time, the grounding of democratic governance in territory can make racial inequalities appear to be no more than the product of the exercise of democratic freedoms. When racial inequalities are translated into spatial inequalities, in other words, they are lent a veneer of innocence.

Students of American political development can inform efforts to challenge and to change such inequalities by removing that veneer. Challenging inegalitarian racial relations, the argument above suggests, requires disturbing not only racist and other discriminatory identity-stories, but also the spatial forms in which those stories have been objectified. Challenging inegalitarian relations structured around material interests requires, similarly, changing the uneven spatial distribution of the benefits and burdens of urban and suburban growth. Finally, challenging inegalitarian limits on the capacity for political action requires institutional reforms that ensure that governance tracks power relations, even crossing territorial boundaries when power does.

Space is not "where politics happens" so much as a crucial site of political development. The challenge for political egalitarians is, first, to understand *how space shapes relations of power*, and then to devise political institutions that prompt it to do so differently.

Notes

1. Karen Orren and Stephen Skowronek, *The Search for American Political Development* (New York: Cambridge University Press, 2004), p. 20.
2. This claim is advanced by Henri Lefebvre, *The Production of Space*, trans. Donald Nicholson-Smith (Oxford: Blackwell, 1991). See also (among others) David Harvey, *Justice, Nature, and the Geography of Difference* (Cambridge, MA: Blackwell, 1996); Doreen Massey, *Space, Place, and Gender* (Minneapolis: University of Minnesota Press, 1994); Edward Soja, *Postmodern Geographies: The Reassertion of Space in Critical Social Theory* (London and New York: Verso, 1980); and Edward Soja, *Thirdspace: Journeys to Los Angeles and Other Real-and-Imagined Places* (Cambridge, MA and Oxford: Blackwell, 1996).
3. See, for instance, Alasdair MacIntyre, *After Virtue*, second edition (Notre Dame, IN: University of Notre Dame Press, 1984); Paul Riceour, "Narrative Identity," *Philosophy Today* (Spring 1991): 73–81; and Charles Taylor, *Sources of the Self: The Making of Modern Identity* (Cambridge, MA: Harvard University Press, 1989).
4. Rogers Smith, *Stories of Peoplehood: The Politics and Morals of Political Membership* (Cambridge: Cambridge University Press, 2003).
5. For a more detailed discussion, see Clarissa Hayward, "The Difference States Make: Democracy, Identity, and the American City," *American Political Science Review* 97, no. 4 (November 2003): 501–514.
6. These include Atlanta, Dallas, and St Louis. In 1917, the US Supreme Court ruled racial zoning in violation of the Fourteenth Amendment (*Buchanan v. Warley* 245 US 60).
7. Robert Fogelson, *Bourgeois Nightmares: Suburbia 1870–1930* (New Haven: Yale University Press, 2005).
8. The study examined deeds for eighty-two subdivisions throughout the United States, and two in Canada. Helen Monchow, *The Use of Deed Restrictions in Suburban Development* (Chicago: Institute for Research in Land Economics and Public Utilities, 1928).
9. David Roediger, *Working Toward Whiteness: How America's Immigrants Became White* (New York: Basic Books, 2005), p. 176.
10. I do not mean to imply that this early twentieth-century racial narrative represented a radical break with the past. To the contrary, it built upon and extended a nineteenth-century narrative that can be traced at least as far back as Georges Cuvier's claim in *Le Regne Animal* that human races are analogous to animal species. Races are permanent biological types (this story goes), which cause differences in behaviors, attributes, abilities, and dispositions. A natural hierarchy exists among the races of humankind, with whites, at the top of that hierarchy, by nature dominant, and blacks, at the bottom, subordinate. See Michael Banton, *Racial Theories*, second edition (Cambridge: Cambridge University Press, 1998), especially ch. 3.
11. David Roediger, among others, has shown that, at the turn of the twentieth century, Southern and Eastern European immigrants to the United States, along with American Jews, occupied an "in-between" place in the country's racial hierarchy. Although they were not regarded as "black," "new immigrants" were not understood to be fully and unambiguously "white." The immigration restrictions of 1924—quotas for legal immigration to the US that were based on would-be immigrants' nations of origin—made possible for the first time in the twentieth century a story of pan-European racial identity that would not threaten those who feared the "mongrelization" of the

American nation. It was at this point that dominant narratives began to distinguish "race"—understood to be permanent, and to be rooted in biology—from what, by mid-century, would be commonly known as "ethnicity"—a form of social difference understood to be based in voluntarily shared practices, and in culture. Roediger, *Working Toward Whiteness*.

12. Historians of the era have documented a fairly constant pattern: When Southern blacks moved to Northern cities, entering relations of power that severely constrained what they could do and what they could be, whites racialized the behavioral regularities these relations produced, circulating stories of race as their *cause*. For instance, because many landlords, real estate agents, and home sellers refused to rent or to sell to black migrant families, the latter were constrained to compete in a dual housing market for over-crowded, over-priced, and often physically deteriorated rental units. Black migrants were excluded from relatively high-paying jobs and discriminated against in lending, as well. Hence it was exceedingly difficult for them to get the capital necessary to purchase their own homes and/or to make much-needed repairs. Whites then racialized the patterns their discriminatory actions produced. See Thomas Sugrue, *Origins of the Urban Crisis: Race and Inequality in Postwar Detroit* (Princeton, NJ: Princeton University Press, 1996).

13. Stanley McMichael and R.F. Bingham's early and influential real estate text stated this position unequivocally: "There is a natural inclination of the colored people to live together in their own communities," McMichael and Bingham wrote. "With the increase in colored people coming to many Northern cities," the authors continued, "they have overrun their old districts and swept into adjoining ones or passed to other sections and formed new ones. This naturally has had a decidedly detrimental effect on land values, for few white people . . . care to live near them." McMichael and Bingham's suggestion for correcting this problem was straightforward: "Frankly, rigid segregation seems to be the only manner in which the difficulty can be effectively controlled." Stanley McMichael and R.F. Bingham, *City Growth and Values* (Cleveland, OH: Stanley McMichael, 1923).

14. See the discussion of a series of articles in the mid-1930s emphasizing the desirability and importance of restrictions in Charles Abrams, *Forbidden Neighbors: A Study of Prejudice in Housing* (New York: Harper and Brothers, 1955), pp. 146–147.

15. Pierre Bourdieu, *Outline of a Theory of Practice*, trans. Richard Nice (Cambridge: Cambridge University Press, 1977).

16. Ibid., ch. 3.

17. Kay Anderson, "The Idea of Chinatown: The Power of Place and Institutional Practice in the Making of a Racial Category," *Annals of the Association of American Geographers* 77, no. 4 (December 1987): 580–598.

18. See John Logan and Harvey Molotch, *Urban Fortunes: The Political Economy of Place* (Berkeley: University of California Press, 1987), ch. 2.

19. Frederick Babcock, *The Valuation of Real Estate* (New York: McGraw, 1932), p. 86, cited in Rose Helper, *Racial Policies and Practices of Real Estate Brokers* (Minneapolis: University of Minnesota Press, 1969). Helper, surveying mid-century real estate text books, appraising manuals, and NAREB publications, finds that almost all endorse this story of the relation between race and property values.

20. Arthur Weimer and Homer Hoyt, *Principles of Urban Real Estate*, second edition (New York: Ronald Press, 1948), cited in Helper, *Racial Policies and Practices of Real Estate Brokers*.

21. Article 34, Part III. This article was in effect from 1924 to 1950, at which point it was revised to veil, without substantively altering, the commitment to promoting racial segregation.

22. That is, discriminating by denying home loans and insurance in particular neighborhoods or areas. The term refers to the color scheme originally devised by the HOLC for its now-notorious Residential Security Maps. Areas deemed too risky for safe investment—areas which consistently included places with a substantial black population—were outlined on the maps in the color red. See Kenneth Jackson, *Crabgrass Frontier: The Suburbanization of the United States* (New York: Oxford University Press, 1985).

23. Quoted in Evan McKenzie, *Privatopia: Homeowner Associations and the Rise of Residential Private Government* (New Haven, CT: Yale University Press, 1994), p. 65.

24. Gregory Squires, "Community Reinvestment: The Privatization of Fair Lending Law Enforcement," in Robert Bullard, J. Eugene Grigsby, III, and Charles Lee, eds., *Residential Apartheid: The American Legacy* (Los Angeles: CAAS, 1994), pp. 257–286.

25. Cheryl Harris, "Whiteness as Property," *Harvard Law Review* 106, no. 8 (June 1993): 1710–1791.

26. Roediger, *Working Toward Whiteness*. Note: This formulation is mine, not Roediger's.

27. Ibid., p. 172.

28. By "political action," I mean, roughly, action that helps shape—whether by destabilizing, reconfiguring, or reinforcing—relations of power.

29. Barry Bluestone and Bennet Harrison, *The Deindustrialization of America: Plant Closings, Community Abandonment, and the Dismantling of Basic Industry* (New York: Basic Books, 1982).

30. Richard Briffault, "Our Localism, Part II—Localism and Legal Theory," *Columbia Law Review* 90, no. 2 (March 1990): 346–454.

31. One of the earliest uses of this term was by Fred Vigman, who claimed in 1955 that American cities were in "in throes of urban crisis." Vigman, *Crisis of the Cities* (Washington, DC: Public Affairs Press, 1955), p. 6, cited in Robert Beauregard, *Voices of Decline: The Postwar Fate of U.S. Cities*, second edition (New York: Routledge, 2003), p. 84.

32. See Richard Thompson Ford's claim that, in the US, the territoriality of political jurisdictions works to legitimize race-based social hierarchies, which would be widely perceived as illegitimate if not perpetuated through this spatial mechanism. Ford, "Law's Territory (A History of Jurisdiction)," *Michigan Law Review* 97, no. 4 (February 1999): 843–930.

33. Robert Beauregard, *Voices of Decline*.

34. Nathan Glazer, *Cities in Trouble* (Chicago: Quadrangle Books, 1970), p. 24, cited in Beauregard, *Voices of Decline*, p. 130.

35. Irving Kristol, "Common Sense about the 'Urban Crisis,'" *Fortune* 76 (October 1967): 234, emphasis added, cited in Beauregard, *Voices of Decline*, p. 172.

8 Placing American Political Development

Cities, Regions, and Regimes, 1789–2008

Philip J. Ethington and David P. Levitus

In this chapter we examine the shape of power within the geopolitical history of the United States since its founding. We place the question of *the urban* in American political development within a wider context of the ways that cities and nations have developed interdependently, as first demonstrated by Max Weber and more recently by Charles Tilly and others.[1] We map the historically developed national state within a network of cities, metropolises, and regions, and propose that there are two broad genres of "regime" that make up the nation. The *national policy regime* is, like "The New Deal," an unstable coalition of regionally emplaced political elites who form their governing coalition with a theme and a distinct bundle of policy goals. *Regional regimes* organize the political economies of the regions that compose the nation state. Especially since the Civil War, these regional regimes have been dominated by leadership based in their respective metropoles. National policy regimes have produced regions and the regimes governing those regions have, at key moments, organized the governing coalitions of the national state, in effect nationalizing its region's political culture.

Regions and regimes construct each other reciprocally. Indeed, *region* and *regime* share a common linguistic root and once meant the same thing.[2] Regions shape both publics and leaders: they are composed of a unique complex of production relations, cultural discourses, and inherited and newly introduced institutions. Regions generate distinctive "political cultures," which set the rules, logic, and parameters of ethics, ideologies, and policy concerns.[3] Success of leadership and policy projects within these milieux requires mastery of the ensemble that makes the region particular. Moreover, political leaders and policies continuously re-shape the economies and cultures of pre-existing regions. Regions, therefore, are profoundly historical, dynamic, and protean. In contrast to the long tradition of sectional analysis of political behavior, which posits the socio-economic structures as bases that explain behavioral outcomes, we see regional regimes as institutional arrangements that are always under construction.[4]

Extending Clarence Stone's model for *urban* regimes, we propose that governance of a *region* requires an adroit combination of political office-holders and economic stakeholders in an informal mix.[5] The dynamism of our historical model proceeds from the fact that certain regional and metropolitan economies have always occupied the leading edge of innovation and wealth-creation. (Silicon Valley is only the most recent example.) In these cases, civil society alone does not drive politics, because governmental policies powerfully influenced the development of leading-edge sectors. Yet at key moments, political entrepreneurs from the leading-edge regional regime have successfully made their own region's political culture the hegemonic one for the nation (and consequently pushed forward new policies). These historical junctures are rare moments of *metonymy*, when a regional part comes to stand for the national whole.

Such moments include the Civil War, the New Deal, and the Republican New Right. The social sciences have long confronted the problem of explaining the transformation from one regime era to another.[6] By looking at the "where" rather than the "when" of power, sweeping changes in the political system become more visible. As we shall argue below, transitions from the national preeminence of one regional regime to that of another can take decades. Change is not abrupt, but continual and uneven as recent work on "intercurrence" emphasizes.[7] Understanding the existence and operation of regional regimes explains a great deal about the dynamics of transition between the major policy regime eras of American history. We present here an account that identifies the ironic way in which national policy regimes ultimately undermine themselves by creating new regional regimes after achieving their "metonymic moment" of national hegemony.

Given limitations of space, we cannot offer a complete case for re-considering American political development within our geo-institutional historical approach. Instead, we outline a case that we hope suggests new avenues of inquiry.[8]

Colonial and Constitutional Foundations

Even before the United States had become an urban nation, federal governing authority had been spatially allocated. As a "settler society," American colonists and then US citizens expected new opportunities to open up spatially, through conquest and expansion across the continent. Parliament's opposition to American colonial expansion across the Appalachians after the costly Seven Years' War was a principal grievance named in the Declaration of Independence. An obsession with territoriality structured the debates on the new Constitution, which enshrined the pre-existing divide between large colonies and small colonies through the Connecticut Compromise, producing a bicameral legislature, with representation in the House of Representatives allocated proportionately to population and with equal representation in the Senate for all states.

Regional differences in economic interests, political culture, and the existence of slavery further divided the Northern and Southern colonies, temporarily mitigated by the notorious three-fifths compromise (counting slaves as three-fifths of a free person for the purposes of apportionment) and the agreement to postpone any ban on the slave trade until 1808. Even the swampland siting of the nation's new capital, the District of Columbia, was a part of a geopolitical compromise between these two major political and economic blocs.[9]

The Constitution was also shaped by the agrarian revolt against urban financiers, most notably Shay's Rebellion, which pushed many of the urban-situated political elite to favor a strong national government, and thus a *federation* in place of the volatile confederation. After the Constitution's ratification, the major conflict of American public life hinged on the competing urban vs. agrarian socio-spatial visions of Alexander Hamilton and Thomas Jefferson—long before many Americans actually lived in urban places.[10] Ultimately the Hamiltonian vision of "intensive development" to concentrate on commerce and manufacturing in Atlantic cities lost out to the Jeffersonian vision of "extensive development," for more than a half century. Based upon its low esteem for cities, this vision successfully re-made the continent through forceful national policies of subsidizing cheap farmland, military campaigns against American Indians, and acquiring more territory via purchase and conquest. The simultaneous drive westward and the economic and cultural divergence between the North and South ultimately led to the Civil War. But if the Hamiltonian vision had triumphed initially, the US might have developed as a tier of states arranged along the Atlantic Coast, remaining east of the Mississippi. The US–Mexican War and the Civil War may never have happened. There were clear policy choices at the time of the Jefferson–Hamilton debates; historical contingencies are such that the Jeffersonian triumph was not inevitable.

Sectional Era, 1800–1860s

The administrations of Jefferson through Jackson and Polk pursued policies that transformed the territoriality of the new nation, and brought cataclysmic conflict onto itself and Mexico. These policies created newer regions within the nascent nation state, and forms of urban development that spearheaded the transformation of those regions.

The urban shapes of power during the period between the 1803 Louisiana Purchase and the 1861 outbreak of the Civil War were diffused throughout a highly variegated agrarian landscape. The defining attributes of the period between the Revolution and the Civil War were bound up with the two great sectional issues of the entire period: slavery's limits and the fate of the great western territories, especially Mexican Cession. Informed by Romantic nationalist movements, the entire Zeitgeist of the era put a premium on achieving political unity both within and between deeply antagonistic regions.[11]

Cities were essential nodes of the regional and global economy during the entire Sectional Period, and also home to nascent industries (often, as with gun manufacture in the Northeast and farm-machinery manufacture in Chicago, stimulated by frontier expansion). While the nation was still heavily agrarian, the rate of urban growth during this period was dramatic. The top ten urban places in 1800 were all along the Atlantic seaboard, with the largest, New York, containing merely 60,000 persons. By 1850, New York had grown by tenfold to 660,000, and six of the top ten cities were western newcomers to the list: Cincinnati, New Orleans, Albany-Troy, Pittsburgh, St Louis, and San Francisco (see Figure 8.1).

During this era the national leadership shifted from a network of elites based until the 1820s along the Atlantic seaboard, to a network of frontier elites, who predominated in presidential elections from Jackson's 1828 victory through Lincoln's 1860 electoral success. While the North–South regional divide was always important, the competing policy visions of the pre-1820 period were the Hamiltonian and Jeffersonian ones, with the former, known as Federalist, constituting the "policy regime" until the "Revolution of 1800," and the latter, to be known as Democratic-Republican, taking control of the presidency and Congress coincident with moving into the new Capitol and lasting until 1828.

The 1829 inauguration of Andrew Jackson marked the advent of a new polarity of policy visions, represented by the two emergent parties of the first genuine "party system": the Democrats and the Whigs. The core principle of the Jacksonian Democratic vision was aggressive territorial expansion westward powered by racial nationalism and executed by military campaigns, but with minimal central control or regulation. The Whig vision was also one of westward expansion, but typified by the policy program of Henry Clay's updated Hamiltonian "American System," favoring a central bank, subsidies for infrastructure, and regulatory laws. The presidencies of this period oscillated between Southerners and Northerners, but the common project of westward expansion forced the problem of slavery increasingly to the surface.

During this entire period, the "Great Triumvirate" in Congress of Daniel Webster, John Calhoun, and Henry Clay represented the tenuously brokered arrangement among the North, South, and trans-Appalachian West that fractured in 1850s under the sectional crisis that westward expansion had provoked. Meanwhile, a new generation of frontier politicians such as Abraham Lincoln learned to join the urban developmental policies of the Whigs with the aspirations of small farmers. Lincoln would form the outlook of these politicians into a coherent vision that grew slowly between 1828 and 1860, emerging clearly with the Whig Party's disintegration and the Republican Party's rise in the 1850s.

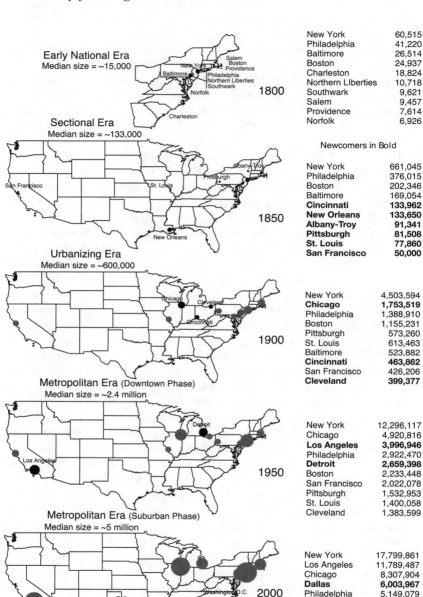

New York	60,515
Philadelphia	41,220
Baltimore	26,514
Boston	24,937
Charleston	18,824
Northern Liberties	10,718
Southwark	9,621
Salem	9,457
Providence	7,614
Norfolk	6,926

Newcomers in Bold

New York	661,045
Philadelphia	376,015
Boston	202,346
Baltimore	169,054
Cincinnati	**133,962**
New Orleans	**133,650**
Albany-Troy	**91,341**
Pittsburgh	**81,508**
St. Louis	**77,860**
San Francisco	**50,000**

New York	4,503,594
Chicago	**1,753,519**
Philadelphia	1,388,910
Boston	1,155,231
Pittsburgh	573,260
St. Louis	613,463
Baltimore	523,882
Cincinnati	**463,862**
San Francisco	426,206
Cleveland	**399,377**

New York	12,296,117
Chicago	4,920,816
Los Angeles	**3,996,946**
Philadelphia	2,922,470
Detroit	**2,659,398**
Boston	2,233,448
San Francisco	2,022,078
Pittsburgh	1,532,953
St. Louis	1,400,058
Cleveland	1,383,599

New York	17,799,861
Los Angeles	11,789,487
Chicago	8,307,904
Dallas	**6,003,967**
Philadelphia	5,149,079
Miami	**4,919,036**
Boston	4,032,484
Washington D.C.	**3,933,920**
Detroit	3,903,377
Houston	**3,822,509**

Figure 8.1 Top ten urban places in five eras

Regional aspirations to establish a national political culture marked the Sectional Era although all attempts failed until after the Civil War. If the defining contrast in the Early National Period was between Jeffersonians and Hamiltonians, the defining contrast for the Sectional Era was between two visions of expansion: free soil, epitomized by Lincoln; and proslavery, epitomized by Calhoun. While radicals in each region proposed forms of secession to preserve their respective political cultures and economies, both Lincoln and Calhoun maintained a commitment to preserving the Union. Calhoun actually proposed a "dual presidency" as a solution to the intractable sectional crisis. Lincoln correctly predicted that the nation could not endure half slave and half free.

National Leadership from Regional Urban Centers

To this point, we have broadly outlined the ways in which political power related to regional and national development. Now we sketch the way that leaders headquartered in specific regional urban centers not only organized those regions but also competed for the authority to claim that their region's political vision best suited the nation as a whole.

During the nation's first years, political leaders allied with New York City's mercantile elite tried to leverage the authority of the national government to benefit their interests. Led by Alexander Hamilton and John Jay and bolstered by strong popular support in New England, their economic program to advance urban commerce and industry soon lost electoral dominance to the Republicans, led by wealthy Virginia planters such as Jefferson, Madison, and Monroe, who favored extensive development.[12] Led by Jefferson, these Southerners consciously battled the political influence of Massachusetts and Connecticut in national politics and the Federalist faction, which dominated those states.[13]

However, these two proto-parties were not simply representatives of the North and South. The Federalist leaders of Congress during the Adams administration, for example, were mostly from Virginia. But the rootedness of these competing visions eventually became clear. During the Virginia-based Democratic-Republican regime that reigned over national politics through the six consecutive terms of Jefferson, Madison, and Monroe (1801–1825), the Federalist Party withered away to its New England base, losing the support of the key middle states, in particular New York. Still sensitive to anti-partisan and consensual norms of governance, Jeffersonian Republicans promoted interlinked policies of universal white male enfranchisement and westward settlement.[14]

In the 1820s, a faction of New York Democratic-Republicans, the Bucktails, led by Martin Van Buren, pioneered a new mode of politicking, first at the state level and then nationally. Later known as the Albany Regency, the Bucktails became the first professional politicians. They had no pretensions to be above partisanship and regarded the existence of permanent opposition as beneficial to the nation. And while the development of frank partisanship was not limited to New York, the state played a particularly strong role in its incubation as a national standard. New York had a comparatively clear division between two opposing political factions. The state stood at the center of the national economy and its electoral votes had long been critical. What came to be known nationally as "the New York philosophy" emerged from the New York scene in a remarkably articulated form.[15] Building on a tradition for pragmatic tolerance and coalition-building that had marked New York City since colonial times, Van Buren drew together the Albany Regency and Virginia's Richmond Junto, cementing a coalition of Southern planters and Northern Republicans. Not surprisingly, a large cadre of Van Buren's associates dominated New York state politics and entered national office. At the federal level, they upheld the traditional resistance to centralization, a principle that coincided with their material interests as New York already had the Erie Canal and had little incentive to fund the improvements of competing states.

While New York became the intellectual and organizational epicenter of American politics, balancing major political parties and sectional disagreements between the North and South, the driving issues of the day emerged from the frontiers, focusing on the settlement and conquest of the trans-Appalachian West as the federal government translated Jefferson's agrarian vision into action.[16] The federal government's purchase of Louisiana followed by cheap widespread grants, surveys and organization of territories, and wars against American Indians made western development possible.[17] Consequently, Van Buren's first national success came in getting Andrew Jackson—"Old Hickory," fresh from the frontier wars—elected president in 1828. From Jackson through the election of Lincoln in 1860, a majority of presidents were either born or resided on the frontier, or fought battles on the frontier against Indians and Mexicans (Jackson, W. Harrison, Polk, Taylor, Pierce, Lincoln). The only exceptions were two New Yorkers (Van Buren, Fillmore) and a Virginian (Tyler).

The western frontier was held together by the transportation system of the Mississippi and Ohio rivers. St Louis was the most important city in the northern reaches of the Mississippi, and the "gateway" to the Far West, at the junction of the Missouri and the Mississippi. It was the headquarters of Andrew Jackson's chief lieutenant in the Senate, and the mastermind of the military expansionists, Thomas Hart Benton. Benton held a string of local offices in St Louis before becoming a Missouri Senator, an office he held from 1821 until 1851. Benton's daughter Jesse Benton Frémont schemed with her father and her husband John C. Frémont, to provoke the war with Mexico, and Frémont became instrumental in the beginnings of California as a key state, with San Francisco sprouting up as a far-flung "instant city" in this western network of cities.[18] Benton, like the other regional leaders, was heavily involved in commercial and real estate ventures that would benefit from his policy positions. For example, Benton's attack on government factories in Indian territories climaxed a lengthy struggle by St Louis merchants to break federal control of the trade along the Missouri River.[19]

The Ohio River Valley was the other central artery of the Midwest Frontier, sprouting a string of important frontier cities: Evansville, Louisville, Cincinnati, and Pittsburgh. The hometown of Henry Clay was Lexington, which sprang up along the Wilderness Road between Louisville and the Cumberland Gap, opened by Daniel Boone in the employ of Jesse Benton (grandfather of Jesse Benton Frémont) in 1775. Clay, like Senator Benton, was an urban lawyer who spoke for his region at the same time that he looked out for the city that provided the base of his operations. When Clay went to the Senate in 1806, he was one of Lexington's most prominent lawyers. But "Clay was so closely tied to Lexington that he never became very popular in Louisville, whose interests so often collided with that of its Kentucky neighbor."[20]

Cities gained political influence in relation to rural areas despite their demographic disadvantage because of "their ability to produce leadership as economic and intellectual centers, [attracting] the talented and ambitious in all fields." Even rural gerrymandering could not prevent urban political leadership. The reason was simple. Long before farmers first plowed the surrounding fields, the towns of the Ohio River Valley facilitated and financed the settlement. In the words of Richard Wade, the towns of Pittsburgh, St Louis, Cincinnati, Louisville, and Lexington were "the spearheads of the frontier."[21]

Urbanizing Era, 1860s–1920s

While the Civil War violently divided the American nation along sectional lines, the resultant economic and political mobilization created the conditions for a new regional regime to emerge. As early as 1840 the most rapid urban growth was among inland river cities such as St Louis, Cincinnati, and Pittsburgh. After the Civil War, railroads shaped the extent and size of urban development, leading to the creation of a dense industrial belt from St Louis and Milwaukee in the West to Baltimore and Boston in the East. Chicago stood at the center of this belt, a transportation and manufacturing hub, spinning goods, services, and capital back and forth from its regional hinterland to the cities of the world.[22]

This antebellum growth was vastly accelerated by the federal policies enacted during the Civil War. The secession of the Confederate states allowed Northern Republicans to push through their program of economic nationalism through industrialization. Within the span of 5 years, the Republican Congress enacted the Homestead Act (1862) to give and cheaply sell (Native American) farmlands, the Morrill Land-Grant

Colleges Act (1862) to create public universities in every state, the Pacific Railway Acts (1862–1866) to create a transcontinental railroad, the National Banking Acts (1863–1864) to create a national system of banks run from New York, higher tariffs in the Morrill Tariffs of 1861–1862, and the first income tax in the Revenue Act of 1861.

The Civil War stimulated a great demand for building materials and for troop provisions; the destruction it left behind created a decades-long "reconstruction" project. These supply demands led to the development of far-flung, vertically integrated corporations, organizing the economy on a grand scale for the first time. J.P. Morgan and John D. Rockefeller had taken advantage of the Union's need for materiel and financing by creating massive corporations.[23] They were just two of a larger cadre of American and European financiers who made Manhattan the world's corporate and financial capital after the war by investing millions and assembling conglomerates such as AT&T, GE, and Standard Oil.

This intense burst of capitalization and organizational growth fueled an urbanizing boom in the Midwest. Mostly mercantile in economic orientation before the Civil War, cities such as Chicago, St Louis, Cincinnati, Cleveland, Detroit, Milwaukee, and Indianapolis became major industrial centers afterwards. Excellent railroad access to eastern city markets and access to raw materials (lumber, iron ore, grain, livestock, coal) combined to make the region a center of explosive growth. Chicago's phenomenal growth was possible because of the centralization of the region's natural abundance, its fortuitous geography, its conscious positioning as the bridge between eastern and western railroad networks, and the favor showered upon it by New York City-based capitalists.[24]

With Cincinnati, Cleveland, and Toledo, Ohio was actually more industrialized than Illinois. Moreover, thanks to Ulysses S. Grant, the Republican Party sank deep roots in Ohio: a thick institutional base for national political action. During the period from 1869 to 1923, a nearly uninterrupted string of Republican presidents came from Ohio.[25] The other great source of "presidential timber," New York, was predictable. All four aberrations from the Ohio pattern were men from New York or New Jersey.[26] Moreover, from 1868 until the nomination of William Jennings Bryan in 1896, every single Democratic presidential candidate was from New York.[27]

Most famously, industrialist Mark Hanna led William McKinley to decisive victory in the presidential election of 1896. A wealthy owner of a coal and iron venture in Cleveland, Hanna branched out into transportation, publishing, and banking. Although working as early as 1880 to secure support for Republicans among industrialists, he dedicated himself to McKinley's political career and helped the former congressmen win two terms as governor of Ohio. In the 1896 election, Hanna drew upon a huge pool of business contributions and reached out with a network of Republican speakers and a massive public relations movement to counter Bryan's popular appeal.[28]

In general, voters in the rapidly growing cities of the Midwest and Northeast saw the Republicans as the party of progress and national authority, in regard to Reconstruction, the Homestead Act, land grants, railroad loans, protective tariffs, and taxes on income and inheritance taxes, through Teddy Roosevelt's bold imperialistic policies, from the war with Spain (1898), the Great White Fleet (1907–1909), to the Panama Canal (1902–1914). Appealing to (increasingly immigrant) urban workers by citing the steady rise in real wages, the party enjoyed the grassroots support that the New Deal would later win away. Just as the Republican Party in this era was an urbanizing party, so the great cities were increasingly Republicanized. Already, in the three presidential elections of the 1880s, the majority of the nation's cities outside the South went Republican, especially Northeastern and Midwestern cities such as Philadelphia, Chicago, Cleveland, Cincinnati, Buffalo, Providence, Milwaukee, Newark, Syracuse, Patterson, and Minneapolis. In 1896 Bryan lost horribly in the Northeast, including the Democratic stronghold of New York. Cities such as San Francisco, Detroit, Indianapolis, Columbus, and St Paul, which had been Democratic, switched to the Republican ticket in 1896 and remained in the GOP's column for decades.[29]

The period of Republican domination from 1896 to 1932 was marked by the shift to Progressive leadership after 1901. The great cities were the proving grounds for the Progressive structural and policy innovations that came to define the national political culture by the 1930s through a regional urban insurgency. Besides re-casting the structure and operations of local government, the urban Progressives proved decisive at the national level in another way. As Elizabeth Sanders has shown, on many occasions legislators from the industrial Northeast deadlocked with those from the agrarian South and West. Urban policy intellectuals supplied the solutions to these deadlocks and representatives from upper Midwestern states with mixed agrarian–industrial economies provided the swing votes in Congress. To gain these votes, agrarian representatives exchanged their own plans for clear-cut statutory action for the proposals of expert bureaucracy of urban intellectuals and professionals.[30]

The urbanization of the political system would have been much more rapid had rural interests not resisted it through spatial means, namely gerrymandering. In an attempt to preserve their political power, rural interests in the South "successfully resisted reapportionment following the 1920 Census—the only time this has happened in American history."[31] In California, as late as 1965, Los Angeles County, with a population of 6 million, had just one state Senator, the same number as two rural counties with a combined population of 14,000.[32] In Georgia, the "county unit" system enacted in 1917 determined congressional and statewide elections on the basis of a similarly tortured arithmetic.[33]

By the 1920s the Democratic Party had divided into a "traditionalist" wing based in the "Solid South" and an "urban liberal" wing primarily based in the big cities, especially New York. While Republicans had been the party of the rising cities and the Northeast in general from the Civil War through the 1920s, urban citizens began voting increasingly Democratic after 1920.[34] In this regard, the fact that Republicans had never dislodged the Democratic Party from New York City would prove fateful for the development of a new national policy regime. New York Democrats of the liberal persuasion were moving to take leadership of an emergent national governing coalition, soon to become the New Deal.

In the 1920s, with Harding, Coolidge, and Hoover at the helm, conservatives increasingly expelled Progressives from the Republican Party. Most of the Democratic Party was rural, Southern, dry, evangelical, racist, or all of the above, but New York City was the crucial exception. For many years, New York Democrats were politically allied with the Jim Crow South and Tammany Hall reigned locally without any liberal inclination.[35] But just as the populist insurgency had pushed national Democrats to accede to agrarian demands, the new Progressive discourse led young up-and-comers in the Democratic Tammany Hall organization to focus on leveraging government authority to benefit the poor, working, and middle-classes of the teeming metropolis. The most important moment was the Triangle Shirtwaist factory fire of 1911 and the shockingly activist Commission that came about as a result. Chaired by Alfred E. Smith and Robert Wagner, most of the Commission's scores of legislative recommendations became state law and then models for state and later federal social policy nationwide.[36]

The 1928 presidential candidacy of Smith was the first fully national manifestation of the shift to urban leadership of both the Democratic Party and the national reform coalition. During Woodrow Wilson's administration, Progressive legislation was the product of a coalition led by populist Democrats from the South, West and Midwest. By contrast, in 1928 Smith won majorities in New York City, Chicago, Cleveland, St Louis, Milwaukee, and San Francisco. Of the twelve largest cities, only Los Angeles went strongly for Hoover. Besides bringing Republican-voting immigrants to his side, he also attracted a tremendous number of *new* voters.[37] When Franklin D. Roosevelt successfully ran for president in 1932 he consummated the marriage between urbanites and the Democratic Party, which would become the backbone of the New Deal regime and inaugurate the Metropolitan Era.

Metropolitan Era, 1930s–2000

The Metropolitan Era was framed by two quintessentially urban moments: Franklin Roosevelt led a coalition of Democrats to lead the federal government in the 1930s and 1940s with central city leaders and constituencies in the vanguard. When Nixon and Reagan led the Republicans back into power in the late 1960s through the 1980s, their vanguard leaders represented Sunbelt cities and suburbs all over the country. Midway through this Metropolitan Era, we can observe a massive shift in the territoriality of power, from the Chicago–Ohio–New York regional regime to the new Washington–Los Angeles regional regime. After a century of domination by politicians from Ohio and New York, politicians from Sunbelt cities, most notably Los Angeles, took the reigns of the national state. Ironically, the New Deal policies that were born and bred in the Chicago–Ohio–New York region spurred the creation of the new regional regime that displaced it.

The Metropolitan Era began in earnest with Roosevelt's 1932 landslide amidst the collapse of the Republican corporate liberal, welfare capitalist, free-market governing coalition (Harding–Coolidge–Hoover administrations). Urban liberalism after 1932, under Roosevelt's masterful leadership, consolidated the network of urban liberals from the Progressive era and then nationalized it. They took full advantage of the new medium of radio—headquartered, via the new "Networks" (RCA, NBC, CBS) in New York City.

FDR's fireside chats, first developed during his tenure as governor of New York, constituted one key mechanism by which Americans came to identify with urban liberalism as national citizens. Millions across the country "looked to Washington to deliver the American dream."[38] His first administration represented a metonymic moment when the part came to speak for the whole; when a metropolitan vision became appealing to a huge majority of Americans. Although he spoke to a diverse public— urban, rural, Northern, Southern, and Western—Roosevelt spoke convincingly on behalf of America and Americans. Yet his idiom, style, and message were the distilled essence of New York-centered urban liberalism.[39]

Great cities were critical to the New Deal coalition. Between 1932 and 1948 the nation's twelve largest cities were decisive in giving the Electoral College majority to the Democrats. Significantly, the only top-ten metropolis that continued to vote Republican in the 1930s was Los Angeles, the city that would eventually become the western pole of the emerging dominant regional regime. As Samuel Eldersveld notes, the ten states with the twelve largest cities, although "geographically not adjacent, constituted a matrix of political strength, together similar in political complexion and trend, but often distinct from their special regions."[40] In other words, the "footprint" of the New Deal coalition was firmly metropolitan. But the metropolis was sprouting suburbs.

Suburbanization after 1940 represents one of the greatest migrations in American history.[41] "In 1950, a quarter of all Americans lived in suburbs; in 1960, a full third; and by 1990, a solid majority."[42] Beginning with the Federal Housing Act of 1934 and the creation of the Federal Housing

Administration (FHA), New Deal policies were largely responsible for enabling a change of this magnitude to occur. Reforming home mortgages to thirty-year amortized loans, then guaranteeing them to bankers with FHA and Veteran's Administration (VA) backing, represented a massive intervention into the landscape of the US. By limiting those new residential landscapes to "whites," the New York-centered New Deal policy regime, compromising as always with its white Southern component, spatially fragmented its core urban constituency along increasingly rigid racial boundaries.[43] The Federal-Aid Highway Act of 1956 further inscribed this new landscape by creating the transportation infrastructure that enabled the relocation of plants and office complexes outside of central cities. This massive construction program developed out of the New Deal's public works agencies, which had created state capacity to plan, build, and transform the American landscape.[44] Suburbanites mystified these federal subsidies underneath an emerging ideology of suburban autonomy, as Matthew Lassiter and other scholars in the recent metropolitan school of urban studies have shown. Nixon and successors would employ not so much of a "Southern Strategy," Kevin Phillips's attempts notwithstanding, but a *suburban* strategy.[45]

As one set of fiscal policies prioritized suburbs over cities, another set of fiscal policies weakened the political ties between urbanites and their local state. The well-known accretion of federal agencies with urban mandates massively shifted cities' revenue base from local property taxes to the federal income tax, and from the city's borrowing powers to those of the United States.[46] When local governments became less dependent on local taxes, local politicians gained more autonomy from their electorates.[47] Emerging municipal and regional "authorities" gained even greater independence from the deliberations of local voters.[48] All of these public officials became more Washington-oriented, seeking the new Manna from Congressional Heaven: funds overlaid on their own local tax base.[49] Lobbying for federal megaprojects such as freeways, or urban renewal projects, thereafter became a bipartisan occupation.

Thus, New Deal policies effectively federalized the metropolis in regard to political mobilization. Although New Deal funds for relief and housing administered by local authorities reinforced the power and influence of existing urban political organizations in the short run, in the long run, urban voters began to make primary connections with national political issues and the federal government, leaving the "local state" in the position of middle-man in the quest for federal largesse. In this new calculus, urban voters rearranged themselves as interest groups negotiating with federal programs and officials rather than as partisans of local machines. This process also federalized urban *issues*. Even when inappropriate, voters began holding presidential and congressional leadership responsible for municipal matters, especially in the case of schooling (Elementary and Secondary Education Acts; anti-busing); civil rights (the movement was primarily to desegregate urban places); urban unrest (Lyndon Johnson's War on Poverty; Nixon's Law and Order campaign); and the tax revolt.

The Solid South would eventually turn away from its century-long Democratic allegiance in reaction to the halting alliance between liberal Democrats and the civil rights movement. As Lyndon B. Johnson knowingly predicted when he signed the Civil Rights Act of 1964: "We [the Democratic Party] have lost the South for a generation." But "the South" was not so solid by the 1960s, as the new suburbs reconfigured interests and constituencies, and these peripheral metropolitan spaces were finding new leadership outside of the Democratic Party. Simultaneously, the pressure of growth policies, begun in the New Deal, steadily dissolved the central-city pillar of the New Deal coalition.

Industrially, the shift from "Snowbelt" economy of Fordist mass production to the "Sunbelt" economy of post-Fordist military and information technology, transformed the peripheral territories of the Cotton South, the Southwest, and the Pacific West, into the new core. As late as 1950, only one metropolitan area of the Sunbelt, Los Angeles, ranked in the top ten of US metros. Fifty years later, five of those top ten were Sunbelt metros: Los Angeles, Miami, Dallas, Washington, DC, and Houston. Among the thirty most populous metro areas in 2000, twenty were in the Sunbelt.[50]

In the shift to the Sunbelt, Washington, DC and Los Angeles became the two leading centers of the new footprint of American political economy, even as New York City and the Midwest remained vital elements of the new configuration of power on the ground. The two emergent poles of the new territorial regime arose according to distinct, but related logics. Both owed their rise to the policies of the military-industrial complex, begun under Roosevelt in 1939 and continued by the Truman and Eisenhower administrations.

Under the New Deal, the District of Columbia finally came into its own as a mighty capital city. Once the federal government became the primary fiscal force, and then as the economy suddenly and lastingly came to revolve around military spending, this mostly administrative metropolis rose to the top rank of the urban hierarchy (see Figure 8.1). Large lobbying and "think-tank" industries developed to influence policy of the rapidly expanded federal government and this "inside-the-Beltway" culture became a main source of political conventional wisdom and policy ideas, first for the Democratic Party and then later for the Republican Party.

Running against the New Deal and Great Society "liberal" (read excessive) spending, and against bloated federal bureaucracies meddling in local affairs, became important planks in the resurgent campaigns of the Republican Right. (Tellingly, however, conservative Republicans created their own Washington "counter-establishment" of think-tanks and media outlets.[51]) The capital city of this anti-Washington dynamic for the rising Republican Right was Los Angeles, home to Richard Nixon and Ronald Reagan.[52]

Los Angeles's role in the rise of the New Right mirrors New York's role in the rise of the New Deal. Prior to their emergence as metropoles of dominant regional regimes, both metropolises had proved stubborn exceptions to nationally dominant political cultures and partisan affiliations. New York had been both a Democratic city among a sea of Republican metropolises and a relatively liberal voice amid Jim Crow and rural conservatism in the first two decades of the twentieth century. Likewise, Los Angeles was a Republican city among a sea of Democratic metropolises and a militant reactionary voice among Eisenhower moderation from the 1930s through the 1950s. Los Angeles was the only top-ten metropolis that continued to vote Republican during the 1930s. From the 1940s through the 1970s, it was the place where many politicians learned the ideologies, rhetoric, and policies that could appeal to voters from the South and the suburbs.

Los Angeles came to occupy an exceptional position in the course of American political development as a result of a confluence of several historical factors: its overlapping positions as an outpost in the violent US–Mexico Borderlands; as the premier site of massive military-industrial activity; as a center of mass communication; and as an embodiment of the new American dream in the popular imagination.

In contrast to most major American metropolises circa 1950, Los Angeles had developed as an outpost in the violent US–Mexico Borderlands. Typified by plantation labor, large migratory pools of labor, and by extractive industries such as oil, gold, and copper, this region had the kind of autocratic ruling class typical of these kinds of economies.[53] This reactionary leadership was personified by the publishers of the *Los Angeles Times*, Harrison Gray Otis and his son-in-law, Harry Chandler.[54] These spokesmen for the anti-union, anti-left orthodoxy of the region's political culture were also massive investors in Mexican plantations and minerals. "Ultimately Americans came to own the majority of land along Mexico's entire periphery."[55] Most of these American investors backed the regime of Porfirio Diaz, favoring his "policies of keeping down popular protest, muzzling the opposition press, preventing the formation of labor unions, and not allowing strikes."[56] This reactionary Borderland political culture reached its maximum definition in the 1920s, just as Richard Nixon came of age as a regional high-school debating champion. Before he could hope to run for Congress in 1946 against New Deal liberal Jerry Voorhis, Nixon sought and received the Chandler family's explicit blessing.[57]

Los Angeles emerged more generally as the global century's new leading-edge technopole in two crucial areas: aircraft/aerospace and mass communications (motion pictures, radio, and later television). No place was better positioned to support the new mass-mediated forms of political leadership than postwar Los Angeles. The sheer propaganda value of Hollywood was pioneered by Louis Mayer during the Hoover Administration and was magnified by the Warner Brothers' pro-war and New Deal cinema. After World War II, Los Angeles's regional culture became the stuff of mass media, leading the nation iconographically with the "Southern California Lifestyle." The media saturation of this seductive lifestyle coupled with the massive Cold War spending on aerospace technologies to bring millions more residents and workers to Southern California, was pushing Los Angeles to displace Chicago as the nation's "second city" by 1970.

Nixon and Reagan came to represent this region's two dominant halves: the military-industrial complex and the "media-political complex." From this base, Nixon and Reagan learned to speak for the vast space-age suburban work force that spread its footprint into wide valleys, southward into Orange County under the shadow of the giant Saturn V rocket engines tested regularly in the hills above the San Fernando Valley. Nixon called this constituency the "Silent Majority" and gave voice to its militarist, anti-radical, anti-civil liberties conservatism. The "suburban" strategy was more generally a Sunbelt strategy, as a chain of Sunbelt cities grew: San Diego, Dallas, Houston, Phoenix, Atlanta, Charlotte, and Miami.[58]

Last but not least, its political culture complemented the Jim Crow political culture of the South. Both shared white supremacy, undemocratic modes of rule, and highly violent rules of engagement for dissidents (civil rights activists, communists, socialists, unions). As such, politicians from Los Angeles were in a unique position to bring together the Sunbelt and the South, suburbanites and disenchanted urban ethnics, under a banner of color-blind racism, militaristic patriotism, and the welfare state without "welfare." As the son of an American oil baron in Mexico, and a Southern mother, William F. Buckley, dean of the conservative movement qua establishment, represents the union of these strains.[59]

The transition from the dominance of the Chicago–Ohio–New York regional regime to the Washington, DC–Los Angeles Sunbelt regime began with the pairing of Ike and Nixon in 1952. Carrying forward the New Deal's suburbanizing infrastructural and housing policies (and of course the military-industrial complex), Eisenhower's administration had its left foot in the New York wing of the party: moderate, internationalist, and very much adapted to the New Deal. Nixon's vice presidency represented the right foot, planted squarely in the headquarters of reactionary Los Angeles. The transition took years to complete, though. In 1960 the Democrats included a Texan on the ticket; the 1964 presidential election pitted a Texan against an Arizonian. Nixon's 1968 and 1972 victories cemented the leadership of the Sunbelt but the "metonymic moment" was not reached until Ronald Reagan's triumph in 1980. Whereas Nixon retained key links to the moderate New York Republican regime and its compromise with welfare statism, Reagan emerged as a paragon of the Republican Right. A true believer, Reagan encapsulated the entire conservative movement from Buckley Jr, Goldwater, Nixon, and the Orange County Christians, into a single message. Like Roosevelt, Ronald Reagan's administration regularly produced "fireside chat" moments for the new governing coalition, speaking for the entire "national character." Reaganism appealed all over suburbia and middle America in part because the Sunbelt lifestyle was largely predicated on a military-industrial complex, which Reagan expanded to record levels with Star Wars and other expensive ventures that boosted Silicon Valley-style university "high tech" park complexes.[60]

By the end of the 1970s, suburban districts gained a plurality of seats in state legislatures and the US Congress.[61] Still during 1990s, most of the Republican leadership in the House of Representatives came from Sunbelt suburbs. Bob Barr (an early advocate of Bill Clinton's impeachment), John Linder (head of the Republican National Congressional Campaign Committee), and Newt Gingrich (Speaker of the House) all represented the fringes of Atlanta. Majority Leader Richard Armey came from a Dallas suburb, while Tom DeLay and Bill Archer came from suburban Houston. When George W. Bush became Governor of Texas in 1994 he received his largest majorities in the ten fastest growing "collar counties" around cities. In office, he attempted to privatize the welfare system and have Lockheed Martin, a pillar of the military-industrial complex, operating it.[62]

A New Cosmopolitan Era?

Writing from the perspective of 2008, the notoriously failed presidency of George W. Bush suggests that the Republican Right regime is nearing its end. While analysis of contemporary developments must remain somewhat speculative, major aspects of the situation today seem to support the model we have proposed in this chapter. To review, we have argued that national policy regimes, such as the New Deal, have profoundly transformed the territorial footprint of American society and economy. New regional regimes have then emerged from those territories, and in several cases have achieved a "metonymic moment," in which a region's distinct political culture and leadership were able to speak to and act in the name of the entire nation. What could we expect to follow the Republican Right policy regime that seems to be ending?

Our starting point is the rise of the Internet, which has vastly transformed American life. The emergence of a networked world and "creative classes" are key new features of the political and economic landscape. But in keeping with our intercurrence model of development, we suggest that these new features are operating in a nexus with persistent features of older regime eras. Indeed, the emphasis of the Sunbelt military-industrial and media complexes on information technologies helped to produce this new landscape. The result is *not* undifferentiated sprawl, but a very specific new geography of politics.

The Democratic primary campaigns of Howard Dean in 2004 and Barack Obama in 2008 built upon a new model of Internet-based progressive organizing. The Internet has lowered the cost of information and cultural production has consequently exploded. The decentralization of the public sphere and cultural production is the key emergent feature of the new era. Narratives and ideologies previously marginalized by corporate-controlled media can now circulate widely. Moreover, the Internet enables increased political participation, tapping into a "cognitive surplus." Instead of watching television, ordinary people can work collaboratively on Internet-based projects such as Wikipedia.[63]

Both Dean and Obama surprised established party leaders by tapping into millions of small donors and organizers via the Internet. As of May 2008, the Obama campaign claimed to have

> more than 800,000 registered users on my.barackobama.com, the campaign's custom-built social network platform, which helped spawn the planning of more than 50,000 offline events and the creation of more than 10,000 local or themed groups in support of the campaign [as well as] more than 1.5 million individual donors.[64]

Such forms of dispersed, networked activism were pioneered in the late 1990s and early 2000s by independent progressive groups. MoveOn.org, formed to oppose President Clinton's impeachment in 1998, which has remained active since in a variety of progressive campaigns, is the most prominent example, but there are scores of others.

These Internet activists, dubbed the "netroots," were not dispersed evenly across the United States, but clustered in "New Economy" metro areas, such as San Francisco, Seattle, Portland, Los Angeles, Boston, New York, Philadelphia, and Washington, DC. The growth of the web phenomenon Craigslist illustrates the trend. Until 2000, only the aforementioned cities plus Sacramento and Chicago had their own city-sites. Since then, Craigslist has rapidly spread, launching into more than 250 small cities between 2006 and 2008 alone.[65] The early concentration in select coastal metropolises was a product of the earlier federal policies. Federal funds enabled the growth of the Silicon Valley-style "high tech" hubs.[66] As Internet access spreads, the geography of participation expands, but as in other regime eras, it seems that the pioneers of the new landscape retain the initiative in formulating new narratives and strategies. Moreover, while Obama is reflecting the changes in the political landscape, he also promises to deepen them through his telecommunications proposals to universalize broadband access and ensure "net neutrality."

If we are correct that the policies of the Republican Right regime have unintentionally produced a new territoriality, then what should follow is the rise of a new regional regime. However, in this case, the "region" is far less geographically contiguous than the regions that have preceded it. Thus the new political culture to match this territoriality will be more cosmopolitan and less dependent upon provincial attachments. On one hand, Republican presidential candidate John McCain is attempting to rely on the political culture of *national* defense and similar tropes, drawing on the dwindling constituencies of the Republican Right. On the other, the Democratic Party and specifically the "netroots" movement within it, has begun to seize the initiative, forging novel strategies and ideologies. Obama represents the cosmopolitan "children" of the recent era of "globalization," bringing together the younger generation, the "creative classes" of professionals, African-Americans (whom Republicans suppressed rhetorically and socially to create their regime), and even many Latino immigrants. His success suggests that American identity has *begun* to transcend old racial, religious, and perhaps national boundaries.[67]

Of course, past performance of our model does not guarantee future results, but the uncertainty lies only in the specific shape that the emerging policy regime might take. And, as we have argued in this chapter, the transition from one regime era to the next is a long and uneven process. Above all, however, our most fundamental argument seems to be holding up very well in the early twenty-first century. That is, analysts of both the American polity and cities need to take seriously the intertwined relationships between national policy regimes, regional regimes, and the territoriality of the American political economy.

Notes

1. Max Weber, *The City*, trans. Don Martindale and Gertrud Neuwirth (New York: The Free Press, 1958); Charles Tilly, *Coercion, Capital and European States: AD 990–1992* (London: Blackwell, 1990); Hendrik Spruyt, *The Sovereign State and Its Competitors* (Princeton, NJ: Princeton University Press, 1996).
2. See "regime" and "region," *Oxford English Dictionary*.
3. Our use of "political culture" descends from the work of Gabriel Almond and Sidney Verba, *The Civic Culture* (Princeton, NJ: Princeton University Press, 1962), but also from its conceptualization as a "script" for persuasion as in Keith Michael Baker, *The Political Culture of the Old Regime*, vol. 1 of *The French Revolution and the Creation of Modern Political Culture* (Oxford: Pergamon Press, 1987), p. xii.
4. The best political scientists in this tradition, such as Richard Bensel, offer much, but remain too geographically determinative. Bensel, *Sectionalism and American Political Development, 1880–1980* (Madison: University of Wisconsin Press, 1984). Regions, as geographer Anssi Paasi shows, emerge from institutional processes. See Paasi, "The Institutionalization of Regions: A Theoretical Framework for Understanding the Emergence of Regions and the Constitution of Regional Identity," *Fennia* 164 (1986): 105–146. We see

institutions as coordinated habits that constitute the fundamental mechanisms of society.

5. Clarence N. Stone, *Regime Politics: Governing Atlanta, 1946–1988* (Lawrence: University Press of Kansas, 1989).

6. We concur with David Mayhew's analysis in Mayhew, *Electoral Realignments: A Critique of an American Genre* (New Haven: Yale University Press, 2002).

7. We owe thanks to John Barnes of the USC Department of Political Science for conversations on this issue. On "intercurrence" see Karen Orren and Stephen Skowronek, *The Search for American Political Development* (New York: Cambridge University Press, 2004). Skowronek's *The Politics Presidents Make* (Cambridge, MA: Harvard University Press, 1997) partly inspired our effort to account for the entire sweep of American history. We see the presidency as a key aspect of regime transformation because "assuming the presidential office and exercising its power has an inherently disruptive effect, and that presidential leadership is a struggle to resolve that effect in the reproduction of a legitimate political order" (*The Politics Presidents Make*, p. xii); For Orren and Skowronek, national regimes are the "working arrangements among institutions" created and managed by a new "governing cadre" that "acts within an intellectual milieu, infusing institutions with meaning, direction and purpose." Orren and Skowroek, "Regimes and Regime Building in American Government" *Political Science Quarterly* 113, no. 4 (Winter 1998/1999): 694.

8. This chapter focuses on the presidency as a key aspect of our dynamic model because of limited space.

9. James H. McGregor, *Washington from the Ground Up* (Cambridge, MA: Belknap Press, 2007).

10. Kenneth R. Bowling shows that these visions tied to the move to DC, in Bowling, *Establishing Congress: The Removal to Washington, D.C., and the Election of 1800* (Athens: Ohio University Press, 2005).

11. Yonatan Eyal, *The Young America Movement and the Transformation of the Democratic Party, 1828–61* (New York: Cambridge University Press, 2007).

12. Martin Shefter, "New York City and American National Politics," in Martin Shefter, ed., *Capital of the American Century: The National and International Influence of New York City* (New York: Russell Sage, 1993), pp. 97–98.

13. Richard Hofstadter, *The Idea of a Party System: The Rise of Legitimate Opposition in the United States, 1780–1840* (Berkeley: University of California Press, 1969), pp. 112, 114–115, 144.

14. Ibid., p. 198.

15. Ibid., pp. 211–231.

16. Shefter, "New York City and American National Politics," pp. 97–98.

17. John Farragher, "Afterword," in *Rereading Frederick Jackson Turner* (New York: Holt, 1994), p. 234.

18. Pamela Herr, *Jessie Benton Frémont: A Biography* (Norman: University of Oklahoma Press, 1988); Gunther Barth, *Instant Cities: Urbanization and the Rise of San Francisco and Denver* (New York: Oxford University Press, 1975).

19. Richard C. Wade, *The Urban Frontier: The Rise of Western Cities, 1790–1830* (Urbana: University of Illinois Press, 1996 [1959]), p. 340.

20. Ibid., p. 115.

21. Ibid., pp. 1, 338–340.

22. Todd Gardner, "Population and Population Growth," in David R. Goldfield, ed., *Encyclopedia of Urban History* (Thousand Oaks, CA: Sage Publications, 2007), p. 592.

23. Robert Beauregard, "The Economy of Cities"; and Dominic Vitiello, "Urban Finance," in Goldfield, ed., *Encyclopedia of Urban History*.
24. William Cronon, *Nature's Metropolis: Chicago and the Great West* (New York: W.W. Norton, 1991).
25. Ulysses S. Grant (1869–1877), Rutherford B. Hayes (1877–1881), James A. Garfield (1881), Benjamin Harrison (1889–1893) (son of Ohio territorial governor and President William Henry Harrison), William McKinley (1897–1901), William Howard Taft (1909–1913), and Warren Harding (1921–1923).
26. Upstate New York Democrat Grover Cleveland, New Yorker Chester A. Arthur, New Yorker Theodore Roosevelt, and New Jersey Democrat Woodrow Wilson.
27. Horatio Seymour, Horace Greeley, Samuel Tilden, Winfield Scott Hancock, and Grover Cleveland.
28. Michael E. McGerr, *The Decline of Popular Politics: The American North, 1865–1928* (New York: Oxford University Press, 1986).
29. Carl N. Degler, "American Political Parties and the Rise of the City: An Interpretation," *Journal of American History* 51, no. 1 (June 1964): 41–59. When Wilson won the presidency in 1912, his margin was small and owed to splintering between Republicans and Progressives.
30. Elizabeth Sanders, *Roots of Reform: Farmers, Workers, and the American State, 1877–1917* (Chicago: University of Chicago Press, 1999), pp. 236–266.
31. Gardner, "Population and Population Growth," p. 594.
32. Bruce W. Robeck, "Urban–Rural and Regional Voting Patterns in the California Senate Before and After Reapportionment," *Western Political Quarterly* 23, no. 4 (December 1970): 786.
33. Kevin M Kruse, *White Flight: Atlanta and the Making of Modern Conservatism* (Princeton, NJ: Princeton University Press, 2005), pp. 21–22. In Georgia, 1920s population figures from http://www.census.gov/population/cencounts/ca190090.txt (accessed October 14, 2007).
34. Samuel J. Eldersveld, "The Influence of Metropolitan Party Pluralities in Presidential Elections Since 1920: A Study of Twelve Key Cities," *American Political Science Review* 43, no. 6 (December 1949): 1189–1206.
35. Terrence J. McDonald, "Introduction," in William L. Riordon, *Plunkitt of Tammany Hall: A Series of Very Plain Talks on Very Practical Politics* (New York: Bedford/St Martins, 1994).
36. J. Joseph Hutmacher, *Senator Robert F. Wagner and the Rise of Urban Liberalism* (New York: Atheneum, 1968).
37. Degler, "American Political Parties and the Rise of the City."
38. Lizabeth Cohen, *Making a New Deal* (New York: Cambridge University Press, 1990), p. 289.
39. Bernard R. Gifford, "New York City and Cosmopolitan Liberalism," *Political Science Quarterly* 93, no. 4 (Winter 1978–1979): 559–584.
40. Eldersveld, "The Influence of Metropolitan Party Pluralities in Presidential Elections Since 1920," p. 1206.
41. Others include the nineteenth-century westward drive and the twentieth-century biracial "southern diaspora." See Matthew D. Lassiter, "Race over Region," *Reviews in American History* 35, no. 1 (2007): 98–104.
42. Kevin M. Kruse and Thomas J. Sugrue, "Introduction," in Kevin M. Kruse and Thomas J. Sugrue, eds., *The New Suburban History* (Chicago: University of Chicago Press, 2006), p. 1.
43. Kenneth Jackson, *Crabgrass Frontier: The Suburbanization of the United States* (New York: Oxford, 1985); Ira Katznelson, *When Affirmative Action Was White: An Untold History of Racial Inequality in Twentieth-Century*

America (New York: W.W. Norton, 2005); David M.P. Freund, *Colored Property: State Policy and White Racial Politics in Suburban America* (Chicago: University of Chicago Press, 2007).

44. Jason Scott Smith, *Building New Deal Liberalism: The Political Economy of Public Works, 1933–1956* (New York: Cambridge University Press, 2006).

45. Matthew D. Lassiter, "Suburban Strategies: The Volatile Center in Postwar American Politics," in Meg Jacobs, William Novak, and Julian Zelizer, eds., *The Democratic Experiment: New Directions in American Political History* (Princeton, NJ: Princeton University Press, 2003). Also see the essays in Kruse and Sugrue, *The New Suburban History.*

46. Eric H. Monkkonen, *The Local State: Public Money And American Cities* (Stanford, CA: Stanford University Press, 1995).

47. Monkkonen, *The Local State*, p. 33.

48. Gail Radford, "From Municipal Socialism to Public Authorities: Institutional Factors in the Shaping of American Public Enterprise," *Journal of American History* 90, no. 3 (2003): 863–890.

49. Thanks to Terrence McDonald for this memorable metaphor.

50. Raymond Mohl, ed., *Searching for the Sunbelt: Historical Perspectives on a Region* (Athens: University of Georgia Press, 1993); Bruce J. Schulman, *From Cotton Belt to Sunbelt: Federal Policy, Economic Development, and the Transformation of the South, 1938–1980* (New York: Oxford University Press, 1991); US Bureau of Census, "Metropolitan and Micropolitan Areas," http://www.census.gov/population/www/estimates/metroarea.html (accessed May 30, 2008).

51. Sidney Blumenthal, *The Rise of the Counter-Establishment* (New York: Times Books, 1986).

52. By "home" we do not mean technically that they were born there, although Nixon was born in Loma Linda, just over the Los Angeles County line, and raised in Whittier, within Los Angeles County. Reagan's entire adult career was based in Hollywood.

53. Terry Lynn Karl, *The Paradox of Plenty: Oil Booms and Petro-States* (Berkeley: University of California Press, 1997).

54. Dennis McDougal, *Privileged Son: Otis Chandler and the Rise and Fall of the L.A. Times Dynasty* (Cambridge, MA: Perseus Publishing, 2001), pp. 73–75.

55. John M. Hart, *Empire and Revolution: The Americans in Mexico since the Civil War* (Berkeley: University of California Press, 2002), p. 172. Hearst's interests are discussed at pp. 170–171.

56. Friedrich Katz, *The Life and Times of Pancho Villa* (Palo Alto, CA: Stanford University Press, 1998), pp. 15–16.

57. For the Chandler endorsement of Nixon, see David Halberstam, *The Powers That Be* (Urbana: University of Illinois Press, 2000).

58. On Atlanta and Charlotte, see Matthew D. Lassiter, *The Silent Majority: Suburban Politics in the Sunbelt South* (Princeton, NJ: Princeton University Press, 2006); on Atlanta only, see Kruse, *White Flight*. Goldwater led an independent node of the new political culture of this Sunbelt regional regime from his base in Phoenix. See Jason LaBau, "Phoenix Rising: Arizona and the Origins of Modern Conservative Politics," PhD dissertation in progress, University of Southern California, History Department.

59. John Judis, *William F. Buckley, Jr: Patron Saint of the Conservatives* (New York: Simon & Schuster, 1988).

60. Ann Markusen et al., *The Rise of the Gunbelt: The Military Remapping of Industrial America* (New York: Oxford University Press, 1991); Margaret

Pugh O'Mara, *Cities of Knowledge: Cold War Science and the Search for the Next Silicon Valley* (Princeton, NJ: Princeton University Press, 2005).

61. Kruse and Sugrue, "Introduction."

62. Kruse, *White Flight*, pp. 259–265.

63. See articles by Chris Bowers on the OpenLeft progressive blog: "Yes, the Medium Is the Movement," May 5, 2008 http://www.openleft.com/showDiary.do?diaryId=5585; "Putting Our Cognitive Surplus to Use," May 6, 2008, http://www.openleft.com/showDiary.do?diaryId=5605; "Obama as a Reflection of the Current Incarnation of the Progressive Movement," May 13, 2008, http://www.openleft.com/showDiary.do?diaryId=5738 (all accessed May 26, 2008).

64. Micah L. Sifry, "What Is Obama's Movement?" May 8, 2008, http://tech president.personaldemocracy.com/blog/entry/25112/what_is_obama_s_movement (accessed May 26, 2008).

65. Noam Cohen, "Craig (of the List) Looks Beyond the Web," *New York Times* May 12, 2008.

66. Markusen et al., *The Rise of the Gunbelt*; O'Mara, *Cities of Knowledge*.

67. Harold Meyerson, "McCain's America," *Washington Post* May 14, 2008, p. A19; Chris Bowers, "The End of the 1960's?" December 14, 2006, http://www.mydd.com/story/2006/12/14/194227/36 (accessed November 9, 2008). See also Chris Bowers, "Growing Demographic Groups Could Provide Obama Victory," *The Nation*, September 1, 2008; and John B. Judis and Ruy Teixeira, "The Re-emergence of the Emerging Democratic Majority," *The American Prospect*, June 19, 2007.

Part IV

The National Significance of Urban Immigrant, Racial, and Ethnic Politics

9 Riots as Critical Junctures

Michael Jones-Correa

Race riots are simultaneously seen as high-profile examples of inter-ethnic tension but also as curiously impotent, having little or no effect in the longer run. The effects of riots have received little attention because the focus in the aftermath has been on governmental response to riots, which is generally acknowledged to be ineffectual. This verdict, however, is based largely on the federal government's response to the race riots of the 1960s: in the broader sweep of the twentieth century this period is the exception rather than the rule.

Historically, the response to riots has more often been *non*-governmental, rather than governmental, and, because riots are primarily local events, the initial response is largely local as well. The response to ethnic violence takes place *first* at the local level and *then* at the national level. Federal agencies rarely create any program *ex nihilo*. Instead, they scavenge among state and local programs for examples of what they want, incorporating local initiatives into federal agendas. Federal intervention is critical, but largely because it reinforces certain local alternatives at the expense of others.

Race riots in the United States have tended to cluster in certain periods—from 1917 to 1921, the 1960s, and from 1980 to 1993—when the rules of race relations are in flux. This chapter argues, first, that at certain historical moments like those of 1917–1921, inter-racial riots in the United States shared common structural conditions and are profitably analyzed as part of a common social process. Second, these riots can be "critical junctures," accelerating institutional shifts in response—for example, in the 1917–1921 period, ushering in an era of racial containment. And third, there are significant parallels and differences between race riots at the beginning and end of the twentieth century. In short, in the right circumstances, race riots can have significant effects, helping to shape new rules of race relations.

Civil Disturbances, 1917–1921

Between 1917 and 1921 there were at least nine major urban civil disturbances in the United States. These riots were symptomatic of rising racism in both North and South. Unlike much of the violence of the late nineteenth century, which was directed at immigrants as well as blacks, by the early twentieth century violence was primarily targeted at African-Americans. Some scholars have suggested that anti-immigrant sentiment in this period waned as immigrants made the transition from "other" to "white," and moreover, that a part of "becoming white" was taking part in violence against black Americans.[1]

These riots have been recounted as part of the broader story of white racism against blacks in the United States, but not as being particularly significant in and of themselves. They have been treated largely as a string of case studies, each illustrating a unique confluence of events, albeit resulting in similar anti-black violence. This is somewhat understandable. Apart from their timing, the nine civil disturbances between 1917 and 1921 seem to have little in common. They are widely dispersed geographically and their causes are seen as essentially non-replicable. Historical accounts have gravitated toward the particularities of the immediate events surrounding the disturbances. The historians Lee Williams and Lee Willliams II, for instance, chronicled several of the riots (Knoxville; Elaine, AR; Tulsa; and Chicago) in hour-by-hour detail without providing any real explanation of why they took place.[2] Elsewhere we learn that the riot in Elaine began over a share-cropping dispute; that Tulsa's began with a gathering outside the courthouse following the arrest of an alleged black rapist; and that Chicago's 1919 riot began after the drowning of a black boy at an all-white beach on Lake Michigan. Washington, DC's riot began after the newspapers began printing lurid stories on black crime, and Atlanta's followed clashes between white sailors and demobilized black soldiers on leave.[3]

It's not that these histories aren't interesting. These were, after all, some of the bloodiest riots in American history—thirty-eight people died in the Chicago riots alone (twenty-three blacks and fifteen whites) and more than 500 persons were injured. Though the riots usually began with whites targeting blacks, blacks were hardly passive victims. Both blacks and whites used rifles, pistols, knives, and firebombs. Both groups tested new technologies in these riots; automobiles were used, for instance, in Washington, DC, and Chicago to drive up and down streets while their occupants fired at bystanders. In Tulsa, there were rumors of airplanes being used to track the movement of blacks, and even to hurl down bombs. There were a lot of rumors in general: of women and children murdered; of black rapes and white looting, of rings of black gun-smugglers in East St Louis and of Mexicans assisting blacks in the manufacture of bombs in Chicago; and of all kinds of secret plots and conspiracies against both whites and blacks.[4] This all took place against a backdrop of political corruption, police incompetence, racist unions, and a sensationalist press.

The best accounts of the period point out structural factors underlying the disturbances. The Chicago Commission on Race Relations' report gathered extensive demographic, economic, and fieldwork data to make the argument that the riots had three main causes: the migration of blacks from the South, the problem of housing for blacks in Chicago, and tense relations at work.[5] Accounts of Chicago,[6] Detroit,[7] Cleveland,[8] and Springfield, IL,[9] have all borrowed from and elaborated on the suggestions of the Chicago Commission's report. But while there have been a number of excellent case histories, historians have not attempted a comparative analysis of riot antecedents. It is far from clear, therefore, whether the structural preconditions apply across riot cities, or really distinguish them from non-riot cities.

There has been only one quantitative effort at analyzing possible commonalities among the riots of the period: sociologists Stanley Lieberson and Arnold Silverman's 1965 study of paired cases of riot and non-riot cities from 1913 to 1963. The study has the advantage of looking at both riot and non-riot cities across a wider pool of cities, but is limited by its methodology, which relies on a simple comparison across cases.[10] They concluded that nothing in particular distinguished riot cities from non-riot cities. A lengthy list of authors have tried and failed to come up with *any* meaningful quantitative comparisons of underlying factors to the urban riots of the 1960s.[11] Their negative findings cast a pall on the use of quantitative tools to explore riots more generally. Further investigation has been put off by the difficulty of getting adequate data to test any hypotheses.[12]

Since 1997, however, the Integrated Public Use Microdata Series (IPUMS) project at the University of Minnesota has made greater comparison of census material across years possible for statistical analysis. IPUMS is a database of randomly sampled census data from 1850 to the present.[13] For the 1910 Census, for instance, the project took a sample of one in every 250 records, providing 113,024 individual records for people who were living in cities with populations over 25,000. For 1920, with a sample of one in every 200 records, there were 172,693 records. These individual records hold person and household data, including information on race, gender, ethnicity, citizenship (and, for immigrants, year of arrival and proficiency in English), city of residence, home ownership, occupation, education levels, and literacy. By aggregating these data to the city level, we can see if there is something particular about the socio-economic conditions of cities that might have led to a riot outcome. These data, then, allow another look at hypotheses regarding the structural conditions underlying inter-racial disturbances.

Using the IPUMS data I tested three hypotheses. The first is whether these riots were related to the urbanization of Southern blacks, who were moving in increasing numbers into cities across the South, North, and Midwest. Black migration from the South to the North and West had been increasing steadily since the 1880s, but the Great Migration really began after 1910. The migration figures are sketchy, but between 1910 and 1920 about 500,000 or more blacks moved out of the South, with most of the migration occurring after 1916 (thirteen Southern states had an absolute loss of black population).[14] The reasons for the migration are various. The devastation of the cotton crop in the South and resulting tensions within the share-cropping system certainly contributed, as did the increase in black lynchings. Anti-immigrant legislation cut off Northern labor supplies, and after the US entered World War I one million men were removed from the labor force.[15] Employers who never would have considered blacks for semi-skilled manufacturing jobs before then began not only hiring but also actively recruiting black migrants.[16] Within a very short period of time African-American populations in Northern and Midwestern cities doubled, tripled, and quadrupled. The population surge was concentrated as well: three out of four black migrants went to Chicago, New York, Detroit, Philadelphia, St Louis, Cleveland, and Cincinnati.[17]

The analysis of the data (see Table 9.1 in the appendix for the full results) indicates that for every increase of 10,000 persons in a city's population, there was a corresponding 1 percent increase in the chance of riot. Holding city population, black population, and foreign-born constant, we see that smaller cities were more likely to experience civil disturbances in this time period. Change in population is significant, which bolsters the migration thesis, though black migration is not significant.[18]

The second hypothesis is that labor competition was increasing between blacks and whites in this period, since blacks were moving increasingly into both skilled and unskilled positions previously occupied only by whites. This period was characterized by increasingly bitter accusations that blacks were being recruited by Northern employers as strikebreakers. In East St Louis, after strikes in 1916 at meat-packing plants and in 1917 at the Aluminum Ore Company, there was considerable resentment on the part of white workers about the hiring of non-unionized blacks.[19] In the Chicago stockyards strike of 1904 and the Teamsters strike of 1905, employers used non-union black workers as strikebreakers.[20] The fact that white immigrants also played the role of scabs and that blacks were discouraged from joining predominantly white unions was conveniently overlooked.[21]

The data show that for every increase of 10,000 black skilled laborers there was a 6.7 percent increase in the chances of rioting; a corresponding decrease in white skilled labor meant a 1.2 percent increase in the likelihood of a disturbance. Thus the main locus of competition between blacks and whites was in the area of skilled labor, rather than unskilled labor or service jobs. This helps confirm a version of the labor competition thesis, with an emphasis on upwardly mobile blacks, rather than those at the bottom rungs of the ladder, the common laborers.

The third hypothesis is that there was competition over housing and public space. Residents of middle- and upper-class neighborhoods who had the resources to move further out to the city's edge or beyond tended to give way in the face of black middle-class incursions, while working-class whites who were irrevocably tied to their investments in their homes were more likely to stay and resist. In Cleveland, for example, areas of black settlement were bounded in some places by native-born settlements, and in other places by neighborhoods of Russian Jews and other Central European immigrants. As African-Americans sought housing, native-born whites in adjacent neighborhoods moved readily to outlying areas. Russian Jews, who were largely renters, moved relatively quickly as well. It was the second-generation immigrant neighborhoods, with fewer resources than the native-born but higher rates of home ownership than Russian Jews, which held fast and at times violently resisted black migration into their neighborhoods.[22] Immigrants in these neighborhoods, "[h]aving raised themselves above poverty, acquired a small home (with perhaps a large mortgage as well) and attained a modest level of income . . . were fearful of association with any group bearing the stigma of low status."[23] There were similar processes at work in other cities: in Chicago's 1919 race riot, historian Dominic Pacyga points out that more blacks were killed in Irish neighborhoods to the east of the "black belt," where middle-class African-Americans were competing for housing, than to the west, where blacks crossed Polish and Italian neighborhoods on the way to work in the meat-packing district.[24] As black neighbors moved in, threatening to devalue the real-estate investments of the Irish lower-middle class, the goal became the removal of African-Americans from the neighborhood.[25]

The analysis of the IPUMS data indicates that for every 10,000 new white homeowners, there was a 2 percent increase in the chances of rioting. Thus the higher the number of white homeowners, the greater the chances of an urban disturbance. This provides some confirmation to the notion that it was the resistance of white homeowners to the increasing movement of blacks into formerly all-white residential neighborhoods that helped contribute to the civil disturbances of the period.

Riots as Critical Junctures

The data thus suggest, contrary to much of the earlier research on race riots in the United States, that in at least some circumstances riots do share common structural characteristics. In particular, the evidence supports historians' contentions that between 1917 and 1921 population change, and consequently competition over housing and jobs, set the stage for inter-racial violence. Yet this still doesn't explain how these riots contribute to our understanding of American race relations, other than to serve as markers of the high-points of inter-ethnic violence. Why do these riots matter?

Scholars looking for answers to similar questions after the period of racial rioting in the 1960s concluded that while riots had psychological

and ideological consequences for the black community, the riots themselves elicited a limited institutional response. In general, studies found
that riot commission reports were almost universally ignored, that rioting
had at best moderate effects on programmatic spending by government
agencies, and that the clearest beneficiaries of the rioting were law
enforcement agencies.[26] The conclusion, on the whole, was that riots
didn't seem to have much of an effect at all.

In order to better understand the significance of these riots we have to
ask a different question: Why is it that even though black migration
accelerated in the 1920s there were no further inter-racial explosions in
that decade? If these earlier riots were post-war phenomena, triggered by
recession, why wasn't there more tension after 1929? The next large-scale
racial disturbances were in Harlem in 1935 and then Detroit in 1943. The
relative absence of large-scale violence after 1921 indicates that these
earlier riots may have been something of a turning point in urban race
relations. But what kind of turning point were they?

One approach to this question is available from the historical institu-
tionalists. Steven Krasner, who writes primarily about international
relations, posits a view of history as a series of "critical junctures" when
periods of institutional stability are disrupted by intermittent exogenous
shocks. [27] Institutions are thrown off-balance by these events and either
adapt through radical change, or collapse, spurring the rise of new institutional arrangements. Stephen Skowronek has written similarly that "crisis
situations tend to become the watersheds in a state's institutional development. Actions taken to meet the challenge often lead to the establishment
of new institutional forms, powers and precedents."[28]

Cities experiencing riots in the period 1917–1921 did not see a massive
breakdown and rebirth of institutions. Yet the riots may be considered
less revolutionary "critical junctures," not challenging the stability of
the state but still acting as a watershed in aspects of state institutional
development. Just as demographic changes and economic competition
contributed to riots, the riots themselves contributed to the rise of institutions that addressed these social tensions, and contained them. These
racial disturbances left behind an "institutional legacy," accelerating
some local organizational and institutional outcomes at the expense of
others, which in turn left a long-lasting mark on national inter-racial
interactions.[29]

Crises such as riots provide simply an *opening* for institutional change
that itself does not guarantee any particular institutional outcome. As
political scientists Ruth Collier and David Collier find in their study of
regime transitions in Latin America, the persistence and stability of
institutional legacies is not automatic, but "rather, is perpetuated through
ongoing . . . political processes."[30] In this view the persistence of
institutions is as much a puzzle as their disruption. As W. Richard Scott
notes,

the persistence of institutions, once created, is an understudied phenomenon . . . persistence is not to be taken for granted. It requires continuing effort . . . if structures are not to erode or dissolve. The conventional term for persistence—inertia—seems on reflection to be too passive and non-problematic.[31]

Institutions are not invulnerable to change, to decay, or to challenge. Attention to the contingent nature of institutional legacies is a departure from Skowronek and Krasner's view, in which the aftermath of critical junctures is relatively unproblematic. For Krasner, it's enough to state that "once crises are past institutional arrangements tend to solidify" without specifying the mechanisms by which this institutional solidity is established.[32] The Colliers, on the other hand, write that "[i]n analyzing the legacy of the critical juncture, it is important to recognize that no legacy lasts forever." Some legacies, "self-destruct" by producing political dynamics that mitigate against the formation of stable institutional patterns.[33] What allows an institution to persist is how it meshes with other institutional processes already underway.

As late as 1910 blacks were less segregated in Midwestern and Northern cities than some recent immigrant groups, notably Italians, Russians, and Romanians.[34] This changed between 1910 and 1920, as African-Americans began increasing in numbers in urban areas and whites began experimenting with ways to minimize contact between black and white populations, particularly by keeping blacks in restricted residential areas. In Chicago, for instance, "the number of census tracts that were over 50% black rose from 4 in 1910 to 16 in 1920; 35% of the city's blacks lived in census tracts that were over 75% black."[35] By the 1920s efforts to maintain racial boundaries had settled on private restrictive agreements or covenants. These were contracts not to sell, rent, or lease property to minority groups, usually blacks (but also Jews and Asians) either among individuals or between individuals and an interested third party such as a developer, real-estate board, or neighborhood improvement agency. As a form of *private* contract covenants were legally enforceable in court and were upheld by the Supreme Court.

The usual story explaining the spread of restrictive covenants is that they were a response to the Supreme Court's ban on racial zoning.[36] Beginning in 1910, several Southern cities had used municipal zoning ordinances to prescribe separate zones for blacks and whites; by 1915 city councils in Baltimore, Richmond, Winston-Salem, Louisville, and Birmingham had enacted segregation ordinances.[37] Dallas followed in 1916, and St Louis held a popular referendum whose results showed the public two-to-one in favor.[38] At the time it seemed that legislated racial zoning had the potential to spread throughout the country, but the National Association for the Advancement of Colored People (NAACP) and its allies took the issue to the Supreme Court, where zoning of this sort was overruled in *Buchanan v. Warely* (1917). Though the court was finding elsewhere that the state could not interfere with private racism, neither could it tolerate the state's enforcement of racial zoning. These ordinances, the court found, interfered with individuals' property rights.[39]

Restrictive covenants came into wider use just around the time the Supreme Court ruled against racial municipal zoning. So it seems reasonable to assume, as many have, that covenants were a response to the court's decision. Yet if covenants were simply substituting for zoning, then covenants should have appeared first in cities mostly in Southern and border states that already had experience with racial zoning. All the evidence points, however, to the appearance of racial restrictive covenants *not* in these cities but in municipalities in the North and West.[40]

Cities in these regions implemented racial restrictive covenants not as part of a continuing campaign of segregation in all forms of public life (as zoning had been in the South),[41] but rather as a response to the rapid demographic shifts occurring in urban areas, awareness of which was dramatically heightened by the racial disturbances of the period. Moreover, racially restrictive covenants became the primary tool to maintain segregated neighborhoods only after the racial disturbances of 1917–1921.

The timing of the implementation of race restrictive covenants seems to support this interpretation of events. Race-specific deed restrictions in St Louis sharply increased in number between 1915 and 1919, around the time of the 1917 disturbances in East St Louis, just across the Mississippi River. Chicago's covenant campaigns didn't begin until the 1920s, in the aftermath of that city's riots in 1919. In both cities, once introduced, covenants spread quickly.[42] The appearance of racial covenants first in the Midwest and the coincidence of the timing of their appearance with the race riots taking place provide evidence of the independent effect of the riots on the introduction of restrictive covenants.

By the late 1920s race-restrictive covenants had spread both within and among cities, particularly in the North and West.[43] Thus blacks in Northern cities continued to have free access to housing in theory, but in practice their choices were increasingly limited. The usual pattern was to have concentrations of restrictive agreements in areas around black neighborhoods, relatively sparse coverage elsewhere in the city, and much more widespread application in newer suburban developments.[44] In Chicago, for instance, by 1947 covenants covered about half of the city's residential sections.[45] With black neighborhoods hemmed in on all sides, either by industrial zones, covenanted neighborhoods or Lake Michigan, the area occupied by blacks remained substantially the same from the 1920s to the 1940s, when covenants were finally ruled unconstitutional.

Riots and National Housing Policy

The rise of restrictive covenants is hardly the whole story. There were *alternative* responses to the riots that were less successful. For example, the 1922 Chicago Commission studying the aftermath of the riot suggested that one solution to the underlying tensions would be for the public sector to become more involved in providing housing for new black migrants and to encourage the dispersal of African-Americans through the city.[46] This clearly did not happen. On the other hand, the spread of the Ku Klux Klan in Northern and Midwestern cities in the early 1920s, in response to immigration and black migration, failed as well.[47] In short, in response to crises, cities spawn a wide range of institutional and organizational responses, some of which persist but many of which do not. To explain why racially restrictive covenants and their cousins—racial steering, block-busting, and redlining—were more successful, institutionally, than their alternatives in the aftermath of the riots, we must explore how the institutional legacies of these kinds of critical junctures are diminished or increased by their interactions with broader institutions that are going through their own processes of change.

In the 1910s and 1920s responses to the perceived incursion of blacks were primarily local and private. The federal government was largely absent from the picture. While the federal judiciary upheld local racial restrictions, the federal government simply did not have the capacity to meddle in any kind of detail in municipal affairs. This is reflected in the figures for federal monetary transfers to the states. Before 1921 transfers were minimal. The passage of the Federal Highway Act that year saw the first significant flow of funds to localities, and it was opposed by urban representatives, who saw it primarily as a boondoggle benefiting rural counties.[48] Metropolitan governments, for their part, did not have the inclination, or the resources, to address the structural issues underlying civil disturbances.

As a result, restrictive covenants and the like were initially sponsored not by the public sector but by private actors. Real-estate boards and their allies, particularly neighborhood and homeowners' associations, endorsed restrictive covenants and mobilized campaigns to collect the necessary signatures for their creation.[49] Local real-estate agents were enjoined by the National Association of Real Estate Boards (NAREB) to avoid "infiltration of inharmonious elements" into neighborhoods. Article 34 of NAREB's code of ethics stated: "A realtor should never be instrumental in introducing into a neighborhood . . . members of any race or nationality . . . whose presence will clearly be detrimental to property values . . ."[50] Real-estate boards could, and did, expel or ostracize members who did not keep to the code.[51] The fact that Chicago was home to NAREB was instrumental not only in the local realtors' enthusiastic support for covenants, but also in the propagation of covenants elsewhere. In 1927

NAREB drafted a standard restrictive covenant document that was then shared with local real-estate boards around the country, and encouraged local boards to form homeowners' associations to sign onto covenant agreements.[52] Together these loose confederations of national and local associations did much of the work of enforcing patterns of racial residential segregation, which kept African-American residents confined to deteriorating urban neighborhoods.

Restrictive covenants succeeded in part because they were in step with the segregationist notions of the time, but their implementation and diffusion was by no means preordained. Like other responses to the riots, racially restrictive covenants ran into challenges from very early on. The NAACP began contesting covenants almost as soon as they were implemented, though they weren't overturned by the Supreme Court until 1948.[53] If racial restrictions on residential housing had relied solely on local efforts, it's likely that residential desegregation would have begun to take place sooner than it did.[54] These racialized institutions would not have been able to sustain themselves if not for the backing of local institutions such as real-estate boards, and later, the federal institutions that played an increasingly important role in the housing market after 1932.

Private, local responses were inherently vulnerable to challenge. While they originated in the *absence* of a strong federal presence, they persisted *because* of that presence. With the Depression, the federal government began to increase its involvement in local affairs, not least in the area of housing. This involvement began with the establishment of the Home Owners Loan Corporation (HOLC) in 1933, which was designed to reduce mortgage foreclosures.[55] HOLC single-handedly established the pattern for long-term mortgage loans. In doing so, it had to make predictions about how housing covered would fare over the life-time of the loan. Housing appraisals became increasingly systematized, rating not only the structural integrity of the homes themselves but also the neighborhoods surrounding them. Areas were rated, with the ratings privileging homogeneous native-born white-collar neighborhoods, and downgrading older, mixed-use, ethnic, or black neighborhoods.[56] As a result, African-American neighborhoods were systematically deprived of mortgages. The patterns established under HOLC persisted after it was folded into the Federal Housing Administration (FHA), which "started its career by accepting prevalent real estate doctrine that nonwhites should be kept out of white neighborhoods in order to protect property values."[57] The FHA's 1938 *Underwriting Manual* instructed appraisers that "if a neighborhood is to retain stability, it is necessary that properties shall continue to be occupied by the same social and racial classes." Appraisers were to predict "the probability of the location being invaded by . . . incompatible racial and social groups."[58] To "preserve" neighborhood character, FHA officials were enjoined to uphold racial restrictive covenants. The *Manual* openly recommended "subdivision regulations and suitable restrictive covenants" that would be "superior to any mortgage."[59] Federal intervention encouraged segregated housing by reinforcing local discriminatory practices, among them race-restrictive covenants.

The story of the federal government's role in promoting segregated housing has been told extensively elsewhere.[60] The point emphasized here is the link between local and federal institutions. As the federal government played a greater role in local affairs during the Depression, it did not step in and invent entirely new institutional structures and practices. More often it melded its new role with existing practices. In the case of housing this meant adopting the standard practices of local real-estate boards and banks, particularly in respecting and upholding local restrictive covenants and racial steering. As HOLC and then the FHA got underway, they were staffed at the federal and local levels by former real-estate professionals who operated under and accepted the realtor profession's racial strictures,[61] and who then transferred these norms into federal practices. For example, Frederick Babcock, a prominent figure in real-estate appraisal, who wrote a widely-used appraising text *The Valuation of Real Estate* (1932) advocating the enforcement of racially segregated neighborhoods,[62] went on to write the FHA's 1938 *Underwriting Manual*, which incorporated similar assumptions of the desirability of neighborhood homogeneity and the pernicious influence of black homeownership on property values.[63] In this and other respects, the FHA's institutional racism was a reflection of local attitudes and policies.

Historian Kenneth Jackson writes that the lasting damage done by the national government was that it "put its seal of approval on ethnic and racial discrimination" and that "more seriously, Washington's actions were later picked up by private interests, so that banks and savings and loan institutions institutionalized the practice of denying mortgages 'solely because of the geographical location of the property'"[64]—that is, redlining. While the role of the federal government in reinforcing racially segregated housing in urban areas was certainly crucial in extending the half-life of race-restrictive covenants and other local segregationist tools, the historical record shows that influence between local and federal institutions ran both ways—the federal government *first* adopted local racial institutions, and in doing so, reinforced them.[65]

Civil Disturbances in the Late Twentieth Century

The structural contexts leading to racial rioting in the 1917–1921 period are not unique in American history. The urban ethnic disturbances from 1980 to 1993, for example, share many of the same characteristics as the earlier riots from 1917 to 1921. These later riots are also characterized by rapid urban demographic shifts and competition among new and old residents over scarce resources, occurring in the context of an economic downturn, and a general shift of resources away from cities.[66] In this more contemporary case, the migrants changing the ethnic and racial demographics of cities are new immigrants arriving to the US after 1965 (many of them since 1980) into particular regions, and to particular cities within those regions.

This immigrant wave is bifurcated between the highly educated and those with relatively few skills. Those with fewer skills tend to settle in areas where they can afford housing, which means settling in areas in or adjacent to poorer black neighborhoods. The black middle class, having more resources, has been moving out of these neighborhoods since the late 1960s, and this trend only accelerated through the 1970s and 1980s. Those left in these neighborhoods are those with the fewest resources. The convergence of two populations with very few resources and overlapping occupational and residential niches has led to friction and occasionally rioting. Four of the top ten immigrant-receiving urban areas had riots in the 1980s and 1990s—Los Angeles, New York, Miami, and Washington, DC.

Similar to the riots of the early twentieth century, it thus seems the riots at the end of the century were caused in large part by population change, job competition, and residential displacement. These hypotheses are tested again using the IPUMS census data. For 1980 there are 515,201 records for individuals residing in cities with populations of 100,000 or more; for 1990 there are 438,482 such records. Aggregating these samples to the city level (134 cities with populations of 100,000 or more for 1980 and 135 in 1990 results in a sample of 103 cases: those cities with populations of 100,000 or more included in both the 1980 and 1990 samples.

The regression results (see Table 9.2 in the appendix) echo those of the model for the earlier period. The greater the change in population, and indirectly in foreign-born population, the greater the likelihood of a city having an inter-ethnic disturbance.[67] For every 10,000 native-born blacks who left factory jobs in the 1980s there was a corresponding 8 percent increase in the likelihood of a riot; thus the more factory jobs lost by African-Americans during the 1980s, the more likely a city was to experience a riot.[68] Finally, the greater the increase in African-American homeownership in the 1980s, the greater the chances of a civil disturbance. For every increase of 10,000 African-American homeowners, there was a 5 percent increase in the likelihood of an inter-ethnic disturbance. The evidence thus suggests that the situation in the 1980s and 1990s parallels that of the 1910s and 1920s, when white homeowners, who were those with the highest stake in changing neighborhoods, resisted the incursions of newcomers. Black homeowners in the 1980s, under considerable economic pressures and seeing their stakes in their neighborhoods at risk, may have reacted the same way.

While there are similarities between the riots at the beginning and end of the twentieth century, it's also important to note at least two differences between these time periods. First, a lot happened in race relations between 1920 and 1980. The Supreme Court's increasing activism in race relations, the civil rights movement, the passage of Civil and Voting Rights acts in the 1960s, and the urban rioting of that decade all helped shape subsequent interactions between blacks and whites, and between blacks and other non-whites. As non-white immigrants entered into cities in the 1980s, there simply weren't the racialized institutions in place that had greeted black migrants to cities in the 1910s and 1920s. And while native-born blacks may mistrust new immigrants, and fear the impact of the new immigration on black opportunities, there simply is not the same kind of racial backlash that greeted black migrants to the North and West in the 1910s and 1920s. Second, with whites moving out of cities following World War II, and with the new immigration after 1965, cities have become much more multi-racial today than they were in the 1920s. Of the cities where major riots occurred in the 1980s and 1990s, Los Angeles, New York, Miami, and Washington, DC, all had non-white majorities.[69] This means that ethnic interactions are more complex, taking place among three and sometimes four groups of ethnic actors.

These differences are important in shaping the outcomes following the disturbances. In the 1980s and 1990s, like the earlier period, the institutional responses in the aftermath of the civil disturbances were more or less likely to persist depending on institutions' capacity to maintain themselves and their interaction with other institutional "layers." Again, like the earlier period, there were competing local responses to the riots. These generally took the form of initiatives to encourage private-sector investment in riot-stricken areas, or attempts at fostering inter-ethnic contact and negotiation. Unlike the 1920s, none of the alternatives were designed to "contain" new immigrants. But race was present (and absent) in interesting ways: while the ethnic negotiation solution was meant to put race and ethnicity on the table for discussion, the private-sector solution was explicitly "de-racialized."

What happened, in a nutshell, is that the turn to the private sector by cities such as Miami and Los Angeles to provide new investments in riot-affected neighborhoods, coincided with, and was reinforced by, the federal government's *own* experimentation with private investment— through Enterprise and Empowerment Zones—as the solution to urban ills. Attempts at inter-ethnic dialogue in the four cities have, for the most part, simply died a quiet death.

Conclusion

Traditional explanations of riots emphasize their contingency and impotence. This chapters argues that, on the contrary, at certain historical moments, such as that around 1917–1921, inter-racial conflicts in the United States share common structural conditions and fall into similar kinds of patterns, and second, that these riots are "critical junctures" because they accelerate institutional shifts, so that riots in the 1917–1921 period, for instance, ushered in an era of racial containment. This argument is particularly significant because it reverses the typical narrative regarding the interaction between institutions and race. In the usual story, institutional intervention is top-down and the federal government is the principal actor. In the events highlighted here, it is local events that are critical, and federal intervention, while important for the long-term patterning of inter-ethnic relations, reinforces racial paradigms only once they are already set into place at the local level.

Notes

1. Susan Olzak, *The Dynamics of Ethnic Competition and Conflict* (Stanford, CA: Stanford University Press, 1992).
2. Lee E. Williams and Lee E. Williams II, *Anatomy of Four Race Riots: Racial Conflict in Knoxville, Elaine (Arkansas), Tulsa, and Chicago 1919–1921* (Jackson: University and College Press of Mississippi, 1972).
3. Herbert Shapiro, *White Violence and Black Response: From Reconstruction to Montgomery* (Amherst: University of Massachusetts Press, 1988).
4. National Advisory Commission on Civil Disorders, *Report of the National Advisory Commission on Civil Disorders* (New York: Bantam Books, 1968), p. 21.
5. Chicago Commission on Race Relations, *The Negro in Chicago: A Study of Race Relations and the Race Riot in 1919* (New York: Arno Press, 1968; originally published by the University of Chicago Press, 1922).
6. Allan Spear, *Black Chicago: The Making of a Negro Ghetto 1890–1920* (Chicago: University of Chicago Press, 1969); William M. Tuttle, "Contested Neighborhoods and Racial Violence: Prelude to the Chicago Riot of 1919," *Journal of Negro History* 55 (1970): 266–288 and Arnold Hirsch, *Making the Second Ghetto: Race and Housing in Chicago, 1940–1960* (New York: Cambridge University Press, 1983).
7. Thomas Sugrue, *The Origins of the Urban Crisis: Race and Inequality in Postwar Detroit* (Princeton, NJ: Princeton University Press, 1996).
8. Kenneth Kusmer, *A Ghetto Takes Shape: Black Cleveland, 1870–1930* (Urbana: University of Illinois Press, 1976).
9. Roberta Senechal, *The Sociogenesis of a Race Riot: Springfield, Illinois in 1908* (Urbana: University of Illinois Press, 1980).
10. Stanley Lieberson and Arnold R. Silverman, "The Precipitants and Underlying Conditions of Race Riots," *American Sociological Review* 30, no. 6 (1965): 887–898. The Lieberson and Silverman study is also flawed by comparing very different kinds of riots, juxtaposing the competition-driven riots of the 1910s and 1920s along with the more politicized riots of the 1960s. Morris Janowitz marks a similar difference, distinguishing between what he called the "communal" riots of the early period with the "commodity riots" of the 1960s. Janowitz, "Patterns of Collective Racial Violence," in Hugh D. Graham and Ted R. Gurr, eds., *The History of Violence in America* (New York: Bantam, 1969), p. 412. See also Allen D. Grimshaw, "Urban Racial Violence in the United States: Changing Ecological Considerations," *American Journal of Sociology* 65 (September 1960): 109–119, who hints at similar distinctions.

11. The National Advisory Commission on Civil Disorders concluded, for instance: "We have been unable to identify constant patterns in all aspects of civil disorders. We have found that they are unusual, irregular, complex and, in the present state of knowledge, unpredictable social processes. Like most human events, they do not unfold in orderly sequences" (*Report of the National Advisory Commission on Civil Disorders*). See also William R. Kelly and Larry Isaac, "The Rise and Fall of Urban Racial Violence in the U.S.: 1948–1979," *Research in Social Movements, Conflict and Change* 7 (1984): 203–233; Peter Eisinger, *The Conditions of Protest Behavior in American Cities* (Madison: University of Wisconsin Press, 1972); Seymour Spilerman, "Structural Characteristics of Cities and the Severity of Racial Disorders," *American Sociological Review* 41 (October 1976): 771–793, "The Causes of Racial Disturbances: Tests of an Explanation," *American Sociological Review* 36 (June 1971): 427–442, and "The Causes of Racial Disturbances: A Comparison of Alternative Explanations," *American Sociological Review* 35 (August 1970): 627–649; and Milton Bloombaum, "The Conditions Underlying Race Riots," *American Sociological Review* 33 (February 1968): 76–91. At least two authors found some evidence for structural effects: Bryan T. Downes, "Social and Political Characteristics of Riot Cities: A Comparative Study," *Social Science Quarterly* 49 (December 1968): 504–520; and William R. Morgan and Terry Nichols Clark, "The Causes of Racial Disorders: A Grievance Level Explanation," *American Sociological Review* 38 (October 1973): 611–624. For a recent re-examination of Spilerman's data see Susan Olzak, Suzanne Shanahan, and Elizabeth McEneaney, "Poverty, Segregation, and Race Riots: 1960–1993," *American Sociological Review* 61 (August 1996): 590–613; and Daniel J. Myers, "Racial Rioting in the 1960s: An Event History Analysis of Local Conditions," *American Sociological Review* 62 (February 1997): 94–112.

12. Though see Susan Olzak and Suzanne Shanahan, "Racial Policy and Racial Conflict in the Urban United States, 1869–1924," *Social Forces* 82, no. 2 (December 2003): 481–517.

13. Steven Ruggles and Matthew Sobek, *Integrated Public Use Microdata Series (IPUMS) 1850–1990* (Minneapolis: Social History Research Laboratory, University of Minnesota, 1990). See http://usa.ipums.org/usa/ (accessed October 20, 2008).

14. For estimates see Florette Henri, *Black Migration: Movement North 1900–1920* (Garden City, NY: Anchor Press/Doubleday, 1975), p. 51; Marcus E. Jones, *Black Migration in the United States with Emphasis on Selected Central Cities* (Saratoga, FL: Century 21 Publishing, 1980), p. 35; Ira Katznelson, *Black Men, White Cities: Race, Politics and Migration in the United States 1900–1930 and Britain 1948–1964* (London: Oxford University Press, 1973), p. 31; Joe William Trotter, "Blacks in the Urban North: The 'Underclass' Question in Historical Perspective," in Michael B. Katz, ed., *The Underclass Debate: Views From History* (Princeton, NJ: Princeton University Press, 1993), p. 68; and Daniel M. Johnson and Rex R. Campbell, *Black Migration in America: A Social Demographic History* (Durham, NC: Duke University Press, 1981), p. 74. This time period also saw a considerable *white* migration from the South (Jones, *Black Migration in the United States*, p. 35).

15. Chicago Commission on Race Relations, *Negro in Chicago*.

16. Johnson and Campbell, *Black Migration in America*, pp. 71, 86.

17. Jones, *Black Migration*, p. 38.

18. Part of the reason for this may be that the population measures are too imprecise. For instance, in addition to the normal hazards of estimating

population, it is generally acknowledged that the Census Bureau did a poor job of counting the black population and migration rates during this period. In addition the decennial Census does not capture year-to-year variance. Much of the black population of East St Louis, for instance, apparently left following the riot in 1917. This Census does not capture this rise and fall.

19. Elliot M. Rudwick, *Race Riot at East St. Louis, July 2, 1917* (Carbondale: Southern Illinois University Press, 1968), pp. 18, 27; Chicago Commission on Race Relations, *Negro in Chicago*, p. 74. For an account of strike-breaking in New York City see Gilbert Osofsky, *Harlem: The Making of a Ghetto* (New York: Harper and Row, 1963).

20. Trotter, "Blacks in the Urban North," p. 63; Spear, *Black Chicago*, p. 36. In a 1919 report the US Department of Labor claimed that black strike-breaking had little effect on labor standards. See Henri, *Black Migration*, note 66 quoting a report by the US Department of Labor, Division of Negro Economics, *Negro Migration in 1916–1917* (Washington, DC: Government Printing Office, 1919), p. 135.

21. Chicago Commission on Race Relations, *Negro in Chicago*, pp. 419–420. Only nine American Federation of Labor unions openly prohibited blacks, but many locals gave blacks second-class membership, allowed locals to bar blacks, which many did, or allowed the segregation of blacks in "Jim Crow" local branches (Kusmer, *A Ghetto Takes Shape*, p. 67).

22. Kusmer, *A Ghetto Takes Shape*, pp. 170–171.

23. Ibid., p. 171.

24. Dominic Pacyga, "Chicago's 1919 Race Riot: Ethnicity, Class and Urban Violence," in Raymond Mohl, ed., *The Making of Urban America* (Wilmington, DE: Scholarly Resources, 1997), pp. 187–207.

25. Pacyga, "Chicago's 1919 Race Riot," p. 205. See also James Grossman, *Land of Hope: Chicago, Black Southerners and the Great Migration* (Chicago: University of Chicago Press, 1989), p. 175.

26. See James W. Button, *Black Violence: The Political Impact of the 1960s Riots* (Princeton, NJ: Princeton University Press, 1978); Michael Lipsky and David J. Olson, *Commission Politics: The Processing of Racial Crisis in America* (New Brunswick, NJ: Transaction Books, 1977).

27. Stephen Krasner, *International Regimes* (Ithaca, NY: Cornell University Press, 1983), p. 234.

28. Stephen Skowronek, *Building a New American State: The Expansion of National Administrative Capacities, 1877–1920* (New York: Cambridge University Press, 1982), p. 10.

29. Ruth Berins Collier and David Collier, *Shaping the Political Arena: Critical Junctures, the Labor Movement and Regime Dynamics in Latin America* (Princeton, NJ: Princeton University Press, 1991), p. 30.

30. Ibid., p. 31.

31. W. Richard Scott, *Institutions and Organizations* (Thousand Oaks, CA: Sage Publications, 1995), p. 90.

32. Krasner, *International Regimes*, p. 234.

33. Collier and Collier, *Shaping the Political Arena*, p. 34.

34. Stanley Lieberson, *A Piece of the Pie: Blacks and White Immigrants Since 1880* (Berkeley: University of California Press, 1980); Karl E. Taeuber and Alma F. Taeuber, *Negroes in Cities* (Chicago: Aldine, 1965), pp. 235–238; Kenneth Kusmer, *A Ghetto Takes Shape: Black Cleveland, 1870–1930* (Urbana: University of Illinois Press 1976), pp. 43, 164.

35. Trotter, "Blacks in the Urban North," pp. 74–75.

36. Spear, *Black Chicago*; Clement Vose, *Caucasians Only: The Supreme Court, The NAACP and the Restrictive Covenant Cases* (Berkeley: University of

California Press, 1959), pp. 5, 9; and Robert C. Weaver, *The Negro Ghetto* (New York: Harcourt and Brace, 1948), p. 231.

37. Glaab and Brown assert that in 1916 only five American cities had zoning ordinances, which is surely an underestimate considering that racial zoning had been in effect for several years in a number of cities by that time. Nonetheless, clearly racial zoning was one of the very first uses of zoning in the US. Charles N. Glaab and A. Theodore Brown, *A History of Urban America* (New York: Macmillan and Company, 1967), p. 291.

38. Vose, *Caucasians Only*, p. 51.

39. *Buchanan v. Warley* 245 US 60 (1917).

40. Historians have paid a great deal more attention to racial restrictive covenants in their heyday and decline (the 1930s and 1940s) than to their origins. The earliest references of covenants in the literature are to residential deed restrictions against Asian immigrants in California, in the 1890s, e.g. the 1892 case *Gandolfo v. Hartman* in which the US Circuit Court refused to enforce an early version of racial covenants (Vose, *Caucasians Only*, pp. 5–6). Robert Weaver dates the first covenant agreement to 1890, in San Francisco (*Negro Ghetto*, p. 231).

41. Just a few years prior to when racial covenants first began appearing in Chicago, for instance, there were a number of bills passed at the state level strengthening the state's civil rights laws. See Weaver, *Negro Ghetto*.

42. Herman H. Long and Charles S. Johnson, *People vs. Property: Race Restrictive Covenants in Housing* (Nashville, TN: Fisk University Press, 1947).

43. Covenants remained more prevalent in some cities (Chicago, Detroit, Los Angeles, Baltimore, Washington, Toledo, and Columbus) than in others (Cleveland, Indianapolis, Pittsburgh, Philadelphia, and New York) (Weaver, *Negro Ghetto*, p. 121). In older cities covenants were more extensive in their suburbs rather in the cities proper.

44. This pattern can be explained by the different costs to establish covenants in urban vs. suburban areas: covenant agreements in older neighborhoods were established only with the agreement of all the property owners in a given area, which could be a time-consuming and expensive process, while in the suburbs, developers often wrote covenants into deeds before new owners moved in (see Weaver, *Negro Ghetto*, p. 212; Long and Johnson, *People vs. Property*, pp. 23–25).

45. This estimate comes from a detailed survey of Chicago's tract indices conducted as part of the court case *Tolbert v. Levy*. Of the 155 square miles examined in the study, 70 were non-residential, and 85 were residential; of these, African American neighborhoods covered 9.5 miles. About half the residential areas not occupied by blacks were covenanted against blacks (Weaver, *Negro Ghetto*, p. 246).

46. Chicago Commission on Race Relations, *Negro in Chicago*, p. 645.

47. Kenneth Jackson, *The Ku Klux Klan in the City, 1915–1930* (Chicago: Ivan R. Dee Publisher, 1992 [1967]), pp. 126, 142, 244.

48. Austin MacDonald, *Federal Aid: A Study of the American Subsidy System* (New York: Thomas Y. Crowell Company, 1928), pp. 239–240.

49. Thomas Philpott, *The Slum and the Ghetto: Neighborhood Deterioration and Middle Class Reform, Chicago, 1880–1930* (New York: Oxford University Press, 1978), pp. 193–196; Long and Johnson, *People vs. Property*, p. 38. Philpott describes the involvement of other voluntary groups in covenant campaigns in Chicago as well, e.g. the YMCA, churches, women's groups, PTAs, Kiwanis clubs, and chambers of commerce (Philpott, *The Slum and the Ghetto*, pp. 189–191.

50. Long and Johnson, *People vs. Property*, p. 58. Article 34 was inserted into NAREB's code of ethics in 1924.

51. Rose Helper, *Racial Policies and Practices of Real Estate Brokers* (Minneapolis: University of Minnesota Press, 1969), pp. 23, 190, 228, 230.

52. Wendy Plotkin, "Neighbors and Boundaries: Racial Restrictive Covenants in Chicago, 1900–1948," presented at the Chicago Historical Society, Urban History Seminar, March 19, 1998; and Helper, *Racial Policies*, pp. 229–230. On the role of neighborhood associations and homeowners' groups in the spread of restrictive covenants see Vose, *Caucasians Only*, p. 8; Long and Johnson, *People vs. Property*, p. 38. On the link between developers and homeowners' associations in keeping the "character" of neighborhoods, see Glaab and Brown, *History of Urban America*, p. 294; Weaver, *Negro Ghetto*, p. 254.

53. The initial effort to overturn racially restrictive covenants failed in *Corrigan v. Buckley* (1926), when the Supreme Court let a lower court decision stand, saying it had no jurisdiction in the case (Vose, *Caucasians Only*, pp. 17–18. Restrictive covenants were finally declared unconstitutional in *Shelley v. Kraemer* 334 US 1 (1948). See Vose, *Caucasians Only*, pp. 17–18; and Weaver, *Negro Ghetto*, p. 243.

54. Some scholars have pointed out that even at their height racially restrictive covenants were not always effective. Hirsch, *Making of the Second Ghetto*, pp. 16, 30; Weaver, *Negro Ghetto*, pp. 212, 234. Hirsch argues that in the 1940s it was neighborhoods without racial covenants (those on Chicago's West Side, for example) that were actually more successful in maintaining racial homogeneity. He attributes this to the fragile sense of community in neighborhoods that had to resort to written contracts to withstand racial demographic pressures (*Making of the Second Ghetto*, p. 217). For Weaver the difference between those neighborhoods resorting to covenants and those that did not was a matter of means: covenants were expensive to implement and enforce (*Negro Ghetto*, p. 233).

55. Between July 1933 and June 1935, HOLC supplied $3 billion in loans, covering more than one in ten owner-occupied non-farm residences in the US. See Kenneth Jackson, "Race, Ethnicity and Real Estate Appraisal: The Home Owners Loan Corporation and the Federal Housing Administration," *Journal of Urban History* 6, no. 4 (August 1980): 419–452 at p. 421; Glaab and Brown, *History of Urban America*, p. 300. Nationally about 40 percent of eligible Americans sought HOLC assistance.

56. Jackson, "Race, Ethnicity, and Real Estate Appraisal," p. 423.

57. Davis McEntire, *Residence and Race: Final and Comprehensive Report to the Commission on Race and Housing* (Berkeley: University of California Press, 1960).

58. Federal Housing Administration, *Underwriting Manual* (1938, Sec. 937), in McEntire, *Residence and Race*, p. 301; see also Long and Johnson, *People vs. Property*, pp. 70–72; Kenneth T. Jackson, *Crabgrass Frontier: The Suburbanization of the United States* (New York: Oxford University Press, 1985), p. 208.

59. Jackson, *Crabgrass Frontier*, p. 208. Explicit racial references were deleted from the FHA underwriting manual only in 1947 (Weaver, *Negro Ghetto*, p. 152).

60. Jackson, *Crabgrass Frontier*; McEntire, *Residence and Race*; Charles Abrams, *Forbidden Neighbors: A Study of Prejudice in Housing* (New York: Harper and Brothers, 1955); Weaver, *Negro Ghetto*. Between 1928 and 1933 housing starts fell by 95 percent and expenditures on home repairs fell by 90 percent.

In response the federal government set up first the HOLC to re-finance mortgages and then the FHA to insure the home mortgages made by private lenders (Jackson, *Crabgrass Frontier*, p. 193).

61. Weaver, *Negro Ghetto*, p. 72.

62. In the *Valuation of Real Estate*, for instance, Babcock writes: "Most of the variations between people are slight and values declines are, as a result, gradual. But there is one difference in people, namely race, which can result in very rapid decline. Usually such declines can be avoided by segregation and this device has always been in common usage in the South where white and Negro populations have been separated." Quoted in Helper, *Racial Policies*, p. 202.

63. Ibid., pp. 197, 202.

64. Jackson, *Crabgrass Frontier*, p. 217.

65. Hirsch makes a similar argument about public housing: "[I]n a literal sense, it was not a 'federal' renewal at all. National legislation simply provided federal assistance, economic and otherwise, for innumerable local programs." Hirsch, *Making the Second Ghetto*, p. 269.

66. Michael Jones-Correa, "Structural Shifts and Institutional Capacity: Possibilities for Ethnic Cooperation and Conflict in Urban Settings," Russell Sage Foundation Working Paper #146, 1999.

67. Change in city population is significant at the 0.1 level. This measure is highly correlated (at the 0.001 level) with change in foreign-born population, so it is also indirectly a measure of foreign-born population change.

68. The variable "change in native born blacks in factory jobs" is significant at the 0.05 level. The estimate of how many blacks leaving factory jobs resulted in a riot was determined from the odds ratio (the exponent of *B*).

69. Las Vegas, NV, St Petersburg, FL, and Knoxville, TN all had riots during this time period as well.

Appendix: Regression Analyses Using IPUMS Data

For the 1910 and 1920 data, individual records are aggregated to the city level, so that instead of 113,000 cases for 1910 there are 230 cases for cities having over 25,000 in population; the individual cases are likewise aggregated 1920 data. Merging the 1910 and 1920 data (dropping those cities that appear in one sample but not the other) there is a final count of 171 cases—cities with a population over 25,000 present in both 1910 and 1920. Out of these 171 cities, six had civil disturbances in this period— East St Louis, Houston, Omaha, Chicago, Knoxville, and Washington, DC (three other cases—Charleston, Tulsa, and Elaine, AR—were dropped for lack of data). The independent variables include measures of migration, labor force participation, and homeownership by race and immigrant status; the dependent variable simply indicates a "riot/no riot" outcome. The multivariate logistical regression model tests which variables contribute to an outcome of "riot."

Measures of cities' population, black population, and foreign-born population in 1910 are all used as controls. The population change hypothesis is tested by measures of change in city population, change in black population, and change in foreign-born population over the decade

1910–1920: the greater the change in a city's population, the greater the chance of a race riot. The labor competition hypothesis is tested by change in numbers of blacks and whites holding jobs in three occupational categories, "skilled labor," "service jobs," and "unskilled labor": the greater the change in these occupational categories, the greater the chance of riot. Finally, with housing competition, as ownership increases, so too should the probability of rioting in that city.

As in Table 9.1, this model is a logistic regression with the dependent variable being a "riot/no riot" outcome for the 103 cities, and the independent variables grouped into three clusters, those measuring population and changes in population, those gauging occupational composition, and those reflecting changes in home ownership.

Table 9.1 Logistical regression effects of population change, labor composition, and housing ownership on race riots in Chicago 1910–1920

	B	SE
Constant	–9.7995**	4.1210
Population change		
City population 1910	–0.000047*	0.0000256
Black population 1910	0.0001	0.0000753
Foreign-born population 1910	0.0000874	0.0000561
Change in city population 1910–1920	0.0001*	0.0000788
Change in black population 1910–1920	–0.0006	0.0005
Change in foreign-born population 1910–1920	–0.0001	0.0001
Labor composition		
Change in black unskilled labor	0.0002	0.0009
Change in blacks in service jobs	0.0027	0.0019
Change in black skilled labor	0.0066*	0.0039
Change in white unskilled labor	–0.0004	0.0003
Change in whites in service jobs	0.0006	0.0006
Change in white skilled labor	–0.0012*	0.0006
Housing ownership		
Change in black ownership	0.0002	0.0003
Change in white ownership	0.0002*	0.0000947

Notes:
N = 171
* = $p < 0.10$; ** = $p < 0.05$
Chi square = 31.085
Degrees of freedom = 14
Significance = 0.0054
Predict = 66.67%

Table 9.2 Logistical regression effects of population change, labor composition, and housing ownership on ethnic riots in cities 1980–1990

	B	*SE*
Constant	−5.4277***	(1.6344)
Population change		
Foreign-born population 1980	0.000018	(0.000011)
Native-born black population 1980	0.000003	(0.000007)
Change in city population 1980–1990	0.000025*	(0.000015)
Labor composition		
Change in foreign-born in service jobs	−0.0002	(0.0002)
Change in foreign-born in factory jobs	0.0001	(0.0002)
Change in native-born blacks in service jobs	−0.0002	(0.0002)
Change in native-born blacks in factory jobs	−0.0008**	(0.0004)
Housing ownership		
Change in foreign-born ownership	0.00005	(0.0002)
Change in native-born black ownership	0.0005**	(0.0002)

Notes:
$N = 103$
* $= p < 0.10$; ** $= p < 0.05$; *** $= p < 0.01$
Model chi square = 24.000
Degrees of freedom = 9
Significance = 0.0043

10 Roots

Baltimore's Long March to the Era of Civil Rights

Matthew A. Crenson

I heard about the Supreme Court's decision in *Brown v. Board of Education* while listening to the car radio from the back seat of my father's 1949 Studebaker. I had just turned eleven, and was about to finish the sixth grade at a legally segregated elementary school in Baltimore. At the time, I thought that the Court's decision would take effect almost immediately. It was, after all, Supreme. I was unaware that the Justices would hold the *Brown* case over for a year so that they could consider arguments about its implementation. The Baltimore Board of School Commissioners, however, acted more quickly than the Court. Three days after the announcement of the *Brown* decision, Board members agreed to confer with local civil rights leaders, and two weeks later voted unanimously to desegregate the city's schools when they reopened in September 1954. A week later, the Board members voted, again unanimously, to approve the desegregation plan that the School Superintendent had drawn up at their direction.[1] My expectations about the speed of the integration process turned out to be roughly accurate. In September, I would be attending a racially integrated, citywide junior high school named, ironically, the Robert E. Lee School.

Under the School Board's freedom-of-choice plan, the number of black students attending formerly white schools was not large, but several black children started with me at Robert E. Lee. We never talked about race. Neither did the teachers. Silence was the school system's conscious policy on integration. The School Board's early and abrupt compliance with the *Brown* decision had been a preemptive strike that minimized political conflict on the issue of race and virtually foreclosed public discussion of integration in the schools.[2]

Keeping quiet was not the same as doing nothing. In fact, the city's leaders had to make significant adjustments in order to minimize public debate about race in Baltimore. The integration of the schools may have been insignificant at first, but by 1957, 26 percent of the city's African American pupils were attending school with whites.[3] Baltimore has had to work hard to restrict the politicization of race. School boards and administrators might find it convenient to pursue strategies that minimized public conflicts about education, but the acquiescence of Baltimoreans in general could not be taken for granted. Thousands of white Southerners had migrated to the city during World War II to work in defense plants,[4] and many native Baltimoreans held traditional attitudes about race and segregation. The city had, after all, named one of its public schools after Robert E. Lee. For the most part, however, Baltimoreans made little or no trouble for their leaders. The muffling of racial conflict was not just a matter of elite convenience but widespread political convention.

Racially Reticent City

A general reluctance to make race a political issue has slowed the political advancement of the city's African Americans. By the mid-1970s, they made up a majority of Baltimore's population. But the city did not elect a black mayor until Kurt Schmoke won the office in 1987. It was not until 1995 that black representatives became a majority of the City Council, and in 2000 Mayor Schmoke was succeeded by a white man, Martin O'Malley, who received endorsements from influential black legislators and clergymen. He also won substantial support among black voters, who passed over his two major black opponents in the Democratic primary to vote for the only white candidate. O'Malley was reelected in 2003.

If race had been a polarizing issue in city politics, the African American majority would almost certainly have risen up to claim its share of Baltimore's government sooner than it did. But racial politics has been unexpectedly muted in Baltimore, a fact that puzzled its first elected black mayor. Shortly before leaving office in 2000, Mayor Kurt Schmoke complained that, in Baltimore, "[i]t's almost as though people would like to ignore the fact that race continues to be a significant factor determining the quality of life in the city and the metropolitan area."[5] Since Schmoke had been mayor of the city for twelve years, one might well ask what kept him from using his own office to promote discussion of the city's racial divisions. Perhaps it was the same culture of avoidance that has generally prevented the race issue from rising high on Baltimore's political agenda. Schmoke himself conceded that he tried to avoid making race a subject of city politics.[6] As for the city as a whole, its capacity to ignore the fact of race is striking, just as Schmoke suggested. Baltimore has a history of legally sanctioned segregation, and when it lost the force of law, segregation retained the force of habit. In the aftermath of the *Brown* decision, whites abandoned public education for the suburbs or private schools. Today the public school population is 88 percent African American.[7] The city is one of the nation's leaders in residential segregation. It contains 60 percent of Maryland's poor households.[8] It has one of the country's highest murder rates, and an estimated 10 percent of its population is addicted to drugs.[9] The poor people and the murder victims are disproportionately African Americans, and the heroin addicts probably are too.

Nothing about the present circumstances of Baltimore seems to explain why its deep racial divisions do not figure more prominently as political divisions. Cleveland, Detroit, and Newark are, like Baltimore, rusty survivors of an industrial age in a post-industrial economy. Cleveland elected its first black mayor in 1967; Newark in 1970; and Detroit in 1973. All three cities had major race riots. Cleveland blew up in 1966. Newark and Detroit both had deadly outbreaks in 1967. Baltimore, though known as Mobtown, did not have its riot until 1968, and then only in response to the assassination of Dr Martin Luther King, an event that triggered violence in more than 100 American cities—including Newark, Cleveland, and Detroit.

There is no reason to believe that Baltimoreans are less prone to racial antagonism than residents of other big cities, but those private animosities seldom come together to form political issues. When political candidates try to make racial appeals, they usually do so indirectly and cautiously, as when a black mayoral candidate in 1999 urged African American residents to "vote for a man who looks like you do."[10] Mayor Schmoke's bumper stickers in his 1995 reelection campaign were red, black, and green—the colors of black nationalism. Though he said almost nothing about race in his campaign, whites accused him of playing the race card, and the Baltimore *Afro-American* took offense at Schmoke's belated discovery of the race issue.[11] Schmoke himself later expressed regret about the design of the stickers. Baltimoreans have delicate sensibilities when it comes to the politics of color.

Other border cities, such as Louisville, are known for their practice of "polite racism." Baltimore's racism is not so much polite as passive aggressive. If whites decline to talk openly about race, they give blacks less reason to talk about it, at least in the sphere of politics. In Louisville, whites frequently discussed race, but for the purpose of instructing African Americans about their place in society and how to "improve" themselves. Black attempts to cross the boundaries set by the city's ex-Confederate patricians could provoke decidedly impolite and even violent responses.[12] Baltimore was different.

The principal reasons for Baltimore's subdued brand of racial politics lie in the city's past—the accumulated layers of urban experience that continue to influence local political practices today. Municipalities are vehicles that carry something of the past into the present. The pull of the past may be even more powerful in cities than in nations. A city represents more than an established political and institutional identity; it is also attached to a durable physical infrastructure that reflects the local usages and populations of the past. Cities are places as well as polities.

An emphasis on the institutions and arrangements of the past has its disadvantages. Some students of American political development (APD) suggest that their historical-institutional approach lends itself much more effectively to the explanation of stability than to the understanding of change.[13] But in Baltimore, at least, staying the same has been a struggle. The preservation of the past requires constant adjustment, especially when urban politics is destabilized by external institutions like the federal government. American politics embraces a multiplicity of political orders, and the tensions and contradictions among them often operate as challenges to stability and impulses to change. "Intercurrence"—the simultaneous operation of competing political orders, regimes, and institutions—has recently emerged as a focal concept among students of American political development. Orren and Skowronek offer it as a more tenable alternative to the singular or unitary views of American politics expounded by scholars such as Louis Hartz and Richard Hofstadter.[14]

Though the study of urban political development is still largely unexplored territory within the larger field of American political development, it can expose the local diversity that underlies and often challenges the institutions and arrangements of national politics. Urban political research also lends itself easily to the comparative approach that is the principal reliance of most APD scholars.[15] And, through comparative analysis, the study of political change in cities may reach beyond the documentation of local peculiarities to uncover the ordering generalizations that explain political change in cities and its transmission to national politics. The path to theoretical synthesis begins, however, with the particularity of place.

Border Town

In 1840, British social reformer James Silk Buckingham made an extended tour of the United States, including a month's stay in Baltimore. He found that Baltimoreans did not defend slavery as residents of New York and other cities did. In fact, they tolerated a variety of opinions on matters of race, but also exhibited a marked reticence on the subject. "In all our intercourse with the people of Baltimore," Buckingham wrote, "and we were continually out in society, we heard less about slaves and slavery than in any other town we had yet visited."[16]

Polite discussion within Baltimore's antebellum "society" reflected its position on the margin between North and South. Its merchant class included gentlemen from Southern Maryland and the Eastern Shore, where slavery was an established institutional presence. But a substantial contingent of Quakers also achieved business success in Baltimore. Their ancestors had begun to arrive in Maryland after the provincial assembly approved the Act of Toleration in 1648. The British occupation of Philadelphia during the Revolution triggered a further migration of Quaker merchants to Baltimore.[17] When Buckingham came to Baltimore in 1840, Quaker abolitionists and proslavery patricians coexisted in Baltimore's elite, socializing and doing business with one another. Among

Baltimoreans who were "out in society," there was one issue that could not become the subject of polite conversation.

Baltimore's location just below the Mason–Dixon Line has made it a place where white Northerners lived with white Southerners. The city's sectional ambivalence helped to mute *public* discussion of race and slavery. Even Quaker abolitionists toned down their expressed principles. They had joined with emancipationists of several other denominations to form the Maryland Society for the Abolition of Slavery in 1789. But the Society disbanded, in Baltimore and the state as a whole, by 1800, and Baltimore abolitionists' attempts to revive it in 1807 failed when some of the town's most prominent Quakers declined to take part. But in 1816, the abolitionists regrouped and formed a Protection Society. Its purpose was not to free the slaves, but to prevent free black people from falling into the hands of slavers.[18] Its members might continue in private to hold to abolitionist principles, but in public at least they adjusted their aims to accommodate the sensibilities of slaveholders. For those in Baltimore's mercantile establishment, at least, careful adjustments were essential for the preservation of peace and position. Stability required change.

The Peculiar Solution

Like other Americans who felt ambivalent about slavery and black people, Baltimoreans proposed to send the whole problem back to Africa. When Buckingham came to Baltimore, the city was a center of the African colonization movement. Its advocates proposed to ease the racial tensions of American society by re-exporting African Americans to Liberia.

The motives of the colonizers varied.[19] Southerners who supported colonization saw it as a means to eliminate free blacks whose presence seemed to threaten the institution of slavery itself. Other advocates of colonization, especially in the North, saw it as a means to end or at least diminish slavery, but without the contentiousness of abolitionism or the inconvenience of harboring a large population of free black people. The conflict between the emancipationists and the slavocracy exploded into an open battle at the fifteenth annual meeting of the American Colonization Society, in 1833.[20] In response, the Maryland auxiliary of the Society, led entirely by eminent citizens of Baltimore, withdrew from the national organization and formed their own independent colonization society with its own separate settlement in Liberia at Las Palmas, which they renamed "Maryland." Back in Baltimore, the leaders of the Maryland Colonization Society managed to straddle the controversy about slavery and African colonization by making no distinctions among the black passengers sailing to Liberia. Unlike the Southern wing of the colonization movement, the Maryland Society included manumitted slaves on the ships bound for Liberia, thereby accommodating anti-slavery sentiment and reaching out for financial support in the North. But they were just as ready to serve the interests of slavery by transporting free black people to Africa.[21]

Changing the Subject

While Maryland sent emigrants to Africa, Baltimoreans turned their attention to immigrants. In 1844, a congregation of nativists met in Baltimore to form a political party, the Native American Party. For Baltimoreans especially, Know-Nothingism was far more than an expression of nativist, anti-Catholic prejudice. It was a refuge from the increasingly contentious slavery controversy, another way to change the subject and sidestep a rancorous conflict about the country's racial status quo, conflict that was sure to set Baltimoreans at odds with one another. During the mid-1840s, the Native American Party made little headway as an above-ground political organization, and its supporters moved into secret fraternal societies. In 1853, Maryland's nativist societies merged into the Order of the Star Spangled Banner and once again began to contest elections,[22] this time achieving meteoric success. The Party occupied the mayor's office and held majorities in both chambers of the City Council. In 1856, Maryland was the only state in the Union to give its electoral votes to the Know-Nothing presidential candidate, Millard Fillmore. By 1858, the Party had seized the state's governorship and a majority of its legislature.[23]

Maryland's Know-Nothings were at least as prone to mob violence as their fellow partisans in New York or Philadelphia,[24] but their political program was much less strident. Baltimore's native Americans, unlike their counterparts elsewhere, expressly disavowed any effort "to interfere with the religious opinions of individuals." The Party was merely "hostile to any combination between church and state."[25] It was, perhaps, an understandable position for a state that had been settled by Catholics and arrived early at the practice of religious toleration, except for Jews. But it also reflected a local preoccupation with conciliation.

For Maryland Know-Nothings, the preservation of the Union eventually became the chief partisan priority, outranking even the nativist anti-Catholicism that was supposed to be the Party's lodestar. In 1855, a Baltimore delegate to the National Council of the American Party tried, unsuccessfully, to persuade the body that native-born Roman Catholics should be eligible to join the Know-Nothings. In the same year, Baltimore Know-Nothing Congressman A.B. Sollers argued in a speech to the House that by sidetracking the slavery debate, the American Party had ended the conflict that was destroying the old parties and, unlike them, had become a truly national party. Know-Nothingism was the solvent of sectionalism, ready to "stand by the Union as it is and the Constitution as it is." By 1859, another Know-Nothing congressman from Baltimore, J. Morrison Harris, was arguing for the formation of still another new political party, an opposition that rejecting all dangerous and useless dogmas, all questions of vain and irritating differences between sections and people will array itself firmly up on the platform of the constitution and win by its moderation, its good sense, its high conservatism, its unquestioned nationality, the good and true men of all parties and sections.

His fellow partisan, Senator Anthony Kennedy, joined him in the call for a party to succeed the Know-Nothings, a "union organization" that would insist on the Constitution and the preservation of the Union and "exclude the slavery question."[26]

Instead of moving toward the anti-slavery camp, like the Massachusetts Know-Nothings, the Marylanders converted their Americanism into a determination to preserve the Union against the forces of sectionalism and the divisions opened up by the issue of slavery. As William Evitts observes: "They were as neutral as their geographic position, Southern sentiment notwithstanding. The agitation over slavery, said most Marylanders, was a politicians' sham, a conflict among 'ultraists,' 'fanatics,' and 'extremists' only." The state's Know-Nothings wanted above all to sidestep the choice between North and South, and Baltimore was the Party's greatest stronghold.[27] On the eve of the Civil War, Baltimoreans were still trying find a safe route around the issues of slavery and race.

Nineteenth-Century Black Capital

From 1810 to the Civil War, Baltimore was home to the largest concentration of free black people in the United States. In 1860, before Lincoln had freed a single slave, more than 90 percent of the city's black population was free, and even Baltimore's slave population achieved a degree of autonomy not evident in other slave states. "Term slavery," for example, was widespread in Baltimore. Term slaves would win their freedom after a fixed period of service. Just as Quaker abolitionists trimmed their principles to live in a slave society, slaveowners compromised with emancipation. The limitations of term bondage represented a gesture to conscience, but they were also expedient. A term slave was less likely to run away than one who could look forward only to a lifetime as chattel, and running away was a practical option in Baltimore.[28] Some owners also permitted their slaves to work for wages so that they could buy their own freedom.[29]

Free black people achieved a critical mass in Baltimore at such an early date that they enjoyed a long head-start over black communities elsewhere in which to construct their own collective life. One of the first and most conspicuous black institutions formed in 1802 when the congregation of the Sharp Street Methodist Church came together and in the same year took control of the African Academy, a private school for black children established by Quakers in 1797. Daniel Coker was hired to teach at the renamed Sharp Street Church School. Coker had learned to read as a young slave in Frederick County, northwest of Baltimore, and then moved to the city where he joined the Methodist Church. From Baltimore, he ran away to New York, where he received an education and was ordained a deacon in the denomination, but returned to Baltimore in 1801. Four members of the Sharp Street Church arranged for his purchase so as to dissolve his master's claims on his freedom, and in 1807 or 1808 he became one of two teachers at the Sharp Street School.[30]

Coker would become one of the first leaders of Baltimore's black community. By 1810, though unordained, he was the minister of the Sharp Street Church as well as head of its school. The Church and its school were only the first elements in an elaborate mosaic of black religious, fraternal, philanthropic, political, and labor organizations, banks, and business firms that helped to transform Baltimore's African American population from "a formless aggregate of transients" into "a society that coalesced around the affirmation of racial distinctions."[31] After the Civil War, the city's black men would even join voluntary military organizations, ready and willing to exchange fire with white antagonists as they marched through the streets of Baltimore on their way to the celebrations and fund-raising affairs of the city's black community.[32]

After emancipation and Appomattox, the fund-raising was usually intended to relieve the destitution of black migrants from the conquered South and rural Maryland. By 1866, the City Trustees of the Poor admitted that they were unable to care for "all worthy persons without regard to nation or color," and federal authorities were unwilling or unable to provide charity to the newcomers. The principal burden of caring for the newly freed blacks was taken up by the free black community of Baltimore. Black orphan asylums, a home for aged women, several churches, and the Lincoln Zouaves all raised money for the ex-slaves.[33]

Organization meant division. The city's African Americans joined different churches, different military units, and different fraternal organizations. Even members of the same organization could fall out with one another. In 1815, for example, Daniel Coker and a minority of the Sharp Street congregation seceded to form the Bethel Methodist Church. Unlike the Sharp Street Church, it was independent of the Methodist Episcopal Church and the whites who governed it. A year later Coker met with other black Methodists in Philadelphia to form a new denomination—the African Methodist Episcopal Church. But by 1820, Coker found that conflict between his former congregation at Sharp Street and his current congregation at Bethel had became so bitter that he decided to take up the Colonization Society's offer and sail for Liberia so that, he said, he "could leave all these divisions behind in America" and return to the land of his ancestors.[34]

African colonization itself exposed another fault line in the black community. William Watkins, who succeeded Coker as a teacher at the Sharp Street School, was one of the most articulate and consistent critics of colonization. He objected, in particular, to the assumption that in America blacks would always be a distinct and inferior caste whose members could never achieve the status of citizens. Even more infuriating to Watkins was the attribution of these views to assemblies of African Americans held at the Sharp Street and Bethel churches and summarized in a memorial published at the end of 1826 in several Baltimore newspapers.[35]

The memorial had probably been drafted by whites and may not even have reflected the sentiments of a majority of the African Americans who attended the meetings, but Watkins responded as a "Colored Baltimorean" taking issue with other colored Baltimoreans.[36] In 1835, he would find himself standing against leaders of the black community, including the pastor of his own church, who sought compromise with the colonizationists. Three black ministers had issued a statement claiming to speak for Baltimore's African Americans in which they declared their sympathy for the cause of African colonization. Writing to William Lloyd Garrison, whose *Liberator* occasionally published his letters, Watkins claimed that the three clergymen had already threatened him with a coat of tar and feathers, and that a meeting had been called just outside the city to discuss ways of silencing his propagandizing for abolition and against colonization. Watkins had been intimidated, and could not speak for his fellow African Americans. But he would not concede the right of the black ministers to act as spokesmen. As he told Garrison, they claimed to express the views of black Baltimore without calling a single public meeting to discuss the desirability of colonization.[37]

The problem was larger than even Watkins recognized. In a black community whose members were divided by denomination, policy, and interest, it was not clear whether anyone could speak for the race as a whole. Black Baltimore's organizational density inhibited its ability to cry out with one voice against racial injustice. Whites, of course, could have solved the problem. African Americans might have unified in the face of a concerted white campaign of public racism. In Baltimore, however, whites had consistently looked for ways to sidestep frank and public discussion of racial divisions. It was no easy matter to rise up in fury against ambivalence and euphemisms. Watkins had faced the problem in trying to mobilize black opposition to African colonization. The movement had many black sympathizers. Daniel Coker had chosen it as an avenue of exit from the tensions of Baltimore's black community. Watkins found his own escape. In the mid-1840s, he was overwhelmed by the conviction that the end of the world was imminent and joined a millenarian movement whose purpose was to prepare for doomsday. The longer the world persisted, the less Baltimoreans listened to him.[38] He eventually moved to Canada.

White ambivalence and black disunity reinforced one another, and they operated together to inhibit the emergence of race as a political issue. Whites avoided public expressions of racism that might have united Baltimore's African Americans in shared outrage. Internal diversity and division in black Baltimore undermined coherent assaults on racial privilege that might have forced whites to abandon their ambivalence and defend their supremacy.

Baltimore in the Storm

The provocation that galvanized black Baltimore originated outside the city. Col. Curtis M. Jacobs, a wealthy Eastern Shore slaveowner and a member of the state legislature, introduced a bill in 1859 that would have sharply curtailed the rights of free black people. "Free-negroism through-out the State," he declared, "must be abolished." Society, thought Jacobs, required slavery. If there were no black slaves, there would be white slaves—the slaves of capitalism and class domination. He envisioned an ambitious program to avert this danger:

> A universal pass system must be adopted. Emancipation by last will and testament, or by any other means, must be prohibited. Negro worship, except in the assembly of a white congregation, and at the stated place and hours of the same, must not be allowed. Free Negroes going out of the State must not be allowed to return on pain of being sold into slavery for life. No free Negro to enter the State, under like penalty.

Jacobs' bill also provided that free African Americans who failed to pay their debts might be re-enslaved. His ultimate aim was to assure that every black resident of Maryland was a slave.[39]

Baltimore's black church congregations rose up as one body. Their members could not vote, but they could lobby. The barbers of Baltimore, who were disproportionately black, urged their customers to sign a petition opposing the Jacobs bill. Black Baltimoreans gathered at Bethel Church at 3:00 a.m. one morning for an entire day of prayer and fasting to summon up the strength to defeat the Jacobs bill. They had white allies. The legislature received a petition from 200 of Baltimore's "best" white women protesting the proposed restrictions on free African Americans, and two of the city's most prominent attorneys signed a petition to the same effect circulated among the male elite. None of Baltimore's news-papers endorsed the bill. All of the proposals were defeated in the House of Delegates, and weakened versions were later rejected by the voters.[40]

The city's display of interracial unity did not last. In Baltimore's labor market, black workers had to contend with the economic competition and racial animosity of a growing immigrant population. Unskilled immigrant workers had driven down wages and reduced opportunities for black labor since the 1840s. But by the late 1850s, white labor engaged in organized campaigns to drive black workers out of jobs. In the shipyards, where black caulkers had dominated their craft for decades, white caulkers, carpenters, and riggers went on strike against yards that employed blacks. Some owners resisted, but most eventually succumbed to pressure. Isaac Myers, the son of free African Americans and a graduate of one of the schools associated with Baltimore's black churches, raised the capital to establish a cooperative, black-owned shipyard, the Chesapeake Marine Railway and Dry Dock Company. The company would eventually provide work for several hundred black caulkers. By the end of the 1860s, Myers was the leader of a new black labor union.[41]

Emancipation intensified the racial resentments of whites. As long as slavery and freedom had coexisted in Baltimore, free African Americans faced the possibility of a return to bondage if their conduct offended whites. Once the slaves were freed, black people were liberated from the sanction that shadowed their freedom, and their new independence fed white antagonism. Christopher Phillips suggests that white animosity grew gradually in Baltimore as the local population of free blacks grew stronger and became better organized, and that white animosity helped to fortify black solidarity. The city's interracial détente, he argues, had almost disappeared by the eve of the Civil War. But the shape of Baltimore race relations continued to change. White attitudes and the internal structure of the black community remained complex and variable. White voters, after all, had overwhelmingly rejected even severely weakened versions of Curtis Jacobs' re-enslavement proposals when they were presented to the electorate in 1860.[42] The Jacobs proposals also succeeded in uniting Baltimore's black congregations, but other issues exposed divisions among them.

Jim Crow Lite

Freedom did not bring Baltimore's African Americans equality or citizenship. Even after Emancipation, they could not serve on juries in Maryland, testify as witnesses in cases involving whites, or practice as attorneys in Maryland courts. A new state constitution in 1867 removed the disqualification for black witnesses. In 1880, the US Supreme Court ruled that states could not exclude African Americans from juries, and five years later a state court decreed that restricting the practice of law to whites was a violation of the Fourteenth Amendment.[43]

Maryland followed many states further South in its imposition of Jim Crow restrictions on black residents following the end of the Civil War and Reconstruction, but there were omissions. The terror, mob violence, and lynchings of the Deep South were rare in Maryland and almost non-existent in Baltimore. The distinctiveness of the city was evident to P.B.S.

Pinchback when he visited in 1891. During Reconstruction, Pinchback had become the first African American governor when he succeeded a governor of Louisiana who had been impeached for corruption. He thought that Baltimore was unique in the South for the economic and educational opportunities that it offered African Americans. "I am at last in a free country," he announced. Pinchback had come to Baltimore to campaign for the reelection of a black member of the City Council, Harry Cummings. Unlike Pinchback, Cummings had actually been voted into office; in 1890 he was the first African American to win an election in Maryland.[44]

Maryland departed from the regime of Jim Crow in one other vital respect. After the ratification of the Fifteenth Amendment, it never by law or artful dodge deprived its black citizens of the right to vote. It was not for lack of trying. Three times the disenfranchisement of blacks came before the voters, and three times it was defeated. Initially, the campaign to exclude African Americans from the electorate had been more partisan than racial. The Democrats had lost control of state government in 1895, and when they returned to power in 1900, they were determined not to give the Republicans another victory. The state's 60,000 eligible black voters were the most reliable Republican base, and eliminating their votes seemed the surest way to prevent the Republicans from returning to power. The General Assembly made several attempts to stem black turnout indirectly by making it more difficult for illiterate and semiliterate voters to understand the ballot. All symbols and party designations were removed from the ballot, for example. The measures all backfired. The Republicans held instructional classes to teach their black supporters how to recognize the names of Republican candidates, and the devices meant to frustrate black Republican voters actually confused many white Democratic voters. Turnout declined for both parties.[45]

The partisan campaign turned malignantly racist. In 1904, the Democrats turned to more direct, constitutional measures to eliminate black voters. The Democratic amendment would allow the vote only to those citizens who had been on the registration rolls before the ratification of the Fifteenth Amendment, or those who were lineal male descendants of such voters. The problem for the architects of Jim Crow in Maryland was that the state's population included a large number of foreign-born whites and voters with foreign-born fathers, concentrated dispro-portionately in Baltimore and in the city's Democratic Party. The amendment would deprive them of the right to vote along with their black fellow citizens. In opposing disenfranchisement, the Republican Party and the black membership of the Maryland Suffrage League were joined by the Maryland League of Foreign-Born Citizens, the German-American Independent Citizens Union, and prominent Reform Democrats. Baltimore, though long a Democratic city, went two to one against disenfranchisement. Four Democratic ward leaders defected and opposed the amendment.[46] In the Baltimore labor market, immigrants and African Americans were rivals. In politics, they became bedfellows, at least temporarily.

Where Goes the Neighborhood?

In 1910 George W.F. McMechen, a black man and successful Yale-educated attorney, moved into one of the most exclusive neighborhoods of Baltimore, near mansion-lined Eutaw Place. The private prejudices of Baltimoreans erupted into the open. A police guard was necessary to protect McMechen's house against ruffians. A mass meeting demanded that city leaders do something to protect white neighborhoods from black incursions. One of the principal arguments in favor of restricting residential integration pointed to the prevalence of disease among black Baltimoreans, especially tuberculosis (TB), which was probably a byproduct of segregation itself. A local housing ordinance prohibited the construction of new "alley housing," where much of the African American population was concentrated, and it was virtually impossible for developers to acquire new land for black housing. Black immigrants were packed into neighborhoods with the cheapest, oldest, and most dilapidated shelter, sometimes no more than shanties, and it was among them that the TB rate soared.[47]

A city ordinance law signed by Mayor J. Barry Mahool in 1910, largely as a response to the firestorm that followed George McMechen's decision to relocate his family to a white neighborhood, prohibited blacks from moving onto blocks where a majority of residents were white, and whites from moving to blocks where a majority of the residents were black. It was the first ordinance of its kind in the country, and would serve as a model for half a dozen other cities, including racially "polite" Louisville. Baltimore was an innovator.[48]

Mayor Mahool was not an ally of the Democrats who had tried to disenfranchise African American voters. He was a progressive who endorsed female suffrage, the eight-hour day, utility regulation, a minimum wage, playgrounds for poor children, and good government. Race was finally a big issue in Baltimore, but the ordinance was clearly designed to push the issue off the city's political agenda and to keep it off. The reformers' intentions were all too abundantly evident from the ponderous title of the statute: "An Ordinance for Preserving Peace, Preventing Conflict and Ill-Feelings Between the White and Colored Races, And Promoting the General Welfare of the City of Baltimore By Providing As Far As Possible for the Use of Separate Blocks By White and Colored People For Residences, Churches, and Schools." The explicit legal justification of the segregation ordinance gave almost exclusive attention to the preservation of racial peace. Before signing the law, Mayor Mahool had sent it to the City Solicitor for an opinion concerning its constitutionality. Solicitor Edgar Allan Poe responded with an even longer but virtually identical justification for the law.[49]

The city's African Americans expressed considerable resentment about the law that restricted their residential choices, but neither they nor Baltimore's whites were of one mind about the segregation ordinance. The *Afro-American* pointedly observed that black lawyers and "real estate men" stayed away from a meeting to protest the segregation ordinance, but that "a few whites opposed to the ordinance" were present. Reporting on a meeting to promote the ordinance, the *Afro-American* mentioned that "Hebrews" were conspicuous by their absence.[50] Targets of residential discrimination themselves, Jews were unlikely to favor measures that subjected other groups to similar restrictions. In the city's racial politics, they seemed to have filled the niche once occupied by Quakers.

The 1910 ordinance was quickly declared unconstitutional by the courts, and a 1911 successor met the same fate. In 1913 the city seemed to reach a constitutionally acceptable formulation, but in 1917 the US Supreme Court declared residential segregation ordinances like the one in Baltimore unconstitutional, not because they were discriminatory but because they interfered with the free disposition of private property. Restrictive covenants would reinforce private patterns of residential segregation, until the Court declared their enforcement unconstitutional in 1948.[51] The Baltimore housing market would then stand wide open to block-busters, operators on the margin of the real estate industry who induced panic selling among whites by moving or threatening to move black residents into formerly white neighborhoods. They were hardly distinctive to Baltimore, but their impact was dramatic. In the city's Edmondson Village neighborhood, for instance, 20,000 blacks displaced 20,000 whites over a period of less than 10 years. While similar changes have occurred in some other cities, white exodus is not a universal response to the encroachment of black residential areas. In Detroit, thousands of whites organized to resist the racial turnover of their neighborhoods. But that required them to make a public issue of race. In Baltimore, they just took flight. One of Edmondson Village's new, black residents captured the ambivalence of the fleeing whites: "They were friendly, but they were prejudiced. They didn't want to live where colored people did . . . They didn't tell you [why they moved]; they just moved."[52] Baltimoreans continued to keep their prejudices to themselves. They said nothing; they just moved. Race was a private problem, not a public issue.

The Shape of Black Politics

The 1911 segregation ordinance was responsible for launching the Baltimore branch of the National Association for the Advancement of Colored People (NAACP), which formed in 1912, just a year before the

State Court of Appeals finally upheld a heavily revised version of the law as constitutional. The branch was only one of many organizations that claimed to speak for black Baltimore, and its voice wavered as its membership dropped. By the 1930s, it was virtually inactive and had only 100 members.[53] A variety of organizations competed for black members in the city, and none had a monopoly—not even the party of Lincoln. The Democrats had been able to claim a significant black constituency in Baltimore long before the New Deal converted African Americans to the party of Franklin Roosevelt. The Democratic connection did not begin well. Jonathan Waters, the first president of the Colored Democratic Association, was shot on a city street in 1872 by someone in a racially integrated mob of Republicans. His successor, however, got a clerical position in the state legislature. He was the first African American to hold a position in state government—one of the early signs that Democrats might be more generous than Republicans in distributing patronage to their black adherents. They also organized African American Democratic clubs at the ward level.[54]

The peaceful coexistence and cooperation of black and white Democrats would have been difficult, perhaps impossible, if race had been an open and contentious issue in city politics. It seldom was. Margaret Callcott counts only three of twenty-three state and federal elections in Maryland from 1871 to 1894 in which racism was a salient feature of the Democratic campaign. The issue was even less prominent in Baltimore than in the state. Five-time mayor Ferdinand C. Latrobe was one of the few Democratic politicians in Maryland who openly courted the black vote. In the early twentieth century, of course, Democrats tried repeatedly to disenfranchise black voters. But those Democrats were not from Baltimore. Baltimore's Democrats were so lukewarm about the constitutional amendment to disenfranchise blacks that state Democratic boss Arthur Pue Gorman accused city boss Isaac Rasin of betrayal and sabotage, arguing that the Baltimore machine had deliberately held back its support for the measure.[55] He was probably right.

The organizational and institutional depth of the black community helped the city to sidestep the race issue. If Baltimore's African Americans had arrived in a giant wave of migrants, uprooted from home communities and disconnected from one another, they would have had only their race in common with one another, and appeals to race would have been the principal means to mobilize them as voters. But the well-established and many-stranded connections that tied black Baltimoreans together through churches, fraternal groups, labor organizations, commerce, and social clubs allowed their leaders to call them to the polls on the basis of direct or indirect acquaintance, not color. "Unlike African American communities in other cities, especially to the North," observes Andor Skotnes, "Baltimore's Black community was never largely a transplant from distant rural areas, and even the Great Migration failed to demographically disrupt its processes of community- and culture-building."[56]

Before the New Deal, the Democratic Party, lacking a Lincoln but burdened by its Confederate affinities, had limited leverage with African Americans. Its chief black operative was Thomas A. Smith, who seems to have worked to suppress the black vote as often as he tried to attract it. The day after an election, Smith would show up at the office of Democratic boss Isaac Rasin to count up the registered black voters who had cast their votes. Smith would be paid according to the number of black voters who failed to show up at the polls. Smith employed violence, persuasion, but especially recreational excursions on election day to keep blacks from voting for Republican candidates.[57]

By the 1930s, when black voters had begun to shift toward the Democrats, black political aspirants in West Baltimore formed the Citizens Democratic Club, whose principal role was to round up black votes for white candidates. In East Baltimore, Clarence "Du" Burns was doing the same for the almost all-white Bohemian Club. Race was not an issue. According to Verda Welcome, a member of the Citizens Democratic Club and one of the first black women elected to the state legislature, race was not mentioned explicitly in electoral politics until the 1970s.[58]

In 1971, black candidates would make their first bid for the mayor's office, following the election of the city's first black judge in 1968. Cleveland, Gary, and Newark had already elected black mayors. Black Baltimore's turn seemed within reach, especially after the incumbent mayor, Thomas D'Alesandro III, announced that he would not seek reelection. But the city's African American activists were unable to unify behind a single candidate. They divided between George Russell, the City Solicitor, and Clarence Mitchell III, a state senator, son of the NAACP's Washington lobbyist Clarence Mitchell, Jr, and nephew of Congressman Parren Mitchell; his mother and grandmother were both revered leaders of the city's NAACP branch. Russell had significant white support. Mitchell had his own political organization and dynastic resources to support him. The two candidates divided the black vote, giving the Democratic nomination and the mayoralty to William Donald Schaefer, who would continue in office until 1986.[59] The organizational density of black Baltimore did not guarantee racial unity, and may actually have impeded it.

But the ability to mobilize African American voters without making appeals to race enabled black politicians to form alliances with white politicians. The most notable beneficiary of such an alliance was Jack Pollack, the white political boss who controlled judges, state legislators, and City Council members. Before coming to politics, Pollack had a storied career as a professional boxer and accused murderer whose criminal records somehow disappeared from the courthouse. Long after his district's electoral majority had become African American, it continued to elect Pollack's white candidates. His chief lieutenant was Loyall Randolph, a black hotel and tavern owner who escorted white candidates through West Baltimore's African American neighborhoods, distributed the patronage that came his way, and helped local merchants cope with zoning or liquor license problems. After one of his candidates for the state legislature was defeated by a black Republican, Pollack began to slate black Democrats, but not always. His last great triumph in city politics was the election of a white State's Attorney in 1974. Baltimore had become a majority African American city, but the majority was divided. The Mitchell family, based in the NAACP, and the Murphy family, which controlled the *Afro-American,* had fallen out with one another, and Pollack's candidate became the city's prosecutor.[60]

Toward the Era of Civil Rights

Thurgood Marshall and Clarence Mitchell, Jr both grew up in Pollack's district. He had risen from ward leader to district boss while they were still in public school, and by the time they had returned from Lincoln University outside Philadelphia, he was in full command. Mitchell and Marshall joined, not the African American supporters of Pollack in the Citizens Democratic Club, but the City-Wide Young People's Forum, a black organization founded in 1931 that could attract as many as 2,000 young African Americans to its Friday evening meetings. The group started at Sharp Street Methodist Church and moved to Bethel Church when the pastor at Sharp Street thought the organization had become too radical. Mitchell joined in 1932, and soon became vice-president, and the Forum's premier orator and debater.[61]

Marshall and Mitchell would both become leading actors in the Forum's most ambitious and dramatic offensive against racial discrimination, the Buy Where You Can Work Campaign, initially aimed at the A&P supermarkets in black Baltimore, which refused to employ African Americans. The Young People's Forum coordinated a boycott with the support of at least forty black churches. Every A&P in an African American neighborhood was picketed. Five hundred adherents of the Young People's Forum and many of their parents participated. A&P agreed to hire three black clerks and promised more. But a few weeks later, the chain fired several black employees as "inefficient." The community reaction was massive, and by early December 1933, A&P had hired 32 black clerks and promised jobs for two black managers.[62]

After its victory over the A&P, the Forum turned on smaller merchants doing business in black neighborhoods. Those in northwest Baltimore had formed an association to resist the pressure and gone to court to get an injunction against the boycott, arguing that since the pickets were not employees of the stores being targeted, their protest was not protected by the Norris–LaGuardia Act. By this time, the chronic contentiousness of

Baltimore's black political community had given rise to divisions, mutual recrimination, and charges of treason. When courts finally decided in favor of the white merchants and against the boycott, they only issued a death certificate for a movement whose time had run out.[63] Direct action had ended in disarray.

Interest in the boycott faded but the focus on the courts remained. Donald Murray, a member of the Young People's Forum and a graduate of Amherst, had applied to the University of Maryland Law School. Like every black applicant since 1889, he had been rejected, and he sued. His case was not simply his own. It was part of a plan mapped out by Carl Murphy, the publisher and president of the *Afro-American* in a letter to NAACP president Walter White. His strategy aimed to improve the quality and accessibility of education for the young people of black Baltimore, beginning with the University of Maryland, which, "with a budget of $1,500,000 a year, excludes Negroes by force rather than by law."[64]

Murphy had been a supporter of the Young People's Forum, and now he was reviving the Baltimore branch of the NAACP, which provided the legal support for Murray's case against the University of Maryland. Murray's attorney was Thurgood Marshall, who had been rejected from the University's law school himself four years earlier. The turn toward Marshall and the litigation strategy offered a means to circumvent the troublesome schisms that undermined the efficacy of black political action in Baltimore. Carl Murphy did not need to achieve community consensus in order to file a lawsuit, just an attorney. Of course, no one realized at the time that he had retained a future Associate Justice of the Supreme Court. Nor were they likely to have guessed that Clarence Mitchell, Jr would emerge, in the 1960s as "the lion in the lobby." Mitchell had been hired by Carl Murphy's *Afro-American*, and he combined journalism with his new role as publicity director of the NAACP branch. His task was not just to give visibility to the resurrected organization, but to hold together the coalition of groups that backed the branch. Baltimore's NAACP was not a free-standing organization. As David Terry points out:

> Though an examination of the rank-and-file of the city's "active" black citizens would reveal various organizational and institutional backgrounds, that which can be characterized as a core leadership displayed a penchant for multiple affiliations, with the common denominator being the NAACP.

All of the branch's ventures were "multi-organizational undertakings."[65]

While Marshall had been preparing the Murray case, Mitchell ran for the state legislature, his first and only quest for elective office. Neither of the major parties attracted him. To Mitchell, it seemed, "the Democrats are a lot of high pressure artists, who will tolerate gambling dens, drinking dives, and houses of prostitution, but refuse to support anything that means uplift and justice." It was a fair assessment of Jack Pollack's Fourth District. But the Republicans were not much better—"a bunch of shilly-shallying reprobates who need to undergo a complete metamorphosis." Mitchell ran as a Socialist and got 1,700 votes.[66] He abandoned electoral politics for the work of mediation, negotiation, and bargaining that was essential for preserving the unity of Baltimore's branch of the NAACP.

Thurgood Marshall moved from his first successful suit against Jim Crow to a series of others aimed at equalizing salaries for black and white teachers in one Maryland county after another, a device for organizing more NAACP branches across the state. His next case, *Williams v. Zimmerman*, carried far-reaching implications for the NAACP strategy of contesting racial discrimination in schooling, foreshadowing *Brown v. The Board of Education*. It was the first of the civil rights cases in Maryland that Marshall lost. The defendant was the principal of an all-white Baltimore County high school. There were no all-black high schools in Baltimore County, and that was why the NAACP filed suit on behalf of Margaret Williams. The County had required her to take a test after the completion of the seventh grade. If she passed, the County would pay her tuition at a black high school in Baltimore City. Margaret had not passed, though she had successfully completed the seventh grade. Marshall argued that the test was a transparent attempt by Baltimore County to deny Margaret equal access to a high school education, and he sued for her admission to a white high school. But, on the advice of NAACP Counsel Charles Houston, he claimed that his real purpose was to get Baltimore County to open a black high school. The NAACP lawyers were concerned that a flat demand for school integration would carry them too far ahead of the courts. In the end, they got neither integration nor a black high school. The Maryland Court of Appeals argued that the remedy Marshall should have requested was the abolition of the test or the creation of a fair test. For white students, of course, there was no test. Reflecting on the result, Marshall noted that,

> for the first time, a court has admitted that some inequalities are inevitable in a separate school system. It is significant and valuable to have a court recognize and state *the mere existence of a separate system, in itself, imparts inequalities.*[67]

By this time, Marshall had been hired as Special Assistant Counsel to Charles Hamilton Houston at NAACP headquarters in New York. It would be ten years before the organization would again challenge educational discrimination in court, and that line of litigation would culminate in *Brown.*[68]

Clarence Mitchell was working as Labor Secretary at the NAACP's Washington Bureau. He came to his new job from the wartime Fair Employment Practices Commission (FEPC), which President Truman had allowed to expire at the war's end. One of Mitchell's objectives was to create a permanent FEPC that would mobilize the authority of the federal government against racial discrimination in employment and labor unions. A critical part of his job was to educate the nation about the systematic character of racial discrimination in the federal government itself. His other task was the construction of a broad lobbying coalition consisting of the NAACP's local branches and a national Labor Committee, including leaders of some of the same unions that had historically excluded black workers. Mitchell's career would continue along the same lines after 1950, when he became the director of the NAACP's Washington Bureau and the coordinating presence in the newly organized Leadership Conference on Civil Rights.[69] In short, Mitchell's work of coalition-building and publicity had much in common with the functions he had performed for the NAACP in Baltimore. He commuted to his job in Washington from Baltimore, where he continued to live for the rest of his life.

Conclusion

Baltimore may help to illustrate one kind of connection between urban political development and national political development. The city contributed two vital leaders to the national struggle for racial equality. They were not masters of confrontation and demonstration, like Montgomery's Martin Luther King or Chicago's Jesse Jackson. Thurgood Marshall and Clarence Mitchell were practitioners of less inflammatory and theatrical modes of racial politics, and both of them represented possible adjustments to Baltimore's racial climate. They confronted whites who were usually intent on soft-peddling the issue of race even as they maintained segregation, and whose practice of Jim Crow was often half-hearted. Segregation in Baltimore was frequently a mere "capitulation" to the decisions of federal courts, and even then white Baltimore frequently lacked the patience for consistent enforcement. Transportation facilities in Baltimore were never successfully segregated, for example, though hotels and schools were.[70] The silence and slackness of white Baltimore limited the aggravations that were likely to galvanize the city's black population for massive racial protest. When black Baltimore did rise up, it was often in response to events that originated outside of the city, such as the state legislature's early twentieth-century attempts to disenfranchise black voters, the 1935 lynching on the Eastern Shore that helped to build black support for a reinvigorated NAACP branch, or the assassination of Martin Luther King.

Local whites seldom supplied the provocations that unified the city's black population, but the black community's organizational complexities and internal divisions also undermined the consensus needed for mass mobilization. Marshall and Mitchell both experienced the problem first-hand as participants in the Buy Where You Can Work boycott. The same problem has also emerged in electoral politics, where the city's African Americans have sometimes been unable to unite behind a single black candidate, and occasionally threw their support to white politicians.

Thurgood Marshall's use of litigation to challenge the practice of discrimination circumvented these problems. But Baltimore could use a Mitchell as well as a Marshall. In a diverse but well-organized black community, where almost all ventures were "multi-organizational under-takings," a skillful negotiator and conciliator could help to maintain the coalitions essential for reasonably coherent interest-group representation in state and city government.

Baltimore did not invent litigation and lobbying, and it hardly explains the civil rights movement, but it may help to reveal the processes that help to introduce change into national politics. The particularities of local political systems generate movements and actors that stand at odds with the established practices and institutions of national politics. Just as states are the "laboratories of democracy," so urban political cultures, conflicts, and practices can trickle up into national movements. In the early twentieth century, Walter Bagehot noticed a similar phenomenon in the making of nations rather than movements:

> A national character is but the successful parish character; just as the national speech is but the successful parish dialect, that is, of the district which came to be more—in many cases but a little more—influential than other districts, and so set its yoke on books and society.[71]

All politics may not be local, but tracing the course of local politics may add to our understanding of national political development.

Notes

1. Howell C. Baum, "How the 'American Dilemma' Limited School Desegregation in A Border City: Liberalism and Race in Baltimore," paper presented at the Thirty-Sixth Annual Meeting of the Urban Affairs Association, Montreal, Canada, p. 6; Elinor Pancoast et al., *Report of a Study on Desegregation in the Baltimore City Schools* (Baltimore: The Maryland Commission on Interracial Problems and the Baltimore Commission on Human Relations, 1956), p. 30.
2. Pancoast et al., *Report of a Study on Desegregation in the Baltimore City Schools*, p. 31; see also Robert L. Crain, *The Politics of School Desegregation* (Garden City, NY: Anchor Books, 1969), pp. 75, 82.

3. George H. Callcott, *Maryland and America, 1940 to 1980* (Baltimore: Johns Hopkins University Press, 1985), p. 152.
4. Kenneth D. Durr, *Behind the Backlash: White Working-Class Politics in Baltimore, 1940–1980* (Chapel Hill: University of North Carolina Press, 2003), pp. 15–16.
5. Tony White, "While City Moves Forward, Schmoke Sees Race Relations at a Standstill," *Afro-American* (Baltimore) December 1, 1999, p. A1.
6. Cameron McWhirter, "Burnout: Once-hailed Mayor Bows Out," *Detroit News* February 13, 2000.
7. Gerald P. Merrell, "A History Lesson on Stage," *Sun* (Baltimore) May 3, 2004.
8. David Rusk, "A Look At . . . Segregation and Poverty: How We Promote Poverty," *Washington Post* May 18, 1997, p. C02.
9. Lynn Anderson, "Survey Backs Drug Treatment: Most Respondents View Programs as Prison Alternative for Adults," *Sun* (Baltimore) June 4, 2006.
10. Marion Orr, "The Struggle for Black Empowerment in Baltimore," in Rufus P. Browning, Dale Rogers Marshall, and David H. Tabb, eds., *Racial Politics in American Cities* (New York: Longman, 2002), p. 270.
11. *Afro-American* (Baltimore) June 10, 1995, p. A4.
12. On Louisville, see George C. Wright, *Life Behind a Veil: Blacks in Louisville, Kentucky, 1865–1930* (Baton Rouge: Louisiana State University Press, 1985).
13. Adam D. Sheingate, "Political Entrepreneurship, Institutional Change, and American Political Development," *Studies in American Political Development* 17 (Fall 2003): 185–203.
14. Karen Orren and Stephen Skowronek, *The Search for American Political Development* (New York: Cambridge University Press, 2004), p. 113.
15. Ibid., pp. 6–7.
16. James Silk Buckingham, *America, Historical, Statistic, and Descriptive* (New York: Harper and Brothers, 1841), vol. I, p. 438.
17. On Quakers in Baltimore, see Leroy Graham, *Baltimore: The Nineteenth Century Black Capital* (Lanham, MD: University Press of America, 1982), pp. 16–18.
18. Ibid., pp. 58–61, 104.
19. P.J. Staudenraus, *The African Colonization Movement, 1816–1865* (New York: Columbia University Press, 1961), pp. 20–21, 28, 33, 193–206; Eric Burin, *Slavery and the Peculiar Solution: A History of the American Colonization Society* (Gainesville: University Press of Florida, 2005), p. 26.
20. Richard L. Hall, *On Africa's Shore: A History of Maryland in Liberia, 1834–1857* (Baltimore: Maryland Historical Society, 2003), p. 27.
21. Burin, *Slavery and the Peculiar Solution*, p. 66; Penelope Campbell, *Maryland in Africa: The Maryland State Colonization Society, 1831–1857* (Urbana: University of Illinois Press, 1971), pp. 60–61; Hall, *On Africa's Shore*, p. 27.
22. William J. Evitts, *A Matter of Allegiances: Maryland from 1850–1861* (Baltimore: Johns Hopkins University Press, 1974), pp. 64–65.
23. Jean H. Baker, *The Politics of Continuity: Maryland Political Parties from 1858 to 1870* (Baltimore: Johns Hopkins University Press, 1973), p. 5.
24. See Tracy Matthew Melton, *Hanging Henry Gambrill: The Violent Career of Baltimore's Plug Uglies, 1854–1860* (Baltimore: Maryland Historical Society, 2005).
25. Carleton Beals, *Brass-Knuckle Crusade: The Great Know-Nothing Conspiracy, 1820–1860* (New York: Hastings House, 1960), pp. 173–174.
26. Ibid., pp. 180–181; Baker, *Politics of Continuity*, p. 34.
27. Evitts, *A Matter of Allegiances*, pp. 25, 82.

28. In 1850, it was estimated that escapes cost the border counties of Maryland about $10,000 in slave property every week. Group escapes were common. On some occasions as many as thirty or forty slaves would abscond at once. Not all of them headed for Pennsylvania. Baltimore was a popular destination for escapees because they could blend in with the city's large population of free African Americans. See Ralph Clayton, *Slavery, Slaveholding, and the Free Black Population of Antebellum Baltimore* (Bowie, MD: Heritage Books, 1993), ch. 7.
29. Christopher Phillips, *Freedom's Port: The African American Community of Baltimore, 1790–1860* (Urbana: University of Illinois Press, 1997), pp. 40–56.
30. Ibid., p. 131; Graham, *Baltimore*, p. 63.
31. Phillips, *Freedom's Port*, p. 145.
32. Graham, *Baltimore*, p. 167.
33. Richard Paul Fuke, *Imperfect Equality: African Americans and the Confines of White Racial Attitudes in Post-Emancipation Maryland* (New York: Fordham University Press, 1999), pp. 117–124.
34. Phillips, *Freedom's Port*, pp. 137–138.
35. Graham, *Baltimore*, pp. 97–100.
36. Bettye J. Gardner, "Opposition to Emigration, A Selected Letter of William Watkins (The Colored Baltimorean),"*Journal of Negro History* 67 (1982): 155–158.
37. Graham, *Baltimore*, p. 119.
38. Ibid., pp. 124–125.
39. Curtis M. Jacobs, *Speech of Col. Curtis M. Jacobs, on the Free Colored Population of Maryland, Delivered before the House of Delegates on the 17th of February, 1860* (Annapolis, MD: Elihu S. Riley, 1860), pp. 7, 10, 12.
40. Graham, *Baltimore*, p. 155.
41. Robert Brugger, *Maryland, a Middle Temperament, 1634–1980* (Baltimore: Johns Hopkins University Press and Maryland Historical Society, 1988), p. 310.
42. Phillips, *Freedom's Port*, pp. 234–238.
43. Margaret Law Callcott, *The Negro in Maryland Politics, 1870–1912* (Baltimore: Johns Hopkins University Press, 1969), pp. 13, 17, 63.
44. David Taft Terry, "'Tramping for Justice': The Dismantling of Jim Crow in Baltimore, 1942–1954," PhD dissertation, Howard University, 2002, p. 6; William George Paul, "The Shadow of Equality: The Negro in Baltimore, 1864–1911," PhD dissertation, University of Wisconsin, 1974, p. 76.
45. Callcott, *The Negro in Maryland Politics*, pp. 105–106.
46. Ibid., pp. 122–123, 125; James B. Crooks, *Politics and Progress: The Rise of Urban Progressivism in Baltimore, 1895–1911* (Baton Rouge: Louisiana State University Press, 1968), pp. 61–64.
47. Sherry H. Olson, *Baltimore: The Building of an American City*, revised edition (Baltimore: Johns Hopkins University Press, 1997), pp. 270–271, 275–276; Garrett Power, "Apartheid Baltimore Style: The Residential Segregation Ordinances of 1910–1913," *Maryland Law Review* 42, no. 2 (1983): 290–291, 298; Roger L. Rice, "Residential Segregation by Law, 1910–1917," *Journal of Southern History* 34 (May 1968): 180–181.
48. Power, "Apartheid Baltimore Style," p. 299.
49. Ibid., pp. 289, 300.
50. "Object to Living Near Respectable Negroes, " *Afro-American Ledger* (Baltimore) October 1, 1910; "Colored Men Protest Against the Passage of the West Ordinance," *Afro-American Ledger* (Baltimore) October 8, 1910.
51. *Buchanan v. Warley*, 245 US 60 (1917); *Shelley v. Kraemer*, 334 US 1 (1948).

52. Edward Orser, *Blockbusting in Baltimore: The Edmondson Village Story* (Lexington: University Press of Kentucky, 1994), p. 1; Thomas J. Sugrue, *The Origins of the Urban Crisis: Race and Inequality in Postwar Detroit* (Princeton, NJ: Princeton University Press, 1996), ch. 8. Another private defense of neighborhood segregation, the restrictive covenant, proved ineffective in halting racial turnover. See Garrett Power, "*Meade v. Dennistone*: The NAACP's Test Case to '. . . Sue Jim Crow Out of Maryland with the Fourteenth Amendment,'" *Maryland Law Review* 63 (2003): 803–804.

53. Power, "*Meade v. Dennistone*," pp. 790, 799.

54. Callcott, *The Negro in Maryland Politics*, pp. 56–57.

55. Ibid., pp. 57, 125.

56. A 1934 study sponsored by the Baltimore Urban League estimated that 400 social clubs operated in the city's black community, more than twenty fraternal organizations, a variety of recreational and social welfare organizations such as the black YMCA, numerous Democratic and Republican neighborhood clubs, women's organizations ranging from a black chapter of the American University Women to the Baltimore Housewives' League, black professional organizations, seventy-one neighborhood clubs with a collective membership of over 5,000, which sponsored activities independently or in cooperation with black churches with a reported attendance of 87,097. There were also four black Catholic churches in Baltimore with a total membership of 9,000 and 216 black Protestant churches. See Andor D. Skotnes, "The Black Freedom Movement and the Workers Movement in Baltimore, 1930–1939," doctoral dissertation, Rutgers University, 1991, pp. 51–52, 78.

57. Frank R. Kent, *The Story of Maryland Politics* (Hatboro, PA: Folklore Associates, 1968 [1911]), p. 308; Verda F. Welcome with James M. Abraham, *My Life and Times* (Englewood Cliffs, NJ: Henry House Publishing, 1991), p. 44.

58. Welcome, *My Life and Times*, pp. 44, 192; Marion Orr, *Black Social Capital: The Politics of School Reform in Baltimore, 1986–1998* (Lawrence: University Press of Kansas, 1999), p. 49.

59. G. James Fleming, *Baltimore's Failure to Elect a Black Mayor in 1971* (Washington: Joint Center for Political Studies, 1972).

60. Welcome, *My Life and Times*, p. 94; Durr, *Behind the Backlash*, pp. 197–198.

61. Skotnes, "The Black Freedom Movement," pp. 193, 197; Denton L. Watson, *Lion in the Lobby: Clarence Mitchell, Jr.'s Struggle for the Passage of Civil Rights Laws* (New York: William Morrow, 1990), p. 89.

62. Genna Rae McNeil, "Youth Initiative in the African American Struggle for Racial Justice and Constitutional Rights: The City-Wide Young People's Forum of Baltimore, 1931–1941," in John Hope Franklin and Genna Rae McNeil, eds., *African Americans and the Living Constitution* (Washington: Smithsonian Institution Press, 1995), pp. 65–66; Skotnes, "The Black Freedom Movement," pp. 221–224.

63. Skotnes, "The Black Freedom Movement," pp. 229–230, 235.

64. Terry, "Tramping for Justice," p. 73.

65. Ibid., p. 71; Callcott, *Maryland and America*, p. 147; Juan Williams, *Thurgood Marshall: American Revolutionary* (New York: Times Books, 1998), pp. 73, 76–77.

66. Watson, *Lion in the Lobby*, p. 99.

67. W. Edward Orser, "Neither Separate Nor Equal: Foreshadowing *Brown* in Baltimore County, 1935–1937," *Maryland Historical Magazine* 92 (Spring 1997): 5–35. Italics added.

68. Mark Tushnet, *The NAACP's Legal Strategy Against Segregated Education, 1925–1950* (Chapel Hill: University of North Carolina Press, 1987), pp. 138–143.
69. Watson, *Lion in the Lobby*, pp. 155–156, 182, 186.
70. Terry, "Tramping for Justice," pp. 35–36; Skotnes, "The Black Freedom Movement," p. 50.
71. Walter Bagehot, *Physics and Politics; or, Thoughts on the Application of "Natural Selection" and "Inheritance" to Political Society* (New York: D. Appleton, 1912), p. 37.

11 Immigration and Institutional Change

The Urban Origins of US Postal Savings Banks

Alethia Jones

Starting in 1910, any member of the public could open a savings account at the post office.[1] With this new service, the federal government expanded its administrative responsibilities. It would collect hundreds of millions in savings deposits, despite the fact that traditional banks offered savings accounts. For American political development scholars, postal banks are a clear-cut case of the expansion of the state's administrative capacities. This policy coup, the introduction of a government bank in a capitalist society, suggests the successful vanquishing of traditionally powerful economic interests. The postal bank case provides solid evidence of the theoretical proposition that unlikely social groups can and do win significant policy victories. Scholars have identified the presence of distinct social movements (agrarian populists and urban social welfare reformers) as well as state actors (high- and mid-level bureaucrats in the Post Office Department) in securing this policy change. Despite scrutinizing the politics of postal banks, these scholars have largely overlooked the critical role of urbanization in furnishing a rationale for bureaucratic expansion and the centrality of "shifts in governing authority" in understanding this institution. As a result, existing scholarship has neither documented nor tried to address the public's reaction to this new service.

The public responded decisively. On August 1, 1911, the Post Office Department allowed branches in Boston, Chicago, and New York to begin accepting savings deposits.[2] Twelve days later, Chicago's postal bank had $108,316 in deposits, New York's $53,029, and Boston's $26,722.[3] In two short years, the Department authorized 12,151 post offices to accept deposits.[4] As the system spread throughout the country, local postmasters reported that they had to turn away customers who had reached the $500 depository limit. Congress eventually raised deposit ceilings to $1,000 in 1916 and to $2,500 in 1918.[5] By 1916, 60 percent of the depositors were foreign-born and their deposits accounted for 75 percent of all the funds in the system, with Greek, Russian, and Italian nationalities heavily represented.[6]

Why were workers, especially urban immigrant workers who had access to private sector banks, hungry for a new style of banking?

Exploring where immigrants banked reveals a distinctly urban element to the origins of postal savings banks, one that is simultaneously local and international. Postal banks presented urban workers, indeed all workers, with a compelling option: it would never lose their savings. In an era where local banks failed and customers regularly lost their deposits, the federal government made a commitment to depositor safety. This safety feature functioned as a form of national deposit insurance, and did so fully 20 years before the New Deal required such insurance of all banks. For some immigrants, the offer of secure banking through the post office was a familiar one. Most European countries created postal savings systems in the 1800s.[7] But this cultural connection only explains part of the story, especially in light of the fact that 50 percent of the system's customers were US-born. In addition to a cultural explanation, a more structural one recognizes that as cities grew in the early twentieth century, urbanization intensified the negative consequences of a laissez-faire regulatory environment. The security of postal bank accounts made them an attractive option for some.

Referred to variously as postal savings accounts, postal savings, postal banks, and postal savings banks, the public's enthusiastic embrace suggests that they filled a niche.[8] We know considerably more about the *politics* of postal banks, than we do of their *purpose*. Why did the introduction of postal banks matter to society or to depositors? How does this new service represent a real shift in government's role and responsibilities, not just a new task or ideological commitment? Distinct features of the urban banking milieu, especially immigrant banking behavior, laid the groundwork for giving government new responsibilities and accounts for its popularity. Postal banks are a distinct case of political development, but the change is registered in the shift in governing authority, rather than in state actors or social movements. If this is indeed the case, then an explanation attentive to identifying such shifts should yield fruit.

Postal Banks as a Shift in Governing Authority

In an important effort to challenge the premises of pluralism's emphasis on economic interest groups, and later rational choice theorizing, theoretically grounded empirical scholarship documented states and social movements as independent political actors.[9] Researchers investigated political institutions, such as legislatures, parties, and agencies, to identify who most influenced the law's passage and identified the social movements and state bureaucrats who successfully persuaded Congress to expand government's responsibilities.

The "who" question has shaped most of the scholarship on postal banks because postal banks are assessed as a political or a bureaucratic institution; research overwhelmingly considers relationships between the Post Office Department, Congress, and various social movements.

Agrarian populists were staunch advocates of postal banks, parcel post, and postal telegraph services as part of an alternative vision of political economy where the federal government owned businesses.[10] A close analysis of the changing coalitions in Congress identifies the diverse coalition and electoral dynamics that sustained postal banks as an issue in Congress from 1873 until its passage in 1910.[11] Daniel Carpenter provides the fullest treatment of postal banks as a bureaucratic institution. He shows that bureaucratic autonomy, the ability of state agencies to persuade Congress to grant the agencies more power and discretion, resulted in agencies acquiring more responsibility. In this role, the Post Office Department identified and mobilized a national coalition of opinion-makers who pressured Congress to act. Post offices are also a site for competition between patronage and civil service staff.[12] In addition, Carpenter identifies a distinct devotion to using the post office to build a "moral economy," that included the desire to teach thrift to the immigrant masses.[13] As political scientists are interested in political institutions, the activity of those who are most politically active naturally gains attention. Explaining the politics of how an agency obtained the authorization to administer a new service is insufficient if one wishes to specify how government's authority actually changed.

Karen Orren and Stephen Skowronek define political development as "a durable shift in governing authority."[14] These three elements combined—durability, a shift, and authority—distinguish development from its generic counterpart, change. In other words, government introduces a new form, function, or role and the change sticks, despite contestation and resistance from affected parties.[15] Two additional elements cement an analysis of American *political* development. First, the development identified must be political in nature, not cultural or economic, though the subject matter may involve culture or economics.[16] Second, American political development scholars are sensitive to issues of temporality. When they employ history, they are often interested in "political time," which uses timing and sequencing to explain political phenomena.[17]

Temporality also figures in Orren and Skowronek's notion of "history as site."[18] Rather than use history as necessary background that provides context to the present, history as site treats history as the foreground where active conflict and contestation for power lives. They note:

> The premise of history as a site leads to a conception of political action as an impingement on the authority of others, and it directs attention to those elements in the larger array that are challenged, displaced, transformed, reformed, or unaffected by new political efforts.[19]

They advise researchers to presume that the space is already occupied. Like Downtown Tokyo, every inch of space is accounted for. Every new institution must be jammed in amongst the institutions that already occupy the space.[20] History as site suggests that if temporal ordering matters, then the roots of shifts in authority lie in conditions that exist before the shift of interest occurs.[21] History as site also suggests identifying the institutions most analogous in form and function to the governmental authority under analysis, the institutions impinged upon by the shift in authority.

Applying "history as site" to postal banks, directs the researcher to the *status quo ante*—the role of government authority in protecting the savings of working-class Americans before 1910, a world dominated by banks and depositors, a world where postal savings banks do not yet exist. The search for analogous institutions situates postal banks among those entities that already offer savings accounts to the general public. Consequently, postal savings banks can be analyzed as financial institutions, instead of political or bureaucratic ones. As a consequence of this approach, the urban dimensions of the origin story of postal banks also come to light because the problems it hoped to address were distinctly urban in nature. They also offered an alternative to locally available banking options by importing a form of banking that was already popular in Europe.

The Myth and Reality of Banking in Early Twentieth-Century Urban America

It is easy to assume that a normal banking system existed in this period; one where commercial banks, with concrete columns, marble floors, and walk-in safes, provided checking and savings accounts to the general public. In this normal banking world, immigrants would have neighborhood-based banks that offered services in their native languages. In addition, credit unions, mutual savings banks, and savings and loans associations encouraged workers to save and granted them low-interest loans. In addition, the government authorized and oversaw all banking operations.

But this image fits banking in the 1920s, not in the early 1900s.[22] By 1910, state and federal governments had not fully institutionalized a modern banking system that served the needs of mass society. There was no Federal Reserve, no single paper currency, most states banned branch banking, and deposit insurance was rare.[23]

By the early 1900s, a new type of banking dominated cities. Colloquially known as "private banks" or "immigrant banks," these informal and unregulated operations provided crucial financial services to the urban masses.[24] Most immigrants banked at grocery stores, bars, rooming houses, bookstores, and small businesses that furnished an array of financial transactions. Private banks accepted deposits, sent remittances overseas, exchanged foreign currency, and sold steamship tickets.[25] An advertisement for Banco Roma, an Italian private bank in New York City, illustrates the array of services offered:

> Remittances in any sum whatever to all the post-offices in Italy, Switzerland, France and Austria, in paper money, gold francs and florins, in the quickest and safest way. Telegraphic orders. Drafts, payable at sight, on all the principal cities of Europe. Notary public; legal advice free. Ocean and R[ail] R[oad] tickets ... Shippers by package post ... Depot for Marsala and table wines. Depot for S[an] Antonio tobacco, imported, prime quality.[26]

In addition to access to people who spoke one's language, private banking often included a social dimension. One's "banker" usually knew local politicians, offered information about job opportunities, and read the newspaper to customers during convenient evening and weekend hours. Because customers communicated with family members in Europe through the mail, some "bankers" wrote and read letters on behalf of illiterate customers.[27] They also sold stamps and received letters on behalf of customers who sojourned to temporary and seasonal work on farms and railroads. As notaries, bankers could witness the signing of citizenship and other legal papers. Many private banks originated when customers asked to leave their cash in a business's safe rather than risk theft or loss. Steamship ticket sellers and real estate agents often received such requests.[28] However, these arrangements could not provide checking accounts, interest on savings, or conventional loans. But savings could be used to gradually pay off steamship and railroad tickets purchased for family members abroad seeking to join an immigrant in the US.[29]

Because banking without a charter was perfectly legal in many states at this time, anyone could open a banking business simply by hanging a "bank" sign in the window.[30] Through an unplanned and unanticipated process, enterprising individuals entered a relatively laissez-faire environment and leveraged the advantages of language and location and provided urgently needed financial transactions to the burgeoning urban population. They grew in number and size through an ad hoc process of adjusting to the immediate needs of a population responding to intense urbanization.

Despite the informality of these banking entities, private banks nonetheless processed millions of dollars. On Sunday, October 2, 1910, the *New York Times* reported that private banks processed roughly $138 million in overseas remittances in 1909. With respect to savings deposits, unincorporated banks held untold millions in their safes.[31] Despite these numbers, the system remained relatively invisible to official entities. The Department of Treasury told the *New York Times* reporter they had "[n]ever heard of such a thing as an immigrant bank," and that "[w]e know nothing of any such institutions here."[32]

The banks in the formal system, though subject to regulation, could not match the services and availability of immigrant private banks. Besides, a combination of exclusionary social norms and geographical inaccessibility meant that most workers did not have access to the type of banking institutions they would have preferred. They were starved for a conveniently located and secure place to deposit their savings.

Before 1910: Government as Bank Regulator

Government authority with major depository institutions operated through charters.[33] Prior to 1910, the government functioned not as a protector of consumer deposits but as a bank regulator, with charters as its primary tool of coercion. Charters specified the legal obligations banks needed to meet to obtain government approval to operate. The requirements defined ownership structures (the size, composition, and duties of the board of directors), inspection requirements by regulatory officials (to ensure honest accounting), and public disclosure requirements (usually by filing quarterly and annual financial reports that a state's banking department subsequently published).[34] Charters also granted privileges, such as the ability to print money, to collect deposits from the public, and to grant loans, but usury laws specified the allowable interest rates. Once legislatures determined a charter's criteria, state agencies approved all applications that met the criteria.[35] Finally, most charters banned branch banking. The country's anti-monopoly culture usually required each bank to be independently owned and operated.[36] The term "national banks" does not refer to banks with branches. Instead it identifies banks with charters defined by Congress and administered by the Department of Treasury. Similarly, "state banks" had charters authorized by a state legislature and overseen by the state's banking department. Even though different types of savings institutions existed, the safest ones were few in number, even in major urban centers.[37]

Government regulated banks that catered to immigrant needs existed. Some shared their business model with colleagues through industry journals. Mr Goddard described how his bank successfully attracted immigrant customers by giving "services in over ten languages" and "cultivated the acquaintanceship of the individual depositor with the hope that he will feel that he is dealing with a personality as well as an institution."[38] They also furnished non-traditional services, such as letter writing services and a desk for a steamship agent that allowed customers to purchase tickets in small installments over time.

But chartered neighborhood banks did not define the field of immigrant community banking until the 1920s, when all state legislatures made government charters mandatory for all businesses that advertised themselves as banks. Until then, private banks easily outnumbered their regulated counterparts.[39] Some of the unchartered private banks operated in traditional bank buildings and offered standard bank services, but they avoided the expense of hiring accountants and inspectors to comply with charter requirements.[40] But many private bankers obtained charters when the law required them to do so.

Acknowledging the need for worker-oriented deposit institutions, state legislatures authorized the creation of nonprofit banks. Collectively known as thrifts, credit unions, mutual savings banks, and building and loan associations (later known as savings and loans associations), they would eventually equal traditional banks in stature and professional management, but only after the 1950s. Until then, most thrift institutions were too small in size or too few in number to accommodate the needs of a growing urban working class. Mutual savings banks, the largest and most well-known of the thrifts, were confined to old east coast cities because bankers in Midwest and western states blocked state laws creating mutuals.[41] From 1880 to 1920, building and loan associations labored at lobbying state legislatures to adapt or replace outdated charter systems.[42] Massachusetts passed the first statewide credit union law in the nation in 1910.[43] Even if thrifts were more geographically dispersed and more numerous, the law often required them to serve only their members. As a result, churches, clubs, lodges, and other member-based associations sponsored thrifts.[44] Furthermore, the cooperative banking model relied on member-volunteers, not professionals, to do the accounting and other managerial tasks.[45] These various restrictions meant that a good thrift was hard to find.

The notion that any member of the general public could utilize a bank's services existed as a legal requirement but social norms undermined the promise of equal access to services. Banks originated to serve the needs of economic and political elites, not the masses. Typically, an area's wealthy population founded commercial banks and through social networks vetted business ventures and granted loans to projects that promoted economic development.[46] Because of the large sizes of these transactions, depository and loan services to corporations and governments, the wealthy assured profitability. The deposits of average people provided easy access to steady streams of capital. But traditional banks demurred from the requisite services. Servicing small accounts diverted staff from profitable customers. Furthermore, English-only tellers and limited "bankers'" hours made traditional banks unappealing to some urban workers.[47]

Bank Failures

Bank failures are unique. The ripple effect of fear caused by a failure caused "bank runs" where depositors descended on the failing bank en masse to withdraw their savings. Depositors who arrived after the bank ran out of cash lost their savings permanently if the bank failed.

Customers redeposited their funds if the bank survived the crisis. Both informal and formal banks experienced runs, and both had incidents of failure. The steep contractions and expansions of cash that occurred as customers withdrew and re-deposited funds destabilized the money supply.

Bank runs had a strong psychological element. Runs on failing banks sparked runs on healthy banks, and vice versa. Ultimately, a bank run reflected a customer's fears more accurately than it did the health of an individual bank. Whether small or large, based on facts or rumors, each run marred the banking industry image by viscerally reminding everyone of the system's fundamental insecurity.[48] Immigrants engaged in runs more frequently than US-born customers. They trusted the banking system less and responded to rumors more.[49] With their disproportionately high number of deposits in unchartered banks, perhaps immigrants felt even most at risk.

It is important not to paint private banks as uniformly deceitful or fraudulent. The system successfully transmitted over $100 million overseas annually by functioning as intermediaries for American Express, Western Union, and the large steamship companies. Although trustworthy bankers existed and perhaps even dominated the field, the number of failures naturally grew as the number of banks grew. But the dynamics of runs amplified any incidence of failure that occurred.

Government Regulation and the Protection of Deposits

Why didn't the charter system protect consumer deposits? In other words, why was this form of governing authority insufficient for the need? In large part, urban realities were grafted on to legal foundations established in an agrarian era. The bank chartering system assumed interpersonal knowledge, especially given its history of serving business and governmental elites. Bankers knew their customers and made loans based on character instead of income and assets, if needed. Thrift institutions embodied this view. Member-based banking organizations functioned through a committee of peers who made loan decisions. Customers, in turn, knew their banker. The inherent information asymmetry in this arrangement, customers would always have less information about banks than banks had of them, expanded as populations increased. Deposit protection resulted from professionally managed banks that made conservative investment decisions and remained profitable; it was not the primary obligation of the business itself and government did not mandate it.[50] The system required customers to be knowledgeable about a bank's management. As society urbanized, it remained up to the individual to choose wisely.

Charters suggested a degree of legitimacy and professionalism that did not always prevail. The combination of federalism and a laissez-faire environment created the classic "patchwork quilt" of laws and institutions that confused customers and failed to protect the public's deposits.[51] National banks, overseen by the Department of Treasury, had the strictest criteria and the most professional management.[52] But the Department of Treasury did not control the nation's banking system, although it would have liked to. When the federal government introduced the National Bank Charter Act of 1863 to raise funds for the Civil War, supporters hoped the new system would replace state banks with a centralized and unified system of national banks. Instead, state banks continued to exist but they stopped printing currency. This overlapping structure required bank owners to choose whether to obtain a national or a state charter. Many of the largest, most established, and most conservatively managed banks traded in their state charters for national ones, giving national banks the reputation for solid management and leaving the country with a dual banking structure that persists today.[53] Banks with weak charters coexisted with banks that had strong charters, which undermined efforts to secure a professionalized banking system. Because state legislatures had over a century's long head start, they granted the vast majority of charters. Each state had its own criteria, leading to wide variations in stringency between states.

For those who relied on evidence of government regulation as a heuristic for a business's trustworthiness and professionalism, such cues provided false comfort. A charter only indicated that a bank met the state's minimum requirements. The charter system regulated banks, not bankers; an approach tantamount to regulating hospitals but not doctors.[54] There was no direct correlation between a charter and professional management, only probabilities.

Immigrants using unchartered private banks also struggled with the true meaning of government designations. In Europe, notaries functioned as lawyers and post offices accepted savings deposits. This mixing of roles meant that many Southern and Eastern European immigrants assumed notaries had the same professional and legal obligations as lawyers in Europe, making them a legitimate place for legal advice as well as banking services. Hence, the "free legal advice" Banco Roma offered. Similarly, some immigrants assumed that postal substations, private organizations permitted to sell stamps, were official branches of the post office and therefore the equivalent of European postal banks.[55]

Facing limited access to conventional banking services, most immigrants and urban workers relied heavily on efficient, ubiquitous, and unregulated private banks. The cost of selecting the wrong bank was significant. But the system placed the burden on customer selection, despite the fact that governmental authority in banking was confusing, diluted, and manipulated.

The banking public effectively had a handful of options: very good but largely inaccessible national banks and thrifts; a bevy of loosely regulated state chartered banks; charter-less private banks; or no banks at all. The latter option included hiding cash at home—under the mattress, buried in the yard, any place that avoided discovery and theft. Some savers purchased money orders in their own name to avoid the problem of excessive cash. Labeled as "hoarding" these practices kept funds out of the money supply where it could be used productively to finance bank loans and investments. Opponents of immigration pointed to hoarding as yet another way that immigrants hurt the US economy, despite the fact that anyone could hoard.[56] Immigrants also mailed money orders or transmitted funds directly to Europe, sometimes for deposit in savings accounts at postal banks in their countries of origin. This route also kept money out of the US where, some argued, it properly belonged. The devotedly risk-averse depositor could create accounts at several types of institutions, thus spreading their risk.

Social location and experiences mediated an individual's choice. Individuals who were well-educated, well-informed, well-financed, well-acculturated, and fluent in English were most likely to know about, choose, and have access to the best banks. Such customers certainly existed, even amongst immigrants. By 1910, the oldest members of the new immigration had been in the US for almost 30 years. But immigrant depositors could be found in all types of banking institutions because personal characteristics (length of time in the US, comfort with English, level of literacy, income, membership in a lodge, congregation, or other association) and geography (proximity to high-status banks either near work or home, population density) probably guided their decision. But in the end, most depositors benefited from a strong dose of luck in their quest to find a safe bank.

The Promise of Postal Savings Accounts

The Post Office Department was well aware of the public's savings practices. In 1909, 80 percent of the $81 million in postal money orders they sold went to six countries: Austria, Great Britain, Hungary, Italy, Norway, and Russia.[57] Reporting on key findings and claims, the *New York Times* reprinted Postmaster General Meyer's arguments in favor of postal banks, as they appeared in the Department's 1907 annual report. They included the following observations:

> [O]n account of its possessors being ignorant of our language and suspicious of our private institutions, [money] is being sent home in order that it may be placed in the postal savings banks of their native countries . . . a great deal of money which does not now find its way into banking channels at all would come into the postal savings bank.[58]

Whether policymakers realized it or not, the fundamental question at issue was whether a modern urban society would have its banking system hinge on the moral fortitude of individual bankers or whether there should be a widely available, publicly accessible alternative suited to a society increasingly defined by mobility and relative anonymity.

Three decades of mass immigration, industrialization, and market forces had still not produced professionally managed, government chartered banks in sufficient quantities to meet the needs of the burgeoning urban masses. Postal banks entered this insecure and inconsistent milieu promising much-needed uniformity, security, and equal access.

Postal savings accounts permitted anyone over 10 years old to make deposits up to an initial $500 dollar limit. Individuals held only one account and deposited up to $100 monthly. If an account holder moved, he or she needed to close the account and re-open it at another location. The funds reverted to the Treasury if no one did so. A system of passbooks and stamps allowed depositor and postal clerk alike to keep track of deposits and withdrawals. The accounts paid 2 percent annual interest while commercial and savings banks paid 4 percent. Organizations and businesses could not have accounts. These and other restrictions meant postal banks would attract customers who had safety as their primary concern.[59] Schools, settlement houses, and other organizations encouraged children to learn how to save by using postal banks.

The Panic of 1907

Congress did not approve postal banks because they solved a banking need. Such an explanation would be functionalist, a claim that "social arrangements exist *because* they meet certain needs of societies or particular powerful actors."[60] Politics matters. Political time, the intersection of political and temporal analysis, helps to explain why Congress authorized the creation of postal banks in 1910. In 1907, postal banks remained at a traditional three-decade impasse. Since 1873, postal bank bills consistently made it through to committee hearings but no further. An exogenous shock broke the legislative impasse: the Panic of 1907 and the widespread bank failures that accompanied it. The longstanding postal bank coalition of agrarians, social welfare reformers, and Post Office administrators seized upon the window of opportunity, as did other coalitions.[61]

In the wake of the Panic and a presidential election in 1908, the sentiment for government action strengthened, while the usual deference granted to the business community weakened and the committee chairs softened their positions. When the dust settled, Congress passed several important banking laws, including the Aldrich–Vreeland Currency Act of 1908, the Postal Savings Act in 1910, and the Federal Reserve Act in 1913.[62] These and other new banking laws brought the country closer to institutionalizing a modern banking system, a project the New Deal would solidify. With these changes in place, bank failures returned to being a routine but manageable fact of life until they reached epidemic proportions with the Great Depression of 1929.[63]

Postal savings banks could not solve the problem of bank runs. Initially, private bankers continued to operate because they offered substantial conveniences well beyond a savings account.[64] When states finally passed mandatory bank charter laws, private bankers usually faced one of three options: exit the banking business; convert to a full-time bank; or become a licensed financial services operator, essentially a nondepository private bank.[65] For those who opted to become banks, generous transition periods facilitated the induction of private bankers into the chartered banking fold.[66] The loose management styles of these numerous small banks are said to account for the large number of bank failures during the Great Depression.[67]

After 1911: From Bank Regulator to People's Banker via Deposit Insurance

In this exploration of postal banks as a shift in governing authority, three questions remain. First, what is the nature of the new grant of governing authority? Second, how did it affect pre-existing institutions? Third, was the shift durable? This new authority, a form of deposit insurance, affected three key constituencies: the banking public, especially immigrants; state regulations; and for-profit banks.

Postal savings banks shifted the government's relationship to the banking public by offering accounts that were fully insulated from loss. This feature and the convenience of post office branch locations expanded the banking options for depositors. Furthermore, this new government role operated on immigrant-friendly terms. In 1918 the post office eventually published deposit forms and documents in twelve languages.[68] The initiative clearly reflected the pre-migration experiences of European immigrants but it possessed the added benefit of expanding banking services to the nation as a whole. The US-born constituted 50 percent of its customers. Postmasters reported that both immigrant and native-born customers brought in "hoarded" cash because they did not have savings accounts at state or national banks. Postal banks established deposit safety as a fundamental responsibility of the federal government.

Postal banks shifted the federal government's relationship to states by implicitly rejecting the uneven nature of state charters. It demonstrated that government could be a source for order in the financial services system. Unlike state regulations, postal savings banks were centrally managed, uniform in operation, and open to all members of the public. Individuals no longer had to guess what the government's presence in banking meant or discover that their confidence in a particular banker was ill-placed. Postal banks operated under a single national standard. Its management, accounting, and investment practices, emanated from a central authority in Washington, DC. As such, the government's presence signaled an undeniable and uniform professionalism and security.

Postal banks clearly upset the status quo in banking. The American Bankers Association (ABA) interpreted postal banks as an invasion of their domain. Its 1908 resolution stated:

> Resolved, that it is the sense of this association that we should condemn in unqualified terms the proposition for the establishment of postal savings banks or any other system by which the government enters directly into banking relations with the people.[69]

The ABA decried the government's departure from its traditional role of working only with banks and leaving the task of working directly with the banking public in the hands of the private sector. The mere existence of a government bank for the people lessened the undisputed primacy of private for-profit entities as the preferred option for the general public. Government banks amounted to unfair competition with a private sector that could not guarantee deposits or operate branches.[70]

Postal banks in 1910 and national deposit insurance in 1932 represent the same grant of authority. They differed in how government offered insurance: one is a case of direct government, in the other government's presence is more indirect. They also differed in political support. The Democratic presidential platform of 1908 explicitly supported national deposit insurance first and postal banks as a last resort. But when William Taft won the election, the Republican Party's preferred solution—postal banks—found favor instead.[71]

The public utilized postal banks as a form of deposit insurance. As the economic crisis of the 1930s unfolded and bank runs became frequent, postal bank customers knew their deposits were safe. To obtain the same protections, bank customers withdrew their funds from checking and savings accounts and redeposited them at the post office.[72] They wished to benefit from its $2,500 depository limit. Total deposits in postal banks topped $1 billion in 1933 and the number of depositors doubled in one year to over 1.5 million in 1932.[73]

The New Deal's deposit insurance law required every chartered bank to join the Federal Deposit Insurance Corporation (FDIC). The law universalized access to government-guaranteed savings by covering all bank accounts, not just those at the post office. In the event a bank failed, the FDIC reimbursed the bank's depositors the full amount in their accounts up to $2,500, the same amount as postal savings accounts.[74]

At last, customers no longer needed to acquire knowledge of an individual bank's management practices to ensure that their deposits would be safe. The universality of the government guarantee eliminated fear and ended the phenomenon of bank runs once and for all. In 1966 the ABA finally persuaded Congress that the systems were redundant and Congress voted to terminate postal savings.[75]

Orren and Skowronek define "durability" as a shift in authority that "holds on for a half-century . . . without getting reversed or deflected."[76] Durability, then, must lie in the form of authority itself, not in the mechanism used to achieve it—that is, the specific institutional form that government authority takes. If this is the case, then political development that takes the form of a "shift in governing authority" need not be coterminous with an institution's life-span. In the case of postal banks, the new principle it institutionalized—that the federal government should protect consumer deposits—lasted well beyond the 56 years of its official existence and continues today in the FDIC.

Conclusion

The population increases that drive urbanization create new patterns and flows that disrupt the social and economic status quo. Marrying urbanization and American political development links population growth to demands that government adopts new roles. A self-consciously authority-centered approach can capture how policies are linked to the actual experiences of the target populations who ultimately must live with these policy changes.

The inherent gap between influential policy advocates and politically weak policy targets is one of the endemic political problems of urbanization. The disjuncture between the empowered groups who advocate for policy changes and the politically dispersed masses raises questions of democracy and representation. A host of reformer-driven policy changes, such as zoning, public health, occupational licensing, juvenile justice, building codes, and the siting of parks, beaches, and highways, remain enmeshed in questions of representation and fairness. Perhaps an authority-centered analysis tied to temporality can shed new light on these questions.

Orren and Skowronek's concept of "shifts in governing authority" combined with the notion of "history as site" point researchers to find politics outside of political institutions. The hunt for entities that possess the authority government seeks to, but does not yet, command invariably leads to a host of private and nongovernmental institutions. Accounting for the experiences of policy targets before government intervenes is one way to bring in the concerns of those who may otherwise be overlooked, outmaneuvered, or silenced in the political process.

No published accounts indicate that immigrants played an important role in advocating for the postal bank law's passage, despite the fact they would benefit from the introduction of this institutional form. By tracing lines of authority, the banking habits of depositors gained new prominence as did the distinctly urban and international elements in the origins of US postal banks. As a potential competitor to the existing purveyors of savings accounts, postal banks can be analyzed as a financial institution, as well as a bureaucratic and political one. In a context defined by the concerns of depositors, instead of bureaucrats, reformers, and bankers, a world of unregulated banks, bank failures, and customer anxiety comes to light. In this context, one can specify the distinctly new element in governing authority that postal banks represent. Because depositors would never lose their funds, postal banks offered a form of deposit insurance for over 20 years before the New Deal's more well-known deposit insurance program leveraged the federal government's power to broaden access to this form of protection.

Going "to the streets" and anchoring the analysis of policy changes in the lived experiences of target populations can highlight why a particular "shift in governing authority" matters. Policymakers' decisions affect whether society creates open and shared institutions or highly segregated and privatized ones. Arguably the product of a paternalistic upper middle-class reform movement, postal banks were simultaneously universal in character because anyone could open an account, yet relevant to immigrants who were accustomed to using postal banks in Europe. Whether by luck or design, postal banks provided a meaningful new service to both the foreign- and native-born. Perhaps, by looking from the ground up at a host of other policy changes, we can specify the nature of new grants of governing authority and identify how they include or exclude marginal and politically weak social groups.

Notes

1. The Postal Savings Act was signed into law on June 15, 1910 but offices began accepting deposits in 1911.
2. In Chicago, the postal bank was located at the main post office branch located in the loop, the city's downtown business district. Only post office branches designated to do so could accept deposits. See "Postals for Central Reserve Cities," *The Chicago Banker: A Weekly Paper Devoted to the Banking and Financial Interests of the Middle West* July 29, 1911, p. 17.
3. Amounts are 1911 dollars. See "Chicago's Postal Bank Leads," *The Chicago Banker: A Weekly Paper Devoted to the Banking and Financial Interests of the Middle West* August 26, 1911, p. 17.
4. Edwin W. Kemmerer, "Six Years of Postal Savings in the United States," *The American Economic Review* 7, no. 1 (1917): 46–90 (see p. 48).
5. Maureen O'Hara and David Easley, "The Postal Savings System in the Depression," *Journal of Economic History* 39, no. 3 (1979): 741–753, quote on p. 744.
6. Kemmerer, "Six Years of Postal Savings in the United States," p. 57.
7. United States National Monetary Commission, *Notes on the Postal Savings Bank Systems of the Leading Countries* (Washington, DC: GPO, 1910).
8. Despite the term "postal bank," the post office did not require or establish separate buildings devoted to banking; the savings accounts were additional services one could obtain at the post office counter.

9. Theda Skocpol, "Bringing the State Back In: Strategies of Analysis in Current Research," in Peter B. Evans, Dietrich Rueschemeyer, and Theda Skocpol, eds., *Bringing the State Back In* (New York: Cambridge University Press, 1985). For an assessment of rational actor approaches from a historical institutionalist perspective, see Paul Pierson, *Politics in Time: History, Institutions, and Social Analysis* (Princeton, NJ: Princeton University Press, 2004).

10. Richard B. Kielbowicz, "Government Goes Into Business: Parcel Post in the Nation's Political Economy, 1880–1915," *Studies in American Political Development* 8 (Spring 1994): 150–172.

11. Jean Reith Schroedel and Bruce Snyder, "People's Banking: The Promise Betrayed?," *Studies in American Political Development* 8 (Spring 1994): 173–193. Splits within the Republican Party figure prominently.

12. Daniel P. Carpenter, *The Forging of Bureaucratic Autonomy: Reputations, Networks, and Policy Innovation in Executive Agencies, 1862–1928.* (Princeton, NJ: Princeton University Press, 2002). See also Carpenter, "State Building through Reputation Building: Coalitions of Esteem and Program Innovation in the National Postal System, 1883–1913," *Studies in American Political Development* 14 (Fall 2000): 121–155.

13. Carpenter, *The Forging of Bureaucratic Autonomy*, ch. 5. The Post Office Department also combated pornography and investment fraud.

14. Karen Orren and Stephen Skowronek, *The Search for American Political Development* (New York: Cambridge University Press, 2004), p. 123.

15. Orren and Skowronek, *The Search for American Political Development*, pp. 123–132.

16. They recognize that cultural and economic ideas often express themselves in institutional form, "which is where they really count as far as politics is concerned." Orren and Skowronek, *The Search for American Political Development*, p. 133. This is especially germane in the field of banking, see Susan Hoffman, *Politics and Banking: Ideas, Public Policy, and the Creation of Financial Institutions* (Baltimore: Johns Hopkins University Press, 2001).

17. More generally, this means attention to "just what ideas about time are most appropriate to the study of politics," which includes intercurrence. See Orren and Skowronek, *The Search for American Political Development*, p. 75.

18. Karen Orren and Stephen Skowronek, "The Study of American Political Development," in I. Katznelson and H.V. Milner, eds., *Political Science: State of the Discipline* (New York: W.W. Norton & Co., 2002). They also delineate history as matrix focused on identifying patterns across cases.

19. Orren and Skowronek, "The Study of American Political Development," p. 751.

20. Orren and Skowronek, *The Search for American Political Development*, p. 22.

21. APD "identif[ies] relevant institutions and the distribution of controls among them before, during, and after the changes in question." Orren and Skowronek, *The Search for American Political Development*, p. 135.

22. Chicago banks pioneered key aspects of the neighborhood bank. See E.N. Baty, *The Story of the Outlying Banks of Chicago* (Chicago: Chicago and Cook County Bankers Association, 1924).

23. For most this country's history, banks printed currency, not the government. With the National Bank Act of 1863, the federal government eventually taxed state-based bank currency out of existence, replacing it with currency created by banks authorized by the Department of Treasury, known as national banks. Today's currency, the Federal Reserve Note, was introduced in 1913

when the Federal Reserve was created and became the sole form of paper currency in 1970. See Kelley L. Ross, "Six Kinds of United States Paper Currency," *The Proceedings of the Friesian School, Fourth Series.* Available at http://www.friesian.com/notes.htm (accessed March 19, 2003).

State-level deposit insurance programs were established in New York in 1829, Vermont 1831, Michigan 1836, Indiana 1834, Ohio 1845, Iowa 1858 but all ended in 1866. Between 1907 and 1917, eleven states adopted deposit insurance for state chartered banks but all were inoperable by 1933. See Carter H. Golembe, "The Deposit Insurance Legislation of 1933: An Examination of Its Antecedents and Its Purposes," *Political Science Quarterly* 75, no. 2 (1960): 181–200.

Clearly, the bias against branching no longer exists but the terms national and state bank continue to refer to a bank's charter, not to branching. Therefore, a national bank can operate in only one state, and in theory, can only have one location. A state-chartered bank can have branches nationwide, but is not a "national bank."

24. Immigrant private banking differs from private banking that originated as a tool for the financial super-elite, such as J.P. Morgan, who used the regulatory freedom to finance unprecedented monopolies in the railroad and steel industries and to bail out the US government. See Richard Sylla, "Forgotten Men of Money: Private Bankers in Early US History," *Journal of Economic History* 36, no. 1 (1976): 173–188; Ron Chernow, *The House of Morgan: An American Banking Dynasty and the Rise of Modern Finance* (New York: Atlantic Monthly Press, 1990).

25. Jared N. Day, "Credit, Capital and Community: Informal Banking in Immigrant Communities in the United States, 1880–1924," *Financial History Review* 9 (2002): 65–78; Lizabeth Cohen, *Making a New Deal: Industrial Workers in Chicago, 1919–1939* (New York: Cambridge University Press, 1990); Perry R. Duis, *The Saloon: Public Drinking in Chicago and Boston 1880–1920* (Urbana: University of Illinois Press, 1983).

26. John Koren, "The Padrone System and Padrone Banks," *Bulletin of the Department of Labor* 9 (March 1897): 113–129. The advertisement appeared in Italian in a New York City paper and is translated and reprinted in Koren's article.

27. In Europe clergy often wrote and read letters from overseas to the entire community. Bankers assumed this function in the US, especially for immigrants who did not have clergy or others available to furnish this service for free or at a convenient time. Marcus Lee Hansen and Arthur Meier Schlesinger, *The Atlantic Migration, 1607–1860: A History of the Continuing Settlement of the United States* (Cambridge, MA: Harvard University Press, 1940); William Isaac Thomas and Florian Znaniecki, *The Polish Peasant in Europe and America* (New York: Dover Publications, Inc., 1958 [1927]).

28. Edith Abbott, *Immigration: Select Documents and Case Records* (Chicago: University of Chicago Press, 1924); Alethia Jones, "Bootstraps and Beltways: The State's Role in Immigrant Community Banking," PhD dissertation, Yale University, 2005.

29. United States Immigration Commission, *Immigrant Banks* (Washington, DC: GPO, 1911), vol. 37, pp. 211–233; Massachusetts Commission on Immigration, *The Problem of Immigration in Massachusetts* (Boston: Wright & Potter Printing Company, 1914).

30. Only banks that issued currency were required to have a charter by state law.

31. Precise statistics on the number of immigrant private banks is impossible to ascertain. Sylla, "Forgotten Men of Money"; George Earnest Barnett, *State*

Banking in the United States since the Passage of the National Bank Act (Baltimore: Johns Hopkins Press, 1902). The only national census comes from the Congressionally-appointed but nativist-oriented Dillingham Commission's volume on immigrant private banks. It concluded that the vast majority of "bankers" were uncountable because they operated as parts of saloons, grocery stores, and other businesses. Those, like Banco Roma, that hung a sign in the window amounted to 2,600 across the nation. Some private banks looked like traditional chartered banks and some actually obtained charters, but banks of this type were too few to count. Despite its bias, the Commission's research was thorough. Even its opponents trusted the particulars of this study. See Abbott, *Immigration*, p. 498.

32. "Immigrants Sent $275,000,000 Abroad in One Year," *New York Times* October 2, 1910.

33. Nondepository financial services entities, such as check cashers, were also largely unregulated at this time. Some states required them to obtain licenses that had considerably fewer requirements than charters, see Massachusetts Commission on Immigration, *The Problem of Immigration in Massachusetts*.

34. See Hoffman, *Politics and Banking*, for a full explanation of these categories.

35. This form of regulation, known as free banking, was institutionalized in the 1830s when state legislatures defined the criteria for obtaining a charter, then an administrative agency would grant charters to all applicants who met the criteria. Prior to this, banks applied directly to state legislatures who crafted charters for an individual institution and voted accordingly, a highly politicized process. Free banking democratized access to bank ownership. See Bray Hammond, *Banks and Politics in America from the Revolution to the Civil War* (Princeton, NJ: Princeton University Press, 1957); David Moss and Sarah Brennan, "Managing Money Risk in Antebellum New York: From Chartered Banking to Free Banking and Beyond," *Studies in American Political Development* 15, no. 2 (2001): 138–162. Thrifts were caught in a similar transition from charters to individual organizations to a free banking system from 1890–1910.

36. Bankers constructed various schemes to circumvent this ban, such as interlocking boards of directors. American Bankers Association, *A Study of Group and Chain Banking; A Survey of the Movement Throughout the United States of Independent Unit Banks into Centrally Directed Systems* (New York: ABA Economic Policy Commission, 1929).

37. Living in a city did not guarantee that individuals had easy and ready access to a bank that met their needs. "It should be stated that prior to this investigation the subject of banking as practiced by immigrants had become one for grave consideration in the State of New York, particularly in New York City, where these concerns flourish as they do nowhere else." US Immigration Commission (Dillingham Commission), *Reports of the Immigration Commission, Volume 37: Steerage Conditions—Importation and Harboring of Women for Immoral Purposes—Immigrant Homes and Aid Societies—Immigrant Banks* (Washington, DC: Government Printing Office, 1911), p. 413.

38. Charles A. Goddard "How a Bank Helps Americanize the Foreign Born," *The Bankers Magazine* December 1918, p. 758.

39. Francis Murray Huston, *Financing An Empire: A History of Banking in Illinois*, 4 vols. (Chicago: S.J. Clarke Publishing Company, 1926). Volumes III and IV contains historical biographies of Chicago's banks. For example, Independence State Bank had its roots in the private banking operation of Kedzie Savings Bank, a private bank founded in 1911, which itself began as a

real estate firm. A new partner joined the bank in 1916, who "divined the spirit" of the neighborhood and determined that "the thing most desired by the local population was some assurance that this bank was safe to deal with, and he offered them the *utmost of safety by submitting to state and government supervision*" (Huston, *Financing An Empire*, vol. III, pp. 105–112, emphasis mine).

40. The House of Pitte, a large private bank in Chicago, with nonprofits and churches among its customers, took in $120,000 in savings and small deposits during its last year of business in 1916. By then, it had been in operation for almost 40 years and was never inspected by the government, see Editorial, *Denni Hlasatel* April 7, 1917 (*Chicago Foreign Language Press Survey*, Bohemian language).

41. Consequently, major cities such as Chicago, St Louis, Michigan, and San Francisco did not have mutual savings banks. See Alan Teck, *Mutual Savings Banks and Savings and Loan Associations: Aspects of Growth* (New York: Columbia University Press, 1968).

42. For example, their charters required all savings be applied *only* to residential homeownership and the organization automatically dissolved once the original members built their homes, requiring a new charter with a new set of members who needed homes built. These features reflected their early origins in 1831. The first mutual savings bank was founded in 1816. Joseph Ewalt, *A Business Reborn: The Savings and Loan Story, 1930–1960* (Chicago: American Savings and Loan Institute Press, 1962).

43. J. Carroll Moody and Gilbert Courtland Fite, *The Credit Union Movement: Origins and Development, 1850–1970* (Lincoln: University of Nebraska Press, 1971). This law was the first to grant credit union charters on a statewide basis using the free banking model, rather than the more cumbersome legislative approval of individual charters model.

44. Credit unions with neighborhood charters could serve anyone who lived or worked in a specific geographic area. See Roy Bergengren, *Crusade: The Fight for Economic Democracy in North America, 1921–1945* (New York: Exposition Press, 1952).

45. Mutual banks could serve the general public and could afford to hire a professional staff because they were often founded by large institutions, such as philanthropically-oriented businesses that wanted to provide workers with a safe and professional place to bank.

46. Naomi Lamoreaux, *Insider Lending: Banks, Personal Connections, and Economic Development in Industrial New England* (New York: Cambridge University Press, 1994); Hammond, *Banks and Politics in America from the Revolution to the Civil War*.

47. See Cohen, *Making a New Deal*.

48. J.N. Higley, "Banks and the Foreigners," *The Bankers Magazine* March 1919, pp. 313–316.

49. The disconnection between runs and actual failures is evident in the experiences of New York City's venerable Emigrant Industrial Savings Bank, which operates today as Emigrant Bank. Founded by Irish Catholics in 1844 to serve immigrant workers, its mutual savings bank charter mandated an investment strategy designed to protect depositors' funds. Recent analysis of customer accounts by economic historians of depositor behavior in the years 1854 and 1857 revealed that immigrant customers opened, closed, and re-opened accounts more frequently than non-immigrant customers, despite the conservative and professional management of the bank. Rumors of failure spread through social networks of Irish immigrants. Cormac O'Grada and

Eugene White, "Who Panics During Panics? Evidence from a Nineteenth Century Savings Bank," NBER Working Paper (November 2002).

50. Moss and Brennan, "Managing Money Risk in Antebellum New York."

51. The term "patchwork quilt" famously captures the result of policymaking in the "state of courts and parties." See Stephen Skowronek, *Building a New American State: The Expansion of National Administrative Capacities, 1877–1920* (New York: Cambridge University Press, 1982).

52. National banks could not offer residential mortgages, seen as risky investments at the time, but state banks could. Most importantly, national banks could issue currency backed by the Treasury bonds deposited at the Office of the Comptroller of the Currency. The elimination of currencies issued by state banks via a 10 percent tax on such notes addressed the fact that by 1860 more than 10,000 different bank notes circulated throughout the country. See The Office of the Comptroller of the Currency, "National Banking System Created, 1832–1864." Available at http://www.occ.treas. gov/exhibits/histor3.htm (accessed May 30, 2008).

53. When Congress created the Federal Reserve system in 1913, only national banks could join.

54. State-level mandatory bank chartering laws permitted a transitional period and temporarily lowered charter requirements to grandfather small banks into the chartered bank system. This preserved many neighborhood private banks that chose to convert to traditional bank form. Consequently, "unprofessional" banking continued, creating an array of small weak banks vulnerable to the pitfalls that the 1929 crash wrought. See Cohen, *Making a New Deal.*

55. Perhaps the biggest case of misdirection exists with the Bank of United States, a private bank in New York City. Many complained that the name led immigrants to believe it was a government bank, perhaps even the original central bank founded by Alexander Hamilton, the Bank of *the* United States. "High-titled Bank can Hold Its Name: Its Rivals Argued East Side Would Think 'Bank of United States' Was Government's," *New York Times* June 24, 1913. See also Joseph Lucia, "The Failure of the Bank of United States: A Reappraisal," *Explorations in Economic History* 22, no. 4 (1985): 402–416.

56. See, for example, W.H. Allen, "Immigrants' Hoards: The Hidden Cause of Financial Panics," *Moody's Magazine: The International Investors' Monthly* VIII, no. 6 (December 1909): 456–460.

57. "Immigrants Sent $275,000,000 Abroad in One Year."

58. "The Postal Savings Bank Suggestion," *New York Times* December 9, 1907.

59. Kemmerer, "Six Years of Postal Savings in the United States."

60. Pierson, *Politics in Time,* p. 8.

61. Graduates of the settlement house movement went on to become staunch advocates for state and national policy changes that benefited immigrants. The agencies they directed pursued resolution of disputes between immigrants and deadbeat employers, exploitative lawyers, landlords, and bankers. In 1911, of the 262 complaints received by New York State's Bureau of Industries and Immigration, 141 were for non-transmission of funds. New York State Department of Labor, *Second Annual Report of the Bureau of Industries and Immigration for the Twelve Months Ended September 30 1912* (Albany, NY: State Department of Labor, 1913), p. 4. See also Christina Ziegler-McPherson, *Americanization in the States: Immigrant Social Welfare Policy, Citizenship, and National Identity in the United States, 1908–1929* (Gainesville: University Press of Florida, forthcoming 2009).

62. Schroedel and Snyder, "People's Banking," see pp. 186–193 on the bill's passage.

63. Before the New Deal, a chartered bank or two failed every day in the United States, averaging 700 failures a year. David M. Kennedy, *Freedom From Fear: The American People in Depression and War, 1929–1945* (New York: Oxford University Press, 1999). In contrast, during the last three months of 1931 over 1,000 banks failed. The Office of the Comptroller of the Currency, "The Changing World of Banking." Available at http://www.occ.treas. gov/exhibits/histor5.htm (accessed May 13, 2008).

64. Massachusetts Commission on Immigration, *The Problem of Immigration in Massachusetts.*

65. Licenses had far fewer requirements than charters because the business did not hold deposits. See ibid.

66. Illinois mandatory bank chartering laws were approved by voters (403,458 to 83,704), temporarily lowered capital requirements, and gave newly declared banks 3 years to come into compliance. It also permitted other businesses to continue accepting deposits but banned them from calling themselves banks. See Jones, "Bootstraps and Beltways," ch. 2.

67. Cohen, *Making a New Deal*; Helen M. Burns, *The American Banking Community and New Deal Banking Reforms, 1933–1935* (Westport, CT: Greenwood Press, 1974). In 1932 the ABA opposed deposit insurance as protecting and subsidizing thousands of small and poorly managed banks.

68. Carpenter, *The Forging of Bureaucratic Autonomy.*

69. Edwin W. Kemmerer, "The United States Postal Savings Bank," *Political Science Quarterly* 26, no. 3 (1911): 462–499, quote on p. 474.

70. The ABA also rejected deposit insurance arguing that it gave comfort to small and poorly managed banks at a cost paid by large banks whose membership fees were higher. Burns, *The American Banking Community and New Deal Banking Reforms.*

71. The Democratic platform read, in part: "We favor a postal savings bank if the guaranteed bank can not be secured . . . ." The Republican platform read, in its entirety: "We favor the establishment of a postal savings bank system for the convenience of the people and the encouragement of thrift." Taft was the sole president to get actively involved in breaking the legislative logjam that kept postal bank bills trapped in committee. Schroedel and Snyder, "People's Banking," p. 187.

72. At least, so claimed the ABA. See American Bankers Association, *The Postal Savings System of the United States* (New York: ABA, 1937).

73. Schroedel and Snyder, "People's Banking," p. 193.

74. The $2,500 figure is from the Office of the Comptroller of the Currency, "The Changing World of Banking."

75. Thrifts also benefited from the deposit insurance idea. The federal government created a similar system to protect deposits in savings and loan associations and credit unions. The New Deal also introduced a national chartering system for thrifts (except mutual savings banks), which allowed applicants to bypass the state laws that remained inconsistent and restrictive.

76. Durability, in particular, is a shift that persists relatively unchanged for over a half-century. Orren and Skowronek, *The Search for American Political Development*, p. 129.

Conclusion

On Diversity and the Accommodation of Injustice: A Coda on Cities, Liberalism, and American Political Development

Ira Katznelson

Not for the first time have large cities—heterogeneous, semi-bounded, partially self-governing built environments that gather and concentrate people, capital, and power—been considered promising vantages from which to understand patterns and processes that transcend their spatial dimensions. Cities of this kind are not typical. Most of humanity resides in other types of places. In the United States, the proportion of the population in cities is at the low end even for the world's wealthy countries. Moreover, its urban inhabitants are different. They possess distinguishing demographic attributes regarding race, immigrant status, religion, ethnicity, and social class that set them apart from more characteristic members of the country's population. Urban political circumstances and activities also are out of the ordinary. As legal wards of state governments, cities have highly contingent powers, yet often obtain and sustain considerable autonomy. They are centers of mass media and the dissemination of ideas and ideologies. Their politics and voting behavior tend to be distinctive. So, too, their national and global economic role, which is focused and particular, not representative.

Yet, precisely because they are uncommon, substantial cities can be revealing. Their very density, accompanied by accelerations in and of time, offers access to central features of modern life that represent a kind of vanguard, a front line of change, for good and for ill. Further, their archetypical characteristics reveal mechanisms and relationships of great scope and significance that may be more difficult to identify and probe in less intense environments.

These assumptions underpin this valuable book. Cities present a privileged viewpoint from which to ask fundamental questions, and deploy systematic historical and social science research and evidence to answer them. The volume's contributions about American history and politics take up this opportunity. Written with a comparative and theoretical sensibility, they reject segregating local studies while insisting that empirical research in cities of various kinds has wide-ranging relevance.

From urban positions, they assess institutions and governance, including the political geography of federalism, land use, and finance. They examine the quest by machine politicians and reformers alike to bias political participation in order to secure durable power. They consider variations across time to cities in national governing coalitions, and they treat the development of competing political ideologies. Concerned with spatial change within metropolitan areas and across regions, and with other economic, discursive, spatial, and policy elements, they explore the meaning of race and ethnicity, and deepen our understanding of struggles for equal rights.

In all, the book reminds us there is much to be gained by paying systematic attention to things urban if we wish to understand configurations of structure and behavior in American political history. Rich with ideas about long-term trends, designs, and relationships, and full of propositions about hierarchies of cause and levels of analysis, *The City in American Political Development* thus presents a down payment for a revivified city-focused research program to illuminate the country's political experience more broadly.

Further, by calling attention to the substantive and analytical possibilities of such city-focused scholarship, these individual chapters suggest that we might fruitfully center an understanding of American political development on themes and orientations that have been important to urban studies. These include the complex of relationships that link other units of governance to cities, sometimes in a tug for power; the resulting character of political space available for municipal governance within a more inclusive institutional mix; wealth, capital, and economic capacity in creating constellations of power that shape these arrangements; legacies of political reform and the layering of institutions; the associational character of civil society; mass participation, mobilization, and violence; the character of urban democracy and its repercussions for national practices and possibilities; the sources, makeup, and persistence of poverty, and the role of neighborhood effects; cities in the development of social reform and the welfare state; the formative or dependent economic capacities of cities; the implications of urban experiments for the national political economy; and cities in global networks of trade, people, and ideas.

This rich set of topics reminds us how, presently, these and other urban lines of inquiry mostly are dormant. Hence this book is also something of an elegy for what has been lost or misplaced. After all, not too many decades ago, leading students of American politics paid systematic attention to cities as a way to deepen knowledge about the larger polity and its relationship to economic and political affairs. Not just Robert Dahl's justly prominent *Who Governs?*,[1] but estimable writing by Wallace Sayre, Herbert Kaufman, Theodore Lowi, Floyd Hunter, James Q. Wilson, Edward Banfield, David Greenstone, Nelson Polsby, Raymond Wolfinger,

Nathan Glazer, and a host of other principal contributors to discussions about ethnicity and race, machines and reform, sources and distributions of power, the character of political representation, the welfare state, and federalism, developed ideas, produced theory, and tested hypotheses about processes and mechanisms in American political life from within the confines of urban political studies.[2]

When I was in graduate school and first started teaching, these writings inspired many of us to set our inquiries about American politics and society on urban ground. The authors of those studies stimulated others to think about pressing contemporary challenges by working through vexing historical and analytical situations with a range of qualitative and quantitative methods. Written at a time of charged social transformation and contention about the character and scope of democracy, these urban studies had a visceral and political as well as intellectual impact. No student of American politics and possibility could avoid them.

The moment passed. The city became less visible in the academy. Whatever the causes, scholarly attention clearly moved to other more aseptic subjects that were more distant from present experience. With this fall off, the chance to investigate big issues in this noteworthy and revealing way sadly declined. We can speculate about the reasons, including demographic change, accelerating suburbanization, the impact of global economic trends, and ideological shifts. As a result, indeed as part of the swing in scholarly attention, the systematic sub-field that came to be called "American political development" (APD) has had surprisingly little to say about cities despite being engaged with many of the same matters, and despite sharing attention to institutions and history.[3] Nourished primarily by large-scale comparative historical scholarship, and focused more on temporality than on space, APD tended to neglect things urban.

There is much ground to make up. This book's project of rectification shows how APD's core concerns—including the meaning of liberalism, the character of the state as an institutional ensemble, and the status of race—can be studied afresh in tandem with urban research. As a goad to do more such work, the volume's chapters also recommend a research program that could further advance some central epistemological commitments of APD, including a sustained connection between the positive and the normative in social research, tight links between history and systematic social science, a refusal to adopt a single methodological orthodoxy, and a willingness to move across boundaries that often separate the material, the symbolic, and the political.

My contribution is less one of reiteration or exhortation than a suggestion about enlarging this agenda. Two closely related questions about the borderland where deep pluralism meets the American liberal political tradition should command additional attention at the intersection of the city and American political development. Each, moreover, also extends the range of literature that might be tapped to investigate circumstances where ideologies and norms meet institutions and power.

First is how citizens who are divided profoundly by background, by culture, by religious practices, and by moral commitments can live together peacefully. "Now the serious problem is this," John Rawls has observed. "A modern democratic society is characterized not simply by a pluralism of comprehensive religious, philosophical, and moral doctrines but by a pluralism of incompatible yet reasonable comprehensive doctrines." This fact generates disputes and trials not just for solidarity, but for a decent social peace. "How is it possible that there may exist over time a stable and just society of free and equal citizens profoundly divided by reasonable though incompatible religious, philosophical, and moral doctrines?" Further, how can such deep pluralism, a pluralism more fundamental than the pluralism of interests that vexed scholars at the high point of urban scholarship, be consistent with, or even promote "the political conception of a constitutional regime"?[4]

America's race relations, robust immigration, religious diversity, and moral crusades—each of which has taken thick form in America's big cities—make this subject matter singularly significant. In the history of the country's political development, this set of qualities has taken an array of forms, dividing slavery from freedom, ascription from equal citizenship, men from women, immigrants from natives, and Protestants from Catholics (and both from Jews and Muslims), as well as supporters from opponents of alcohol, abortion, capital punishment, and other non-divisible ethical issues. Such sharp arenas of disagreement frequently have generated ugly rhetoric, private and public violence, and deep physical insecurity.

Second is the character and bases of stability for liberal political regimes. We may ask, as Mark Graber does in a provocative book about the infamous 1857 *Dred Scott* decision that validated slavery in the territories and refused access to American citizenship to black residents, free as well as slave, how much accommodation to injustice is tolerable, and perhaps even required, within the framework of liberal democracy. What is the power and appropriate responsibility of popular majorities who support such decisions? When racism has commanded a majority of the white majority, and when racist institutional practices have been reinforced through the normal institutions of participation and political representation, what should the responsibility of liberal constitutionalism and politics have been? Graber calls this the problem of constitutional evil, "the practice and theory of sharing civic space with people committed to evil practices or pledging allegiance to a constitutional text and tradition saturated with concessions to evil."[5] As the Civil War demonstrated, this dilemma defines and inhabits a zone of great moral uncertainty. How does one weigh up the choice between the eradication of the profound evil of slavery and the saturation of the country in the blood of some 600,000 dead by battle and disease, or the death of 36,000 (one in five) black Union troops?

The first might be designated the test of toleration; the second the test of injustice. Both, together, press us to deepen our understanding and investigation of the Western liberal tradition beyond the rather thin references to Lockeanism in Louis Hartz's influential study of *The Liberal Tradition in America*,[6] or the compartmentalization of liberalism and ascription proffered by Rogers Smith in his powerful assessment of conflicting ideas about citizenship in *Civic Ideals*.[7] Indeed, an odd aspect of APD is how it has combined a persistent fascination and anxiety for the status of political liberalism with a relative neglect of the range and depth of relevant considerations extant in political theory and systematic philosophy. Liberalism cannot just be identified in an epigrammatic way as "Lockean" and considered as crisply separate from other traditions like republicanism,[8] or treated as inherently universal and egalitarian and regarded as a body of values that transcend the solution of determinate specific and grounded historical predicaments. If students of American political development are to deepen their understanding of liberalism, they will have to enhance their conceptual range and amplify their accounts of times past.

The city provides an important position from which such work can move ahead. There are, of course, many ways to advance such inquiry. Rawls primarily worked by deductive reason; Graber by the analysis of jurisprudence in historical time. But in the mix of methods and approaches, studies within and about dense, diverse, and unequal city environments are especially promising. Read together, the reciprocal treatments by Rawls and Graber of how constitutional democracies must deal with deep polarization in more than one dimension has broad relevance for this book's intellectual quest to link cities to larger American patterns.

The Test of Toleration

One familiar way to think about toleration is to celebrate its enlargement. Persecution of individuals and groups because of how they worship or how they look is much less common today than in prior decades and centuries. This welcome progress risks understating the persistence of actual and potential conflict about deep differences, legacies of intolerance joined to deep inequality, and the fragility of toleration. The history of the past century—a century that began with celebrations of enlightened reason but soon experienced unprecedented violence and radical evil in the heart of the "civilized" West—reminds us that grim circumstances and outcomes are latent possibilities. Moreover, as vectors of difference and demographic facts change, new opportunities for intolerance arise.

Cities beckon, in light of their continuing, if shifting, heterogeneity and arrangements of unequal power. Though Rawls, of course, is not an empirical social scientist or an urbanist, the reasoning he offers in *Political Liberalism* can fruitfully help impel urban-based APD research on toleration.

In his monumental *Theory of Justice*,[9] Rawls presented a theory of social cohesion with a family resemblance to Hartz's account. *The Liberal Tradition in America* claims that liberalism in the United States is more than a basic set of norms about rights, consent, and political representation or a portrayal of the country's institutional arrangements marked by a separation of powers and federalism. Though Lockeanism includes these features for Hartz, the liberalism he describes is an enveloping ideology so pervasive that it simultaneously is hegemonic and invisible. It structures and limits possibilities, forcing actual and potential dimensions of conflict and mobilization into a simplified enclosure of thought. As a disciplining body of implicit ideas, liberalism functions as the country's source of social integration, shaping its ability to cope with deep fissures of region, race, and class inequality.

Likewise for Rawls, a well-ordered liberal regime based on what he called justice as fairness and the cooperation of citizens is made stable by an extensively shared liberal conception. As he noted retrospectively, the idea of "a well-ordered society as it appears in *Theory*" requires "that all its citizens endorse this conception on the basis of what I now call a comprehensive philosophical doctrine." Like Hartz's *Liberalism*, Rawls' *Justice* contained no appreciation of the heterogeneity of American and other modern societies, a circumstance in which individuals cluster in groups of various types with often incompatible values, preferences, and moral fundamentals of the kind he later put front and center in *Political Liberalism*. In contemporary societies, there are some doctrines, to be sure, that are "unreasonable and irrational, and even mad" where "the problem is to contain them so they do not undermine the unity and justice of society." But most are not unreasonable, irrational, or mad, only contrary and discordant.[10] How can they come to share common political space?

Legitimate stability thus presents itself in a new way. *A Theory of Justice* is placeless and beyond the vagaries and details of actual history. *Political Liberalism*, while not a work of history, is rooted implicitly in definite locations, populations, and circumstances. The difficulty is not how to discern a holistic singular means with which to integrate the social order, but how to find a basis for constancy that is compatible with deep pluralism. For "our individual and associative points of view, intellectual affinities, and affective attachments, are too diverse, especially in a free society, to enable those doctrines to serve as the basis of lasting and reasoned political agreement."[11] What might substitute?

Even before turning to the elements of Rawls' solution, based on a distinction between the nonpublic and the public realm of citizenship and the idea of an overlapping consensus, it is worth noting that the basic assertion he makes about pluralism and modernity is factual. Like all empirical claims, it invites verification based on systematic conceptualization and measurement. The type and degree of pluralism can be arrayed on different dimensions that have to be identified and investigated. Cities are privileged sites for such inquiries. More than other settings, they tend to be on the high side of pluralism's extent while varying with regard to type. If deep pluralism constitutes the central contextual dynamic of Rawls' modern world, urban studies offer potentially powerful means with which to appraise its qualities, and assess the extent to which any particular configuration might pose powerful challenges to stability and justice.

In light of the uncommon degree of immigration, religious diversity, demographic heterogeneity, and competing ethical viewpoints in the United States, and the tandem absence of a singular transcendent non-civic nationalism, a refined account of the character and vectors of deep diversity is urgent. When citizens are profoundly divided, and when there is no prospect that their differences can be eliminated or reconciled, how can they together constitute a just and stable political society? In *A Theory of Justice*, Rawls elided this subject by a deductive device that positioned imagined individuals in circumstances of ignorance about their identities, beliefs, attachments, aims, and interests, and asked them to reason together about principles of justice. The result of the contract they would negotiate he famously characterized as an ethical consensus with two main principles: the first secures rights and basic liberties; a second assures that inequalities rebound to the benefit of the least advantaged members of society.

In *Political Liberalism* Rawls did not replace these principles, to which he continued to adhere. But he rejected the idea that stability can be produced by an all-embracing liberal consensus. Instead, he offered what he hoped would be a more realistic formula for decent social unity in the here and now, in a world marked by profound and irreconcilable differences, a formula that is not sectarian or parochial. How, he wanted to know, could agreement about liberal political fundamentals, what he calls "a political conception of justice," survive, perhaps even secure support from, civil society's cultural and moral pluralism? This inquiry is of fundamental importance because it bears on whether

> a just democratic society is possible and can be stable for the right reasons . . . .. The wars of this century with their extreme violence and increasing destructiveness, culminating in the manic evil of the Holocaust raise in an acute way the question whether political relations must be governed by power and coercion alone.[12]

Rawls' formula for a mutual accommodation of difference within a common public frame is based on three key ideas. First, the modern state should be conceptualized as neither an association nor a community. Associations are partial and voluntary, but sovereign states are inclusive and compulsory. Communities are homogeneous in that they are composed by people sharing identities and comprehensive views, but states must incorporate and recognize pluralism. Second, the difference between reasonable and unreasonable pluralism lies in the capacity of the former to enter into the domain of public reason, a zone where reciprocity among equal citizens is an axial principle. Reasonableness connotes the willingness to identify and act on standards of fair cooperation despite substantial differences among groups of citizens. Third, a liberal principle of legitimacy can be discerned in the region of an "overlapping consensus" about political rights, institutions, and procedures—"consensus" because it is shared; "overlapping" because the agreement is grounded in the different reasons generated from within often incommensurable doctrines. "Each citizen affirms both a comprehensive doctrine and the focal political conception, somehow related."[13]

Cities are not associations or communities, nor are they inclusive and compulsory polities. They offer exit and entry options, which can be freely exercised, certainly in liberal democracies such as the United States. Those who choose to live in such heterogeneous places without fleeing to more simple and uniform environments are more likely, we might hypothesize, to render their pluralism reasonable and seek an overlapping consensus. If the Rawlsian formula is to successfully operate anywhere, it should work here.

From this perspective, cities are locations within which to put the proposition of the possibility of an overlapping consensus to the test in the face of objections to the effect that Rawls' formulation for just stability is too naive, because disagreements run too deep for such a consensus to be discovered, and too weak, because it leaves potentially illiberal commitments too much potential to penetrate and bruise the liberal public square. To qualify as reasonable, how much must deeply held identities and preferences be modified? How much separation is assumed to exist between social groupings pursuing discrete and dissimilar ways of life? Is not the assumption of different zones of public and private rather too orderly? Can incommensurability be kept outside the public realm and be introduced there only when capable of contributing to an overlapping consensus? What if civil society conflicts spill over into the political realm?

Considerations of these issues in cities, joined to the historical and analytical advantages of APD, can transform both Rawls' claims and grounds for doubt into theoretically directed empirical research. Through urban research, his concepts and ideas can be operationalized. How diverse groups do, or do not, craft a common liberal political space can be rigorously compared in time and space. Such a project would also demand, APD-style, an institutional imagination that transcends Rawls' rather abstract reasoning, for only through the elaboration of particular sets of institutions could the Rawlsian prescription actually operate to produce acceptable provisional outcomes by way of negotiation, compromise, and arbitration.

The Test of Injustice

Rawls looked for solutions to create a common liberal and democratic polity despite deep differences in human commitments about the good. In a complementary move (though one without any reference to Rawls), Mark Graber invites us to think about a common liberal and democratic polity based on agreements to set aside or not pursue to their logical conclusion profound disagreements in the public realm about matters as basic as whether a liberal society can tolerate chattel slavery. His *Dred Scott and the Problem of Constitutional Evil* is concerned to think about how "problems of constitutional evil arise in large, diverse polities," with "the crux of the problem" identified with the fact that citizens do not agree about what in fact constitutes evil.[14] An overlapping consensus can do more than provide justifiable stability; it also can ratify ugliness.

Graber proceeds by way of a surprising appreciation for *Dred Scott v. Sandford*.[15] Often described as ghastly, odious, and tragic, the decision, he shows, was more than plausible in its context. It affirmed the bisectional agreement between the free and slave parts of the Republic that had been enshrined—indeed hard-wired—in the Constitution, and reinforced in subsequent jurisprudence and lawmaking, the central activities of America's liberal political order. As the election of 1860 and the Civil War that quickly followed soon demonstrated, the withdrawal of consent for compromises with evil threatened to dissolve, and then produced, the termination of the country's common polity. Without a formula to cross the deep divide between freedom and slavery, the United States could not exist, except by compulsion fashioned by the application of unprecedented force. Peace required injustice; justice required war.

America's overlapping consensus thus was charged with moral ambiguity and the potential for collapse into a war of all against all. *Dred Scott*, from this vantage, was less an ethical abomination (which, of course, it was) than a desperate quest to find grounds to maintain a crosssectional consensus sufficient for the Union to persist. Graber tells us in deeply unsettling prose:

> We celebrate Lincoln, only by recognizing that in 1861 he chose justice over constitutionality, or at least that he refused to accommodate slavery to the extent necessary to maintain the old constitutional order. The devastation wrought by Union forces starkly demonstrates that the choice between constitutionality and justice rarely amounts to a simple decision between good and evil. Injustices

deeply rooted, as slavery was in 1860, can be swiftly eradicated only by actions that kill, maim, and devastate millions of persons, many of whom bear little responsibility for the evil in question.[16]

In this way, Graber identifies difficulties that lie just on the other side of the quest for legitimate stability advanced by Rawls. Read together, we can see why accounts of the United States as simply liberal all the way down can be on the mark, yet also terribly elusive about the formation and import of a liberal public sphere in the face of, and with accommodations to, deep pluralism. American constitutional democracy has functioned well not only when, as in the 1960s, it confronted racial demons, but, disturbingly, also when, as in the rightly celebrated New Deal period, it maintained a balance of sectional power that protected racist beliefs and practices.[17] Yet treating American history as the story of competing traditions, as if they are free-standing and independent, also is insufficient. Over the course of the country's political development, political liberalism has not thrived, or even existed, independently. It has, rather, been experienced, shaped, and shaded, in large cities and other locations, by the manner of its braiding with profoundly illiberal constellations of thought and activity.[18]

It thus is easy to see why the heterogeneity, complexity, variation, and density of cities offer not so much a unique but an advantaged site of inquiry and adjudication for the range of concerns that Karen Orren and Steven Skowronek have called the search for durable governing authority, the theme they emplace at the center of APD.[19] From their perspective, American political institutions and arrangements are not a singular, stable constant, but a historically formed and reformed governing order based on provisional constellations of authority. This conceptualization has an obvious affinity with Rawls' puzzle about how stable and just liberal polities can form under circumstances of profound pluralism, and Graber's concern for the character of the necessary compromises and the costs they entail both when they are endured and when they are contested.

Cities summon APD scholarship because as places of deep pluralism they cannot but convene efforts to produce the "good" of a shared public sphere of discourse, institutions, and adjudication. Simultaneously, they also force us to see that such agreements can include spatial, social, economic, and political inscriptions of the "bad" of inter-group accommodations that can range from the merely unpleasant to the profoundly evil, at least as judged by liberal normative standards.

In cities, APD can join hands with the Rawls–Graber agenda to extend systematic studies of the most basic and vexing features of liberal democracy in the United States. Their cultural specificity, marked by the differentiated preferences and powers of groups, the uneven quest for political order, and often compartmentalized histories dealing with America's profound racial divide—key areas for discussion in this book—

offers up mechanisms and processes that collide in urban space. These traits bid us to discover how to turn the theoretical apparatus of Rawls and the constitutional assessment of Graber into a sustained program of urban inquiry that can reflect directly on APD's core scholarly concerns and normative commitments. If, as we were reminded in the Introduction, Charles Merriam's survey of progress in his 1926 American Political Science Association presidential address could announce that "one of the most striking advances in research ... has been centering" since the Association's 1903 founding "around the problem of the modern city," in a manner both "scientific and practical,"[20] this forceful book likewise has the potential to motivate and help direct local studies into accounts of the great challenges that torment liberal democracy in the United States.

Notes

1. Robert A. Dahl, *Who Governs? Democracy and Power in an American City* (New Haven: Yale University Press, 1961).
2. See Wallace S. Sayre and Herbert Kaufman, *Governing New York City: Politics in the Metropolis* (New York: Russell Sage Foundation, 1961); Theodore J. Lowi, *At the Pleasure of the Mayor: Patronage and Power in New York City, 1898–1958* (Glencoe, IL: Free Press, 1964); Floyd Hunter, *Community Power Structure: A Study of Decision-Makers* (Chapel Hill: University of North Carolina Press, 1953); Edward Banfield and James Q. Wilson, *City Politics* (Cambridge, MA: Harvard University Press, 1963); J. David Greenstone and Paul E. Peterson, *Race and Authority in Urban Politics: Community Participation and the War on Poverty* (New York: Russell Sage Foundation, 1973); Nelson W. Polsby, *Community Power and Political Theory* (New Haven: Yale University Press, 1963); Raymond E. Wolfinger, *The Politics of Progress* (Englewood Cliffs, NJ: Prentice-Hall, 1973); Nathan Glazer and Daniel Patrick Moynihan, *Beyond the Melting Pot: The Negroes, Puerto Ricans, Jews, Italians, and Irish of New York City* (Cambridge, MA: MIT Press, 1963).
3. Important exceptions include Amy Bridges, *City in the Republic: Antebellum New York and the Origins of Machine Politics* (Cambridge: Cambridge University Press, 1984); Amy Bridges, *Morning Glories: Municipal Reform in the Southwest* (Princeton, NJ: Princeton University Press, 1997); and Stephen P. Erie, *Rainbow's End: Irish-Americans and the Dilemmas of Urban Machine Politics, 1840–1985* (Berkeley: University of California Press, 1985).
4. John Rawls, *Political Liberalism. Expanded Edition* (New York: Columbia University Press, 2005), pp. xvi, xviii, xxxvii.
5. Mark A. Graber, *Dred Scott and the Problem of Constitutional Evil* (Cambridge: Cambridge University Press, 2006), p. 1.
6. Louis Hartz, *The Liberal Tradition in America* (New York: Harcourt Brace and World, 1955).
7. Rogers M. Smith, *Civic Ideals: Conflicting Visions of Citizenship in U.S. History* (New Haven: Yale University Press, 1997).
8. This is a central theme in Ira Katznelson and Andreas Kalyvas, *Liberal Beginnings: Making a Republic for the Moderns* (Cambridge: Cambridge University Press, 2008).

9. John Rawls, *A Theory of Justice* (Oxford: Clarendon Press, 1972).
10. Rawls, *Political Liberalism*, p. xvi.
11. Ibid., p. 58.
12. Ibid., pp. lix–lx.
13. Ibid., pp.132–172, xix.
14. Graber, *Dred Scott*, pp. 8–9.
15. 60 US 393 (1857).
16. Graber, *Dred Scott*, pp. 13–14.
17. For a discussion, see Ira Katznelson, *When Affirmative Action Was White: An Untold History of Racial Inequality in Twentieth-Century America* (New York: W.W. Norton, 2005).
18. An exemplary treatment of such an imbrication is Stephen Skowronek, "The Reassociation of Ideas and Purposes: Racism, Liberalism, and the American Liberal Tradition," *American Political Science Review* 100 (August 2006): 385–401.
19. Karen Orren and Stephen Skowronek, *The Search for American Political Development* (Cambridge: Cambridge University Press, 2004).
20. Charles Merriam, "Progress in Political Research," *American Political Science Review* 20 (February 1926): 1.

Index